Pioneer's Progress

ILLINOIS COLLEGE, 1829–1979

BY
CHARLES E. FRANK
PIXLEY PROFESSOR OF HUMANITIES
Illinois College

Foreword by Donald C. Mundinger

Introduction by William N. Clark

Published for
ILLINOIS COLLEGE
by
SOUTHERN ILLINOIS UNIVERSITY PRESS
1979

Part 1 of *Pioneer's Progress* is an abridged edition of *Illinois College: A Centennial History, 1829–1929* by Charles Henry Rammelkamp. Copyright 1928 by Charles Henry Rammelkamp. Copyright renewed 1955 by The Trustees of Illinois College.

Printed in the United States of America
Designed by Bob Nance

Library of Congress Cataloging in Publication Data

Frank, Charles Edward.
   Pioneer's progress.

   Pt. 1 is an abridgment of Illinois College, a centennial history, 1829–1929, by C. H. Rammelkamp.
   Bibliography: p.
   Includes index.
   1. Illinois College, Jacksonville—History. I. Rammelkamp, Charles Henry, 1874–1932 Illinois College. II. Title.
LD2341.I52F72   378.773'463   78-10275
ISBN 0-8093-0892-4

Dedicated to

The Eleven Presidents and Several Acting Presidents

OF ILLINOIS COLLEGE

for whom
LEADERSHIP HAS BEEN A BURDEN ALWAYS
AND A JOY SOMETIMES

The eleven presidents of Illinois College are presented at length in the several chapters devoted to them, but the acting presidents, except for Rufus Crampton, are mentioned only in passing. They deserve to be listed separately, because they got very little of the joy of leadership while bearing more than a fair share of the burden. They are:

Professor Rufus C. Crampton, 1876–1882
Professor E. W. Milligan, Dec. 1891–Oct. 1892
Dean Milton E. Churchill, 1899–1900
Trustee Julius E. Strawn, Jan.–April 1905
Professor John Griffith Ames, 1929–1930; April 1932–June 1933
Dean Ernest G. Hildner, Jr., Aug. 1955–Jan. 1956

Contents

Illustrations

Foreword

By Donald C. Mundinger
President, Illinois College

The one hundred and fiftieth anniversary of an institution is an important event. It is especially so when it is the sesquicentennial of the first college in the state to award a baccalaureate degree. A special obligation is incumbent upon that institution to record its history accurately and perceptively. This responsibility Illinois College has enthusiastically embraced.

Dr. Charles E. Frank, the A. Boyd Pixley Professor of Humanities, has lovingly researched and written the history of Illinois College. His goal was to recount the record of Illinois College in higher liberal education. Illinois College has remained faithful to the mandate of its founders—to provide a fountain of knowledge at which students could freely drink. In 1979, we rededicate ourselves to that mission—to teach the ablest students we can attract, at the highest level of their capacity, to use their talents in the service of God and their fellow man. That mission and that promise are sounded clearly in this history by Professor Frank.

A special word of gratitude is in order to Robert and Jessica Sibert, Jacksonville, Illinois, who have generously underwritten the publication of this history of Illinois College. Robert and Jessica, people of vision and a humane spirit, are keenly sensitive to the responsibility and privilege which accompanies their achievement and success. As a result, they have underwritten the Illinois College history and other major College projects. The enlightened spirit of Robert and Jessica Sibert will continue to serve Illinois College well into the twenty-first century as students, alumni and friends read and reread the inspiring story of Old Illinois College.

Introduction

By William N. Clark
Chairman, Board of Trustees, Illinois College

One thing about anniversaries—they provide special impetus for doing things that ought to be done anyway. Updating the story of Illinois College is a case in point. Fifty years have passed since the publication of Dr. Charles Henry Rammelkamp's superb and scholarly *Illinois College: A Centennial History*. To suggest that in the more recent of those years the fields of academia have been littered with institutional casualties may sound hyperbolic, but it isn't. Accelerating costs and a host of other factors, not the least of which is the enormous growth of the tax-supported university, have thinned the ranks of small, privately-endowed colleges. Some have hung on by virtue of merger, yielding traditional identities in exchange for survival of sorts. Others have simply vanished.

Illinois College, first in the state to graduate a class, keeps going. It does better than that; it enters its sesquicentennial year with its finances, its physical plant and—most important—its teaching capability all in the very best of good health.

Why?

Has Illinois College somehow been spared the challenges that have proved too much for so many others? (It has not.) Were there lean years during which the future of Illinois College was seriously in doubt? (Indeed there were.) Are there no dark pages in the records of some who have influenced the college's destiny? (Unfortunately, one or two.)

It is important that these questions be raised and the answers be documented, not just for those who have had a personal involvement of one kind or another with Illinois College but for all who care about the future of small, private colleges in our total educational system.

The reasons, then, for making a record of Illinois College's third fifty years are many and compelling. No problem getting a "go ahead" for the project. Next step—who should be the author? And what about format?

The choice of author came first. After all, the writer, whoever he might be, should have a good deal to say about format. But shall he be an outsider or an insider? Might the presentation of the Illinois College history benefit from the objectivity someone without personal ties to the college would bring to the assignment?

It didn't really take much time to decide that, whatever the advantages of outside treatment, they would be overshadowed by a host of benefits to be derived from placing the project in the lap of Dr. Charles E. Frank.

Charles Frank has a unique combination of qualifications for an Illinois College historian. First off, he's a scholar—a member of Phi Beta Kappa who earned his doctorate at Princeton. His scholarly achievements and his teaching talent have been recognized in many ways by his peers and by his students. Now, as the A. Boyd Pixley Professor of Humanities he is the distinguished first occupant of a chair established in memory of a late benefactor of the college.

Credentials other than those as a scholar and teacher also weighed heavily in Dr. Frank's favor. He came to Illinois College as a young assistant professor of English in 1939. There was a four-year interruption for military service, but Charles Frank's career association with Illinois College remains among the longest recorded by any one person—longer even than that of the revered president and centennial historian, Dr. Rammelkamp. He has been positioned to follow the fortunes of the college at close hand under four presidents, but with the perspective provided by freedom from central administration responsibility.

But there is more to Charles Frank than scholar, professor, and strategically-placed observer. His warm and spritely account of a family trip to Europe, *Six Franks Abroad*, was successful in the popular market and served as a convincing demonstration that though he is undeniably a scholar he is no pedant. Frank professes to see some of the qualities of James Hilton's Mr. Chips in the late Professor "Johnny" Ames, but there is at least as much of Chips in Frank himself. The ebullience his students remember so well comes bubbling through in the pages that follow.

One other point is worthy of mention. Reared and educated in the east, Frank has no family ties in Jacksonville save those with his own wife and children—another advantage for the present assignment.

So, the project is approved and the author selected. But what about format? Should the new book be cast as a sequel to the Rammelkamp centennial history, picking up where the first left off and simply reciting what happened next, and next, and next? From the author's standpoint this probably would have been the easiest treatment. However, those desiring to read a complete history of Illinois College would have been confronted with a formidable amount of material—a forbidding amount, it was feared, to some.

Dr. Frank's solution is ingenious. By excerpting and paraphrasing the Rammelkamp history and adding a penetrating account of the decades since, Frank has produced a comprehensive but thoroughly digestible one-volume history of the college. At the same time, the Rammelkamp work, a model of integrity and scholarship, stands as completely satisfying reading for anyone wishing to explore the developments of the first one hundred years in greater detail. The two books have subject matter in common but each stands on its own.

Though Illinois College survives and, currently, thrives, the last fifty years have been less than tranquil. To a degree that no doubt would surprise some of the neighbors across the street from the beautiful campus, the college has mirrored the troubles of its times and has come up with a few uniquely its own. Frank glosses over none of these, and that's the way a history should be.

Nevertheless, the durability of the old school suggests that in times of stress good men and women have been on hand or have come along to handle the situation. Any enterprise that maintains continuity of operation for a century and a half has had the services of good people. At Illinois College, that has made the difference. Acceptance of mediocrity—a willingness merely to "get by"—would not have provided the fuel to keep the engines going for one hundred and fifty years.

Finally, a personal note; a confession of sorts. Though I stand behind every word in this introduction it is possible that an unsympathetic reader could call my objectivity into question. From earliest memory until my own graduation from Illinois College I lived a scant half-block from the campus. It was a childhood playground. From pre-kindergarten years onwards my comings and goings seemed at least as much ordered by the bell in Sturtevant Tower as were those of a long succession of student bodies. Later, as an Illinois College student, I met the young lady who was to become my wife, and still later our first born took his baccalaureate degree from Illinois College.

If this were not enough, I have had the privilege of serving on the board of trustees for twenty-one years as of this writing, and have enjoyed the friendship of Charlie Frank since his arrival in Jacksonville, briefly as a next door neighbor, some thirty-nine years ago.

So much, perhaps, for objectivity.

However, none of this has any bearing on why Illinois College has made it through one hundred fifty years and is in such fine fettle for its sesquicentennial celebration. What Dr. Frank has to say does. I commend his words to your attention.

PART ONE

1829–1925

"It was not long after I came to Illinois College as Professor of History and Political Science that I began to realize that the College had a history which was not only interesting but of some real importance in the general story of the development of education and culture in the Middle West. The sketch of that history in the interesting *Autobiography* of President Sturtevant whetted my appetite for more knowledge and when, through the kindness of Dr. Sturtevant's family and of other friends of the College, I came into possession of hundreds of private letters throwing light on the history of the institution and its relation to the progress of learning in the pioneer state of Illinois, I became convinced that the whole story ought to be told. And so for many years, as opportunity offered, I have sought refuge from the pressing and often harassing duties of a college president by delving among the records of the past century."

—CHARLES HENRY RAMMELKAMP, Preface to *Illinois College:*
A Centennial History, 1829–1929

I

PROLOGUE

Where Have You Been, Illinois College?

People like to celebrate anniversaries, and certain anniversaries seem to them more important than others. Institutions, especially colleges, have a similar penchant. Sometimes it seems that just having survived is worthy of note, but if, in addition, one can see growth and maturity and wisdom resulting from the aging process, a person or a college has justification for a special observance, a party complete with bells and cakes and candles, poems and songs and toasts. Illinois College has had such observances commemorating her twenty-fifth, fiftieth, seventy-fifth, one-hundredth, and one-hundred-twenty-fifth birthdays. Some of these celebrations have been as flamboyant as academic celebrations are likely to get; others have been muted.

The College is now preparing, as these words are written, for its sesquicentennial birthday. It is altogether proper on such an occasion to look back over one's shoulder and examine the path that has been traveled. It can be a chastening experience; it can also be an exhilarating one. When I undertook the job of bringing the history of Illinois College down to 1979, as a part of the sesquicentennial celebration, I was aware of several problems. The existence of the Rammelkamp *Centennial History* was not only challenging, but because of its excellence, somewhat intimidating.

The simplest solution to that problem would have been to reprint Rammelkamp and then produce a new volume dealing with the third half-century of the College's history. But Rammelkamp's bulk would have made reprinting costly and impractical. Furthermore, even had it been practicable, that would not have solved the problem of interrelating the earlier and the more recent history. Cross-referencing between volumes would have been tedious and awkward. It occurred to me that a better, more practical, solution would be to abridge Rammelkamp and use the abridgement as the beginning of a new, compact history of the College.

I suspect that I will find myself in ample and good company if I admit that I had never before read Rammelkamp through, carefully and consecutively, though I had often consulted the book on specific points, as one consults an encyclopedia or dictionary. A careful, consecutive reading was illuminating. First, it confirmed my belief that Rammelkamp had unearthed excellent source materials, had organized them effectively, and had presented them in an orderly, readable way. Second, I became convinced that although some of the challenges of the third half-century were new ones, many of them were old ones under new guises. Third, I decided that sometimes Dr. Rammelkamp had presented more details than the general reader needed, that his meticulous giving of credit to each of hundreds of people who had in some way contributed to the growth and health of the College impeded the common reader's movement. I found these qualities more noticeable as Dr. Rammelkamp approached the end of his task. He wanted to be objective even when he was most involved, and he wanted to reveal his involvement without sacrificing a scholar's objectivity. Moreover, the climactic events of his administration—the strengthening of the endowment funds of the College, the building of Tanner Library and Baxter Dining Hall, the celebration of the Centennial, the achievement of a chapter of Phi Beta Kappa—all these were in the future as he began the final paragraph of his *Centennial History*: "We are not only at the end of an old century, but we stand on the threshold of a new era. The future beckons us to still greater achievement in the cause of higher education and public service."

For obvious reasons, Rammelkamp did not attempt any evaluation of his own administration. Perhaps if he had lived to a ripe old age he might have been able to arrive at a calm and fair judgment of his achievement, but he died in full career at the age of fifty-eight and was denied any opportunity of making such a judgment.

Most of us have had to summarize the work of others and we know how difficult it is to get the gist of a complex matter and re-state it clearly and accurately. In Part 1 of this history I have reduced the bulk of Rammelkamp by approximately 80 percent. It is likely that different readers will regret the loss of different things. It may even be that those things I have regarded as most dispensable—the many photographs, the lists of names of men and women involved in various collegiate activities, the changing personnel of faculty and trustees, the winners of all manner of contests—will seem essential to admirers of Rammelkamp. To all such I can only say that these details are preserved for all time in the original text, which the curi-ous reader may and should consult. To assist such readers, I have cited, in Appendix A, the appropriate pages of Rammelkamp, chap-ter by chapter.

Some may object to my throwing overboard those hallmarks of scholarship—footnotes, Latin abbreviations, indications of elision and emendation. I have done this with some regret, but when I con-sidered the confusion that would have resulted if I had attempted to impose my footnotes on those of Dr. Rammelkamp and to distin-guish his elisions from my own, I thought it better to aim at reada-bility and clarity rather than the appearance of scholarship. The Rammelkamp history is notably free of errors of all kinds, but where I have found any, I have quietly corrected them.

In Part 1, I have kept the original chapter divisions and the titles for them. So far as I could, I have retained Rammelkamp's wording, even where it is a little more formal and courtly than is currently in vogue. Some passages I have cut severely and others I have kept very nearly intact, but I have tried to keep Rammelkamp's emphasis and proportions. I have not re-evaluated his source materials nor altered his judgments upon them.

To check my policies and practices, I have had several knowledge-able and judicious critics read over my abridgement, and I have re-ceived valuable suggestions on it. I express my thanks especially to friends and colleagues, Ruth Bump, Alma Churchill Smith, the late Ernest Hildner, and Iver Yeager. I want also to acknowledge my indebtedness to Julian Sturtevant Rammelkamp and other members of the Rammelkamp family who have been warmly supportive of this undertaking. Of course, I accept full responsibility for the final result and particularly for any errors of commission or omission.

Members of the Rammelkamp family have done more than I could have asked them to do. Among other things, they have let me sort through the class lecture notes which Dr. Rammelkamp made and preserved for courses he gave over a period of thirty years, in English history, colonial American and constitutional history, and the like, notes for talks he gave in chapel, addresses to alumni at regional banquets in New York and Chicago and St. Louis, comments to fellow educators about common problems. Three file drawers full! So, when I say, as I do, that the man was meticulous, I know whereof I speak.

Most helpful in establishing a sense of intimacy and understanding has been a collection of courtship letters exchanged by Charles Henry Rammelkamp and Rhoda Jeannette Capps, who were later married. She was a native of Jacksonville, away at college, and her family had been closely connected with Illinois College for many years. In many ways, she knew more of the College than he did in his third year of service on the faculty. So when he wrote to her that one of the trustees had asked permission to submit his name to the committee searching for a new president, he naturally sought her advice. Her answer was a marvelous consideration of all the pros and cons—including what this change in situation might do to and for their prospective marriage. Finally, she left the decision to him. For one who like me remembers Jeannette Rammelkamp well and recalls her absolute devotion to Illinois College, what a delightful shock it was to see her write: "I can't bear to think of my sweetheart all worried and burdened with the cares of that octopus. And yet, I know it is not a thing to be lightly rejected. Personally, I should dread it for you and for myself, but I know I should not be childish and cowardly if you think it is best."

There have been some interesting problems in dealing with the Rammelkamp administration. My solution has been to devote two separate chapters to the Rammelkamp years. There is precedent for this in the *Centennial History*; the long administration of President Sturtevant is divided into two chapters. Next to Sturtevant, Rammelkamp has had the longest tenure of any president of Illinois College, and so deserves more extended treatment. I have placed the first chapter on Rammelkamp in Part 1 and called it "Mostly First Person," and the second chapter on him in Part 2 and subtitled it "Partly Third Person."

College histories, like county histories, are legion, and it must be admitted that many of them are miscellaneous and long-winded and self-serving. Only alma mater and her most devoted children could love them. Is there room for another? I trust there is. John Milton said of books that it was "of greatest concernment to the Commonwealth to have a vigilant eye how they demean themselves, for they are not absolutely dead things, but do contain a potency of life in them." I believe a good college is like a good book and does indeed contain a potency of life within it. It therefore should be periodically examined to see how it is demeaning itself.

Any institution is affected by the character of its leadership, but the small college is especially subject to the shaping hand of its presidents. A long-time faculty member, now emeritus, put it succinctly: "The success of Illinois College has been very largely determined by the character and judgment of its presidents. Those presidents who have identified themselves wholly with the College and have lived for it have been successful. Those who have not, even though they were conscientious administrators, have not been successful." That is not an infallible yardstick to measure by, but one could do worse.

Colleges are sometimes thought of as ivory towers and the professors therein as abstract and withdrawn, as if they could or would live apart from the rest of the world. That seems to me a pernicious notion. It has never been true of Illinois College. From its very beginnings, this College has had a great influence in Jacksonville and Morgan County and the State of Illinois, and it has made some ripples beyond these regional environs. Equally, it has been subject to the winds and currents of its time and place. It can be regarded both as unique and typical. If that appears to be a paradoxical statement, I ask you to read on, suspending judgment until you reach the end of *Pioneer's Progress*.

2

A New Missionary Arrives

One day in the early fall of 1825 a new missionary wandered into the old town of Kaskaskia, Illinois. Although fresh from an eastern seminary, he was not exactly a young man, for he had learned and practiced the trade of a tanner even before he entered Dartmouth College, and was already past thirty when he was ordained to the ministry in the Old South Church, Boston. Although Illinois College was not founded by any single individual, it was this itinerant missionary, John Millot Ellis, who started the movement which led to the founding of the College. Born in Keene, New Hampshire, in 1793, Mr. Ellis, like most New England boys, had spent his early days on a farm. It is not surprising also to learn that his father and mother were people of deep piety.

In college young Ellis seems to have made a good, although perhaps not a remarkable record. His seminary course having been completed at Andover, he set out for the West as an agent of the United Domestic Missionary Society, which soon became the better known American Home Missionary Society. When Ellis arrived at Kaskaskia, Illinois had been enjoying the privileges of statehood barely seven years. It was still part of the frontier of the United States. Roughly speaking, only the southern half of the state had been even sparsely settled, the northern half being an almost unbroken wilderness from which the Indian tribes had not yet been banished. At the time of the admission of the state, the population was about forty thousand; by 1830, or five years after the arrival of Mr. Ellis, the population had quadrupled.

Most of the settlers had come from the South, especially from Kentucky, Virginia, and Tennessee. A few Pennsylvania Dutch seem also to have settled in the region, but by 1825 people from New England and New York likewise began to come to Illinois, and the stream from that direction was destined soon to increase in volume. The Easterners came mostly to the northern part of the state and seemed more inclined than the Southerners to gather in small villages and towns. The "Yankees," as they were usually called, were not always popular among their fellow settlers from the South. They seemed always more intent on business and were a little less hospitable than their neighbors. It was this eastern element that gave a strong impetus to the movement for improving the educational facilities on the frontier.

Both the Ordinance of 1787 and the Enabling Act for Illinois recognized the importance of education. "Religion, morality and knowledge being necessary to good government and the happiness of mankind, schools and the means of education shall forever be encouraged" declares the familiar clause in that ordinance which established certain great principles for all the states of the Northwest Territory. Furthermore, in each of the states carved out of the Northwest Territory, one or two entire townships were reserved by Congress for the support of a college, or, as it was called in the case of Illinois, a "seminary of learning." It is likewise interesting and significant that the Illinois Enabling Act, instead of setting aside the usual 5 percent of the proceeds of federal land sales for roads and canals, directed that 3 percent of the 5 percent should be used "for the encouragement of learning."

The study of these documents might lead one to conclude that the road to learning in early Illinois was an easy one. However, it must be conceded that notwithstanding these great declarations, the frontiersmen of Illinois experienced many difficulties in educating their children. Indeed many of them were not particularly concerned about the education of their children, for they were too fully occupied with the stern struggle for existence to think about such things.

The missionary on the American frontier was a pioneer not only of religion but of education and civilization as well. Mr. Ellis belonged to a new band of educated ministers of the gospel who heard and heeded the call from the western country. The older group of backwoods preachers were inclined to look with jealous eyes at the new missionaries who began to come to the Illinois frontier in the late twenties and early thirties. They feared that "they were now about to be superseded and thrown aside for nice, well dressed young men from college, whom they stigmatized as having no religion in their hearts, and with knowing nothing about it, except what they learned at school." However, the personal histories of these new men proved them to be fully as religious as the earlier group and hardly a single step removed from them in the pioneering spirit. Like their forerunners they traveled to and fro over the face of the country, now along the narrow trails through the primitive forests and again over the trackless prairies.

3

The Foundations Laid

Mr. Ellis had not been long in Illinois before he saw the urgent need of better educational facilities for the settlers. Indeed, the educational needs of the country rested almost as heavily as the religious emergency upon his conscience. He realized, as have many other missionaries, that there can be no substantial progress in morality and religion without adequate educational opportunities. Therefore, almost from the beginning of his labors among the pioneers of the West, he urged that some kind of higher school, or "seminary of learning," should be established. The education provided was to be not only theoretical but also practical. Nor is it to be overlooked that the plan also contemplated some provision for the education of girls, or "females" as they were then usually called.

Of all the early settlers, the people who had gathered in various settlements along Shoal Creek in Bond County seemed to manifest the most interest in the educational dream of Mr. Ellis. They were ready immediately to cooperate with him in an effort to establish a seminary of learning. They had his plan printed and began to solicit subscriptions. According to Presbyterian ecclesiastical arrangements, at that time Illinois belonged to the presbytery of Missouri, and both Illinois and Missouri were a part of the synod of Indiana. Perhaps fortunately for the plans of Mr. Ellis and the Shoal Creek enthusiasts, presbytery met that fall of 1827 in Edwardsville, Illinois. A committee consisting of Mr. Ellis, the Rev. Salmon Giddings of St. Louis, the Rev. Hiram Chamberlain, and the elder Thomas Lippincott were appointed to confer with the trustees at Shoal Creek and to report to presbytery the next spring.

In due time the committee, or at least two members of it, Ellis and Lippincott, held a conference with the Shoal Creek trustees. The latter were eager to push forward their plans and commence at once the actual construction of a building, but fortunately a few other friends, including especially Samuel D. Lockwood, then a justice of the supreme court of the state, advised the committee not to commit itself definitely regarding a site for the proposed college until conditions in other counties further north were investigated. Mr. Ellis and Mr. Lippincott took this advice and accordingly, in January 1828, began a tour of investigation through the counties of Greene, Morgan, and Sangamon.

Traveling must have been difficult at the time of year when these two men went about the country looking for a site on which to establish a college. As Lippincott remarks in his very interesting account of the tour, the early settlements through which they passed "were yet in the gristle and thinly scattered along the road." The committee spent several days in the little village of Jacksonville, and the courtesy extended to them and the interest shown in their plans made a decidedly favorable impression on them. Several attractive sites were examined, and in particular a knoll on Mound Road, a mile or two west of Jacksonville, where Mr. Lippincott, impressed with the beauty of the spot, believed the school should be located.

It was not long before the time came when the committee must make its report to the spring meeting of presbytery, convening on this occasion in St. Louis. The friends of the enterprise were naturally anxious to have the support of presbytery. The latter's endorsement would at once give the project a standing among people in both the West and East, which it otherwise could hardly secure. However, presbytery refused to give its endorsement. The reason for the opposition to such a worthy movement was explained by the fact that it was proposed to establish the seminary "on the wrong side of the river."

Although disheartened, Mr. Ellis, it need hardly be remarked, was not the kind of man who easily gave up. Presbytery might refuse its support, but it could not in that way thwart the enterprise. As his chief fellow worker remarks, Mr. Ellis's "hope was in God and cheered by a word of encouragement from his friends, he proceeded in the work." He prepared a new subscription paper, in which it was set forth that the institution was to be located "within five miles of Jacksonville in Morgan County," and proceeded to secure subscriptions on this basis. This document, in the handwriting of Mr. Ellis, dated May 1828, yellow and brittle with age, is still in existence. The subscription list bears eloquent testimony to the interest of all classes, both rich and poor, in the enterprise.

While Ellis and his friends were laboring in the West, a group of young men at far-distant Yale in the East were wondering how they might make their lives count for something worth while in the world. How these two groups ultimately joined hands in the cause of education and religion is, indeed, an interesting story. Nor is it strange that some believed Divine Providence itself guided these two groups into a happy and fruitful union. Illinois College certainly could not have been founded without the help which came from the East.

A strong and growing interest in the cause of home missions was just then manifesting itself among the students in the theological seminary at Yale College. The West was attracting from year to year an increasing number of settlers, and these young students realized, as did many others, that the new country beyond the mountains was destined to play an important part in the history of the United States, and they felt, in spite of their youth, a grave sense of responsibility for the welfare of the region. Among the seminary students there existed a Society of Inquiry Respecting Missions, and one evening late in November 1828 one of its members, Theron Baldwin, read an essay on "The Encouragements to Active Individual Efforts in the Cause of Christ," which seems to have aroused great interest among his friends. Writes Julian Sturtevant, "Returning to his room after the meeting that night, Mr. Baldwin fell in with his college classmate, Mason Grosvenor," who had been pondering for some time upon a certain missionary and educational scheme. Grosvenor outlined his ideas to his friend, and these suggestions became the basis of a new association among the divinity students of Yale, which proved the chief factor in the founding of Illinois College.

Briefly stated, Grosvenor's idea was to combine religion and education, to form an association whose members should pledge themselves to go out to one of the new western states or territories and there establish an institution of learning. All members of the association were to cooperate for the welfare of the proposed college, some as teachers in the school, and others as missionaries, working in the respective communities, preaching the gospel, establishing churches and Sabbath schools, and sending promising young men to the college. As the plan was suggested to various fellow students, it met with hearty approval. But to what particular locality should they go? Grosvenor almost immediately busied himself trying to find an answer to that question and in order to get further light turned to *The Home Missionary*, a recently established religious periodical.

Grosvenor's attention was especially attracted by a letter in the current number written by the Rev. J. M. Ellis and dated Jacksonville, Morgan Co., Illinois, September 25, 1828. It told of the encouraging prospects in the little Presbyterian Church to whose pulpit Mr. Ellis had so recently come. After emphasizing the urgent need for more missionaries, the letter concluded in two paragraphs, which deserve to be quoted at length on account of their influence in shaping the thoughts of these young men who were to become founders of Illinois College.

A SEMINARY OF LEARNING

Is projected to go into operation next fall. The subscription now stands at between 2 and $3,000. The site is selected in this county, Morgan, and the selection made with considerable deliberation, by a committee appointed for that purpose; and is one in which the public sentiment perfectly coincides. The half quarter section purchased for the site, is certainly the most delightful spot I have ever seen. It is about one mile north of the celebrated Diamond Grove, at the east end of Wilson Grove, on an eminence overlooking the town and country for several miles around.

The object of the Seminary is popular, and it is my deliberate opinion that there never was in our country a more promising opportunity for any who desire it, to bestow a few thousand dollars in the cause of education, and of Missions. The posture of things now is such, as to show to all the intelligent people the good effects of your society, and to secure their co-operation in a happy degree in all the great benevolent objects of the day, if such aid can now be afforded in the objects above mentioned.

It is easy to imagine with what keen and absorbing interest Grosvenor read that letter. Here, apparently, was the very opportunity which he and his friends were seeking. The college had not yet been established; only a beginning had been made in the enterprise, and it might be possible, therefore, to carry out their great plan by uniting with these western friends. Mr. Grosvenor at once dispatched a letter of inquiry to the author of this article.

Illinois College is decidedly fortunate in possessing much of the contemporary material relating to the earliest beginnings of the school, and among the archives is the original letter dated December 5, 1828, which young Grosvenor sent to Mr. Ellis from New Haven. He asks for general information regarding this section of the western country, its climate, its diseases, and especially its moral and religious condition. He outlined for his western correspondent the plan which he and his fellow students of the seminary had been discussing. "It would be their intention," he explains, "to select a spot, the most favorable for exerting an influence, with a view of taking up their abode for life. It would also be desirable for them to settle as near each other as circumstances would allow with the expectation of having their number increased yearly. One of their first objects would be to establish a seminary of learning where in due time young men may acquire a thorough education, both collegiate and theological, and thus be prepared for the ministry. From your statements," he continues, "this section of the western country seems to strike our minds as a favorable spot for such efforts."

In the meantime, all unconscious of the interest which the article in the *Home Missionary* had aroused in the East, the local friends of the enterprise were proceeding further with their plans. On the third of January 1829, the trustees had held another meeting and adopted a plan for a building prepared by James Kerr. One of the group, Mr. Posey, has left an account of what happened that day. Says he: "We were on our horses on our way to set the stakes for the seminary. As we passed Dr. Chandler's, Mr. Ellis came out and called to us. 'I have something to show you' said he. We stopped and he read to us the letter from Mr. Grosvenor. You can't imagine how much it encouraged and animated us. It seemed to come to us from the Lord in answer to prayer. We received it as such."

While impatiently awaiting a reply from Illinois, young Grosvenor and the friends who shared his enthusiasm sought further knowledge and advice. The young men grew more enthusiastic about their great design every day and steps were soon taken to perfect their organization. A constitution, drafted by Grosvenor and a fellow student, Sturtevant, was duly adopted. A few days later a solemn pledge, or compact, was adopted and signed.

Believing in the entire alienation of the natural heart from God, in the necessity of the influences of the Holy Spirit for its renovation, and that these influences are not to be expected without the use of means; deeply impressed also with the destitute condition of the western sections of our country and the urgent claims of its inhabitants upon the benevolent at the East, and in view of the fearful crisis evidently approaching, and which we believe can only be averted by speedy and energetic measures on the part of the friends of religion and literature in the older states, and believing that evangelical religion and education must go hand in hand in order to the successful accomplishment of this desirable object; we the undersigned hereby express our readiness to go to the state of Illinois for the purpose of establishing a seminary of learning such as shall be best adapted to the exigencies of that country—a part of us to engage as instructors in the seminary—the others to occupy—as preachers—important stations in the surrounding country—provided the undertaking be deemed practicable, and the location approved by intelligent men—and provided also the Providence of God permit us to engage in it.

Theological Department	THERON BALDWIN
	JOHN F. BROOKS
Yale College—Feb. 21, 1829	MASON GROSVENOR
	ELISHA JENNEY
	WILLIAM KIRBY
	JULIAN M. STURTEVANT
	ASA TURNER, JR.

Two days later the compact was certified by Professor Nath. W. Taylor and Professor Josiah W. Gibbs and further endorsed by the President of Yale College, Jeremiah Day: "I fully concur in the above recommendations, being familiarly acquainted with a majority of the Gentlemen and having satisfactory information concerning the others."

The next step was to get the formal endorsement of the American Home Missionary Society; Mr. Sturtevant was accordingly sent to New York as the representative of the association. He met with the directors of the Missionary Society, who accepted the plan as practicable and "appeared perfectly willing to lend all their influence and contribute funds to its support." A little later a formal agreement with the Illinois stockholders was prepared and sent to Mr. Ellis. About the same time Theron Baldwin and Julian M. Sturtevant were selected as the representatives of the association to go out to Illinois in the fall. If they could come to an agreement with the Illinois shareholders regarding a few fundamental principles, they were ready to enter heart and soul into the undertaking. These general principles were two: (1) a board of trustees of a limited number should have full control of the seminary "independent of any extraneous influence"; (2) the board of trustees should have full power to fill their own vacancies. If a union could be effected on the basis of these principles, they were ready to furnish ten thousand dollars for the institution, two thousand payable at the time of union and the balance within two years.

Young Sturtevant was engaged to be married, and consequently before signing the compact it was necessary for him to consult the wishes of a certain Miss Fayerweather, who if he went West would have to share with him the discomforts and dangers of life on the frontier. However, the young lady, loyal to her lover and herself inspired with high motives, proved ready to face any difficulties and discomforts. "The whole subject," says Sturtevant, "was laid before Miss Fayerweather and without the least attempt to conceal the trials incident to the location of our home five hundred miles west of civilization. She was far from being a romantic girl. At twenty-two years of age, she was a woman of rare thoughtfulness and sobriety, and judging correctly of the future, cheerfully approved the plan."

The western trustees in due time received the proposed terms of union and agreed to them unanimously. In fact, they regarded the terms as "liberal and generous." At a meeting of the local trustees held before the communication was received, Mr. Ellis had already been appointed an agent to solicit subscriptions in the East. Furthermore, the ecclesiastical clouds were clearing away, for about this time the Presbytery of Illinois, which had in the meantime been separated from that of Missouri, met in Jacksonville and warmly endorsed the seminary enterprise.

On account of the pressure of other interests, it was not considered wise just then to conduct a public campaign for funds in Boston, but the matter was presented to several individuals there. Furthermore, Mr. Ellis secured in Boston several hundred books for the proposed school. At Andover, both faculty and students showed a warm interest in the project, while in New Haven a public meeting was held in one of the churches on Sabbath evening and subscriptions amounting to some twelve hundred dollars were secured. Asa Turner was appointed to visit Albany, Troy, and New York in company with Mr. Ellis, and in October subscriptions were more actively solicited in Boston. The effort succeeded even beyond the expectations of the friends of the cause. The ten thousand dollars were soon raised, and the Association was ready to consummate its plans. Mr. Sturtevant was formally designated as an instructor in the seminary at an annual salary of four hundred dollars and requested to begin his teaching immediately upon his arrival in Illinois. Near the end of August both he and Baldwin were ordained to the ministry at Woodbury, Connecticut, and a few days later Mr. Sturtevant and Miss Fayerweather were married. After short visits with a few relatives the bride and groom went to New Haven to attend the annual college commencement at which the groom received his master's degree.

In October the long wedding journey to the West began. For the young man it was a journey not away from his home but towards it, for his parents had been pioneers in their day, and were now residing in the village of Tallmadge in northeastern Ohio. Descended from Mayflower stock, Mr. Sturtevant was born in Warren, Litchfield County, Connecticut, in 1805. His earliest schooling in the rudimentary subjects of reading, writing, spelling, and arithmetic was received in the typical New England school district of Warren, and his earliest religious impressions and experiences were those of the typical New England home, supplemented by the services of the village meeting-house. Occasionally the boy was privileged to listen to the "eloquent preaching" of Dr. Lyman Beecher, who, following a good old custom of New England, often exchanged pulpits with the local pastor. Prospects in Warren, however, were not very bright for the Sturtevant family. They belonged to the "frugal farmer" class, but the most rigid frugality could not extract much profit from the "rugged and barren" soil of their farm, not to mention the economic depression created throughout New England by the War of 1812. Like many other New England farmers, the elder Sturtevant therefore decided to move West with his wife and four children. And so it happened that Julian when hardly eleven years of age made his first journey to the western frontier. To the childhood experiences of stern New England was now added the strenuous life of the wilderness.

Education and character building must not be neglected. It was decided that both Julian and his elder brother should go to college, and accordingly during the winter months, they began their preparation in Latin and Greek in an academy which fortunately had been established in Tallmadge. Yale was the college selected, but when the time came for making the trip, there was no cash in the family treasury to pay for the journey, to say nothing of later expenses in college. One marvels with Mr. Sturtevant that their parents "should consent that two sons, one of whom had not reached the age of seventeen, while the other was scarcely nineteen, should try their fortunes at Yale with absolutely no resources to depend upon. It was a venture which nothing could excuse but their firm trust in Providence." Very practical efforts were made, however, to assist a benevolent Providence.

The young man who was starting west with his bride on that October day in 1829 was no green novice in the life of a pioneer. The interesting details of this wedding journey from the hills of Connecticut to the prairies of Illinois are duly recorded in President Sturtevant's *Autobiography*. By various stagecoaches, canal boats, river steamboats, and finally a "team and driver," they reached the end of their journey. It was Sunday morning, November 15, 1829, when they entered the little village of Jacksonville, where a hearty welcome awaited them at the home of Mr. Ellis.

Mr. Sturtevant's duties began at once. "When breakfast and family worship were over, it was time for church," he recalled later, and he was called upon "to preach the sermon." This he was not ready to do, for he had prepared no manuscript. He soon learned that on the frontier a preacher who needed a manuscript was not very well regarded. So, with all his other problems, he had to wrestle with that of preaching without a manuscript.

The College building was not yet completed, and for a few weeks he was not very busy. About a month after the arrival of the Sturtevants, a meeting of the local subscribers, or stockholders, was held in order to perfect the organization of the school. The meeting took place "amid the shavings and carpenter benches" of the building still in progress of construction. "The President of the meeting had no seat but the carpenter's bench, and the members stood." The communication from the "Illinois Association" (later known as the "Yale Band") which Sturtevant and Baldwin had brought with them was formally presented to the meeting. The eastern friends expressed in this document their readiness to consummate the plans for the proposed union. Not only had the promised ten thousand dollars been secured but they were confident of raising a still larger amount; two thousand dollars was now being forwarded to the West by the hands of Sturtevant and Baldwin, the remainder of the money, as collected, would be deposited in the East, where it might be drawn on by the local trustees as the needs of the College required. The terms of the agreement were unanimously accepted and resolutions expressing deep appreciation of the assistance from the East were passed. Before the meeting adjourned another important step was taken—the new school was christened "Illinois College."

A little later on in the day the trustees elected Samuel D. Lockwood their President, J. M. Sturtevant, Secretary pro tem, and J. P. Wilkinson, Treasurer. At this meeting Mr. Sturtevant's appointment as first instructor in Illinois College was confirmed.

4

President Beecher, 1830–1844

Instruction began in Illinois College on the morning of Monday, January 4, 1830. Sturtevant wrote to Thomas Lippincott some weeks later:

> I repaired to the building and found the floors completed, and the building quite enclosed, but no lathing or plastering, no stove, no teacher's desk and only a part of the seats for the pupils completed. But we were pledged to commence instruction at that time. Nine students had presented themselves for instruction. I was accompanied and assisted by Wm. C. Posey, Esq. to whose active efforts to nurse its infancy, the college owes much. Our first business was to put up a stove, which occupied us about two hours, carpenters and teacher, and trustee and students co-operating in the work. Pupils were then called to order. I addressed them a few words and among other things told them what my heart felt and believed, that we had come there that morning to open a fountain for future generations to drink at. We then commended ourselves and the whole great enterprise to God in prayer. It was to me a season never to be forgotten, whatever the fate of the college may be. I then proceeded to inquire into the intellectual condition of my pupils. Not one of them had ever studied English grammar or geography, a few had learned the ground rules of arithmetic and two had some knowledge of the rudiments of Latin.

As a matter of fact for the first few years of its existence, the College was little more than a preparatory school. How could it have been otherwise, for there was probably not a young man in the whole

President Edward Beecher

state really prepared to begin collegiate studies. It was not until 1831 that the first fully prepared collegiate class was admitted.

While Mr. Sturtevant continued as the sole instructor, steps were being taken to find a president and additional teachers for the new school. The local trustees wisely delegated the power of selecting a president to their eastern colleagues, who naturally conferred with President Day and the faculty of Yale about the matter. After several months of deliberation the position was offered to Edward Beecher, pastor of the Park Street Church, Boston. He accepted. It proved a fortunate choice for the infant college, for Edward Beecher was a member of Lyman Beecher's family, who possessed not only an attractive personality but also real intellectual ability and great moral courage. When the news of the selection reached Jacksonville, Sturtevant, who already knew him rejoiced "that the leading responsibility of the institution was soon to pass into the hands of a man so competent, so strong and so devoted." The selection established an interesting connection between the College and this family which has achieved such distinction in American history. That Mr. Beecher was willing to give up the pastorate of an important church on Boston Common in order to become the president of an obscure, struggling school on the western frontier shows what motives dominated his life and character. The same zeal and motives influenced, however, practically all of the early faculty of the College.

Regular collegiate instruction had begun in 1831, it being in that year that the first regular freshman class was admitted into the College. Mr. Sturtevant had continued as the sole instructor in collegiate studies while one Erastus Colton acted as instructor in preparatory studies. William Kirby, another member of the Illinois Association, or "Yale Band," had come west in 1831 and gave some assistance in the work of instruction as a tutor from 1831 to 1833. A full faculty and the establishment of new courses became necessary only when other classes entered and the students already in the institution were prepared for more advanced work.

Near the end of the year 1832, Truman M. Post, a recent graduate of Middlebury College, Vermont, came to the city of Washington. He was a nephew of Reuben Post, at that time pastor of a Presbyterian Church in that city and Chaplain of the United States Senate.

Able and ambitious, young Post was filled with a high purpose to dedicate his life to some useful calling. He had tried teaching, had studied law and also dipped into theology, but was still uncertain and restless. In Washington he hoped to see and hear some of the great statesmen of the day—Webster, Clay, Calhoun, Marshall, and others. His wish was gratified, and these men made a deep impression upon his mind, but a chance acquaintance with a modest congressman from Illinois, General Joseph Duncan, exerted a more potent influence upon his career. At the urgent invitation of General Duncan, young Post made a trip to the West in the spring of 1833. He writes later in life:

I remember one day soon after my arrival in Jacksonville a call from Rev. Edward Beecher and Rev. J. M. Sturtevant, who were teachers in the college just opened, and whose names the west and the whole country have since learned to know. They inquired if I would for a little while aid them in the classical department in the new college, as they were at that time in need of a teacher and had learned that I had been engaged in teaching at Middlebury College. The proposition struck me favorably, attractively; my sphere of life was, I felt, yet unfixed; my determination of thought and action between educational, political, clerical, literary and legal pursuits was yet unsettled. "The world was all before me where to choose," and so I consented to the proposition made me, as a temporary arrangement.

The "temporary arrangement" proved the beginning of nineteen years of loyal and efficient service on the faculty of the College.

The same spring of 1833 another young man was added to the instructional staff. President Beecher had written to President Day of Yale College asking him to recommend a teacher, and the latter had suggested a young man who was just then completing his senior year at Yale—Jonathan Baldwin Turner. He evidently was a youth of ability and promise, and his subsequent career amply demonstrated the good judgment of the man who had recommended him. President Day excused this senior from his final examinations and promised to send him his diploma. Early in the spring, therefore, young Turner set forth on his journey to the West, arriving in Jacksonville on the eighth of May 1833. The following year the trustees formally appointed Mr. Turner Professor of Rhetoric and Belles Lettres.

A few years later Samuel Adams was appointed Professor of Chemistry, Mineralogy, and Geology. A graduate of Bowdoin, where he had been a student in the days when Longfellow held the chair of modern languages, Adams proved a worthy colleague of the men who had preceded him to this western college. After graduation from college he had taught school for one year and then turned to the study of medicine. His Alma Mater conferred the degree of M.D. upon him in 1836, and it was two years later that the call to Illinois came. He was to remain on the faculty for over thirty-eight years.

These five men, Beecher, Sturtevant, Post, Turner, and Adams, with a few temporary instructors or tutors, constituted the early faculty of the College. It was, indeed, a remarkable group. They were all men of real ability, fired by that youthful enthusiasm which enabled them to conquer difficulties and endure hardships which would have discouraged older men. Of the number, Sturtevant was, perhaps, intellectually the most able. He was a keen, thorough student with a fertile, logical mind. Turner was, without doubt, the most versatile and independent member of the group. Interested in many different fields of knowledge, active in many enterprises, he was always perfectly fearless in expressing his convictions. Post commanded a brilliant style. As a writer, and perhaps still more as a speaker, he was always witty and entertaining. The fact that President Beecher commanded the respect and devotion of such men as these is sufficient testimony to his own worth. In intellectual ability, moral character, and administrative capacity, he proved a worthy leader of this group of able young scholars. With such a faculty it is not surprising that the College grew and prospered, weathering several storms that threatened to destroy it in its infancy.

The course of study during these early days deserves a word. Illinois College, like every other institution of higher learning at that time, made its students follow closely a prescribed course of study. Modern science with its laboratory equipment and experimental methods was unknown either East or West, and modern languages were barely beginning to receive attention. The whole field of modern history, politics, and economics was practically neglected, and therefore to appreciate the curriculum and standards of Illinois College in that day one must bear in mind the educational limitations of the age. The modern college with its bewildering variety of elective courses had not come into existence anywhere.

The student studied in his freshman year algebra, geometry, trigonometry, Graeca Majora with Lysias and Isocrates, Livy and Roman antiquities; there were optional courses in rhetoric and belles lettres. Sophomores wrestled with plane and spherical trigonometry, mensuration, navigation, conic sections, mechanics and hydrostatics, Graeca Majora, volume 1 completed, and extracts from Homer. In Latin, they read Horace. Juniors studied outlines of ancient and modern history and a variety of subjects called pneumatics, electricity, magnetism, and optics, subjects which later developed into the science of physics. They likewise studied astronomy, Tacitus, and De Officiis. Optional studies for juniors included such subjects as experiments in natural philosophy, history of the Latin and Greek languages, philosophy, and chemistry. Seniors were required to take intellectual and moral philosophy, logic, natural theology and evidences of Christianity, a critical study of selected Greek and Latin authors, political economy (such as it was), American law, and rhetoric. In Illinois College, as in every other institution of that period, Greek, Latin, and mathematics formed the backbone of the course. Experiments in natural philosophy, English literature, and chemistry were optional studies for seniors.

There was also an organization known as the Rhetorical Society which embraced in its membership "all members of the college classes and as many others as chose to unite themselves with it." The society held periodic "exhibitions" at which declamations were delivered and compositions criticized. Occasionally a formal public lecture was delivered before this society as when, for example, Henry Ward Beecher came over from Indianapolis in 1843 to address the society.

On completing the college course, students were to be "faithfully examined by the Faculty and such Committee as the Trustees may appoint, together with such other gentlemen of a liberal education as may be present." During ten weeks previous to annual commencement seniors reviewed the studies of the entire course.

The college calendar of the earliest years differed materially from the present arrangements. Perhaps the chief difference is found in the fact that the long vacation did not occur during the summer months. On the contrary, instruction continued throughout the hot season, and commencement, instead of occurring in June, was celebrated in September. The laws of 1837 declared that the annual commencement should be held on the third Wednesday in September; there were two vacations, one of eight weeks from commencement day and the other of four weeks from the Wednesday preceding the seventh day of April. This arrangement continued until the academic year 1839–40, when commencement day was changed to the last Wednesday in June.

The year in which Post and Turner joined the faculty proved a trying time to both College and village, for it was the year when a terrible cholera epidemic carried off many of the settlers. During the early summer of 1833 several towns of the Mississippi Valley had been devastated by the scourge, and in July it broke out in Jacksonville. The town then had a population of about eighteen hundred. It is difficult to estimate the number of the stricken. Over one hundred people died, and it is said nearly one-half of the population fled from the city. Young Turner wrote to his sweetheart in the East: "To meet a man at night and attend his funeral in the morning has ceased to alarm, much less to surprise. Some die in three hours, seldom do they live twelve and very rarely twenty-four."

Among the very first families stricken was that of the Rev. J. M. Ellis. Mrs. Ellis, her two children and a niece all succumbed to the malady within a few days, mother and one child being buried in the same grave. Ellis, himself, was away in Indiana at the time. When, apparently unconscious of what had happened in his absence, he returned to Jacksonville he stopped at his church "to attend prayer meeting before going to his home. . . . As he entered the door he heard a friend praying for their stricken pastor, so suddenly bereft of all his family. He fell to the floor as if he had been struck by a butcher's ax." Mrs. Beecher and Mrs. Sturtevant were also stricken, but it was after the disease had somewhat "spent itself" and they both recovered.

The college community, possibly because of its situation on higher ground some distance from the village, escaped the worst ravages of the disease. College work proceeded, but the closing exercises of 1833 were indefinitely postponed, and students were given permission to go to their homes. Although many students were afflicted, apparently only one died. Students and faculty courageously assisted their stricken friends, watching them night after night, and administering to their needs. The professors "gave up Latin and Greek and turned to cooks, bottle-washers, etc. The College was a perfect hospital for more than two weeks."

Almost from the very beginning of the movement for the establishment of the College, thoughts were entertained of introducing a system of manual labor for the benefit of the students. How important the idea seemed to the founders is evident from the fact that the state legislature recognized the system in the charter which was eventually granted to the College. In such a new country there were many young men of slender means, and the founders of the College were eager to lend a helping hand to every deserving youth. The interest of the trustees and early faculty in a system of manual labor was prompted not only by the desire to help worthy young men but also by the necessity of securing laborers for the College. Skilled mechanics and ordinary laborers were scarce in the West of those days. Land was so cheap and promised such large returns that only the highest wages would attract men. Under such circumstances why would it not be an excellent plan to utilize students, especially since their labor could be secured so cheaply? The idea was embraced with enthusiasm.

The College thus maintained both a shop and a farm, and the catalogue announced that students who wished to work their way through college might find an opportunity to do so. The original plans for providing board for students were closely related to this scheme of manual labor. Mr. Baldwin was strongly opposed to the idea of a college commons. Recalling the bread and butter rebellions at Yale, he feared that a college commons in the West would be even "more prolific in rebellions than at the East." But the trustees proposed "to furnish the necessary buildings, utensils, etc. and rent them to the students." They proposed also "to rent them land for gardens where they might raise all their vegetables." Some years later Sturtevant expressed the opinion that if the money wasted in the manual labor scheme and the large student dormitory had been otherwise invested "the College would have known much less of pecuniary embarrassment."

Meanwhile the College was operating without a charter. It is somewhat curious that such pronounced opposition to the legal incorporation of the College should have manifested itself, but there evidently existed in the state a widespread suspicion of the whole movement to establish colleges—a suspicion which members of the state legislature shared. A bill for a charter was introduced, but the members of the legislature gave it a cold reception. Some said it was a scheme for uniting church and state, while others suspected it might be a conspiracy of land speculators to get control of large tracts of land.

It was not until 1835 that Illinois College finally obtained a charter from the legislature. What ignorance and prejudice the friends of learning had to overcome even in that session is evident from the declaration of a member on the floor of the lower house who proudly proclaimed that he was "born in a briar thicket, rocked in a hog trough and had never had his genius cramped by the pestilential air of a college." However, influential friends, including especially Governor Duncan and Judge Lockwood, had now become interested in the cause. Also, Mr. Theron Baldwin was asked by the Senate Committee on Petitions, to whom the request for a charter was submitted, to draw up arguments in favor of granting the request. So this friend of the College supplied persuasive reasons for adopting the proposal. If the state was to have a good system of common schools, where could teachers be trained for their work? The time had certainly come when the state of Illinois should have too much pride to depend upon other states for the training of its teachers. The fear of such institutions was entirely unfounded, argued the committee's report. "Not only do facts prove the safety of such literary corporations, but the nature of the case also shows that they are exposed to fewer influences which may lead to a perversion than almost any other class of corporations." Asked the committee, "Shall Illinois, with its unrivalled location, beauty, fertility, and natural resources, which prepare it to stand preeminent in the confederacy, degrade itself in the eyes of the whole nation by refusing to foster literary institutions?" This time, the legislature was convinced and passed the bill.

The act provided for the incorporation not only of Illinois College but of three other institutions. The objects of these institutions were declared to be "the promotion of the general interests of education, and to qualify young men to engage in the several employments and professions of society and to discharge honorably and usefully the various duties of life." The boards of trustees named in the charter were given power to elect their successors, and other broad powers of control were conferred upon them. However, in one or two respects, their powers were very strictly limited. For example, the establishment of a theological department in any of the colleges was absolutely prohibited, nor might any one of the colleges hold more than 640 acres of land. To insure an observance of the principle of religious toleration in the management of these colleges, the charter provided that the schools should be open to "all denominations of Christians and the profession of any particular religious faith shall not be required of those who become students."

The design for the seal of the College was recommended by President Beecher. It will be noted that the device in the center is surrounded by the words "Sigillum Collegii Illinoiensis." The device itself represents three pillars—Religion, Liberty, and Science—resting on the foundation of the Word of God and supporting the arch of Rights and Laws. We are informed by the trustees' record that the "import of the device may be thus briefly stated: The Word of God is the only sure foundation of science, true liberty and religion, the three pillars of the social system, and these alone can maintain inviolate our laws and rights." The figure standing between the pillars of liberty and knowledge represents the "civil magistrate bearing the sword of justice to demand liberty and check licentiousness."

The first collegiate class was graduated from the College in 1835. The graduates on this interesting occasion were two in number—Richard Yates, who became the war governor of Illinois, and Jonathan Spillman, later a minister of the gospel who wrote appropriate music to the lines, "Flow Gently, Sweet Afton." The latter was valedictorian, but consented, as a consolation to his classmate, that Yates should be the first to receive a diploma from the College. Two masters' degrees (honorary) were also conferred, and the printed program of this commencement shows that many other students spoke; the exercises occupied both the forenoon and afternoon of the day.

The College had not been in operation a year when a meeting was held at the home of one of the trustees, John P. Wilkinson, to consider the question of establishing "a Female Seminary in the town of Jacksonville." The committee recommended on October 2, 1830, "that an Academy ought to be immediately established to be devoted to female education" and that Jacksonville was "a situation highly favorable for the successful operation of such an institution." The school was not incorporated until 1835, when it received a charter from the same legislature which granted articles of incorporation to Illinois College. The first principal of the Academy was Miss Sarah C. Crocker, who was first recommended to the trustees by that well-known pioneer in the movement for the higher education of women in the United States, Mary Lyon of South Hadley, Massachusetts.

Nor would the history of these times be complete without mention of the Ladies' Education Society—that pioneer organization which has really accomplished large things for the education of women in the Middle West through the financial aid which it has extended and still extends to worthy young women who are seeking an education. It was in 1832 that this society under the earlier name of The Ladies' Association for Educating Females was organized, with the help of the wives of the members of the college faculty.

The student life of these early years arouses our interest and curiosity. In some respects it has much in common with the student life of our own time; in other respects, however, there were differences. The spirit of discipline was totally different from that of our own day. The early professor was a sort of policeman, and the student aimed to make his life as uncomfortable as possible. Practical jokes upon members of the faculty seem to have been the chief aim of student frolics. Professors inquired minutely into the daily life of students; rules and restrictions were numerous, even corporal pun-

ishment being occasionally administered. College athletics, that
great safety valve for superabundant student energy, were, of course,
unknown. The absence of many of the modern conveniences and the
general conditions of frontier life made necessary many regulations
which have since become obsolete.

The religious life of the students was carefully and even strenu-
ously regulated. There were morning and evening prayers in the college chapel, which all students were required to attend. Morning
prayers were held "half an hour after the ringing of the second bell
for breakfast" (which apparently meant prayer at the early hour of
five), "and evening prayers at 6 in the summer and at 5 in the winter
term." Students were also required to attend chapel service every
Sabbath, unless their parents specifically requested that they be allowed to attend services at some other place of worship in the village.

The "laws" of 1837 solemnly enjoined students to treat the members of the faculty not only "with that politeness which is required
by the rules of refined society, but also with that respect and defer-
ence which is due to them as the executors of the laws, and the constituted guardians of the institution." This college code declared that
the penalties for breaches of discipline should be "chiefly moral,
addressed to the conscience and the principles of honor and shame,"
but the term "moral" had a wide application, for moral punishments
were enumerated as "admonition, private or before the faculty, or
the class, or the students at large, suspension, limited or indefinite,
dismission and expulsion." It was an age when pecuniary fines still
played an important part in college discipline. Professor Turner used
a system of fines to encourage students to attend to their work in his
"Rhetorical Exercises," and students who retained a book from the
college library longer than two weeks were fined 6¼ cents for the
first week beyond the specified time, 12½ cents for the second and
25 cents for every subsequent week.

Students were held responsible for any disturbance taking place in
their rooms unless it could be clearly shown that the disturbance
occurred without their knowledge or consent. An instructor had
authority to enter the room of a student at any time. It was a standing rule of the faculty that an instructor should visit all of the rooms
of the students at least once a week. If a student refused to open his

door when requested to do so by a member of the faculty, the latter might break open the door and the student was to bear the expense of repairing the damage.

On the whole, college students of those days were treated more like boys than men. It was a common thing to compel students to make public confession of their guilt not only before the faculty but before the whole body of their fellow students. Sometimes a member of the faculty wrote out a confession which the student was then compelled to sign and publicly read.

One of the most important problems which caused much work and worry for both trustees and faculty was the financial problem. If the members of the faculty had not been inspired with such missionary zeal and a willingness to make large sacrifices, the College could not possibly have weathered the financial storms which broke upon it again and again. By 1835 a determined movement was started to increase the financial resources of the institution. Practically all the members of the faculty were authorized by the trustees to go forth on this crusade for more funds. It was hoped to raise one-hundred thousand dollars "to be appropriated to the erection of new buildings, payment of debts, support of a professor of chemistry, enlargement of library and apparatus," etc. The movement evidently met with considerable success. It was a time of high hopes and unbounded speculation in the financial affairs of the nation, and the College evidently felt the thrill of the general financial prosperity. Plans were undertaken to enlarge still further the work of the institution. However, the terrible financial crash of 1837, which paralyzed every business enterprise of the country, also proved a severe blow to the College. The "magnificent sum" which had been raised during the previous two years was almost entirely in the form of subscription notes and now, since the subscribers had failed, it melted away.

At the beginning of the year 1843, the College owed the president and professors $7,497, a sum which was more than the faculty salary budget for an entire year. Other bills were apparently being paid, and the result was that the members of the faculty complained of the administration of the finances of the treasurer, Nathaniel Coffin. The latter, in defense of his methods, insisted that there were certain bills that must be paid to maintain the general credit of the institution and that for the same reason his own personal credit must be maintained, even if the salaries of the professors could not be paid in full.

Not only Illinois College but a number of other western institutions such as Western Reserve, Wabash, Marietta, and Knox were having similar difficulties, and their agents were all flocking to the East begging for funds. Friends who were interested in these colleges realized that something must be done to systematize these appeals and save the colleges. It was under these circumstances that the Society for the Promotion of Collegiate and Theological Education at the West was organized in the city of New York in 1843. This society under the direction of Theron Baldwin, who became its secretary, proved to be of great assistance to many of the early colleges which are today among the strongest in the West. The first year of its existence, it appropriated to Illinois College $3,774, and it continued to grant additional aid from time to time.

Begging for money was a task which President Beecher never enjoyed, and as the financial clouds kept gathering, he became more and more discouraged. He thought that relief might be secured if he could only work in the East for a longer period, and accordingly when he went East in 1842, he took his family with him. He never returned to his duties as president. In February 1844 he wrote to the prudential committee asking to be relieved of the presidency of the College. Although he may have lost confidence in his own ability to perform the task just then most urgent, he had not in the least lost interest in the College. On the contrary he believed his position in the East would afford him an opportunity to help the cause. He wrote to his colleagues on the faculty: "Illinois College, and all its interests are deeply engraven on my heart, and I love with undiminished affection my former associates there, and in bidding farewell to college hill and its endeared occupants, and its delightful scenery and sacred associations, I sunder some of my strongest earthly ties." The trustees accepted the resignation with sincere regret and asked for his aid in the selection of a successor.

5

The Medical School

The trustees and faculty were ambitious to widen the field of instruction in the institution so as to include both law and medicine, as well as theology. Although the prohibition against the teaching of theology inserted in the original charter was repealed in 1841, no school of theology was ever organized, in spite of the strong desire adequately to prepare young men for service in the Christian ministry. Nor was a school or professorship of law ever established. However, more definite progress was made at an early date in the field of medical instruction. In fact the first medical school established in the state was that organized at Illinois College, antedating by a few months the founding of Rush Medical College in Chicago.

Four professorships were created and the following doctors elected to fill the chairs: David Prince of Quincy, anatomy and surgery; Samuel Adams, Illinois College, chemistry, etc.; Daniel Stahl, Quincy, theory and practice of medicine; Henry Jones, Jacksonville, obstetrics, etc. On November 1, 1843, actual instruction in medicine began in the College. The first year fourteen students were in attendance of whom five were graduated in 1845 with the degree of M.D.

The course of lectures extended over a period of sixteen weeks, beginning the first of November. The charge for the full course was sixty dollars and an extra fee of five dollars had to be paid for "tickets for private dissections." Prospective missionaries, "wishing to pursue medical studies for that purpose," were to be admitted to the lectures without expense. The requirements for the degree of M.D. deserve to be quoted at length, illustrating, as they do, the general standards of medical education in the country at that time. The following qualifications were to "entitle a young gentleman to the degree of Doctor of Medicine":

1. He must possess a competent acquaintance with the Latin language, and a sufficient knowledge of all the usual branches of an English education.
2. He must have pursued a thorough course of study with some regular practitioner.
3. He must have attended two full courses of medical lectures, the last of which must be at this institution; provided, however, that experience in the practice of medicine may be accepted in the place of one course of lectures.
4. He must pass a satisfactory examination in all branches of medical study, before the Medical Faculty, assisted by a board of Censors, annually appointed for that purpose by the Trustees.
5. He must publicly read and defend a dissertation on some medical subject.
N.B. This Institution does not require any definite term of study as a condition of graduation. A thorough knowledge of all the branches of medical science, whether acquired in a longer or shorter time, must, however, be exhibited at the examination.

Judged by the number of its students, the Medical School must have achieved a fair degree of prosperity. In the 1846–47 academic year, for example, it enrolled thirty-nine students. The following year there were thirty students in the medical department, or three more than in the College. Yet in spite of its apparent prosperity the school abruptly ceased operations at the end of the academic year 1847–48. Not a word of explanation appears in the minutes of the board of trustees, and no statement was made in the catalogue. Uncertainty and perhaps even mystery shroud the end of this pioneer medical school. Dr. Carl Black believed that the "anatomy question"—that is, the rumors about methods used to acquire cadavers for dissection—was more important than any other single factor in the discontinuation, but Dr. Samuel Willard, one of its well-known graduates, gives a more prosaic but possibly the correct reason: "The school was discontinued because it did not pay the professors who came from abroad to lose their practice at home for all they got by the professorship. For the most part they had promissory notes, the payment of which was indefinite."

6

Illinois College and the Antislavery Movement

Illinois College played more than a minor role in the antislavery movement in Illinois and the Middle West. Its relation to the great struggle over the slavery question possesses more than a merely temporary or local interest. The importance of the issues involved, the prominence of the men who participated in the struggle, the bitterness of the dispute in a community where people from New England and the South met face to face give the story a significance that extends beyond the walls of the College and the limits of Jacksonville.

The characteristics of the early population of Illinois have already been mentioned. Not only did the fertile prairies of the state attract the ambitious, thrifty Yankee but the fact that Illinois was forever dedicated to freedom by the Ordinance of 1787 probably also influenced the pioneer from New England to settle within its bounds. The New Englander naturally brought with him his antagonism to the system of slavery. But these fertile fields were just as attractive to people from the slave states of Kentucky and Virginia. Although the Southerners could not bring their slaves to till the free soil of Illinois and although some left the South because they desired to escape direct contact with slavery, they could not entirely shake off their proslavery sympathies.

The Southerners settled chiefly in the southern counties of the state while the New Englanders selected farms in the northern and central counties. It happened that Jacksonville was situated in the borderland region where the streams of migration from the North and South met. Mingling waters are usually turbulent. The conflicts over the slavery issue were numerous and bitter.

Although situated in a community where a large proportion of the inhabitants were opposed to the abolition of slavery, the College, on account of the views of its professors, soon became identified with the antislavery movement. This attitude of the faculty tended to check the growth and prosperity of the institution. Near the end of his life, Dr. Sturtevant, in his address on the fiftieth anniversary of the College, said: "Of the difficulties under which this college labored, in the times in which the martyr Lovejoy fell, and his printing press was thrown into the Mississippi for the advocacy of a very mild form of abolitionism, no man can form any just estimate, who was not himself an actor in those scenes. The same power that ordered and obtained the martyrdom of Lovejoy, was dogging the footsteps of the prominent teachers of this College by night and by day and ever ready to let loose upon them the dogs of war. My soul hath those times in remembrance and is humble. That the College did not die in that struggle is success and ought to be glory enough." Whatever may be the truth in Dr. Sturtevant's assertion, certain it is that a strong opposition to the school soon developed. Since the College was receiving some of its students from families of Southern sympathies, the antislavery attitude of the faculty drove away patronage.

William H. Herndon, an early student who later became the law partner of Lincoln, bears testimony in his biography of the Great Emancipator to the antislavery influence of the faculty and its effect in leading proslavery families to withdraw their sons from the institution. Mr. Herndon, in writing of the death of Lovejoy in 1837, continues: "This cruel and uncalled for murder had aroused the antislavery sentiment everywhere. It penetrated the College and both faculty and students were loud and unrestrained in their denunciation of the crime. My father, who was thoroughly pro-slavery in his ideas, believing that the College was too strongly permeated with the virus of abolitionism, forced me to withdraw from the institution and return home. But it was too late. My soul had absorbed too much of what my father believed was rank poison."

It will be worth while to examine somewhat more in detail the attitude of the faculty and founders on the subject of slavery. Kirby, Baldwin, Sturtevant, and Asa Turner of the Yale Band, all became more or less identified with the antislavery movement of the Middle

West. President Beecher, a member of that family famous in American history for the vigorous blows which it struck at the institution of slavery, also allied himself with the anti-slavery cause. Professor Sturtevant was, of course, closely associated with President Beecher in the days of conflict over the slavery question, but he probably was less radical than the president. Like Mr. Beecher, he appreciated the delicate position of the College in a proslavery community, although no one could imagine Mr. Sturtevant ever permitting mere expediency to control his views or actions. He was inclined, however, to counsel moderation. Sturtevant, like his friend Abraham Lincoln, belonged to that large class who hesitated to advocate total and immediate abolition in the slave states themselves but who looked with fear and abhorrence upon the threatened spread of slavery to free territory and the attempt of the slave power to stifle free speech. He very soon came to regard the slavery question as the paramount political issue before the country.

Professor Jonathan B. Turner, much more radical than either Beecher or Sturtevant, was undoubtedly the most independent member of the faculty, if not of the community, and the term abolitionist might much more appropriately be applied to him than to any of the others. Both in the expression of his views and in his activity on the Underground Railway, Mr. Turner showed himself a most determined opponent of slavery. When others hesitated on account of natural conservatism or expediency, Turner moved forward with a decisive step. He was ever ready to lend a hand to the abolitionists of the town in helping some poor slave on the way to freedom. Professor Post's convictions were likewise strongly in favor of the anti-slavery cause although he hesitated, perhaps more than any of the other members of the faculty, frankly to express his opinions. Still, speaking on the same platform with President Beecher, Post declared, years before Lincoln made his famous declaration about a "house divided against itself," that "American slavery and American liberty cannot co-exist on the same soil." Most of the early trustees of the College, such as Judge Samuel D. Lockwood, the Rev. Gideon Blackburn, Thomas Lippincott, and David A. Smith, as well as the members of the Yale Band, were opposed to slavery.

The connection of the College with the Lovejoy tragedy, which stirred so deeply the animosities of people not only in Illinois but in other parts of the Union, was an intimate one. President Beecher had become a close friend and adviser of Elijah P. Lovejoy; his *Narrative of Riots at Alton* gives a participant's view of the troubles which led to Lovejoy's martyrdom. Through the activities of its president, the College became closely identified with the controversy, especially in the mind of the proslavery element. Criticism and vituperation were aimed at Mr. Beecher, and vigorous protests were made against the antislavery influence of the college faculty. The papers of St. Louis were violent in their attacks upon both the president and his college. The *Missouri Republican* was particularly outspoken in its denunciations of Beecher and most frank in its advice to the College. Even before the death of Lovejoy it had regretted "that the head of Jacksonville college had become identified with the course of these fanatics." Policy and propriety, in the opinion of this newspaper, "should have induced the reverend gentleman to have been at least a silent spectator, rather than a busy participator in the movements of a party, whose every step is viewed with jealousy and every act attended with more or less excitement."

Beecher was held responsible for the trouble. Lovejoy would never have held out as he did if Beecher and others had not urged him to maintain his ground. The paper published a communication signed by "A Sucker," who claimed that he had heard Edward Beecher and his father, Lyman, pleading for funds in the East and that they had both argued that contributions to western colleges would advance the cause of abolitionism. The writer was sure that "the people of the East, and particularly of New England, had been grossly humbugged in relation to the intellectual and religious wants of the West and by no individuals more effectually than the Messrs. Beecher." A little later, the *Missouri Republican* renewed its attack.

We have ever with pride and pleasure marked the advance of Illinois College. Not that State alone, but this and the whole West are interested in its prosperity and the sentiments and professions of those who may preside over its destiny. Many of the young men of Missouri have been sent there for their education, and under proper auspices, we trust this would continue to be the case; but with one so deeply identified with the abolition cause as the Rev. E.

Beecher now is esteemed by all to be, it cannot expect either a continuance of the support of the citizens of this or of many of that state.

Among the students, Samuel Willard, William C. Carter and J. A. Coleman were strongly abolitionist in their sympathies; in fact, all three belonged to families prominent in the Underground Railway. One episode may be mentioned to illustrate student activity in the cause. A southern lady, Mrs. Lisle from Louisiana, came to Jacksonville to visit relatives. She had brought with her a child and its nurse, a black slave of about eighteen years. Illinois being free territory, the slave, it was contended, could legally claim her freedom. The students attempted to pilot the girl northward on the Underground Railway. The attempt failed, but the episode aroused great excitement in Jacksonville. A public meeting was held at the Courthouse February 23, 1843, and resolutions were passed, stating among other things:

That the citizens of Jacksonville will at all times extend the hand of friendship and hospitality to their acquaintances in the South, and will be pleased to reciprocate the friendly relations of neighbors, ready at all times and on all occasions, promptly and efficiently to aid and protect them in the enjoyment of their property. And to that end, having reasons to believe that there are regular bands of abolitionists, organized with depots and relays of horses to run negroes through our State to Canada, and that one of them is in this town, we will form an Anti-Negro Stealing Society, as we heretofore formed an Anti-Horse Stealing Society, and that we will, in this neighborhood, break up the one as we broke up the other.
That although young Willard who stole the negro, and young Carter who assisted to conceal the negro are students of Illinois College, and as yet have not been dealt with by said College; yet it may be proper for this meeting to abstain from any action in relation to the case, leaving it to the College to defend her own reputation.

The bitterness of the opposition to the College is further evident from a very threatening anonymous letter sent to Professor Turner from Louisville, Kentucky, in 1842. The letter came from a person who professed sympathy with the antislavery views of Mr. Turner. It warned him that an association of slaveholders in Missouri was conspiring to kidnap him and destroy the College. If kidnapping failed, the professor was comforted with the assurance that "a little poison, or a hemp cord on your neck, or a messenger of lead, or a bowie knife, would be certain in time."

One must avoid overestimating the antislavery influence of the College. The proslavery element in Illinois and the South, always supersensitive to criticism, may have exaggerated the active opposition of the college faculty to the institution of slavery. Furthermore, with the resignation of President Beecher and the election of Professor Sturtevant to the presidency, the College possibly became more conservative on the slavery issue. Yet in spite of his good common sense and somewhat conservative attitude, Sturtevant never really dodged an issue, and could always be counted on to take a firm and open stand when the occasion demanded it. It was shortly after he had been elected to the presidency that Arthur Tappan, the well-known antislavery business man of New York, wrote him asking whether black students would be admitted to Illinois College. Sturtevant replied "that while in view of public sentiment around the institution, he should question the expediency of sending such students there—yet if the trustees were to vote against their reception, he would instantly resign his position." From the facts presented it is clear that Illinois College was one of the powerful antislavery forces in the state. In spite of severe criticism and the loss of patronage, it consistently maintained its antislavery attitude. Through its faculty and the young men who had studied within its walls, like Herndon, Willard, Fagg, Yates, and a host of others, the College exerted an influence that powerfully moulded public opinion on the slavery issue both in the state and outside it.

7

Fundamentalism and Modernism in the Early Days

Ignorance is the mother of prejudice. Since the light of learning was only flickering on the Illinois prairies of those days, enlightenment in religion was hardly to be expected. It might seem, however, that under such conditions educated Christian people would have united and worked harmoniously for the advancement of the kingdom of God, but, on the contrary, strife and faction rent the forces of righteousness. Young Sturtevant, coming from his studies at New Haven, was greatly distressed by the discord which divided Christian people on the frontier. "In Illinois," he writes, "I met for the first time a divided Christian community, and was plunged without warning or preparation into a sea of sectarian rivalries, which was kept in constant agitation, not only by real differences of opinion, but by ill-judged discussions and unfortunate personalities among ambitious men. No words can express the shock which my mind experienced."

These theological discussions in the early history of the College were greatly intensified by the general feeling of antagonism which existed between the Congregationalists and Presbyterians. In those days there were comparatively few Congregationalists in the Middle West. Indeed, it will be remembered that the two denominations had, early in the nineteenth century, entered into a scheme of friendly cooperation known as the "Plan of Union." The agreement resulted, practically, in turning over the pioneer West to the Presbyterians. The young men from Yale were of course familiar with the "Plan

of Union" and to a certain extent acquiesced in the terms of that
agreement, even consenting in the beginning that the College should
be "Presbyterian in character." Nevertheless, they could not entirely
throw off their Congregational sympathies. Although they and their
friends joined the local Presbyterian churches in Illinois and united
with that denomination in missionary and general religious work,
they still longed for that system of church organization which they
had left behind in New England.

The Presbyterians soon became suspicious of their Congregational
friends, and, naturally, this suspicion and antagonism fertilized the
soil for the growth of sectarian controversy. When members of the
college faculty began to show tendencies towards even slight liberalism in religion, the more orthodox brethren at once raised a protest.
Beecher, Turner, Adams, and Sturtevant were all guilty of these
liberal tendencies. Professor Sturtevant was greatly disturbed by this
controversy. As we might expect, he stood firmly for a reasonable
freedom of the faculty to discuss religious and theological problems.
He insisted that the only question which the public had a right to ask
regarding a member of the faculty was this: Is he a good man and
a capable teacher? Writing to his friend Theron Baldwin in May
1843, Sturtevant acknowledged that some of the faculty might have
acted or spoken indiscreetly, but:

The Faculty of this College have rights; they have claims upon the
justice, the kindness, and the sympathy of the friends of learning and
religion in this State which cannot be disregarded without offending
God and bringing disaster upon the interests of Society. We are in
circumstances of great difficulty and trial. We are called to sacrifice
almost everything we have to the public weal. We not infrequently
find it very difficult to get the means of purchasing the necessities
of life for our families. Now how long is it to be expected that we
will continue in these circumstances if we still find that those who
should sustain us and sympathize with us—distrust us—speak evil of
us—and suspect us? As these murmurs have come in upon me during
the past six months I have many times felt that this addition to my
burden is more than I can bear.
I have no idea of resigning—no this is my home and I shall bear
as well as I can what is laid on me here—I shall not flee—but if this
course is persisted in, will it not be likely to disorganize our Faculty?

If so can we organize another as good or nearly as good? Is there not a danger in this direction which threatens the College and which ought to be looked to? You cannot perhaps very easily imagine the faintness of heart which has resulted from these causes during the present year. I feel that the Trustees must look into these matters and unless there are some good reasons to the contrary, afford us the assurance of their confidence and cordial support—especially that they will be ready to defend our right to that latitude of opinion which we must enjoy or we can neither respect ourselves or be respected by others.

A little later this theological controversy became so serious that a committee was appointed by the Presbyterian Synod of the state to investigate the charges of heresy against the faculty of the College. It may easily be imagined that the members of the faculty were greatly aroused by the appointment of this committee and the formal presentation of charges. Sturtevant was convinced that "if Synod had wished to kill the College at a blow, they would have found it difficult to devise a step more directly tending to the result." This time, he began to think of resigning. "No event has ever occurred which distressed me so much and brought me so near the point of instantly resigning all connexion with the College. The meeting of the Trustees is just at hand and if the subject is met by them in the same spirit as by the Synod, I shall feel that I have little more to do here."

After listening to the discussions, the trustees, however, were not convinced that the College was harboring a set of heretical professors, and passed a series of resolutions as evidence of the confidence in the religious views of the instructors. Perhaps more important than these resolutions as evidence of the confidence of the trustees in the faculty was the action of the board at this same meeting of November 28, 1844, in electing one of the so-called heretics, Professor Sturtevant, president of the College.

It was suspected by some that these charges had been made with the purpose of preventing the selection of Professor Sturtevant as the successor of President Beecher. If that was the purpose, it had failed most signally. Furthermore, the committee appointed by Synod never made a formal report, and that body finally dismissed the matter, wishing "it understood that the Synod have preferred no charges and they do not endorse any of the rumors unfavorably affecting the College." But as the years came and went, the theological thunderclouds kept gathering and their reverberations caused many a conflict among people who should have stood shoulder to shoulder for the great cause of religion and education.

8

The Literary Societies

The literary societies of Illinois College constitute one of the most interesting and important phases of student life "on the Hill." Furthermore, contrary to the experience of most of the older colleges and universities of the country, these societies have proved to be an enduring tradition in the student life of the institution. They have maintained themselves in spite of the changes in student ideals and activities.

The first literary society established in the College was probably the so-called Rhetorical Society. Membership in this association was evidently open to any student who cared to join. Possibly one or two similar societies had once existed, for President Sturtevant referred on one occasion to "several attempted literary societies" which had failed to maintain their existence.

Sigma Pi was founded in 1843, near the end of President Beecher's administration. A group of students who evidently were leaders in discussions on various grave topics in philosophy, theology, and other fields of learning matured their plans carefully. Among the objects which these students had in view was that of making the proposed society restricted in its membership. The earlier societies had included practically the whole student body, a principle not likely to promote permanent success as these young men saw it. Fifteen students were present for the meeting of June 24, 1843, at which time a constitution was adopted and the society definitely organized. The principle of a restricted membership and a slight element of secrecy characterized the Sigma Pi society. However, there never were any grips or passwords nor any of the other "secrets" which usually characterize college fraternities.

It was not long before another society came into existence. What one group had done might also be accomplished by another. Little is known about the conferences which led to the organization of the rival society, but the motive which called the new society into being is reflected in a bit of reminiscence by one of the founders: "We felt that there was an outside element of good fellows, who ought to be united. We might not be as pious as others; we did not claim, as they did, any great amount of intellect or culture; still, we hoped we had some, and finally determined to band ourselves together and have a society of our own." So on Thursday evening, September 25, 1845, seven students gathered in the northeast corner of the third floor of the old dormitory and resolved to form another literary society.

It is easy to overemphasize contrasts, but it seems on the whole true to say that Phi Alpha has built on a foundation of broader democracy in the selection of members. It is probably true that greater harmony of purpose and a warmer spirit of fraternity have characterized the membership of Sigma Pi, while a refreshing independence and individual freedom have been the glory of Phi Alpha. It is not surprising, therefore, that Phi Alpha attracted during the controversy over slavery men of both parties.

In addition to their own rather formally and solemnly structured meetings the societies conducted "lecture courses." In the days when the lecture platform was popular throughout the country, these lectures often brought a little money into the society treasuries and gave both students and citizens an opportunity to see and hear men of national reputation. Among others, Mark Twain, Horace Greeley, Frederick Douglass, and Wendell Phillips lectured under the auspices of one society or the other.

Among the lecturers engaged by Phi Alpha was Abraham Lincoln, who came over from Springfield in February 1859. The proceeds of the lecture were not sufficient to pay Mr. Lincoln's fee and leave anything for the benefit of the society library. Recognizing the fact, Lincoln said to the society president, "I have not made much money for you tonight. Well, boys, be hopeful; pay me my railroad fare and

50 cents for my supper at the hotel and we are square." Possibly he wished to show a little appreciation of the action of the society a few days earlier in electing him to honorary membership.

As the years came and went, Sigma Pi and Phi Alpha grew or languished with the alternating prosperity and adversity of the College itself. When the students increased in numbers, other societies like Gamma Nu and Beta Upsilon and Pi Pi Rho sprang into existence, and with the women came also Philomathian, Gamma Delta, Sigma Phi Epsilon, Agora (later Chi Beta), and Alpha Eta Pi. Most of these societies have prepared their own histories, and some of these have been published.

President Julian M. Sturtevant

9

President Sturtevant: The Early Years, 1844–1858

When the board of trustees met in July 1844, some five months after Beecher's resignation had been received, the members were not ready to make a decision, and accordingly postponed the election of a president until the following November. In the meantime, a committee consisting of Smith, Baldwin, and Lippincott was to investigate possible candidates. It will be remembered that Mr. Beecher was also asked to cooperate in the search for a new president. Various candidates had been mentioned, among them, Baldwin and Sturtevant. The precarious state of college finances seemed to make it necessary to reduce the number of the faculty. In other words, it was questionable whether a new man could be called unless some member of the present faculty resigned. Sturtevant, quick to see the situation, at once assured his friend Baldwin that he himself would gladly resign, if the trustees wished to call a new man to the presidency, and if in consequence there must be retrenchment.

When the trustees reassembled on the twenty-eighth of November 1844, they apparently had made up their minds, for they unanimously elected Professor Sturtevant to the presidency. His selection was enthusiastically endorsed by the student body. In the evening all the windows of the main college building were illuminated, the candles being ingeniously arranged in the fourteen windows of the fourth story so as to spell the name of the new president. The college bell rang out the news, and the president-elect was summoned to the front of the building where "three times three cheers" were given for him. He writes: "I was greeted with a great burst of applause and returned to my house astonished, bewildered and humbled. I felt myself utterly unworthy of such demonstrations." He did not at once accept the position, but took about two weeks to consider the offer.

The honor and the responsibility were finally accepted, and for a period of thirty-two years Julian M. Sturtevant guided the destinies of the College. In accepting the presidency, he gave up his classes in mathematics and physics and took the professorship of Mental and Moral Science. The formal inauguration occurred at the following commencement, the exercises being held in a natural amphitheater in the college grove. The president's inaugural address was devoted to the subject of "The Relation of our Collegiate System to our National Civilization." It was a very thoughtful discourse, in which Mr. Sturtevant sought to show the intimate connection between a nation's ideals and its system of liberal education.

It was not an easy problem that confronted the new president. The school had really never recovered from the financial ruin caused by the panic of 1837. Not only was there no endowment, but the annual deficits had gone on accumulating until the load now threatened to drag the College over the precipice. Members of the faculty had been paid so little that their families were in want and the professors were, therefore, losing heart in the cause. The trustees, hardly less despondent than the faculty, were planning to make a final, supreme effort and, if it failed, apparently no alternative would be left except "to suspend instruction and sell the buildings."

In the midst of the financial gloom a ray of hope finally appeared. It was a gift of some 14,500 acres of land from the trustees of what was known as the Blackburn Fund. However, this gift proved to be illusory, and in addition to the false hopes it aroused, it was the cause of embarrassment and litigation.

Two key members of the faculty, Turner and Post, resigned in 1847; the circumstances are interesting. Jonathan Baldwin Turner was a born radical. He belonged to that class of men who blaze the way so that others may follow, and often they follow at a safe distance, spending their time hurling epithets at the guide who is making the trail easy for them. As the years passed, the trustees became more and more convinced that Turner's presence on the faculty was a cause of trouble to the College; his liberal tendencies in religion caused even more apprehension than his antislavery principles. However, since the College owed Mr. Turner at this time about one thousand dollars of back salary, the problem was not so simple as it might otherwise have been. At length, in June 1847, Turner's resignation was presented and accepted. The board made arrangements for paying his back salary, and in accepting the resignation passed the following resolution of appreciation: "Resolved, that in accepting the resignation of Prof. Turner the Trustees wish to express their high regard for his moral and religious character and for the distinguished ability, faithfulness, and perseverence with which he has fulfilled the important and onerous duties of his station and their grateful sense of the self denying zeal he has evinced in sustaining, with his associates, the Institution under the difficulties incident to an early enterprise."

It is not easy for a man in middle life to give up his cherished profession and turn to a new career. He thought for a time of studying medicine, but in the end decided to devote himself to "horticulture and osage orange culture." He went to work with characteristic zeal, and in time large success crowned his efforts. His resignation from the college faculty proved to be but the beginning of a much larger and more important work. He soon became deeply interested in promoting a more practical education than that which was dominated by the old classical tradition. As will be noted later, he made an important contribution to the movement for the establishment of the federal land grant colleges in the United States.

Post's resignation came about as a result of persistent efforts of other institutions to get his services. In 1846, Middlebury, his alma mater, offered him the chair of rhetoric and English literature. The temptation to accept must have been great, but the personal ties and professional opportunities which bound him to Illinois College were also great, and he declined the call. Meanwhile, the officers of the Third Presbyterian Church of St. Louis persistently continued to urge their call upon him. They evidently were willing to risk his views on slavery, especially since they had confidence in his common sense. In the end, since his debts kept "constantly pressing more and more, with no prospect of relief" where he was, Professor Post decided to accept the call. It is evident that he left with a heavy heart and with a lingering hope that he might at the end of four years return to the work that so strongly attracted him. The resignation, coming as it did at the beginning of a college year, proved very embarrassing to the trustees. When it is remembered that religious and financial difficulties were also harassing the president at this particular time, it is no wonder that he wrote: "It seems lonely here, and I am sometimes almost ready to sink in deep water."

It is not practical to pursue the many problems of staffing the faculty, but two appointments merit brief notice, the first one being J. B. Turner's successor. After several unsuccessful efforts had been made to fill his place, the Reverend William D. Sanders, pastor of a church in Ravenna, Ohio, was appointed Professor of Rhetoric and Elocution. A graduate of Hudson College or, as it was later called, Western Reserve College, Professor Sanders soon proved himself to be a teacher of ability, a ready public speaker, and a man of strong convictions on the public questions of the day. He remained on the faculty for over fourteen years, occasionally the storm center of controversies but always a distinct educational force both in the College and in the community. The second was Rufus C. Crampton, who was appointed Professor of Mathematics and Astronomy in 1853 and remained on the faculty for thirty-five years, his term being one of the longest and his services among the most efficient and honorable rendered to the College by any member of the faculty.

Much of Sturtevant's energy as president had to go into the raising of money. Passing reference has been made to the unhappy outcome of the Blackburn bequest. In the meantime, the effort to raise the new endowment of fifty thousand dollars had been continued, and finally in 1852 the College was given permission to begin active operations on the eastern field for a sum of twenty thousand dollars on condition that the institution should make no further claims for aid from the eastern Society after that amount was raised. Of course the Society promised its cooperation in the effort. Success finally

crowned the persistent efforts of years. At noon, on the last day of
May 1858, President Sturtevant telegraphed his friend Theron Baldwin: "Fifty-eight thousand," and wrote at length the next day:

I was half sorry I had promised to telegraph for I thought you
would be too incredulous of so large an amount that you would suspect some mistake. We have been borne up to a point we had no
thought of reaching. The part of Jacksonville and vicinity in this
matter is most interesting. At the commencement of this enterprise
our friends here subscribed $5000. Last week we got $14,205. The
Pisgah subscription should be added, only eight miles out. It is
$2180. These sums make $21,385 given in this immediate vicinity to
this, our enterprise. A few months previous we had raised about
$10,000 from the same field for the new building. We have certainly
no occasion to say hereafter that the College has no friends at home.
The earnest support of Quincy, Alton, Springfield, Griggsville, and
Pittsfield is also cheering. Illinois College dwells among its own
people. *It is at home*.

In Illinois College, as in other institutions, the old curriculum was
followed year after year with few changes. However, by the middle
of the century the College began to feel a demand for other courses
than those of the old classical dispensation, and accordingly in 1852
a so-called scientific department was established. That the trustees
and faculty were progressive in this matter is evident when we recall
that it was only in the preceding year that Harvard had conferred
the first degree of bachelor of science ever given in this country.
Thus the instructors at Illinois College were among the first in the
country to give recognition to the importance of science and the
modern languages in a college curriculum.
    According to the catalogue, the new department was designed for
that class of young men, "believed to be very numerous," who desired a scientific and English education and were "yet hindered by
their circumstances from attempting to explore a field so vast as that
to which the study of the classics is designed to introduce the student." Candidates for admission into the new scientific course escaped the examinations in Latin and Greek, being examined only in
such subjects as English grammar, geography, arithmetic, and ele-

mentary algebra. Furthermore, instead of being required to take four years, the students in this department studied only three, and for two of those years they were required to be in attendance only twenty-six weeks; only for the last year were they required to be in residence the usual forty weeks. In the first year the scientific students studied rhetoric and mathematics, including navigation and surveying; in the second year they went on with the higher branches of mathematics, although calculus was optional, and were required to take natural philosophy and chemistry; French was an optional study. The last year, they had a strange mixture of intellectual philosophy, astronomy, logic, natural theology, moral sciences, Paley's *Evidences of Christianity*, rhetoric, political economy, history, etc. The trustees felt it necessary to assure the public that in establishing the scientific course, they had no intention to lower the standards of the institution or "in the least to depreciate the classics." It was also announced that instruction in civil engineering would be offered as soon as the demand for instruction in that study justified the creation of such a professorship. The first time the degree of bachelor of science was conferred by Illinois College was in 1854. The next year the length of the scientific term for the first two years was changed from twenty-six to forty weeks, thus bringing the length of the course in both classical and scientific departments more nearly in harmony and doubtless greatly improving the quality of the work in the latter department.

A fire on the night of December 30, 1852, destroyed most of the main college building. It occurred when nearly all the students were away on their Christmas vacation. "It was an awful night, never, never to be forgotten," writes President Sturtevant. "When the morning dawned, the walls were all standing in desolate, awful loneliness. While we were at breakfast, the middle partition wall, owing to the consumption of some timbers which were wrought into its structure gave way and drew along with it the side walls in one, huge indiscriminate ruin, leaving three of the tall chimney stacks—standing like monuments of desolation projected upon the beautiful grove in the rear."

But, perhaps, after all, the disaster might be a blessing in disguise. Instead of rebuilding the dormitory, it was decided to construct a dignified building for general college purposes and thereafter "to trust entirely to private accommodations for students." Plans for the building were prepared by Mr. Rumbold, an able and well-known architect of St. Louis—the same architect who designed the beautiful dome of the old courthouse in that city. It was not until 1855 that the construction of the present Sturtevant Hall with its graceful tower was commenced. The cornerstone was laid on the seventh of October.

Also in 1855, the College celebrated its twenty-fifth anniversary. According to the program, many old friends of the College must have been present. The invocation was offered by Theron Baldwin, and the principal address, delivered by President Sturtevant, proved to be a very interesting, dignified, historical account of the founding and progress of the College. He traced the beginnings of the movement in the West; the union with the band of young men from Yale; the simplicity and vicissitudes of the first years; the early progress of the institution followed by a financial crisis which brought it almost to the point of extinction; its recovery and the brighter outlook which was then filling all with great hope. "We began in the midst of poverty—we are now called to carry forward the work in the midst of wealth. We began almost single handed—we have now more than a hundred living alumni to sustain us in our work. We began in youthful inexperience—we have now the benefit of a quarter of a century of experience. Let us then be strong and acquit us like men."

The sectarian controversies of the early years did not by any means subside in the administration of President Sturtevant. Indeed, the president's views on church government, as well as the liberal tendencies of some of his colleagues, helped to draw the religious lines more sharply. The old controversy between Presbyterianism and Congregationalism was still at the bottom of the trouble. Presbyterians looked with jealous eyes at the growing strength of the Congregationalists in the West, and Presbyterians on the board of trustees insisted that their interests in the College should be more securely safeguarded.

In 1846 a committee of two clergymen, Mr. Eddy and Mr. Towne, had been sent out by the eastern Society to investigate the western colleges. The scope of their investigations apparently was broad, extending to religious as well as educational and financial conditions. A few extracts from the committee's report will suffice:

> During their stay at Jacksonville, they spent an entire week in the most full and free conversation with the people of the village, and with the faculty themselves, hearing all that was to be alleged on the one side and the explanations that were to be made on the other. And we are happy to state it to be our firm conviction that so far as regards President Sturtevant, and Professors Post and Adams, nothing can be objected which can in the least shake the confidence of the Christian public and the patrons of learning in them. They are men of great independence of mind, it is true. They are men of great transparency of character. Their views are too enlarged and elevated to admit of their being bigots in religion or partizans in politics. It gives us pleasure to add that they have a hold on leading minds in the state of Illinois which could not be easily loosened.

The independent spirit of President Sturtevant and his devotion to the cause of intellectual freedom in the college are evident from his attitude in connection with an article which he had published in the *New Englander* in the fall of 1857. The article, dealing in a frank spirit with certain controverted questions, aroused criticism and feeling in some quarters, and in the midst of the campaign for funds, a member of the board of trustees expressed to the president his disapproval of the article and warned him "of the evil consequences likely to result from such publications." This trustee furthermore attempted to induce Mr. Sturtevant to pledge himself to a policy of silence on such subjects in the future. The president's reply was what might have been expected; evidently aroused by the interview, he told the board member in plain words that he would resign at once if the trustees of the College believed that he had "in the smallest degree violated the strictest proprieties" of his position. He insisted that he did not care to retain his place "at the expense of the smallest portion of his freedom of utterance." It was certainly a fine, courageous reply, and it must have made a wholesome impression on the complaining trustee, for the latter at once assured the president that no thought of his resignation could be entertained. Undoubtedly President Sturtevant was doing a great service for the cause of higher education not only in Illinois College but throughout the West by his vigorous protest against denominational control of colleges. It is doubtful whether there was any educator in the country at that time who saw more clearly the dangers of a narrow, sectarian control of higher education. He restated his position a few years later in another *New Englander* article when he said: "The very spirit and principle of Denominationalism must be adjured in our Colleges. We must found them upon a broad and comprehensive platform of Evangelic faith. We must cooperate in sustaining them as Christians and not as Sectarians. We must esteem them as precious, not as the instruments of aggrandizing our Denomination, but as blessings to our country, to mankind, and to the distant future." It was in the early part of President Sturtevant's administration that Illinois College began to feel the competition of other institutions. Knox, founded in 1837, was beginning to compete with Illinois College for both money and students, and since both institutions expected financial aid and patronage from common sources, there was more or less rivalry. Perhaps still more keenly, however, did the friends of Illinois College feel the competition of the Methodists at McKendree and of the Baptists at Shurtleff. More distant institutions like Western Reserve, Oberlin, Wabash, and Beloit, while not competing with Illinois College for students, were nevertheless keen competitors for eastern contributions.

By the late fifties the College had begun to exert a perceptible influence upon the community and state through its alumni. Graduates of the early years had now been out of college long enough to begin to play a part in the affairs of the world. As might be expected, a large percentage of them had entered the field of the Christian ministry. The record of the occupations of the early alumni is not by any means complete, but fully 44 percent of the graduates of the first twenty years entered the Christian ministry. The founders must, indeed, have felt that one of their great objects in establishing the College was being achieved. Nineteen percent of the graduates of the first twenty years went into law, and about 11 percent became physicians. Many of these ministers, lawyers, and doctors undoubtedly taught school during the first few years after they were out of college. A total of 130 had been graduated during these two decades. President Sturtevant saw with pride and pleasure this extension of the influence of the College. There is little doubt that Illinois College was at that time, through the influence of its faculty, trustees, and alumni, the most important institution of higher learning in the state.

IO

President Sturtevant: The Last Years, 1858–1876

Beginning approximately with the period of the Civil War, not only was the College itself torn by the great conflict but the financial question again loomed large, and certain other problems, like the decreasing attendance, the relation of the College to the plans for a state university, and the adaptation of the curriculum to changing educational aims, especially in the field of science, called for solution. Hovering in the background, and sometimes at the very front of the stage, was always the annoying ghost of sectarianism. As the years rolled on and the controversy over slavery and the fundamental nature of our government became more acute, the college community was more than once a storm center. The faculty remained ardently loyal and continued to exert its strong influence for the Union and against slavery. However, the surrounding community, as might be expected from its predominantly southern origin, continued to show at times a strong sympathy with the policy of the Democratic party in its opposition to extreme war measures and to advanced opinions on the abolition of slavery.

If Professor Turner was the radical leader on the faculty for the cause of freedom in the earlier years, it was Professor Sanders, his successor in the chair of rhetoric, who became the outstanding faculty champion of the antislavery cause in these later years. "When feeling is up, he is apt to throw oil in the fire," wrote President Sturtevant of this colleague. The professor of rhetoric was always a watchful and sharp censor, allowing no oration or declamation to be delivered which reflected the views of the proslavery party. The result was that Professor Sanders and his students more than once locked horns over these issues.

William M. Springer, in later life a distinguished member of Congress, Chairman of its Ways and Means Committee, was the student whose independent views and fearless defense of his right to free speech brought on a controversy with the faculty. The Junior Exhibition was for a great many years, next to commencement, the chief oratorical festival on the college calendar. Young Springer chose as the subject of his oration for the 1857 exhibition the question: "Is Agitation Necessary as a Means of Reform?" When the young man presented a brief of his speech for criticism to the professor of rhetoric, the latter cut out part of the oration "on the ground that it was political," and returned it with the comment that "the Junior Exhibition is not a pothouse caucus; it is a Literary Festival." Professor Sanders went on to explain, in his comments on the oration, that the Junior Exhibition should be a "time of genial feeling"; that the audience were, in effect "the invited guests" of the speakers, and therefore should not have their sensibilities shocked; no small portion of the audience, he felt sure, would regard Springer's "tirade of abuse against those who believe in the Declaration of Independence as a gross and gratuitous outrage." "With due respect for your high position, I ask, Professor," said the young man in a very formal note to his instructor, "are my sentiments thus to be crushed to the ground, or am I to have that liberty of speech, which a year ago, you granted to Mr. Symonds?"

Apparently some progress was made towards conciliation and compromise between the professor and student; at least according to the story of the boy, he "accepted all changes and corrections excepting the striking out of a few sentences." It seems that the main ideas of the offending paragraph and the quotation in the last sentence were taken from a Thanksgiving sermon by the most prominent preacher of the town, Livingston M. Glover, of the Presbyterian Church. The young man had, therefore, buttressed his position by borrowing a few sentences from a local preacher of powerful influence. The professor, however, was not intimidated. The oration would be delivered as corrected or not at all, was his final dictum. The next step in the controversy was a meeting of the junior class,

Sturtevant Hall. Drawing by Louise Boring Wood

which sent a petition to the president respectfully requesting that their classmate, "having conceded everything which honor and respect for his instructor demand," be allowed to deliver his oration as corrected. President Sturtevant, however, refused to interfere, explaining in a talk to the class that neither he nor the faculty had any jurisdiction in the matter, but that the whole responsibility and authority rested in the hands of Professor Sanders. The young man, although not allowed to appear at the Exhibition, was determined not to be entirely frustrated in what he regarded as his rights, and so when the audience gathered for the contest, a broadside, carefully prepared by young Springer, was distributed to the assembled friends. Whatever the merits of the oration may have been, there is no doubt that Springer made a very strong and dignified presentation of his side of the case in this circular. But it was an offense which the faculty could not well allow to pass unnoticed, and they therefore dismissed the young man, who later took his bachelor's degree at another institution. With the passage of time, overheated feelings cooled and when the war was long past and Mr. Springer had won the distinctions already mentioned, the College, which had dismissed him, invited him to receive one of its highest honors, the degree of Doctor of Laws. That he accepted the degree showed that Mr. Springer could also forget and forgive, as well as fight.

The episode attracted more than local attention, for after the faculty thought it had dismissed the case as well as the student, certain Democratic papers in Illinois and Missouri took up the cudgels for young Springer. The influential *Illinois State Register* of Springfield devoted editorial after editorial to the case, and, as it warmed to the fight, became very violent in its attacks upon Professor Sanders and his colleagues on the college faculty. Two quotations from the editorials which appeared in the *Register* show how strongly many Democrats in the state felt about the College. Under date of April 10, 1857, after paying his respects to President Beecher for the aid which he had given to the "notorious" Lovejoy at Alton, the editor states: "After the resignation of Beecher, better things were promised and expected from the institution. The promises have never been realized and at present it is a mere manufactory of abolitionism, higher-lawism. Two of its present officials are President Sturtevant and Professor Sanders. These two dignitaries have prostituted their position and have devoted themselves to furthering the cause of abolitionism and treason to the government and the constitution." Another hot blast came from the editorial offices of the *Register* a few days later:

The Illinois College has sailed under false colors ever since its inauguration. It has by false pretense, preyed upon a portion of the people of the state of Illinois. It has by deception and false pretense drawn largely upon the purse of the community. To expose this fact and to set this institution in a proper light and in its true colors before the community is our object, and, as we firmly believe, our duty. Let the Illinois College at Jacksonville be known as the fountain and hot-bed of ultra abolitionism. To the people of Illinois we say, beware of what you do. Remember that while you contribute one dollar to this institution, you are accountable to your country and to your conscience, for you are aiding to spread the most dangerous influence that our government has to encounter.

As one reads these editorials and many more like them, he is not surprised to learn that President Sturtevant always regarded the slavery issue as one of the greatest obstacles to the progress of the College. Sturtevant, by nature conservative and never inclined to hotheaded radicalism, was, nevertheless, pleased to see the lines tighten, and the issue between freedom and slavery more clearly defined.

The firing on Fort Sumter produced excitement on the Illinois College campus as it did everywhere else in the North. The question was now no longer an academic one; the day of compromise was over, and when President Lincoln issued his first appeal for volunteers, in the spring of 1861, twenty-six Illinois College men at once answered the call. The record of the College in the war was indeed a very honorable one. In measuring the value of that service to the Union cause, one thinks not only of the 240 or more Illinois College men who served in the Union army and navy but also of the services of such men as Richard Yates, '35, who in his position as chief executive of Illinois became one of the outstanding war governors of the time, and of President Sturtevant and the other members of the faculty who had for years in their teaching and public addresses been promoting the cause of freedom and of the Union in a state where many held other opinions.

Among the Illinois College men who served in the union army were 7 Brigadier Generals, 12 Colonels, 2 Lieutenant Colonels, 8 Majors and 19 Captains. It may be of interest to compare the 240 men whom Illinois College sent into the service with the numbers contributed to the Union service by other colleges with which com-

parisons might be made. For example, Bowdoin sent 267 of her sons
into the service; Williams 308; Amherst 273; Rutgers 70; Princeton
150; Knox 58. When it is remembered that the eastern colleges
named were without exception older than Illinois and undoubtedly
had larger bodies of students and alumni, the record of Illinois College is one of which every alumnus may well be proud. Since some—
the exact number is hard to determine, but Rammelkamp lists by
name and class and unit, twelve—Illinois College men served under
the Confederate flag, it is not surprising that occasionally during the
course of the war they found themselves in opposing fighting units.
And occasionally, Illinois College men belonging to the same family
fought on opposite sides, as in the case of the Van Eaton and Bristow
brothers.

   During the course of the war another and sharper controversy
arose between faculty and students over the question of free speech.
This time it was members of the senior class who got into difficulty
on account of their orations for the commencement of 1862. Members of the class petitioned the professor of rhetoric, William Sanders, "to consider if it would not be compatible with the interests of
the commencement to adopt one or the other of the following rules:
Either to exclude every sentiment which had recently been the subject of party debate and excitement; or to permit each side of those
questions to be fairly represented." They were informed that political opinions could be expressed but the professor "would be sove-
reign judge of their truth and propriety." When asked by the peti-
tioning students whether they might express the belief "that a little
of our present national danger might be traced to extreme Abolitionism," he is said to have replied, "It will not be tolerated, it is false,
it is party slang." Four members of the class continued to argue
the question of free speech with the autocratic Professor Sanders, but
without softening him. Finally, only one speech was disallowed, that
by a Mathew Patton, Jr. Three of his classmates stood by Patton and
refused to give their speeches unless he were allowed to give his. All
four were denied their diplomas by the faculty. The boys then issued
a manifesto "To the Public," defending their position, and on the
invitation of a large group of local citizens all four delivered their
orations at a sort of rump commencement, which is said to have been

even more largely attended than were the regular commencement exercises. The story of the episode would be incomplete without adding that in later years all four men were granted their diplomas and restored to the class.

The year 1862–63 looked especially gloomy to the authorities of the College. In the words of the president, "College became rather a dull place to teachers who lectured to empty seats and to the few students who were hindered by various considerations from going to the war." It was at this time of gloom and uncertainty, when he was wondering what was left for him to do, that Mr. Sturtevant received an offer from his friend, Eliphalet W. Blatchford, to pay the expenses of a trip to England. As is well known to students of this period of our history, public opinion in England was not running strongly in favor of the northern cause. Others had tried to change this state of affairs, including Henry Ward Beecher, but with little success. Nonetheless, Mr. Blatchford evidently thought that Sturtevant, on such a mission, could render a substantial service to his country. Sturtevant hesitated, but Theron Baldwin wired him urging acceptance, and the college trustees agreed that the president ought not to decline the offer, and voted to continue his salary during his absence. Accordingly, in early April of 1863, Sturtevant was on his way to England, encouraged by President Lincoln and armed with letters of introduction. Secretary of the Treasury Chase wrote him: "It will gladden my heart if you succeed in giving to the British people a clearer idea of the true situation here. Once rightly informed, it seems impossible to believe that they will permit the illicit aid and countenance now given to the rebellion in England."

Sturtevant met with cold antipathy in most places, often being enjoined not even to mention the American war. Personal conversations with men like Richard Cobden presented opportunities for explaining the cause of the Union, but rarely did he venture to speak about the war in his sermons or other public addresses. He was back on the campus by the opening of college in the fall of 1863. After his return, he lectured occasionally on his experience in England and also wrote an occasional article or report which helped the people of the North to gain a better understanding of public opinion in England.

During and immediately after the war, discouragement settled like a cloud over the campus. The chief cause of the renewed financial worries was, it need hardly be explained, the war, both in its immediate and remote effects. The drop in attendance materially reduced the income from tuition, for after the Civil War, contrary to recent experience, there was no revival of attendance and, of course, no renewal of income from tuition. Therefore, even if full interest had been realized on the new endowment, the financial situation would have been bad enough, but other circumstances aggravated the situation still further. As so often happened in the financial history of the College, subscriptions had been accepted on long terms of payment, and when the hard times of war came on, the friends of the College were not able to fulfill their promises. In 1864 the president was convinced that a "new system of effort must be undertaken or the enterprise of our lives will prove a mortifying failure. The time has fully come when the College is compelled to be much more than it is or nothing at all." The governor had appointed him on the commission which was to determine the disposition of the lands which had been granted to the state under the terms of the Federal Land Grant Act for the establishment of a college of agriculture and mechanic arts, and he dared to hope that Illinois College might secure that magnificent grant.

Meantime, another supreme effort had to be made to keep the college alive. "I cannot feel content to die or to resign my place in Illinois College," said Sturtevant, "until it is in some such manner provided for its great mission." In this campaign, as in nearly every other effort to increase the funds of the College, the troublesome denominational question threatened to create discord among its friends. A joint meeting of the faculty and the prudential committee of the board was held "to consult and provide for the success of the undertaking."

The leaders of the Presbyterian faction of the faculty were Professors William Sanders and Rufus Nutting, both of whom had been appointed to the faculty to placate Presbyterian friends in the board of trustees and out of it. At the joint meeting of faculty and trustees, Sanders, a man of no mean oratorical ability, delivered a strong address advocating that in the future all appointments to the board of trustees and faculty should be equally divided between the New School Presbyterians and Congregationalists and that future presidents of the College should be alternately Presbyterian and Congregational. On the other hand, President Sturtevant urged a very different course on the trustees, that they should assure the friends of the College that the institution would never be conducted in the interests of any particular denomination. The College, he urged, must be conducted "not for the aggrandizement of one or of two denominations but for learning, for our country, for the whole Church of God." The trustees sided with Sturtevant and adopted unanimously resolutions that put the College on record as opposed to any policy of sectarian control.

Shortly after commencement, 1866, the president was again hard at work in the East. About the middle of July he declared he would not return until the fund was completed, even if it took until the following January. By October the amount was evidently pledged, for the president was again at his post of duty at the College. Contrary to the experience in many previous financial campaigns, subscriptions were paid with commendable promptness.

The relations between the president and Professor Sanders continued strained. A teacher of pronounced ability and a man of strong opinions, Professor Sanders was always an aggressive partisan of any cause which he espoused. It was in 1864 that he had established the Young Ladies' Athenaeum, a school for girls that soon won a good reputation and became an active competitor of the Jacksonville Female Academy. President Sturtevant objected very strongly to this outside activity of one of his professors, claiming that members of the faculty were employed to give their full time to the College and that Sanders' action was arousing the opposition of some very good friends of the College. He evidently felt that the only satisfactory solution was to secure Sanders' resignation. The controversy, involving, as it did, some elements of the old denominational fight, assumed a threatening aspect and unfortunately involved considerable personal feeling. Not only did Professor Sanders personally appear before the trustees to present his side of the case, but a committee of three citizens requested and were granted a hearing on the subject, and articles on the controversy appeared in the local press. Professor Sanders claimed in his address to the trustees that the real motive of the opposition to him was to oust him from the College because he was a Presbyterian and that his connection with the Athenaeum was a mere pretext. The trustees, always hoping that the troubled waters would of themselves subside, evidently were not ready to force the resignation of Professor Sanders. Finally at the end of the college year 1868–69, Professor Sanders himself brought the controversy to an end by handing in his resignation, and the trustees unanimously accepted it.

The dream of state aid had more than once flashed through the mind of President Sturtevant. The state of Illinois, according to the terms of its admission into the Union and the regulations governing the sale of public lands within its territorial limits, had in its possession certain funds known as the Seminary and the College or University Funds, amounting in the forties to over one-hundred thousand dollars, and growing from year to year, at least theoretically, as interest was added to the principal. The denominational colleges of the state all looked with longing eyes upon these state educational funds and from time to time made suggestions for their division among them. Furthermore, the idea of allying Illinois College with a state university was somewhat of a natural development of the president's thoughts on university administration. Possibly his ideas on this subject had been influenced more or less by what he had observed at Oxford and Cambridge when he was abroad during the war. If England could built up great universities by a community of independent and semi-independent colleges, why could not the same thing be done in America? Why, for example, provide the general cultural courses, leaving to the other departments the work in agriculture and mechanic arts? These thoughts and hopes were quickened when Congress passed the Morrill Land Grant Act.

This act, passed by the Congress in 1862 while the country was torn by civil war, is undoubtedly the most significant piece of legislation ever enacted in this country for the encouragement of higher education in the practical branches of agriculture and the mechanic arts, and it must always be a matter of pride to the alumni and friends of Illinois College that a former member of her faculty played an important role in this movement. There seems little doubt that Jonathan Baldwin Turner sponsored the movement which ultimately bore fruit in the Morrill Act appropriating those millions of acres of public lands to the various states for the establishment of colleges in which the leading subjects of the curriculum, without excluding other courses, should be agriculture and the mechanic arts. Professor Turner, since leaving the faculty of the College in 1847, had been devoting himself to the cultivation of various plants like osage orange and the red raspberry and to the invention of agricultural implements, not to mention his continued activity in the antislavery movement and other causes. In a few years this former professor of rhetoric became deeply interested in the promotion of industrial education or the education of the masses along practical lines. "As things are now," he said, "our best farmers and mechanics by their own native force of mind, by the slow process of individual experience, come to know at forty what they might have been taught in six months at twenty; while a still greater number of less fortunate or less gifted stumble on through life almost as ignorant of every true principle of their art as when they began."

When the passage of the Morrill Land Grant Act finally settled it that Illinois, like the other states of the Union, would have thousands of acres of public lands at her disposal for the establishment of a university, the contest for the location of the proposed institution became very keen and even bitter. The college men of the state, with the single exception of President Sturtevant, strongly advocated a division of the fund among the various denominational colleges. The action of certain eastern states—Massachusetts gave its share of the fund to Amherst, Connecticut made Yale the beneficiary of its fund, and New Hampshire assigned its share to Dartmouth—encouraged the college men of Illinois to believe that the Illinois fund might be divided among the colleges already in existence. The state conference of colleges appointed a committee on legislative aid, which brought in a carefully prepared report, outlining the position of the denominational colleges and recommending that application be made to the state legislature for aid. J. B. Turner was one of the most incisive critics of the college presidents, becoming at times a bit personal in his arguments:

We need no further proof of the utter incapacity of these gentlemen to manage these funds than their own published reports give us. They evidently have no just conception of what the fund is really for. The miserable sham which they propose is not worthy of the name of an university. It would be a disgrace to any people who should inaugurate it. Just look at it: More than a round hundred corporators, gathered promiscuously, by a sort of accidental drag-net, from all classes, professions, and conditions in life, without the least possible regard to their knowledge of educational interests; and set to do what? Why, simply to dole out and watch the miserable pittance of two thousand dollars a year, distributed among some twenty or more rival colleges agreed in nothing but a present want of funds. Who, thereupon, are to teach "agriculture and mechanics, one or both, to all our youth, male and female." What troops of crinoline carpenters and farmers the state would then have! Outdoor labor would then be nothing but one everlasting honeymoon and all sorrow and tears as well as all university funds, would soon fly away.

Turner's wit and wisdom carried the day. President Sturtevant's intimate association with Turner must have greatly influenced his own concepts of the new state university. It cannot be denied that Sturtevant was working to promote the interests of the particular college over which he presided, but he never lost sight of the larger good of the whole state. He was eager to see the proposed university located in Jacksonville and connected in some way with Illinois College, but he always held the belief that whether the institution was located in Jacksonville or elsewhere, the fund must be kept intact; there must be one university and not several, located in different parts of the state: "I am satisfied that the system of education in this great state will culminate in a state university. I think it our duty to cooperate in the founding of that university, and to exert all the influence and use all the wisdom acquired by our experience to mould it right. The best thing, then, which we can do is to ally it with Illinois College, or rather engraft it upon Illinois College."

Theron Baldwin's response to the letter just quoted partly agreed and partly disagreed with Sturtevant's views. He believed that there would always be a place for denominational colleges of high standards, no matter what the outcome of the state university might be. He quoted from a recent report of the State Superintendent of Public Instruction: "Let church colleges keep right on in their appointed course, neither abandoning the whole field to public systems of education, nor yet courting the favor and patronage of the state. Their work is unique and peculiar and its successful accomplishment demands freedom from outside control; it is utterly incompatible with the embarrassing restrictions of legislative supervision." This was a telling judgment from one of Sturtevant's own protégés, Newton Bateman, class of 1843.

In the end, four counties, Champaign, Logan, McLean, and Morgan, became serious contenders for the prize. Whatever advantages the other countries may have offered, there is no doubt that the best organized group was the "Champaign crowd," as it was often called. Morgan County labored under the disadvantage of already having three state institutions—schools for the blind, for the deaf, and the State Hospital—and, if there were to be any reciprocity or fairness in the distribution of favors, people said it did not deserve to have another. However, the citizens of the county apparently had only whetted their appetites for another plum, and in 1866 began actively to prepare their bid for presentation to the state authorities. President Sturtevant interested himself energetically in the movement, especially insofar as it concerned Illinois College. In June of 1866 the trustees of the College instructed their prudential committee to "inquire whether anything can be done to facilitate the wise location and successful working of the proposed Industrial University of Illinois." According to their charter and the terms of their trust, the trustees did not feel empowered to turn over to the state the complete, unrestricted ownership of this property, but they were willing to agree, if the university were located in Jacksonville, that Illinois College should become a department or one college in the proposed university.

The legislature appointed a committee to visit the competing localities and make a report on the various bids. These were estimated as follows: Morgan, $491,000; McLean, $470,000; Logan, $385,000; and Champaign, $285,000. In spite of this evaluation by their committee, the legislature decided to locate the university in Champaign County. The result of the long and bitter struggle was a sore disappointment to many of the best friends of the movement. Turner was discouraged. It was the first time in his life, said Turner, that he had ever known "a valuable piece of property to be knocked down to the lowest bidder." Thus the attempt to ally Illinois College with the state university failed, and the College was compelled to work out her salvation along other lines.

Various experiments were tried. The preparatory school was discontinued, and then when that proved to be an unwise decision, was re-established, with the help of a ten-thousand-dollar gift from Dr. Samuel L. Whipple. Accepting the offer, the trustees voted to call the school "The Whipple Academy" in honor of the donor.

There were occasional changes in the faculty, none as traumatic as the earlier departures of Turner and Sanders, but the inevitable, yet nonetheless significant ebbs and flows of an academic community occurred. On the board there were changes too. The founders of the College and those associated with it in its earliest years began to give way to younger men. Theron Baldwin, who died in the spring of 1870, deserves more than a passing word. From the day when with Sturtevant and his college friends he had solemnly signed that New Haven compact dedicating his life to the cause of education and home missions in the West, Baldwin had ever faithfully and efficiently kept his pledge. Not only Illinois College but such institutions as Wabash, Beloit, Western Reserve, Marietta, and Knox, as well as Lane and Chicago theological seminaries, all felt his strong influence in the early and formative years of their existence. His intimate personal friendship with President Sturtevant, not to mention his active part in the founding of Illinois College and his official position as a trustee, made both his interest and influence stronger here than in any other college. It may be said that Dr. Sturtevant almost never took an important step in the affairs of Illinois College without consulting his friend Baldwin, and, in practically every case, the advice received proved sound. A broad outlook over the whole field of higher education and a detachment from local and personal feelings always gave added value to Baldwin's advice. And what a fortunate thing it has proved for the historian of the College that these two friends lived apart and therefore corresponded with one another so regularly. Their hundreds of letters, so fortunately preserved, are not only a rich mine of historical information but bear testimony to a rare and beautiful friendship and disclose to our intimate view two really great personalities.

The appointment of Edward P. Kirby, '54, as Treasurer of the College resulted in considerable improvement in the institution's accounting system. During the course of years, more-or-less loose methods of accounting had grown up. It seemed uncertain, for example, on whose authority bills were to be paid; special funds were handled by others and not by the regular treasurer of the board; there was a large number of miscellaneous endowment funds, some of which might well be consolidated; trust funds were not always being strictly applied to the objects for which they had been established, etc. When Kirby was asked to take the treasurership, he said that he would not be willing to act as treasurer unless "some person or committee be authorized to draw upon the treasurer for such expenditures as may be necessary, upon whose warrants alone money shall be paid out by the treasurer." As a result of Mr. Kirby's recommendations it was now ordered that the treasurer should be the sole custodian of all college funds and that monies should be paid out by him only on warrant duly signed by the chairman of the prudential committee, after authorization by that committee; that the principal of no fund should be borrowed or used in any way that might be a violation of the conditions upon which the fund had been given to the College. These were good methods and high ideals of accounting, and it is only to be regretted that they were not always observed in the subsequent history of college finances.

When the old dormitory had burned in 1852, President Sturtevant was not totally unhappy because he was getting rid of an annoying problem of discipline. Now, twenty years later, the conviction was growing that the College must build another. The maintenance of proper discipline in such a building might present difficulties but students must be conveniently housed at moderate rates. Some thought it would never get out of the rut into which it had sunk unless a new dormitory were provided. Professor Crampton evidently shared that view. At any rate, the College is chiefly indebted to him for the dormitory which now bears his name. He began to seek funds soon after he was appointed financial agent, and in the fall of 1874 the new dormitory was ready for occupancy.

At the end of the year 1875–76, Dr. Sturtevant, after thirty-two years of notable service as president of the College, asked the trustees to relieve him of the duties of that office, expressing a willingness to continue his work as professor. For nearly another decade he continued his duties as Professor of Mental and Moral Philosophy, contributed many articles to current magazines, wrote two books, and lectured in various parts of the country. He was not exactly a popular teacher, but his students admired him and caught real inspiration in his classroom. Wrote one of them: "Dr. Sturtevant taught his students to think for themselves. Almost every professor tells his pupils, in words, to do their own thinking. But very few manifest real pleasure in freedom of thought on the part of their pupils when it reveals itself in the earnest questioning of their expressed opinions. But it seemed to me that Dr. Sturtevant enjoyed the respectful boldness of a student who dared to controvert his declared views."

II

Acting-President Crampton, 1876–1882

Professor Rufus C. Crampton succeeded Dr. Sturtevant as president of the College in 1876, assuming the office, however, as acting-president. Apparently Professor Crampton could have had the appointment as a permanent position, but he preferred to serve only until a more permanent selection could be made. It is not surprising that the trustees turned to him at this time for executive guidance. He had already assumed such heavy responsibilities in connection with the administration of the College that the new appointment meant little more than a continuance of former duties with added responsibility and authority.

The commencement of 1879 was a memorable one because it marked the fiftieth anniversary of the founding of the College. The time had come when some people began to refer to the school as "Old Illinois." Careful and elaborate preparations were made by a committee of which Professor Edward Tanner, '57, of the faculty was chairman. Many founders and friends of the early days, as well as alumni and former students, returned for the celebration. Of the seven original members of the Yale Band five still survived, and three of them, John Brooks, Mason Grosvenor, and Julian Sturtevant, were present, Elisha Jenney and Asa Turner being too feeble in health to come.

Wednesday, June 4, the day preceding the commencement exercises, was set apart for the semicentennial celebration. Without doubt the most notable address of the occasion was delivered by Dr. Sturtevant. Who could be better qualified in ability and experience than

he to voice on such an anniversary the spirit of the past and the hope
for the future. If he could not interpret the meaning of the years that
had gone and look forward into the years still to come, who could
do it? Said he: "No society can grow, nor long live, that has not
thinkers, independent thinkers, seers, and that is not governed by
them. Such men must carry their own credentials with them; they
must wait for the endorsement of no hierarchy; they must be sustained by no authority but the authority of truth and righteousness
and God. The function of a college is to aid in raising up such men
and qualifying them to perform their high office." He pointed out
how the founders of Illinois College, true to their own convictions
on education, religion, and the perplexing political issues of the
times, had tried to build, not for temporary prosperity, but for the
ages. The two greatest obstacles to the success of the College, he
insisted, had been the slavery issue and theological controversies.
The former trouble was now out of the way, but he almost despaired
of a solution of the theological problem. The influence of sectarian
narrowness in the field of higher education seemed an almost insur-
mountable obstacle destined, in his opinion, to cause difficulty for
years to come. He frankly declared that he did not look with hope
upon state universities, with their lack of positive religious influences, as a solution to the problem. His final word was a renewed
plea for the Christian college—on a voluntary, nonsectarian foundation:

We have no sectarian ends to accomplish. We never had. We
meant to build upon this spot a college sacred to Christ and His
Church Universal, sacred to religion, to humanity, to well regulated
liberty, to civilization. If anyone thinks he can better provide for
that great want of our state and our civilization which I have pointed
out, by rejecting these foundations, and building on some other, do
it—in the name of God do it—and build with all your might. But if
you cannot, I pray you build here. We are no bigots. We acknowledge the greatness and difficulty of the subject and the limitation of
our wisdom. Give us your wisdom, but while you offer that, do not
withhold your active co-operation in a work so great and excellent.

One of the most interesting and important features of the rather brief
administration of Professor Crampton is found in the development

of student life in that period. The spirit of student activities under-
went change; new student customs were introduced; and it is to this
period that we can trace the beginnings of intercollegiate debate and
sports and also campus journalism of an organized kind. Prior to this
period, intercollegiate competition of any kind was unknown, but
now began a very vigorous intercollegiate competition in oratory,
and students likewise began, in a somewhat feeble and irregular fashion, their intercollegiate contests in athletics. It was shortly before
this administration that the Illinois Intercollegiate Oratorical Association originated and that Illinois College students began to play baseball with the students of other colleges. The first annual oratorical
contest was held at Bloomington, November 20, 1874. Besides Illinois College and Illinois Wesleyan University, the other institutions
represented in this initial contest were: Chicago University (an institution earlier than the present University of Chicago, which was
founded in 1891), Monmouth, Northwestern University, Knox,
Shurtleff, and the Illinois Industrial University (now the University
of Illinois).

The interstate oratorical contest held in Jacksonville in the spring
of 1881 was undoubtedly the outstanding event in student activities
in the administration of President Crampton and one of the greatest
events in the history of student activities at Illinois College. The
affair was felt to be a great honor to the College and the city, for
it must be remembered that this was the first student intercollegiate
contest of any kind for which competitors were coming from various
states. Six states were represented in the oratorical competition: Minnesota by Carleton College; Iowa by Upper Iowa University; Wisconsin by Beloit College; Illinois by Monmouth College; Indiana by
Asbury University, now DePauw; and Ohio by Oberlin College.
The oratorical contest was to be held on Wednesday evening, May
4, but there were both preliminaries and subsequent events. Delegates began arriving on Monday: the Industrial University sent a
delegation of over 60, Monmouth 85, and Knox 35. It is worth noting that among the visitors was a young girl from Rockford College
destined later to achieve high fame—Jane Addams, who came apparently to request the admission of her college into the association.

The oratorical contest took place in the opera house, and brought

Crampton Hall. Drawing by Louise Boring Wood

out, in spite of rain, "such an audience as even the 'Athens of the West' itself has seldom, if ever, seen." Mr. Coffin of Asbury University won the first prize for his oration on "The Philosophy of Skepticism," while second honors went to Mr. Morris of Carleton for his oration on "Progress, its Sources and Laws." The next evening in the auditorium of the School for the Deaf, the literary societies of Illinois College and Knox College held a debate and literary contest. Although Phi Alpha won the debate, Adelphi of Knox won the competitions in essay, declamation, and oratory, and, therefore, was declared the winner of the contest as a whole. This is probably the first occasion of an intercollegiate debate at Illinois College. The *Rambler* made its contribution to the occasion by publishing a special interstate edition of twelve hundred copies. There was a reception at the Illinois Female College (now MacMurray), a banquet for three hundred at the Armory Hall, and a dance. The baseball tournament was washed out by rain, but not before Illinois College had defeated the Illinois Industrial University, 14–13. One wonders whether it would be possible in these later days, when athletics have become a major interest and not a mere appendage, to arouse such interest in oratory in any college or university of the land.

Baseball seems to have been the first sport which started among the students in any organized form. The sport must have been in existence prior to President Crampton's administration, but the absence of a student newspaper makes it difficult to trace the beginnings of organized baseball at the College. The sport must have been sporadic until the middle or late seventies. It should be noted that the first regular nine was organized at Princeton apparently as early as 1858 and that Harvard and Yale played their first series in 1868. In those early years of the sport, both organized and unorganized, it was played in the fall months as well as in the spring, football not yet having established itself as the fall sport. The diamond on which the Illinois College games were played was located east of the dormitory. As far as tradition and records show, Illinois College's first intercollegiate game of baseball, and perhaps the first intercollegiate athletic game of any kind, was played with Shurtleff College in October 1878. It is evident that baseball and oratory greatly promoted intercollegiate relations in this period. Almost always, there seems to have been a baseball tournament arranged in connection with the oratorical contest. The Illinois College boys were rather active in urging the formation of a regular intercollegiate association for the playing of baseball, but this attempt did not bear fruit for some time.

The faint beginnings of football may also be traced back to these years, if the kicking of something called a football about the campus may be cited as the beginning of that sport. Whether this kind of romping can be called football is perhaps very doubtful. But that student interest in sports was increasing is indicated by the provision made for a sort of gymnasium in the basement of the dormitory. The students, aided by the faculty and friends, purchased some parallel bars, dumbbells, a trapeze, mattress, etc., from the "Turners," a local German association, and installed this equipment in a basement room of Crampton. In good weather, this apparatus seems to have been brought out into the open air.

The College Young Men's Christian Association began its existence in Illinois College during the period of President Crampton. The general Y.M.C.A. organization had already established branches in many of the colleges of the state, and from time to time the question of establishing a branch in Illinois College had been agitated by the students. It was, finally, on February 11, 1882, that a group of students met in the city Y.M.C.A. rooms and organized the College Association.

The first number of the *College Rambler* appeared in December 1877. It seems that a few years earlier a paper called *The Athenian* had been published, but it did not survive beyond a few issues. The publication of student papers in some of the other colleges of the state probably helped to stimulate interest in a similar enterprise among the students of Illinois College; at any rate, before the *Rambler* came into existence, *The Illini* had been started at the Industrial University, the *Student's Journal* at Wesleyan, and the *College Courier* at Monmouth. The original *Rambler* was a monthly publication, but in the spring of 1881 it began to be issued semimonthly. As originally published, the *Rambler* was an organ of the Student Association, which apparently had also assumed financial responsibility for the publication. At the end of the first year, that organization, evidently discouraged over the financial prospects of the next year, refused to continue publication. It is good testimony to the energy and determination of the leaders among the students of that day that they would not sit by and see the new college paper die without making an effort to keep it alive. After thorough discussion, it was decided to try a new scheme for financing the enterprise. A stock company was to be formed, with twenty shares of a value of five dollars each. These shares were to be offered to the students at auction and sold to the highest bidders. The plan worked even better than its authors expected, and shares sold at a premium. Sixty-seven dollars was realized above the par value of the stock. "The wheels of the *Rambler's* life once more began to move." Only one issue was missed, the first number under the new management appearing in February 1879. The publication of the *Rambler* has continued without serious interruption from that day to this.

Professor Crampton continued to work energetically at the difficult task of increasing the endowment of the College, and made trip after trip to the East and various parts of the West. The burden of teaching and of administrative responsibility bore with increasing weight upon his shoulders. In the fall of 1881 his health became so much impaired that the trustees felt obliged to appoint Professor Tanner to take up Crampton's work as financial agent. Though he found it necessary to limit his activities, Mr. Crampton continued to serve as the Hitchcock Professor of Mathematics and Astronomy until 1888. His death in that year removed from the college family one who had given long, valuable, and heroic service to the institution. Although of strong physique and originally of robust health, he had worn himself out in his labors for the College. Coming to Jacksonville almost immediately after his graduation from Yale, he had been a member of the faculty for some thirty-five years. What he accomplished for the financial rehabilitation of the College in those trying years of the seventies were notable achievements that helped to save Illinois College from extinction.

12

President Tanner, 1882–1892

The trustees finally in the spring of 1882 elected as president Edward Allan Tanner, the Professor of Latin on the College faculty. A better choice could not have been made, and the only surprising thing about the election is the fact that it was so long delayed. Professor Tanner was an alumnus of Illinois College. The year of his elevation to the presidency marked the twenty-fifth anniversary of his graduation and the seventeenth year of his service on the faculty. He had many of the qualities which go to make up a successful college president. He was a painstaking scholar, a good teacher, and an eloquent preacher, and he combined with these qualities great energy as an administrator. In the seventeen years during which he had been serving on the faculty, a large number of students, many now successful young alumni, had passed through his classes. He was well known and greatly liked among the citizens of the town, and his occasional sermons in various parts of the state had widened still further his circle of friends. Furthermore, as an aide to Acting-President Crampton during the last year or two, Mr. Tanner had clearly demonstrated that he had pronounced ability as a money-raiser, an occupation in which many a college president has exhausted his strength.

One of the first things to which the president-elect gave prompt and vigorous attention was the campus and the college plant. At an earlier time of financial stress, the acreage of the campus had been reduced by the sale of a row of lots on the east side, along Park Street. Even before the new president took formal charge, he started a movement which resulted in the recovery of this property by the college authorities. It was, indeed, a fortunate thing for Illinois College to recover this land. When one thinks of a row of small, private dwellings on the west side of Park Street and further allows his imagination to picture the dismal prospect, as one might look down from Sturtevant Hall into back yards with their fences, sheds, and garages, he appreciates the real service which Dr. Tanner performed for the College in this instance. Furthermore, it was at this time that the old, unsightly Osage orange hedge which surrounded the campus was grubbed out. One day in May of 1882 Professor Tanner announced in chapel that if the students were willing all recitations would be omitted the following Friday while students and faculty went out together to grub up the Osage orange hedge. Then, as ever, a holiday was a bait which students were quick to follow. The *Rambler* describes what happened.

Friday, May 5th will always be remembered as an eventful day in college history, for upon that day students and faculty made an assault on the old ragged hedge which had stood for so many years. The sun failed to put in an appearance in the morning and fears were entertained that the rain which had poured down unceasingly during the week, would not permit the work to be undertaken but immediately after breakfast Prof. Tanner arrived, and, saying that it would at least be a cool day to labor, advised the boys to procure their axes and spades. Some time before the hour appointed, the boys from the dormitory and town were swarming along the hedge cutting away as if their lives depended on the work being done at that particular moment. After dinner the boys worked until four o'clock, when they had cut down the hedge and grubbed up the roots. Lemonade was furnished on the campus Osage day.

Noteworthy financial progress also immediately occurred. It was that same spring of 1882 that Professor Tanner, who had been appointed by the trustees to take up the financial solicitation which President Crampton could no longer prosecute vigorously on account of his failing health, completed the thirty thousand dollars necessary to secure the Stone bequest. This was a gift made in the latter part of 1880 by Mrs. Valeria G. Stone of Malden, Massachusetts, conditional upon the raising of an additional thirty thousand dollars by the College. The successful conclusion of this campaign meant the addition of fifty thousand dollars to the permanent endowment of the institution.

Educationally, a new era also began. The completion of the Stone Fund made possible an enlargement of the faculty, or at least a filling of vacancies on the instructing staff. The appointment of Dr. Harvey W. Milligan as professor of rhetoric, history, and English literature, Edward B. Clapp as instructor in Greek, Harold W. Johnston as instructor in Latin, and Joseph R. Harker as principal of Whipple Academy were early and distinguished appointments of the Tanner Administration. Not only was the variety of courses increased and the quality of instruction improved as a result of these appointments, but other steps were taken to raise the educational standards of the College. For example, the entrance requirements were raised by adding practically another year of preparatory work to the previous requirements.

The problem of avoiding the blighting annual deficits also commanded Tanner's early attention. Order and system were introduced into the management of college business. The new president began to present carefully prepared annual reports to his trustees which reviewed the history of the current year and recommended definite policies for future development. He paid special attention to the preparation of a budget with carefully worked out plans for making expenditures and income balance.

Everybody had had such a good time grubbing out the Osage orange hedge in the spring of 1882 that when the next year rolled around there was a general demand for an observance of Osage Orange Day. Evidently, President Tanner and the faculty entered heartily into the plans for an annual celebration of the day. It was resolved to make it an occasion of varied activities—athletics, music, speeches, a picnic lunch, and a general good time. Alumni and local citizens, as well as students and faculty, began to assemble on the campus early in the morning, so that a crowd of considerable size had gathered when the Fifth Regiment Band marched to the campus about ten o'clock. Athletic events constituted the first part of the program. By the time the athletic games were ended, it was far past the noon hour, and the hungry multitude was fed with a picnic

President Edward Allan Tanner

lunch. About three o'clock, the crowd marched behind the band to a spot near the east entrance to the campus, where a pine and Osage were planted side by side and where was performed a ceremony, "the wedding of the Osage and the pine," in which President Tanner served as the officiating clergyman, and the principals were the Illinois College boys, and girls from the Female Academy, the Athenaeum, the Methodist Female College, and the City of Jacksonville. The ceremony was evidently intended to symbolize the harmonious interests of the various educational institutions of the city.

Then came the heavier part of the program, when the people assembled at the rostrum and President Tanner introduced the Honorable Paul Selby, '53, of the *Springfield State Journal*, as the chairman of the literary exercises. Mr. Selby, having replied in a speech of some length, called upon a long list of alumni and students to make brief remarks. Those were the days when intercollegiate and high school athletics had not yet developed, and so Osage Orange Day, in a few years, became the most important event on the college calendar, with the exception of commencement. Incidentally, the annual athletic program and celebration did much to promote local interest and alumni loyalty. Alumni and friends drove in from miles around to witness the event and others came on trains from a farther distance; the public schools of Jacksonville were dismissed for the day, and many of the merchants closed their stores. When the weather happened to be favorable, several thousand people often came to the campus. It was a great day for the town, as well as for the College. The merchants of the city usually contributed the prizes offered in the various athletic events. Although the athletic program tended to overshadow other activities, oratory, the picnic luncheon, and the music by band and glee club continued for many years to play a part in the program. Press dispatches in the newspapers of St. Louis and Chicago made note of the day.

Having grasped the opportunity offered by Osage Orange Day to win a more hearty support for the College from local friends and alumni, President Tanner next determined to widen the constituency of the institution. As he once expressed himself, he proposed to work from the center to the circumference. Local citizens and alumni must first be warmed into a new interest and loyalty, and then gradually a wider circle of new friends must be won. Partly to win these new friends among the farmers, and partly to enable the College to perform a greater and more practical service to the section of the country where it was located, Mr. Tanner resolved to introduce instruction in agriculture into the college curriculum. "We must," he said in his 1883 report to the trustees, "recognize the nature of our environment; it is agricultural. The wealth of the future is buried in this fertile soil. Let the College then seek to bless the farmer as it has never done, and then convert him from an indifferent and hostile neighbor into an open-hearted, open-handed friend." Without lowering traditional ideals and standards, he proposed "to reach, and elevate and transform into college builders, a powerful class."

Specialized, practical courses with experimental facilities could hardly be attempted. "Culture for agriculture and agriculture for culture" was to be the slogan of the department, and this perhaps represents fairly well the goal of the college authorities. The catalogue stated: "The course in this department, though primarily intended for those who expect to make agriculture their vocation, is not a course in farming. The institution neither has, nor desires to have, an experimental farm—the design is to meet the wants of young men that can devote only six months of the twelve to books, but who wish to continue their studies through a number of years, sufficient to give them thorough training in the sciences connected with outdoor occupations, as well as in those liberalizing branches which may be pursued profitably, without the aid of foreign languages." Ambitious young men from the farms were encouraged to register by the promise that the course would teach "how to mix brains with the soil, so that the latter may yield a hundred fold," and in a somewhat high-sounding phrase it was proposed to "dignify labor by elevating agriculture to the rank of a learned profession."

Thus, in a variety of ways, President Tanner made heroic efforts to solve the financial problem of the College. Nearly every year witnessed an increase in the endowment resources of the institution, at least as measured in terms of subscription notes. Mr. Tanner pointed out emphatically to friends of the College that they must cease to depend upon the East for pecuniary support. "More and more," the East would be inclined to say, "Illinois with all her magnificent resources, must henceforth provide for her own institutions." The president himself acted on his own advice, and practically all the funds which he raised were secured in the West. The financial history of the period as reflected in the expense and income account bears out the conclusions drawn in discussing the history of the endowment fund. Income was steadily growing, but it never permanently caught up with expenditures. It is pathetic to watch this devoted and self-sacrificing president put forth every ounce of his strength to wipe out that everlasting deficit and fail again and again. One cannot help believing that this uphill, nerve-wracking fight contributed to the worry which eventually broke down the president's health. According to the treasurer's reports, there was a deficit every year of the Tanner administration except one, but fortunately the deficits were comparatively small.

It may be said that the president in making new appointments continued, with few exceptions, to show that insight which marked him as a discriminating college executive. Among these were Samuel W. Parr, who became professor of agricultural science, and Dr. Hiram K. Jones, who was appointed professor of philosophy. One of the most loyal and generous alumni who ever graduated from the College, Dr. Jones was a philosopher of some reputation, not to mention his standing in the medical profession of his generation. He had been graduated from Illinois College with the class of 1844 and belonged to that small group who had studied medicine in the medical department of the College. In the field of philosophy he had made a distinct impression not only upon the local community but also upon a wider circle as a student of Plato and of German idealism. He was associated with that interesting and influential group of idealists who conducted the Concord School of Philosophy in Massachusetts. McCosh of Princeton referred to him as "a genuine and representative member" of this school of philosophers. Dr. Jones counted both Bronson Alcott and Ralph Waldo Emerson among his friends, and entertained them when they visited Jacksonville.

A comparison of the courses at the beginning and the end of the Tanner administration shows that there was considerable expansion in the curriculum. Most of this expansion occurred, as might be expected, in the field of science. Although a scientific course was scheduled in the earlier years, it meant little more than that the "scientifics" escaped Greek and for a time got through college in three years instead of four; otherwise, the classical and scientific courses had been nearly identical. It was the inauguration of the agricultural department which helped in time to improve the general instruction in science. However little that department did for practical agriculture, it did much to improve science instruction in the College. Chemistry with laboratory practice, botany, physiology and histology, invertebrate zoology and entomology now found a place in the curriculum.

Towards the end of the Tanner administration, the so-called philosophical course, leading to the degree of Ph.B., was introduced. This course required Latin, which was now no longer a requirement in the science course. In 1891 there existed the following courses or departments of work: the old classical course (A.B.); the philosophical course (Ph.B.); the scientific course (B.Sc.); and the agricultural course, whose registrants, the catalogue stated, "will be encouraged to become candidates for the degree of bachelor of science, which they may do by remaining at the College and pursuing the studies of the senior year in the scientific course."

The administration of President Tanner witnessed a remarkable development of student activities. The days of simple diversions when students were satisfied to swing from bars in the college grove and join a Peripatetic Club, whose members sought recreation in walking, were gone forever. To a certain extent this rising tide of student activities at Illinois College was part of that general development of student life in American colleges and universities, due chiefly to the growing interest in athletics and also, one must not forget, to those constantly increasing facilities for transportation which made intercollegiate contests among students more practicable. The Tanner administration not only witnessed important developments in baseball but it saw the beginning of football as an organized sport and the beginning of track and field athletics; it contributed to our college history the first regularly organized and trained glee club; it saw the beginning of tennis on the campus, of cycling, and, in a very amateurish way, also of student dramatics. The social life of the students likewise expanded, for it was in this administration, in spite of strong discouragement from the college authorities, that the dance finally won a place as a recognized student activity. President Tanner's own home, filled by a family of attractive daughters and active sons and presided over by a gracious wife, became the center of a most wholesome social life.

Baseball remained the chief athletic sport in the decade of the Tanner administration. It continued to be played in the fall as well as in the spring, and to make the nine was the chief ambition of the student who had athletic ability. During these years, as in the preceding period, young faculty members who had the ability and agility continued to play on the nine, apparently without protest from competing colleges, which doubtless followed the same policy. Professor Johnston, of the Latin department, playing on second base, and Professor Parr, of the agricultural department, on first base, were among the best players on the team. In addition, Professor Johnston served for a time as manager of the team, a circumstance which probably further explains the unusual success of the sport in Illinois College during those years. In 1887, when T. W. Smith and Edward Capps, seniors who had been members of the baseball team, were promised positions on the faculty, the *Rambler* remarked that the trustees had given "Mr. T. W. Smith, our heavy batter, and Mr. Edward Capps, our able fielder, places in the college faculty, there to play with first baseman Parr and second baseman Johnston for the interests of the College and the College nine. Some objection has been raised because Mr. John C. Rice, also chosen a tutor, does not play ball. However, as he is a man of steady nerve, cool judgment and great courage, he may develop into an excellent umpire, so that this one infelicity can be overlooked."

The first suggestion for the organization of a glee club seems to have been made in the spring of 1883, when a number of students with some ability as songsters were brought together by Professor Clapp and drilled to sing at the Junior Exhibition of that year. Their singing was very much appreciated, and at once the thought of a regular college glee club began to take form. As soon as the students returned for the following fall, the subject was again taken up, and in October at a meeting held in the college chapel a club was definitely organized. In the spring of 1884, the club gave its first concert as a benefit for the college Y.M.C.A., to enable that organization to purchase some furnishings for its new quarters in Sturtevant Hall. The concert was evidently a success musically and financially, the club turning over about one hundred dollars to the Christian Association. The boys also sang at the Osage Orange Day festivities that spring. The club consisted of about thirty members, little attempt being made to restrict membership to those who could really sing.

Another student enterprise which attained a high measure of success was the *College Rambler*. The claim was made that "the *College Rambler* has become in size and circulation, the leading college paper of the state." In tone and quality it must have compared favorably with any college periodical of that time, conducted on the combined plan of furnishing news and providing a medium for the literary expression of the student body. It is true that this literary expression consisted mostly of the reprinting of essays and orations that had been submitted in various college competitions. It is not these essays and orations but rather the distinctly well-written editorials and news items that attract one's attention. Furthermore, the paper's general policy and attitude towards student affairs, involving occasionally stirring problems of student discipline, was dignified and independent. The editors did not hesitate at times even to support the faculty in spite of the pressure of student public opinion.

The Y.M.C.A., started in President Crampton's administration, grew to enlarged strength and activity in the time of President Tanner, although there was a lapse of interest and activity in the last year or two. The new president supported it heartily, doing what he could to give it not only inspiration but also material help. Very early in his administration quarters were assigned to the association in Sturtevant Hall, a neatly furnished room being provided where magazines and newspapers could be found and where conferences and meetings of all kinds could be held. In the fall of 1891, the state convention of the Y.M.C.A. was held in Jacksonville—a meeting worth noting since it was addressed by John R. Mott, then a young man recently out of college but already showing himself a peerless leader of young men in their religious aspirations.

Another contribution which the students of this generation made to student activities was the college annual. The first Illinois College annual was the *Cerberus*, published by the class of 1892 in the spring of 1891. The next class was small in numbers, and for a time it looked as if *Cerberus* would be allowed to slumber, but a successor, called *Hercules*, was published, dedicated to the late president and containing a fine tribute to Dr. Tanner.

Still another creation of the time was the Dorm Court. The original object of the Dorm Court was (1) to give dormitory boys who might be interested an opportunity for a little practice in moot court work; (2) to deal out justice and penalties to dormitory residents who interfered with the comfort of their fellow students; and (3) to provide amusement and refreshments. It was a court of dormitory boys for dormitory boys, and to a certain extent represented an attempt at self-government in the turbulent life of Crampton. The *Rambler* of January 27, 1883, reports a typical incident:

> The dormitory court held its first session last Saturday evening, with Judge Tomlinson in the chair. The case brought forward for trial was, Dormitory vs. Pope, Clymer and Galbreth, on a charge of embezzlement. Stevenson and Hull conducted the case for the people, and Bond and Beggs for the defense. After a rigid examination of witnesses the case was given to the jury and the verdict of "not guilty" was rendered. The judge, jury, lawyers and spectators then devoured a half-bushel of apples at the expense of the prosecution. The court was then adjourned *sine die*.

It is evident that while there was a great deal of fun connected with the proceedings and, doubtless at times, some boisterous conduct, there was also a vein of serious purpose running through the whole thing. If a student damaged another's property, he was likely to be haled before the court and dormitory abuses of various kinds were thereby held in check. Protests were made against purely trumped-up charges and against the punishment of the guiltless.

In the spring of 1886 occurred a case of hazing which was probably the source of the most unpleasant controversy of the Tanner administration. One evening a group of boys entered the room of a newcomer and subjected him to some indignities. The student reported the names of his harassers to the authorities, and President Tanner called in five of the boys and warned them to desist from any further harassment, but somewhat later further damage was done to the young man's property, the ringleader in the renewed mischief being one of the boys who had led the first assault. The president took the following action: one student, apparently the ringleader, was ordered permanently to vacate the dormitory and the commons; furthermore, he was to be reprimanded in chapel and his parents notified. Lesser punishments were decreed for the other offenders. President Tanner delivered the reprimands publicly and forcefully. Among other reasons given for the expulsion from the dormitory was that the culprit was "a beneficiary of the institution and had never paid a cent of tuition." The boy and his friends were angered by this reference and they drew up a petition which was signed by seven members of the senior class and delivered to the president as an ultimatum. One can imagine how a person of Dr. Tanner's temperament would receive such a document. The faculty refused to grant the petition and sustained the president absolutely. The president then demanded that the seven seniors remove their names from the petition. Feelings grew intense, but the erasure of the names soon began. Later when the trustees met in their annual meeting they endorsed the stand of the president and the faculty and passed a resolution strongly condemning the practice of hazing. More remarkable, the *Rambler* gave general support to the president and faculty: "Taking everything into consideration, we are glad to see the stand the authorities have taken in this matter. All advocates of law and order, all believers in healthy discipline, all haters of hazing, all lovers of Illinois College, should rejoice in this manifestation of backbone."

In the early nineties the question of alumni representation on the board of trustees began to be seriously agitated. Among the board members, of course, were many graduates of the College, but the alumni were not represented by members whom they themselves were regularly choosing. As a matter of fact, the trustees had several years previously invited the alumni to nominate members of the board, and they had actually done so. Julius E. Strawn was elected to the board upon nomination by the alumni in 1876 and Marshall P. Ayers in 1879. Illinois College was among the first colleges in the country to recognize the right of the alumni to representation on the board of trustees, but it was not until the time of Dr. Tanner's successor that the problem of alumni representation on the board of trustees was finally and satisfactorily solved.

The increasing interest of the alumni in their alma mater manifested itself in the spring of 1892 by the organization of two alumni associations—one at Quincy and the other in Chicago. The movement for the establishment of such organizations started first among the Chicago alumni, although it happened that the men of Quincy and its vicinity held the first banquet. As might be expected, President Tanner and some of the trustees had been active in promoting the idea of such local associations of Illinois College alumni. The general Alumni Association began its existence many years earlier. In 1839, only four years after the first class was graduated, the alumni held a meeting in the office of Richard Yates, '35, and organized themselves into an association "for the purposes of mutual improvement and of perpetuating the feelings and friendships of collegiate life." The Illinois College Alumni Association therefore takes its place among the oldest associations of this kind in the country, the first perhaps being that organized at Williams in 1821, followed by Princeton in 1826 and the University of Virginia in 1838. Interesting to relate, the original Illinois College minute book contains continuous minutes from September 19, 1839, to June 5, 1912.

Public lectures were given at the College intermittently during these years, with occasional successes and more frequent failures. In the spring of 1882, Oscar Wilde had come to Jacksonville under the auspices of Sigma Pi, but for several years after that neither society seemed ready to undertake the financial risks incident to a lecture course. Some years later, Phi Alpha, Sigma Pi, the Methodist Female College, and the Female Academy all united to sponsor a lecture course. There was a profit of $272, which was divided among the four institutions.

The beginnings of bathing on the campus deserve to be recorded. Cleanliness and athletics developed in the same decade. When the dormitory was constructed in 1873, it had not yet become customary to include bath rooms in the plans, but nine years later a Bath Room Association was organized to agitate the question of providing bathing facilities in the dormitory. W. N. Lewis, evidently a lad with a little money and an eye for business, proposed to advance $250 to fit up a bath room in the basement of the dormitory providing he might charge a reasonable fee for the use of the facilities. His proposal was accepted, and accordingly in the fall of 1882 the Lewis Bath Room, "elegantly fitted up with all the necessary appointments," opened for business. The following year, however, young Lewis despairingly reported that the "College bath rooms are meeting but a scanty patronage from the students." But the college catalogue of 1883–84 announced: "Hot and cold baths are furnished at the College bath rooms to all students at a nominal charge. Experience has shown this to be a very healthful and pleasant feature of dormitory life." Still later, according to the *Rambler*: "The Athletic Association will try to make up their deficiency of $150 by the sale of bath room tickets. Shower baths have been arranged, a dressing room and all modern conveniences fitted up, and any member can wash and be clean at any and all hours of the day. Every student is expected to indulge in at least one bath during the year."

In 1888, the student athletic association began agitating the question of securing a gymnasium building for the College. A sum of fifteen thousand dollars was mentioned as a possible goal, and a committee on solicitation was soon appointed. The classes of 1891 and 1892 were especially active in the enterprise, pledging eight hundred dollars and five hundred dollars respectively. The next Osage Orange Day program proclaimed: *Gymnasium erectandum est*, but funds accumulated very slowly. President Tanner took up the cause, and in the spring of 1891 ground was broken for the construction of the building. In the spring of 1892 the building was finally ready for use. The first dedicatory event was an athletic dinner held the evening of May 2, followed the next evening by two plays. The social dedication came during the commencement week when the senior class gave its promenade in the new gymnasium, the college glee club having given a benefit concert on the preceding evening. The gymnasium was, as the *Rambler* declared it to be, "a monument to the student spirit of Illinois College." In its day, the gymnasium was one of the first and best college gymnasiums in the state.

The strain of his strenuous labors for the College began to tell upon the president. He had little chance for rest or relaxation. Preaching, teaching, ever seeking more endowment, harassed by annoying problems of student discipline and of faculty changes, desperately striving for an ideal not yet attained, wasting hours of precious time on petty details of college administration, President Tanner began to show signs of failing health. In the spring of 1891 he suffered a breakdown, and the trustees relieved him of his duties until he might be able to resume his work. When college opened in the fall, he was on hand as usual, but by December illness again gripped him, apparently a nervous trouble. For a few weeks longer with characteristic energy and determination, he attended to pressing duties, but in the middle of January an attack of influenza aggravated his trouble, and he had to give up. Even in his final illness, he insisted on taking up college affairs, and when the doctor remonstrated, his reply was: "You might as well ask a man to take out his heart and lay it aside." He died February 8, 1892, at the age of fifty-four.

Illinois College was fortunate in the presidents who had guided her destiny during these formative years. Beecher, Sturtevant, Crampton, and Tanner were all men of outstanding ability who not only gave valuable service to the College but made real contributions to the cause of higher education in the Middle West.

13

President Bradley, 1892–1899

The death of President Tanner was a bewildering blow to the friends of Illinois College. Temporary provision was made for the administration of the College by appointing Professor H. W. Milligan Chairman of the Faculty and Acting-President—in fact this arrangement had been made even before President Tanner died. Professor Milligan continued to act until a new president arrived. An interregnum is seldom a happy era either in politics or in education, for a sense of authority and responsibility rarely characterizes that kind of government. At a meeting held in April 1892, a committee of five was appointed to seek a new president. Although requested to report, if possible, by the following commencement, the committee asked for more time. Their choice eventually fell upon Dr. John E. Bradley, who, however, did not come to Jacksonville to undertake his duties until the last of October. It is of interest to observe that the board had not chosen a minister. Dr. Bradley was what one would call a public school man, of good training and of varied and successful experience. He was a graduate of Williams College, and had secured the degree of doctor of philosophy from New York University. He was called to the presidency of Illinois College from Minneapolis, where he had been serving for some six years as superintendent of the city schools. Both Dr. Bradley and his wife possessed attractive social qualities, and their home in Jacksonville was destined to become a social center for faculty, students, and townspeople. The new president undertook his work with high hopes and genuine enthusiasm.

The administration of President Bradley proved to be comparatively brief. Although in some respects phenomenal progress had been made in the previous administration and the College had won a high position in the educational world, Dr. Bradley soon found that some very perplexing problems awaited him. He was following a popular, as well as able, predecessor, and many wondered whether he could carry on. Most people did not know that the financial foundations of the institution were far from secure. Many of the subscriptions to the various endowment funds which President Tanner had raised remained unpaid, and the old problem of making bricks without straw soon worried Dr. Bradley, as it had worried and harassed every one of his predecessors. The new gymnasium increased the ordinary overhead expenses of the College, and certain promises of promotion and of increases in salary made to faculty members added to the difficulties of the situation. Nor is it to be forgotten that it was a period when, on account of the widening field of collegiate education and the rapid growth of the state university and other large institutions, all small colleges in the state had hard sledding.

Dr. Bradley's inauguration was a simple ceremony following the commencement exercises of 1893. Edward P. Kirby, secretary and treasurer of the board of trustees, presented the key of the College to the new president, and Dr. Bradley, after accepting this symbol of privilege and responsibility, delivered an inaugural address on the general subject of "The American College." Although hardly a notable address, it was a sane and stimulating discussion of the function of the college. "The college is a training school," said the new president; "it should yield for each life which it helps to fashion, strength, culture and character."

There is a general feeling that educational standards declined somewhat in the administration of President Bradley. Whatever basis there may be for such an opinion, it is not to be denied that, so far as financial limitations permitted, an effort was made to bring the College into line with the developments in higher education elsewhere in the country. One of the first policies suggested by the new president was a further extension of the elective system in the college curriculum. Among the more progressive colleges and universities, the range of studies in such fields as science, history, politics, English

President John E. Bradley

literature, etc., was steadily increasing. Dr. Bradley was not only in touch with this new movement from the point of view of the public schools but he spent part of the time between his election as president of Illinois College and his arrival on the campus in a tour of investigation among the colleges of the East and West. These visits to other colleges must have opened his eyes to the progress that was being made in the best colleges and universities of the country. The faculty adopted his new policies, and in the first catalogue issued in Dr. Bradley's administration the plan of elective studies was duly announced. The work of the freshman year was all to be required as previously, but for the sophomore, junior, and senior years, with the exception of five or six hours each term in history, English, and philosophy, the work was all to be elective, although a few years later the number of required subjects in the last three years was slightly increased.

"To my mind," reported the president to the trustees, "the object of elective studies is not so much to permit a student to choose those branches which bear upon his future work as to enable him to select such as will interest him and thus lead his mind to act with greatest vigor. The problem of education, so far as it relates to the intellect, is to develop thought power, the ability to grasp and firmly hold related ideas until their scope and relations can be exactly determined. Feeble and apathetic operations of the mind will not accomplish the desired training. Every condition should conduce to vigor and spontaneity of action. It is believed that the wide range of electives now offered will greatly strengthen and enrich the work of the College." The students hailed their new freedom with delight.

A comparison of the curriculum at the end of the Tanner period and in the middle of the Bradley administration shows clearly that a greater variety of courses was being offered in the latter period. There was a considerable offering of elective courses in Latin, a stimulating variety of courses in the history of English literature, including a course in Anglo-Saxon. Much less expansion occurred in history, economics, philosophy, and Greek. In French there was practically no expansion, but a third year of German was offered as well as an elective course in scientific German. But the departments which showed the greatest expansion in elective courses were mathematics and the sciences.

President Bradley still further extended the program of courses by providing additional lectures by well-known scholars who were not regular members of the faculty. For examples, not only did Dr. Hiram K. Jones continue to give his lectures on philosophy to the members of the senior class but Dr. Frank Parsons Norbury offered a course on psycho-physics, and Professor Harry Pratt Judson came down from the University of Chicago to supplement the work in political science. Other nonresident lecturers included such men as James E. Rogers, the president of Blackburn College, and Professor Albert Hurd, of Knox College, as well as some Jacksonville scholars.

In a time when the new spirit of scientific study was permeating the educational system of America, it is refreshing to find that the faculty of Illinois College gave a warm welcome to the new methods and spirit of scientific investigation. An interesting episode occurred in the neighboring village of Franklin. The principal of the high school was threatened with dismissal because he allowed the theory of evolution to be taught in his school. A meeting of the board of education and patrons of the school was called to give the principal a hearing, and Professor Carter of the Illinois College science department was invited to expound the new doctrine at this hearing, with special reference to its bearing on the Christian religion. Unlike the fate of the public school teacher a generation later, at whose trial in Dayton, Tennessee, a famous alumnus of Illinois College appeared as the champion of medievalism, this superintendent was acquitted and allowed to proceed with the course.

An indication of the scholastic standing of the College, as well as the relation of the new president to the educational movements of the time, is given by the fact that Illinois College was invited to become one of the charter members of the North Central Association of Colleges and Preparatory Schools—one of the very few colleges of the state to which such an invitation was extended at the time.

At the end of the first year of the Bradley administration the College lost one of the most efficient members of its faculty. This was Joseph R. Harker, the principal of the Academy and professor of pedagogy, who resigned in order to accept the presidency of what was then called the Illinois Female College. In the years of his service on the faculty, Mr. Harker had succeeded in building up a strong preparatory department both in the number of students and efficiency of instruction. The trustees recognized the value of his services to the College by granting him an honorary degree. His presidency of the Female College marked the beginning of more friendly relations between the boys on the Hill and the girls in the eastern end of town. Other faculty losses included Professor Johnston, Professor Shaw, Professor Clapp, and Professor Milligan. Milligan retired but continued on as librarian. As vacancies occurred near the end of this administration, instructors were uniformly appointed, probably because the trustees could not afford to appoint experienced professors.

The preparatory department continued to attract a goodly number of students. The time had not yet come when the state of Illinois was ready to guarantee a free high school education to the youth of the state, and there continued to be a fruitful field for a private preparatory school of the type of Whipple Academy.

In no branch of student enterprises was there more activity than in athletics, and if professionalism sometimes appeared, as it undoubtedly did, it is not to be forgotten that it was an age of low ethical standards in college athletics. Although members of the faculty had ceased playing on the teams, it was no uncommon thing, especially during the earlier years of the Bradley administration, to have men on the football and baseball teams who could be regarded as students only by a wide stretch of a strong imagination. "They all do it," was the excuse. However, at Illinois College, as elsewhere, the evil became so flagrant that the faculty began to awake to its responsibility and eventually made an effort to improve conditions. Even the student *Rambler* grew incensed at the practice:

No fair-minded thinker can possibly object to scholarships, either in principle or practice, provided they are judiciously conferred. But there has arisen in these later years a bird of strange plumage which might be styled the "Athletic Scholarship." We are referring to the growing practice of paying, by private subscription or from the treasury of the college athletic association, the expenses, in whole or in part, of one or more athletes, men who come to college on the express stipulation that they are to make athletics their chief study and have their college bills paid for so doing.

There are two very valid reasons why such action is not advisable. First, it is a poor business venture; second, it is poor policy. To pay the expenses of even one man is expensive. If the number of "hired students" increases, the cost is augmented. And even when all is done, and the specialists are hired, there is no certainty of victory. Paying specialists to be our athletes is, in the second place, a poor policy. It discourages honest, hard training on the part of the genuine college students. What incentive to conscientious and often irksome training can any college man find in the knowledge that he may be set aside, dropped from the football or baseball team at the last moment and a hireling substituted for him? Moreover, such a policy is fatal to a genuine, hearty college spirit. Can an intense college fervor or glowing enthusiasm be generated over a football game, in which the college is represented by paid outsiders?

A new athletic constitution adopted in 1895 provided for a joint committee of control, consisting of three members of the faculty, three alumni and five students. The encouraging sign was that the students themselves wanted this control. Football had been introduced in the later years of Dr. Tanner's administration and became more popular in the early years of the Bradley administration. The team of 1894 won all but one of its games, and its schedule included not only Knox and Monmouth and Eureka but Illinois Normal and Washington University, and the representatives of the Peoria Athletic Association and the "Pastimes" of St. Louis. No doubt, the difficulty of the schedule was partly responsible for the hiring of players.

The class of 1894, while juniors, brought out the first volume of the *Rig Veda*, a name which eventually caught on for the college annual, although the 1897 issue proved obnoxious to the faculty because it carried a cartoon reflecting on the president. Publication of the *Rig Veda* was ordered suspended for the future, but the next class got around the ban by publishing an annual under another name.

It was in this administration, largely on the suggestion of President Bradley, that the joint debate between the literary societies was revived and became an annual event on the college calendar. On Fri-

Jones Memorial Chapel. Drawing by Louise Boring Wood

day, March 10, 1893, a large crowd of students and townspeople filled the gymnasium for a program featuring songs by the glee club, an essay, a declamation, a reading, and an oration. The debate was on the subject: "Resolves that Man is Evolved from a Lower Order of Animals," Sigma Pi upholding the affirmative and Phi Alpha the negative. No decision was given for the debate, the *Rambler* reporting that it would have been very hard to render a decision.

Three important events in the history of the literary societies occurred during these years. Sigma Pi and Phi Alpha celebrated their fiftieth anniversaries, and a new society was established. The anniversary celebrations were very elaborate affairs with impressive programs and banquets and reunions of oldtimers. The increasing number of students created a demand for another literary society and led to the organization of Gamma Nu in the fall of 1897. At that time, 118 students were registered at the College. Sigma Pi limited its membership to 30, and although Phi Alpha had no constitutional limits, its membership numbered that year about 40. Obviously, unless a third society were organized, a considerable number of men in college could not be members of any society. The name and motto of this new society gave some difficulty. According to one of the founders, the motto "Know Thyself" was favored, but the Greek for that motto, *Gnothi Seauton*, would have given Gamma Sigma, and the founders "could not have anything to do with Sigma." They did like the name Gamma Nu, and it was therefore suggested that they accept the motto and simply capitalize the first and last letters, Gnothi seautoN. "This met with unanimous approval, although it was very amusing to our Greek Professor." The two older societies apparently gave a cordial welcome to the new society.

The increasing number of students and the demands for better library and laboratory facilities called for an expansion of the college plant. The College obviously could not hold its own in competition with the growing universities of the state and other stronger colleges unless better equipment could be provided. At the commencement of 1895 a resident alumnus, who wished to remain anonymous, promised to donate twenty thousand dollars for a new library and chapel building provided others would subscribe an equal amount. Financial conditions were not especially propitious in the country

during those years of 1895 and 1896, but at the annual meeting of
the board in June 1896, the president was able to announce not only
that the necessary twenty thousand dollars had been raised but that
an additional five thousand dollars for endowed scholarships had
been provided. The corner stone of Jones Memorial Chapel was laid
early in the fall, and in June of 1897 it was dedicated. The exercises
included a symposium on philosophy which brought to the campus
some well-known scholars, including Professor Tufts of the University
of Chicago, Dr. William T. Harris, the U.S. Commissioner of
Education, and President Charles F. Thwing of Western Reserve
University.

Political activities also came to the campus from time to time. The
College, as well as the city, took a great interest in the candidacy
of William Jennings Bryan, '81, for the presidency of the United
States in 1896. Mr. Bryan had made his mark as a student. Entering
as a young and modest prep in 1875, he had come into college with
the freshman class two years later. Although he was not among those
students who were constantly in the limelight by their participation
in many activities, he won the recognition of his instructors and fellow students by those qualities of character which in the course of
years made him one of the most influential political leaders of his
generation.

Mr. Bryan had been present at the Sigma Pi Triennial in the commencement week of June 1896, and spoke on the subject "Job and his
Boils; Our Government and the Ills which Beset It." It was only a
few weeks later that he delivered his "Cross of Gold" speech and
won the nomination for the presidency. Early in the fall, the *Rambler*
published a special Bryan number, containing several reminiscent
articles of interest and value in any study of the career of Mr. Bryan.
In late October the candidate came back to the campus and spoke at
the morning chapel service. There was much curiosity, not only in
Jacksonville but elsewhere, as to how this candidate, whom the Yale
boys had heckled in New Haven, would be received by the students
of his alma mater. He was given a sincere, nonpartisan reception
in the chapel, and his address to the students was in every respect
worthy of the occasion—eloquent, dignified, shrewd, and forceful,
making an appeal for support. A little controversy followed because

Mr. Bryan made several references to Dr. Sturtevant's book, *Economics, or the Science of Wealth*, and implied that in advocating free silver he was only applying principles which he had learned at Illinois College. The family of Dr. Sturtevant very much resented Mr. Bryan's effort to connect their father with the "free silver heresy."

The war with Spain stirred up patriotic fervor on the campus of Illinois College as it did among college youth everywhere. When war broke out, several students enlisted, in spite of the conservative attitude of the faculty and of the president who, in a chapel talk, advised students "to consider carefully before deciding to enlist." Nonetheless, the faculty voted that any seniors who did enlist should receive full credit for the term's work, and when commencement occurred, three men who were in service received diplomas *in absentia*. So far as it has been possible to trace the records, some thirty-five students and alumni enlisted in the Spanish-American War.

The importance of alumni to the College received formal recognition during this administration. At the annual meeting in June 1893, the trustees resolved "that it is desirable that some arrangement should be made whereby a portion of the board of trustees, to hold their office for a limited time, should be annually elected by the alumni of the College." At the meeting of the alumni association that commencement, Judge Kirby advised the association of the action of the board and a committee was appointed to arrange the details of the election for the next year. The term of these alumni trustees was to be three years; the first selection was to be made at the annual meeting in June 1895, and an additional trustee was to be elected each succeeding year. At this meeting of the board, it was decided also to make the total number of trustees henceforth twenty-five.

Considerable improvement was made in the organization and routine work of the board in this administration. A new plan of standing committees was adopted in 1897, including: (1) Prudential Committee, which continued to be virtually an executive committee; (2) Auditing Committee; (3) Building and Grounds Committee; (4) Committee on Memorials; and (5) Finance Committee. Somewhat later, a Committee on Honorary Degrees and the Investment Committee were added to the list.

Dr. Bradley, like many another college president, met his Water-loo on the field of college finances. It is said that when he accepted the presidency of the College he was assured by the trustees that they would manage the finances, including the raising of endowment. Whether or not such a promise was ever made, it did not take the new president long to discover that if additional funds were to be secured he must raise them. In justice to Dr. Bradley it must be admitted that whatever advantages Illinois College may have had when he was entrusted with its administration, the institution was not in a sound financial condition. When Dr. Tanner died, the Col-lege was far from having an endowment sufficient to provide an adequate income. Furthermore, thousands of dollars of subscriptions remained unpaid, and the deficits, sad to relate, went on accumulat-ing with annual regularity. The accumulated indebtedness during the seven years of Dr. Bradley's presidency was nearly $52,000.

Finally at the annual meeting of the board in June 1898, the presi-dent was "authorized and directed to undertake to raise the sum of one hundred thousand dollars." Arrangements were made to relieve him of his teaching and other duties so that he might give his un-divided attention to the supreme need of the hour. The Auditing Committee was instructed to make a detailed investigation of the fi-nances of the College and especially to prepare and present to the board "a statement showing to what extent, if any, the permanent or endowment fund may have been encroached upon, to meet the current expenses of the College, or for any other purposes, begin-ning with the year 1890 and continuing year by year to the present time."

As the end of the year 1898–99 approached, the president, dis-couraged because he had not made more substantial progress in the financial campaign and possibly for other reasons, decided to offer his resignation. A few days before the annual meeting, he called a special meeting of the Prudential Committee and disclosed his inten-tion to its members and asked for their advice. Apparently they did not attempt to persuade him to alter his intention, and after some discussion the committee adjourned. When the trustees assembled for the annual meeting, the president reported that he had secured an offer of twenty-five thousand dollars on condition that the whole amount of the proposed fund of one-hundred thousand dollars be raised, but for some reason there were practically no other subscriptions. In the middle of the proceedings, he withdrew, leaving his resignation with the board. It was accepted.

The trustees, in their formal resolution accepting the resignation, expressed their high personal regard for the president and their appreciation of the work he had done for the College. The financial problem of the College was not being solved, and the trustees evidently felt, like the president himself, that another man must be called to the task. Possibly there were other reasons for the resignation, for it is not often that such actions are determined by a single circumstance. The president, although a man of many admirable qualities and of demonstrated ability in certain fields of education, seemed to lack the vigor just then needed by a college struggling for existence. Fortunately for all concerned, the change took place with good feeling on both sides, and the fact that President Bradley and his wife remembered the College in their wills shows that there could have been no wounds which left a scar.

14

President Barnes, 1900–1905

On the resignation of President Bradley, Professor Milton E. Churchill became Dean and Acting-President of the College, a position he held during the 1899–1900 academic year. The trustees had appointed a Committee on Inquiry and Correspondence to seek a new president, and by June of 1900 that committee agreed upon and recommended to the board Clifford Webster Barnes. Mr. Barnes was a graduate of Yale and had also taken the divinity course at Yale. He had served a short time as secretary of the Young Men's Christian Association at his alma mater, had travelled and studied abroad, and had worked at Hull House in Chicago. At the time of his appointment at Illinois College, he was serving as an instructor in sociology at the University of Chicago, where he had received his master's degree.

The conditions on which Mr. Barnes accepted the presidency of Illinois College are clearly set forth in his letter to the trustees, which the board unanimously approved. They included the following points: (1) The permanent endowment fund was to be kept intact; (2) a vigorous effort was to be made to "increase the endowment to $500,000 by the first of June, 1904—the seventy-fifth anniversary of the College"; (3) in the meantime, a guarantee fund of $7,000 a year for three years was to be raised to help pay running expenses; and finally, the college plant was to be put "in a perfectly satisfactory condition for the opening of the fall term." The new president agreed himself to contribute $500 annually to the guarantee fund, it being understood that his salary would be $2,500 a year.

President Clifford W. Barnes

The trustees concluded this contract on June 13, 1900, and early the next morning, which was commencement day, the new president arrived from Chicago. He presided at the adjourned meeting of the trustees and was presented to the commencement audience by Judge Kirby. Once more hope blossomed. The new president, with his confident spirit and optimistic enthusiasm, restored confidence in the future of the College. The fact that, like the founders, he had come from Yale appealed to the sentiment of many friends, and his connections with men and women of large means held out hopes of early financial recuperation. Mr. Barnes showed himself to be a man of high ideals with a broad vision, ready to plunge at once into the hard work that awaited him. A new day appeared to dawn, and large developments seemed to loom on the horizon.

At a meeting of the Prudential Committee, held only a few weeks later, Mr. Barnes submitted a proposal to build at his own expense and on certain other conditions a commodious president's house on the campus. The trustees were to repay him the cost of the house "out of the first money raised for the new endowment fund." He proposed, furthermore, to pay an annual rental for it. The trustees accepted the proposal on the terms suggested, and the house was soon in process of construction. Now known as Barnes House, it has proved a beautiful, as well as most useful, addition to the college plant. Other housekeeping improvements were made that first summer.

Still more significant were the radical changes made in the membership of both the board of trustees and the faculty. In the course of about two years both bodies were almost totally reorganized. Of the permanent trustees who held office at the beginning of the administration, only seven were still on the board at the end of the second year, and of those one resigned early in the following fall. In order to give the College a wider constituency and also to win the financial backing of wealthy and influential persons, the policy was adopted of filling several of these vacancies by the election of Chicago men of some financial standing. Still further to promote an interest in the College in the city of Chicago, the semiannual meetings of the board were regularly held in that city. A new set of by-laws was adopted, reorganizing the committees and more clearly defining the functions of the president and the faculty.

In the same period the faculty changed even more completely. At the beginning of the year 1902, only one man remained whom President Barnes found on the faculty when he came, and that man left at the end of that year. The new members of the faculty were, without exception, young men who had had specialized training in the universities of America, England, and Germany; when a short time later the College became co-educational, a few young women were added. In the midst of so many changes, a few questionable appointments were· inevitable, but, on the whole, it was an able faculty that President Barnes gathered about him.

With this revolutionary change in the personnel of the faculty came also important modifications of the curriculum and of the general educational policy of the institution. New and more advanced courses were introduced, and a new spirit of instruction stirred the atmosphere of the old campus. Higher and more exacting standards were established, requirements for both entrance and graduation being stiffened. In the middle of his second year, when the new members of the faculty had been able to work out their plans, the president reported to his trustees the organization of twelve distinct departments and the introduction of the group system of studies with an expansion of the opportunity for elective courses. The faculty, so the president reported, were now offering "132 different courses of study," as compared with about 80 courses offered at the end of the previous administration; furthermore, a carefully worked-out plan for extension lectures in nearby towns was announced in the catalogue. Much of this expansion proved to be illusory.

In spite of the substantial improvements in the college plant and the expansion in the curriculum, students did not come in any larger numbers. In fact, the number of students, on the whole, declined during these years. College attendance steadily declined from 100 in 1899–1900 to 67 in 1902–3, although the admission of women in the fall of 1903 led to a substantial increase, bringing college attendance for the year 1903–4 to 105. The next fall there was again a slight decrease. The attendance in the preparatory department followed the same tendency, dropping from 79 in 1899–1900 to 40 in 1901–2. Under the circumstances, there were few students to take the new advanced courses, and it was exceedingly difficult to maintain the various student activities on a successful basis, not to mention the constantly disheartening effect when a report was made for the year on the reduced income from tuition and fees.

All student enterprises encountered difficulties during these years. In athletics, with the possible exception of the track team, it was not a period of any noteworthy achievements. With a declining attendance and no regular athletic director on the staff, it is perhaps surprising that the students accomplished as much as they did in sports. A lively interest continued to be manifested in oratory, debate, and dramatics, but the decrease in the number of students made it difficult to maintain three literary societies; Gamma Nu, organized in the Bradley administration, ceased to function in the year 1901–2.

One of the outstanding events in the administration of President Barnes was the celebration of the seventy-fifth anniversary of the College in the early fall of 1904. Whatever may be said of other notable Illinois College celebrations, no occasion had ever brought to the campus or to the city of Jacksonville such a large number of distinguished scholars, scientists, and educators. Representatives from Edinburgh, Princeton, Yale, Johns Hopkins, and the University of Amsterdam, and the presidents of Stanford, California, Indiana, Chicago, Minnesota, and Colorado College participated in the celebration. The staff of Governor Yates and Company I of the Fifth Regiment of the Illinois National Guard added a touch of official and military color to the academic procession.

The enlargement of the faculty and the repairs and improvements of the plant imperatively required additional funds. Could these be obtained, all might go well, but if they were not forthcoming, there was bound to be trouble ahead. Reference has already been made to the so-called Guarantee Fund. With wisdom and foresight Mr. Barnes had asked the trustees, as one of the conditions on which he had accepted the presidency, to raise annually for three years an expense fund of seven thousand dollars. Approximately this amount seems to have been subscribed. It was to provide for the running of the College without a deficit while the president and trustees were seeking more endowment.

Expectation continued to run high regarding the achievements of Mr. Barnes in the financial field. Trustees and friends thought that the old financial problems would surely be solved, and to the credit of Mr. Barnes, it must be said that he went about the task with energy and confidence. In the presence of a large audience gathered in the gymnasium one evening in February 1901 to listen to a joint debate between the literary societies, Dean Churchill read a telegram from the new president announcing that Dr. D. K. Pearsons of Chicago had made the College an offer. Pearsons was a New England medical man who had given up his practice and come West to make a fortune in land deals. He was a hard-headed philanthropist who always required the recipients of his gifts to raise matching money on their own. He made challenging offers to fifteen colleges other than Illinois College, including Beloit, Colorado, Drury, Mount Holyoke, Olivet, and Whitman. There appeared to be no special consistency in his academic giving, except that the colleges really needed money and were willing to raise a good part of it on their own. During a long lifetime he gave away five million dollars, which resulted in the raising of at least ten million dollars more. "I had a good time making my money," said Pearsons, "but have had a better time spending it." Pearsons had offered President Barnes $50,000 on the condition that an additional $150,000 be raised. "We will do it," the president had added in his telegram, and the audience applauded. However, the task was not to prove an easy one.

When the trustees assembled in Chicago in December of that year, the prospects were not encouraging. In spite of the attractive offerings in the enlarged curriculum and the improvements in laboratory and library facilities, as we have seen, attendance had fallen, so that the income from tuition and fees was likely to be three thousand dollars under the estimate. Even with the full payment of the Guarantee Fund, the year would probably still show a deficit of three thousand dollars. "To sum up the matter very briefly," reported the president, "with our present endowment and with even a fair increase in our attendance, we have to face an annual deficit of about

$10,000. If the Guarantee Fund of $7,000 can be promptly and entirely collected, we shall still have at least $3,000 per year for the next two years to make up and after that the larger sum of $10,000." Furthermore, almost nothing had been accomplished in meeting the offer from Dr. Pearsons. President Barnes put it squarely up to the trustees:

> We cannot afford to be sentimental over a question which requires the coolest and most critical judgment, but perhaps we may be pardoned just a moment's wondering query as to what our predecessors would have done under circumstances such as confront us at present. I think of the missionary zeal of the early founders, of the brave Yale band who turned their backs on eastern comfort to endure the hardships of western life, of the rude log hut which they built for shelter, though the winter's snow crept through the cracks. I think of Beecher, full of hope and promise in his chosen field, beloved by the great church on Boston Common, who gladly left it all to give the best years of his life to this pioneer College, and as it all comes back to memory what these men endured and how they struggled in those early days, my mind finds it hard to even consider the question of closing our doors. "Our doors," did I say? Their doors; for by prayer and blood they bought this College and only asked of us to keep it safe for posterity.

Fortunately, Dr. Pearsons agreed to extend the time limit on his offer for one year, and accordingly plans moved forward for arousing the alumni and friends. The more modern methods of campaigning for funds had not yet been evolved, but president and trustees exerted themselves here and there as opportunity afforded. Other possibilities of insuring survival were explored, including a merger with Blackburn College of Carlinville. That fell through, but a proposal for a union with the Jacksonville Female Academy began to take more definite shape. Judge C. A. Barnes, no relative of President Barnes, stated to the board that the trustees of the Jacksonville Female Academy, of which he was a member, favored the proposed union, but they were not willing to take any action, "until the trustees of Illinois College shall have taken definite action."

The action called for was more drastic than some would have liked, but the possibility of increasing college resources by two hundred thousand dollars was a strong inducement, and if the Pearsons offer of one-quarter of the sum was not to be lost, there was no time for prolonged deliberation. Radical and permanent changes of policy were required, and they would have to be carried out expeditiously. When the alliance with the Jacksonville Female Academy was consummated, Illinois College became co-educational and Presbyterian. The agreement with the Academy trustees included these provisions: (1) A majority of the trustees of Illinois College were henceforth to be Presbyterians; (2) Illinois College was to become co-educational, affording to women all "educational privileges that are or shall be" afforded to men; (3) Fifty thousand dollars of the new fund was to be definitely set aside for the "purpose of female education," that amount to be refunded to the trustees of the Academy if at any time in the future Illinois College ceased to be co-educational; (4) The trustees of the College were to assume all the indebtedness and obligations of the Academy, including specifically a mortgage of twenty thousand dollars on the Academy property.

On these terms the property of the Academy was deeded to the Trustees of Illinois College at a valuation of fifty thousand dollars, an amount which Dr. Pearsons accepted as a partial fulfillment of the terms of his offer. A subscription of fifty thousand dollars was made by President Barnes and accepted, with the condition that the trustees would purchase the president's house at a price of twenty-five thousand dollars and repay him "the sum of fifty thousand dollars out of the first additional endowment funds secured for the College"—conditions which subsequently were to cause difficulty and embarrassment. Other subscriptions by trustees and generous friends completed the fund. Dr. Pearsons was notified and promptly paid his pledge of fifty thousand dollars in stock of the First National Bank of Chicago.

While these things were being accomplished, one other step had been taken which aroused keen interest among alumni and friends of the College. A plan was developed for affiliating Illinois College with the University of Chicago. Although completed in all essential particulars, this scheme of affiliation was never put into operation. The venture was part of a general scheme which the fertile mind of President William Rainey Harper had conceived for bringing the smaller colleges of the West into closer relationship with the Univer-

sity of Chicago. The College agreed to maintain educational standards conforming to those of the University; faculty appointments
were to be made only after consultation with the University; degrees
might be conferred "conjointly with the College" on students who,
after three years of study at the College, completed three quarters
at the University; furthermore, under certain conditions the University was to grant its degree to graduates of the College for one
quarter's work at the University; and it was also stipulated that Illinois College students might take their senior year for professional
study in the University, and at the same time retain their residence
in the College, presumably with the privilege of receiving a degree
from the College.

That all of these radical changes not only excited interest but also
produced some discontent among alumni and friends of the College,
may well be imagined. Dr. Sturtevant had struggled throughout his
presidency to keep the College free from any direct denominational
control; that was one of the cardinal principles of his policy in the
administration of Illinois College. Furthermore, many of the alumni
were strongly opposed to the admission of women into the College;
nor were the alumnae of the old Jacksonville Female Academy happy
over the absorption of their alma mater. It was perhaps hardly to be
expected that either of these groups fully understood the crisis which
made it imperative for the trustees to depart from the historic policy
and practice of nearly seventy-five years. The air was full of rumors,
gossip, misunderstandings, and criticisms.

Early in 1903 appropriate exercises were held to celebrate the completion of the fund and to prepare alumni and friends for the new
era in the history of the College. The chief guest and speaker of the
occasion was President Harper. He spoke on "The Future of the
Small College" at a large afternoon meeting and again less formally
at a banquet in the evening. "The question," he declared, "is not
what the University may gain, but what it may do for the College."
William Jennings Bryan and Governor Yates, both alumni trustees
of the College, had been invited to the banquet but neither came.

To complete the enumeration of the changes introduced into the
College that winter, it should be added that a Conservatory of Music

came into the fold with the Female Academy. This Conservatory was an old school of good reputation, originally established in 1871 and later made a part of the Jacksonville Female Academy. This new department helped not only to expand the work of the College but unfortunately increased still further its financial difficulties.

To no class were these radical changes of more direct and vital concern than to members of the faculty. With one exception, all had come to the College very recently; so historic traditions and a sentimental regard for the past had little influence on them. Most of these men had previously studied and taught in co-educational institutions. The faculty, although not responsible for the changes, were inclined to defend the president against the wave of criticism which followed the changes. Six members of the teaching staff left at the end of that academic year, but not necessarily because of the changes the president had brought about.

As the year 1903–4 drew to its close the financial shadows darkened. It became evident that, in spite of the new endowment fund, the financial foundations of the College, on account of the burden of debt created by the extensive repairs and improvements, were growing more shaky than ever. At the annual meeting of the trustees in 1904, the finance committee reported a total deficit for the year of $29,000, of which staggering amount nearly $15,000 had been spent for repairs and permanent improvements. The fact that the annual Guarantee Fund of $7,000 had ceased with the year 1902–3 made the situation still more critical. A policy of retrenchment was obviously imperative. The president undertook it, first by making certain readjustments among the faculty that would reduce the faculty salary account by 12 percent for the coming year. Furthermore, repairs for the following year were to be kept at a minimum. But in spite of these substantial reductions in appropriations, another deficit in the budget for the next year was inevitable.

When the trustees assembled in December for their regular semi-annual meeting and learned that the president contemplated resigning, the situation assumed a still more critical aspect. Various propositions and counter-propositions were made by the president and his trustees, but no solution seemed possible, and so at a special meeting

of the board near the end of the month Mr. Barnes definitely resigned the presidency of the College, effective the first of January
1905. The board accepted his resignation.

His administration was a period of transition in the history of the
College. Many changes had to be made, whether they were popular
or not. Some of these, like the introduction of co-education and the
readjustment of the religious affiliations of the College, caused hard
feeling among many alumni and old friends. At the same time, many
of them were adopted, not so much out of policy but to meet emergencies which at the time it seemed impossible to meet in any other
way. Cordial relations between the president and his young faculty
generally existed. His successor, then a member of that faculty, said,
"We felt that in our president we had not only a true friend, but
one who understood what we were trying to accomplish for our students and the College."

15

President Rammelkamp: Mostly First Person, 1905–1925

The history of Illinois College had been one long succession of financial crises, and we certainly faced another in that early winter of 1905. Discouragement and despair darkened the skies. Confidence was almost totally gone. At this critical juncture, the most prominent alumnus of Illinois College came to the rescue of his alma mater. From the day when as a student in an eastern university I cast my first ballot in a presidential election against Mr. Bryan to the present, I have found it difficult to accept his political, economic, educational, or theological views, but I cheerfully and gratefully acknowledge the great service which he rendered to his alma mater in this hour of need.* Undoubtedly it was Mr. Bryan's warm interest and timely help which restored confidence in the future of the College. I do not refer to any large financial support contributed by Mr. Bryan or his friends, but to the hope and enthusiasm which his interest and his speeches created for an apparently losing cause. When he placed his strong shoulders to the wheel, friends instinctively felt that the cause could not fail.

It was less than a week after the resignation of Mr. Barnes that the trustees, assembled in a special meeting, listened with keen interest to a letter from Mr. Bryan written to his personal friend, Mr.

---

* The reader will have noticed the rather abrupt shift from third to first person that takes place at this point. The subjective handling of the narrative here seems to me inevitable, justifiable, and delightful. The reader will find a more objective view of the Rammelkamp administration in Part 2 of this history.—C. E. F.

M. F. Dunlap. The Great Commoner had intimated in this letter that he might be willing to extend a helping hand, and the trustees at once asked Mr. Dunlap to communicate with Mr. Bryan and "arrange to have him meet the board and talk over the situation." In the meantime, the trustees had elected Julius E. Strawn chairman of the board and acting-president of the College, designating Dean F. S. Hayden as chairman of the faculty.

In about a week Mr. Bryan came to Jacksonville for the proposed conference with the trustees. Before he went into this conference, the trustees, perhaps to make the path a little smoother for him, voted to dissolve the affiliation with the University of Chicago, that institution "established with Standard Oil money." Only then did Mr. Bryan enter the meeting. He was elected first a member and then immediately chairman of the board. His expression of deep interest in the College and of his purpose to do all in his power to promote its welfare gave great encouragement to the members of the board. A little later the board adjourned in order to give Mr. Bryan an opportunity to speak to the students in chapel. I recall the enthusiasm which his appearance in chapel at that particular time created. He declared: "I want to be instrumental in doing something in my humble way for this dear College on the Hill, which I love. I want to do more in the future than I have done in the past, although I have always been deeply interested in my alma mater." In the evening he spoke again in the chapel, this time more especially to the large number of local citizens who crowded into the small auditorium with the students. He urged the citizens to support the College. "I want this College," said he, "to be an ideal college in an ideal town and if we work together we may make it what we will." A few weeks later Mr. Bryan returned to the city to deliver an address on behalf of the College before a large audience in the local opera house and to confer with the trustees about some of the practical details of college business. He opened the business session of the board with a proposal to donate twenty-five hundred dollars towards paying the accumulated deficit and other members soon promised enough more to make a total subscription of about fifteen thousand dollars, which was later still further increased. But the sad fact may as well at once be stated that most of the subscriptions were never paid, since they were made on condition that the whole amount of the deficit be subscribed—a goal which was never achieved.

One of the main problems just then before the trustees was, of course, the selection of a new president. Many hoped that Mr. Bryan himself would accept the office, but he declared positively that he could not entertain the thought. Some consideration was also given to other candidates, without result. I confess I was greatly surprised when the chairman of the committee approached me on the subject, for I certainly had no thought of being a candidate for the presidency of the College. I was devoted to my work of teaching and longed for the time when I might devote myself more energetically to research in the field of American history, and I had only recently accepted an offer to teach on the faculty of the University of Illinois during the next summer session. I admit that I felt somewhat flattered by the suggestion, in spite of the fact that I realized that the presidency of Illinois College at that particular time was not a bed of roses. I had had practically no experience in administrative work, and, I suppose, the chief consideration in my favor was the impossibility of finding any other suitable candidate to undertake a task so difficult and discouraging.

I had come to Illinois College in the fall of 1902. It was for me a new experience. In many ways I was unprepared to teach in such a college, but fortunately I was young and willing to learn. I had received most of my own college training, both undergraduate and postgraduate, in an eastern institution, Cornell University. For three years, I had also taught there as an instructor in American history. After a year of travel and study abroad, including a semester at the University of Berlin, I had gone to Leland Stanford University, accepting a temporary appointment as instructor in history. It was from Stanford that I came to Illinois College as professor of history. My training and experience had therefore been altogether in large universities, and I was chiefly interested in the ideals of specialized scholarship which dominated university work. At Cornell, my teaching had been confined largely to a course on American colonial

history and another on the history of the State of New York; at
Stanford, it was American colonial history and modern English history which occupied my attention. I had learned to do concentrated
and somewhat thorough work in very limited fields. How different
were the conditions in a small college. How much I had to learn and
unlearn. That first year, besides teaching two courses in the more or
less familiar fields of American and English history, I was obliged
to conduct courses in general European history, the Reformation and
the French Revolution, economics, public finance, money and bank-
ing, political science, and international law. At first I floundered so
in this sea that it hardly seemed possible to keep afloat, but in time
I learned to swim. I had at one time and another taken courses at
either Cornell or Berlin in all of these various subjects, and I soon
discovered that however little I might know, I at least knew more
than the students in my classes. Furthermore, in time, I came to appreciate the stimulating opportunity of dealing with subjects of large,
general importance in various fields instead of confining my studies
to smaller problems of more limited range.

The intimate personal relations both among the members of the
faculty and between faculty and students were also a new and pleasant experience for me. When I came to Illinois College, it was an
institution exclusively for men. To have only men in my classes was
therefore another new experience, and I missed the refining influence
of the women and their faithful performance of the daily tasks of the
classroom. It took a little time for the boys and me to understand
one another. Like many young instructors, I was perhaps severely
exacting in my requirements, but in a short time I believe I won the
confidence and respect of my students. At any rate, I do not recall
that, as an instructor, I ever had any serious disagreement or case
of discipline in my classes.

I found on the faculty of Illinois College a group of men, young
like myself, and with a training and experience very similar to my
own. It soon became evident to me that a radical change had recently
taken place in the personnel of the faculty and that this circumstance,
together with the changes in courses and methods of instruction, had
created a spirit of unrest on the campus and perhaps also in the town.
Now I was being asked to do more than teach my classes. My task

would be to restore confidence in the institution, both on the campus and in the community.

After a brief consideration of the chairman's inquiry, I advised the committee that I would accept the proposal on certain conditions, chief among which was the promise on the part of the trustees themselves to raise the deficit by the end of the next college year. Furthermore, when I mentioned to the committee that I had had no experience whatever in raising money and that I certainly had no wealthy friends to whom I might appeal for aid, the committee assured me that the trustees themselves would also assume the burden of raising additional endowment. *That would not be a part of my duty.* What a promise!

My conditions were accepted and accordingly in April 1905, I began my work as president of Illinois College. As I now look back to those days, I realize more than I could possibly have done at the time that I was taking a big chance—in fact, it was only because I was young and ignorant of the size and difficulty of the task that I was willing to undertake it. The hopeless jobs in life usually await young men who have more enthusiasm than knowledge and who do not weigh too cautiously the chances of failure. The students, young like myself, seemed pleased with the choice of the trustees, but I cannot help suspecting that many alumni and older friends of the College wondered whether a serious mistake had not been made. Be that as it may, I at least felt a sincere devotion to the old College and was firmly resolved, with God's help, to do the best I could.

I had no thought of any formal inaugural ceremonies nor evidently had the trustees, for not one spoke to me about any such exercises. It was undoubtedly well that no formal inauguration was planned, for the College certainly had no money to spend on unnecessaries. The next morning in chapel Mr. Strawn, on behalf of the trustees, presented me to the students, and after a few informal words I ventured, as the first act of my administration, to declare a holiday. The students promptly provided a carriage in which, headed by an ex-cowboy in full regalia, they hauled me and Mr. Strawn and my colleagues, Principal Stoops and Professor Ames, through the streets of the city, past the campus of the Woman's College.

It was not ceremonies and celebrations which Illinois College needed just then, but hard work. I realized soon that the College was in a struggle for existence and until that fight was won there was little use in giving thought to the development of any particular educational policies. I agreed to serve during the remainder of that spring without any increase in salary and also to continue my full schedule of teaching in addition to the new administrative duties. Not only were we members of the faculty overloaded with work but peculiar and strange combinations of departments had to be made in order to save on expenses. I certainly should be sorry to have my ideas on educational policies judged by some of the things which dire necessity compelled us to do in those trying years. It was not a time for developing ideal educational policies. How to win the confidence of alumni and local friends; how to increase the student body and get a little more money—these were the pressing questions of the hour. Educational policies must wait.

Nominally, the College had then, in addition to the plant, an endowment fund of $228,000, but included in that amount were so many questionable personal notes and other doubtful securities that the net invested endowment of the College that spring of 1905 was certainly not more than $155,000. To throw further light on the actual financial situation at that time, it should be stated that the current deficit at the end of the year 1904–5 was nearly $8,000, and the year had not been one of unusual expenditures. This, then, was our chief problem—to save a college which had a debt of over $36,000 and was running behind, even on a greatly reduced educational program, at the rate of about $8,000 a year. For a while there seemed nothing to do but let the old boat drift in the current, constantly drawing nearer the brink of financial disaster. The conditional pledges of some $16,000 already made by the trustees towards the payment of the deficit and the active support of Mr. Bryan made us all feel that a little patience and courage would enable us to bring the boat to a safe landing.

There were some hopeful signs. Mr. Andrew Carnegie began about that time to turn his attention to colleges, and the General Education Board, established a few years earlier by John D. Rockefeller, was just then beginning to make those stimulating grants to higher education. It was only a few months after my election to the presidency of the College that we read of the gift of ten million dollars to that board by Mr. Rockefeller. Naturally, many of us hoped that Illinois College might secure aid from these sources. President Harper, who at one time had been deeply interested in Illinois College, was a member of the General Education Board. True, he had been treated somewhat curtly, if not discourteously, when the affiliation with the University of Chicago was broken off, but I dared to hope that he might still be willing to speak for Illinois College. We had even more confident hope of getting into touch with Mr. Carnegie. Mr. Frank A. Vanderlip was our reliance in the possible approach to Mr. Carnegie; he had recently rendered valuable service to Mr. Carnegie in regard to the pension system which the great ironmaster had established for the benefit of college professors. It happened that Miss Rhoda Jeannette Capps, to whom I was engaged to be married, was an intimate friend of Mr. Vanderlip and his family. Himself a native of Illinois and warmly interested in the cause of higher education, Mr. Vanderlip listened sympathetically to our story when Miss Capps and I met him in Chicago. He promised to do what he could to interest Mr. Carnegie in the College.

But now it was that new and unexpected dangers appeared in the stream. Mr. Bryan would not listen to the plan, for in his opinion the money of Mr. Rockefeller and Mr. Carnegie was tainted and he would have none of it. How very strongly he felt on the subject did not at once appear to me, for I had never had any personal conversation with him on the matter. In my first annual report to the trustees in June of 1905 I recommended innocently "that immediate steps be taken to get into touch with Mr. Carnegie and that a committee be appointed to present to him the needs of the College." This at once precipitated a warm discussion among the members of the board on the question of tainted money. Mr. Bryan was, of course, presiding at the meeting. In a restrained but nevertheless perfectly unmistakable manner, he let his colleagues see how strongly he felt on the question. No action was taken, for we all hoped, even in spite of the solemn words of our chairman, that it might still be possible for us to reconcile our differences. Perhaps some also thought that a little delay might give Mr. Bryan a chance to win other help that would make unnecessary the proposed appeal to Carnegie and Rockefeller.

I need hardly say that I had no sympathy with Mr. Bryan's doctrine of tainted money. So long as a gift leaves the beneficiary perfectly free to act according to his conscience and principles, there can hardly be any taint attached to the money. Furthermore, it was obvious that Mr. Carnegie was attaching no conditions, directly or indirectly, to his gifts, which would interfere with the freedom of teaching in colleges which might become his beneficiaries. Perhaps, in justice to Mr. Bryan, the issue should have been definitely decided at that first discussion. It looked as if he might resign on the spot, and we, therefore, hesitated at once to press the matter to a final conclusion. Friends of Mr. Bryan on the board later insisted that an injustice had been done him in not taking definite action at the time; the failure to act, they insisted, gave him the impression that the trustees would not press the matter.

I soon became convinced that I could accomplish nothing for Illinois College unless I could present the cause to such philanthropists as Mr. Carnegie and such a body as the General Education Board. I had had further communications with Mr. Vanderlip and felt encouraged to believe that we might really succeed in interesting Mr. Carnegie. I resolved, therefore, a few months later to put the issue squarely before the trustees and ask for a decision. Accordingly, I called the trustees in special meeting early in November and, laying before them the critical situation of the College, I personally offered a general resolution assuring "acceptance of any funds solicited by individual members of the board and given under conditions which made acceptance possible." Although the resolution was a little vague in terms, its import was well understood by all the members. After full and free discussion, the resolution was passed by the substantial majority of 11 to 2, the two members voting against it being close personal and political friends of Mr. Bryan. These two members immediately offered their resignations, but very considerately, upon the request of their colleagues who wished to avoid, if possible, a public discussion of internal difficulties among board members, consented to allow their resignations temporarily to lie on the table.

A copy of the resolution was ordered to be cabled immediately to Mr. Bryan who then happened to be in the Far East on a trip around the world. It took several weeks for the message to reach him, but when he learned of the action of the board, he immediately mailed his resignation. From Hong Kong he wrote in explanation:

The issue presented seems to me to be a vital one, and even if Carnegie refused, the same question is likely to arise if some other trust magnate invites requests. Our College cannot serve God and Mammon. It cannot be a College for the people and at the same time commend itself to the commercial highwaymen who are now subsidizing the colleges to prevent the teaching of economic truth. It grieves me to have my Alma Mater converted into an ally of plutocracy, but having done what I could to prevent it, I have no other recourse than to withdraw from its management. I regret the action, if it was to be taken, was not taken before I gave my notes, for I regard money given as worse than wasted, if the College is to be under the shadow of a great monopoly.

Wide publicity was immediately given to the resignation in the public press of the country, editorial comment naturally reflecting the political sympathies of the editors. A few months later, Mr. Bryan wrote again from London, requesting that his name be taken from a prize which he had established and that, if possible, his name be also dropped from the list of alumni. He evidently felt deeply on the subject.

As I look back at this early episode in the history of my administration, I do not have the slightest doubt that we acted wisely. To break with this prominent and influential alumnus, who had so loyally and enthusiastically come to the rescue of his alma mater in a time of supreme need, was indeed no light matter. But we could not do otherwise. I saw then and see now that, in view of the position which Mr. Bryan had taken in public life, condemning unreservedly the business methods of Mr. Carnegie and Mr. Rockefeller, it would have been embarrassing to him, as chairman of our board, to accept gifts for his alma mater from these very gentlemen. I only regret that he could not have withdrawn more quietly and without any political fireworks.

It is perhaps worth while to add that Mr. Bryan never afterwards became fully reconciled to the College. While he was Secretary of State in the Wilson administration, our New York Alumni Association invited him to attend its annual banquet which that particular year was given in special tribute to Mrs. Edward A. Tanner, widow of the man who was Bryan's own teacher and valued friend in college and who performed the wedding ceremony when he married Miss Baird. But he would not come. On the other hand, when Mr. Bryan made his last visit to Jacksonville a few weeks before the Dayton trial, he paid glowing tribute to his alma mater in a public address, acknowledging her beneficent influence on his life. I am glad to say that the differences of opinion which arose regarding college policies never disturbed the friendly personal relations between Mr. Bryan and me. Fortunately, I never had to discuss with him the doctrine of evolution—the earlier break with him on the issue of tainted money at least prevented any later attempt to interfere with the teaching of scientific truth in the College.

Mr. Bryan had resigned even before a subscription of any kind had been received from Mr. Carnegie. We had burned our bridges behind us. Eventually in May, with the assistance of Mr. Vanderlip who personally called on Mr. Carnegie, we received an offer of fifty thousand dollars towards an endowment fund of one hundred thousand dollars. Although it was not as large a subscription as we had hoped for, the offer of dollar for dollar was much more generous than the subscriptions which Mr. Carnegie was generally making to colleges at the time.

I shall not attempt to narrate the details of the campaign—its alternating hopes and disappointments, my own inexperience, and the great difficulty of arousing the alumni to a sense of responsibility for saving their alma mater from extinction. I had to work largely alone, traveling from one end of the country to the other, getting help mostly in small amounts from twenty-five dollars to one hundred dollars. A subscription of five hundred dollars or one thousand dollars was a rare occurrence. However, before we had gone far in the campaign, a substantial bequest put hope and even confidence into our hearts. Mrs. Phebe Gates Strawn had died in February 1906, and when her will was probated some weeks later, it was discovered that she had made a bequest of twenty thousand dollars to Illinois College for the establishment of a department of agriculture and another bequest of ten thousand dollars to the Jacksonville Female Academy. Since the Academy had been absorbed by the College, it seemed likely that this additional amount would also come to the College.

At the commencement of 1907 we were able to announce that the new endowment fund of one hundred thousand dollars had been fully subscribed, although it was to take several months before the subscriptions could be collected, as required by the terms of Mr. Carnegie's offer. This was accomplished by the following January. Although we were by no means out of the woods, substantial progress had been made. About 25 percent of the alumni and former students whose addresses we had on our very incomplete list had given. At least we had made a beginning in securing the support of the alumni for their alma mater. I wish also to bear testimony to the cordial support given to the campaign by the alumnae of the old Jacksonville Female Academy.

In January 1908, I journeyed to New York to claim Mr. Carnegie's fifty thousand dollars and also to attend the annual banquet of the New York Alumni Association. Among the special guests present on this occasion was Mr. Vanderlip, whom I had asked to act as our representative in advising Mr. Carnegie that we were ready to claim his fifty thousand dollars. I sat next to Mr. Vanderlip at the supper and I noticed that he seemed very uncommunicative. When it came his turn to make a few remarks, it soon became evident why he had not been eager to engage in conversation earlier in the evening. He told of his visit that afternoon to the home of Mr. Carnegie —how after telling him that we had completed our fund, he had immediately asked for another fifty thousand dollars for Illinois College. When we learned in the next sentence that the ironmaster had said he would give it, we jumped from our seats. When the applause subsided Mr. Vanderlip proceeded to say quietly that after Mr. Carnegie had learned a little more about the College, its history, and especially the great struggle we were making in the face of the most discouraging difficulties, he said, of his own accord, that he would like to change his offer—that he would give seventy-five thousand dollars. It can easily be imagined how our hearts beat with joy. I have attended many annual banquets of the alumni of Illinois College, but none has ever given me the thrill and courage which this little gathering did that evening.

The only condition was that we were to raise an equal amount in "cash or marketable securities." The gift, when paid, was to become the Frank A. Vanderlip Endowment Fund, but absolutely no restrictions were imposed regarding the use of the other half which we ourselves were to raise. This freedom was very important, for it gave us the opportunity to pay off that horrible debt which hung like a millstone about the neck of the College. Thus we were immediately launched upon another financial campaign, and it now really seemed possible to place the College on a solid financial footing. This possibility gave us all great courage and enthusiasm. Friends and alumni who had given in the other campaign were asked to give again, and since their first subscriptions had been in comparatively small amounts, most of them responded favorably. These two campaigns, adding a quarter of a million dollars to the funds of the College, had been concluded in a little less than six years. The struggle for existence was now ended.

In the fall of 1908, the Reverend William A. Sunday came to Jacksonville. It was inevitable that his meetings and methods should stir our college community. Whatever may be said about the good which he possibly accomplished among certain classes of people, he certainly was not a leader of college students in their religious thinking and convictions. A man who announces that "Darwin is sizzling in hell" and that "all scientists can go plumb to hell, so far as I care," can hardly be expected to make a convincing and lasting appeal to thoughtful students, however much he may for the moment stir their emotions. In a burst of eloquence one evening, he shouted: "What we want is to tear down the seminaries and stand the professors on their heads in mud puddles. A seminary and its teachings are no more use to preaching than a crane's legs are to a setting hen."

I had noticed the newspaper accounts of the sermons of this fire-eating evangelist long before he came to our city and I deeply regretted his coming. Anxious, however, as I was to maintain and promote a spirit of friendly cooperation between the College and the churches of the city, I resolved, so far as possible, to refrain from criticism and to give the movement our support. But an attitude of friendly neutrality soon proved impossible. In spite of every effort to avoid trouble, a clash between the evangelist and the College could not be avoided. When the converts did not hit the sawdust trail in as large numbers as the success of the meetings demanded, Illinois College was made the scapegoat. The *Rambler* took a dignified and independent position in the midst of the religious excitement which spread over the campus and the city. One evening I was called on the telephone by Mr. Sunday's manager and told in somewhat peremptory terms that the college paper was about to publish an attack on Mr. Sunday and that I must suppress the edition or he would that very evening make a public declaration against the College. Upon investigation I found that the issue in question, which had already been run off the press, contained a very excellent and entirely sane article on "Evolution in the Educational World" and also an editorial, mild and dignified in tone, defending the College against aspersions which were being cast upon its alleged lack of religious spirit. I saw at once that unless I was ready to stultify myself as a student and leader of an educational institution of fine traditions, I could not order the suppression of the paper. In fact, it never occurred to me to do so. The public declaration was not made against the College that evening, but subsequently, as opportunity offered, many a poisoned dart was shot at the College in both sermon and prayer. It was an unhappy episode, but throughout it all, I am glad to say, Illinois College remained true to its principles as an educational institution with high Christian ideals.

The Commencement of 1906, the second at which I presided, deserves mention because it witnessed the graduation of the first class including women, four of them. Little progress was made in educational policies during these first half-dozen years; we were satisfied simply to keep the ship afloat. But members of the faculty were aggressive and constructive leaders in efforts for higher standards. Illinois College was one of the charter members of the North Central

Association of Colleges and Secondary Schools, but for some reason it had allowed its membership to lapse. The College was now, upon application, restored to full membership in this organization.

Few college presidents, I suppose, entirely escape misunderstanding with their faculties. On the whole, I believe I have been fortunate in my relations with my colleagues on the faculty. At least so it has seemed from my point of view. I gratefully appreciate the loyal service and friendly tolerance shown by my colleagues during the many years we have worked together. So far as my recollection goes, the only occasion when a serious difficulty arose between us was in the year 1910–11 when the trustees, on my recommendation, resolved to introduce courses in education into the curriculum, without first receiving the approval of the faculty. It was a mistake, I freely admit, but it was made innocently by president and trustees. Certain members of the faculty, I suspect, had personal objections to the instructor appointed, and this helped to strengthen convictions and deepen feelings. A formal and very dignified protest was sent to the trustees. The latter expressed regret at the misunderstanding and assured the faculty that the failure to consult them "in this instance was an oversight and not an intentional slight." The incident helped to clarify more precisely the relative functions of trustees and faculty in the administration of the College and led to the adoption of the following bylaw: "All matters of discipline are entrusted to the president and faculty. They shall arrange the course of study and the hours of recitation. They shall have general jurisdiction of the students. If in the opinion of the president, any measure passed by the faculty seriously affects the general welfare of the College, he may, in his discretion, require the consideration and approval of the measure by the board of trustees, before it is finally put into operation." So far as I recall, this is the only occasion when I felt distinctly unhappy in my relations to my colleagues on the faculty.

Mention was made earlier of some irregularities in the athletic program that had occurred in the Bradley administration. In subsequent years, the athletic programs were played down to such a degree that they did little to create or maintain a wholesome spirit on the campus. However, in the fall of 1910, Bill Harmon, '07, had returned to the campus of his alma mater as director of athletics and instructor in preparatory mathematics. Although when Mr. Harmon returned to the College a more regular system of coaching had been introduced, there was still not much encouragement in the outlook. His first football team that fall of 1910 not only failed to win a single game but did not even score a single point. The results in basketball that winter were hardly more encouraging, the team winning only three games out of fourteen. Basketball had begun at Illinois College in the year 1904–5 and became a major sport in the year 1908–9. The baseball and track teams of the spring of 1911, however, gave us a little hope. And the finances of the Athletic Association were greatly improved when the College Book Store was established with the arrangement that its profits were to be devoted to the benefit of athletics and still further when, in the fall of 1911, the trustees were finally persuaded to establish a compulsory athletic fee. The faculty also passed during these years various regulations making decent scholastic work a prerequisite for athletic competition.

The constantly growing loyalty of the alumni during recent years meant much to me in my efforts to build a better college. Alumni loyalty, when based not only on enthusiasm for athletics but on an intelligent appreciation of educational standards and achievements is the most precious endowment which a college can possess. The greatest achievement of the alumni during my connection with Illinois College has undoubtedly been the establishment of the Alumni Fund. I think not only of what the Fund has meant to the College financially but still more of what it has done for the alumni themselves in creating among them a finer sentiment of loyalty and in making them realize more clearly that they are an integral part of the College with real influence in its affairs. The results achieved by the Alumni Fund Association have been so noteworthy and the management of the Association so sound that the trustees of the College cannot fail to pay respectful attention to any request which the directors of the Fund may make. It has been the policy of the Association to confine its appropriations, as far as possible, to the general expense fund of the College, thereby avoiding the temptation to help certain projects according to the influence which special interests might exert on the board of directors. One of the most interesting achievements of the Association is found in its "In Memoriam Memberships."

These are permanent memorial memberships established by friends and relatives in honor of deceased alumni and former students. In the words of a chairman of the Association:

The final test of a college is the lives of those who have enjoyed its privileges as students. It is for their training in character and intellect that the College was founded and is maintained, and it is by the standard of the results of this training, as shown in the character and achievements of its students, that the College will be judged. While the living are doing their part in the world, we desire to commemorate in every possible way those who are dead, not only by testifying to their loyalty to the College while living, but also by keeping alive, in intimate connection with their alma mater, the memory of the place they won in the world and in the hearts of their associates. The endowed membership has proved a simple and effective means to this end.

When Illinois College admitted women in 1903, it also acquired a Conservatory of Music. Organized in 1871 by Professor Sanders, this school had achieved a solid reputation. At the time of the merger of the College and the Academy, however, the Conservatory had fallen considerably from its earlier prosperity. In the summer of 1928, a plan was consummated for the union of the conservatories of Illinois College and the Illinois Woman's College. Although this action has caused some regret, it seemed then a wise thing to do, for the city of Jacksonville is hardly large enough to provide patronage for two music schools of high grade.

During the early years of my administration, many efforts were made to improve the financial stability of the College, and some of them were successful. As a result of correspondence begun in the winter of 1915–16, the Eli B. and Harriet B. Williams Memorial Scholarship Fund was established. Hobart W. Williams, the donor, was an elderly, shrinkingly modest bachelor residing in Cheshire, Connecticut. His parents, in whose memory the gift was made, were early settlers of Chicago, and their fortune originated in property in the Loop district. Hobart Williams himself was born in Chicago and had lived most of his life there. Illinois College was one of ten beneficiaries of the original trust fund and of the residuary estate after his death. This scholarship fund has enabled Illinois College, as well as the other institutions named in the trust, to perform a truly great service for that group of worthy young men and women of slender financial means who are ambitious to secure a college education. Hobart W. Williams deserves a place among the great benefactors of his country.

Like other colleges and universities of the land, Illinois College tried to do her duty when the United States entered World War I. Reflecting the attitude of the Middle West from which all of its students and most of its faculty came, the College was at first somewhat conservative on the question of aiding the Allies, but when in the early spring of 1917 the war clouds became darker, both trustees and faculty passed resolutions pledging the unqualified support of the College to the government in whatever measures it might adopt. The faculty was the first to act. On March 28 it sent to the President of the United States a resolution expressing its "firm conviction of the need of adequate preparation and vigorous action to maintain the dignity and interests of our nation," and the trustees followed shortly with a resolution to "place at the disposal of the government of the United States the laboratories, plant and equipment of Illinois College, to be used in such manner as the needs of the future may determine and the resources of the College may permit."

A few days after the declaration of a state of war the faculty promised full credit for the balance of the year to all students in good standing who might enter the service of the government, including an assurance of degrees to seniors who might enlist. The ordinary activities of the campus were soon thrown into confusion by the supreme need of the hour. Since our student body was small, it was difficult to get any consideration from the government in plans for formal military training on our campus. In May I went to Washington to attend the conference of colleges and universities, called by the Council of National Defense to consider possible plans for cooperation between the colleges and the government. We listened to an able address by Newton D. Baker, the Secretary of War, who advised that the colleges should, as far as possible, maintain their regular work and that "all young men below the age of liability to the selective draft and those not recommended for special service" should be urged to continue their studies. The colleges were asked to modify their calendars and curricula so as to meet more fully the needs of the nation.

Great uncertainty prevailed regarding the probable conditions that might exist at the opening of college in the fall, but carrying out the conclusion of the Washington Conference, we resolved to continue our work, with such modifications of the course of study as attendance and other circumstances might dictate. When college opened in September there was a decrease of about twenty-five students, almost all men. Of the men who were in college at the outbreak of the war, about 34 percent had entered the service by the end of the academic year 1917–18. Our roll of honor at that time, including both the students who had dropped out of college and alumni and former students, listed about 175 names. The faculty made provision this year for awarding special "War Certificates" to all students who gave up their college work in order to enter the service.

As the war proceeded and the determination of the government to mobilize the whole available man power of the nation became more clearly evident, the continued presence of large groups of young men of military age in our colleges and universities became a still more serious problem. Communications received from the War Department late in the spring of 1918 disclosed the general purpose of the government to make more direct and effective use of the colleges for the purpose of military training. The government announced its intention of establishing a military unit in every college that could furnish a minimum of one hundred able-bodied men of military age. Before the end of the summer, these plans took more definite shape and led to the establishment of the Student Army Training Corps.

The experiences of Illinois College in the year 1918–19 were probably not very different from those of other colleges and universities. Instead of a large decrease in attendance, as had been expected earlier in the summer, the S.A.T.C. brought to the campus a larger group of students than we had ever had, the total registration that year being 242, of whom 164 were registered as freshmen. Our unit of the S.A.T.C., as finally inducted into the service, included 118 men. For the first few weeks of the year the Illinois College unit and that at James Millikin University of Decatur were placed under the same commanding officer. This man, because of his overbearing spirit, not to mention other undesirable qualities, proved utterly unfit for the post. One day in October I received a telephone call from the president of Millikin asking how I liked our commanding officer. The result of our conversation was an early trip to Washington to ask for the removal of this gentleman. The request was at once granted, and the very morning when I returned to the campus, I saw the lordly captain taking his leave. We were greatly pleased with his successor, Lieutenant Gordon Coons, who was detailed for service exclusively at Illinois College. Considering the peculiar duties of the position, I do not see how we could have had a better qualified officer for the unit. Lieutenant Coons, or Captain Coons as he soon became, had some comprehension of the functions of an educational institution and was ever ready to cooperate in that spirit which produced the best results for the military unit, the College and the country.

The men of our unit had to do their training under great discouragement. Equipment was slow arriving from the War Department— as a matter of fact uniforms were not received until after the Armistice, and guns did not arrive much earlier. Furthermore, training had been in progress only a few weeks when the "flu" invaded the city and the campus, resulting in the practical quarantine of the men during the whole period of enlistment. However, since not a single death occurred in the unit or student body, we had every reason to be thankful. Nearly all ordinary student activities were now suspended. The men's literary societies, after feeble attempts to maintain their regular meetings, practically adjourned *sine die*. There was practically no football that fall, and only a few numbers of the *Rambler* were issued. The Armistice was declared before any considerable number of the Illinois College unit were called into more active service.

It was fortunate that we were not obliged to engage in any extensive construction projects in order to care for our unit of the S.A.T.C. I am glad to say that we eventually made a very reasonable settlement with the War Department on the contract for the establishment and maintenance of our unit. The order for demobilization came on November 26, and by the Christmas holidays, peace once more reigned on the campus. Altogether, slightly over 400 Illinois College men, including the Student Army Training Corps of 118, had joined the colors. We were fortunate in our casualty list, for only 9 had to make the supreme sacrifice.

Although no student succumbed to the "flu" in that troubled year of the S.A.T.C., the disease did claim one of the ablest members of our faculty, Professor Stella L. Cole, head of the modern languages department. In teaching ability and scholarly qualities Professor Cole had few equals and no superiors on the faculty during the years of my association with the College. The absurd charge of disloyalty was brought against her during the war. It was made so definitely and from such a source that the trustees felt obliged to have a conference with her on the subject. Well do I remember that conference which took place in my office one Sunday afternoon in the fall of 1918. A committee of three trustees, including the chairman of the board, were present. Whatever emotions may have stirred her heart, Professor Cole was cool and undaunted as she answered question after question, and when it was all over and she had left the room, the committee unanimously agreed that, whatever indiscretions of utterance may have led to the charge, there could be no question of her real loyalty. She simply refused to be swept off her feet by that war hysteria which sought to abolish all German art, music, and literature, and she refused, as she explained to the committee, to think ill of German friends whose characters she had learned to respect and whose friendship had meant so much to her in her student days in Germany.

Whipple Academy, the preparatory department, was finally abolished in the spring of 1920. From the earliest years and almost continuously throughout its history, the College had maintained a preparatory department. Although, like the College of which it was an integral part, the preparatory school had struggled against serious financial handicaps, it had supplied for many years a real educational need in this part of the state. But with the development of the modern community high schools the Academy came to the end of its days.

In the summer of 1920 occurred a disastrous fire, which in the end proved a blessing in disguise. I had just returned late one August day from my summer vacation, and as I happened to awake from my

Whipple Academy. Drawing by Louise Boring Wood

sleep about midnight, I heard a peculiar, crackling sound. I looked out of an east window and saw the campus lighted up with a great fire. The upper story of Sturtevant Hall was a mass of flames. I ran out expecting to see the fire engines already on the ground, but not a person was in sight and I myself turned in the alarm. It looked as if Old Sturtevant were doomed, and I urged the firemen to do what they could to save the beautiful tower. They worked manfully and to good purpose. Fortunately there was little wind, and when the slate roof fell in, it helped to protect the lower story. Although the second story was completely burned out, the flames did not eat their way very far towards the first floor. The solid construction of the old walls kept them standing and made it possible to restore the building without changing its exterior lines.

The soaring prices of the war period created serious problems for the colleges and universities of the country. Endowments, which might have been adequate previously, were now proving absolutely insufficient to meet running expenses. The most crying need was additional income to enable colleges to pay their professors a living wage. At the outbreak of the European War the salary scale for full professors at Illinois College was only fifteen hundred dollars. At the end of the war full professors were receiving sixteen hundred dollars with a bonus of two hundred dollars for married men. Obviously, it was not enough to enable a family to meet bare living expenses. Something must be done.

After much discussion and an attempt to start a new endowment campaign while the war was still in progress, it was finally settled in 1919 that an effort should be made to secure a new fund of $500,000, of which amount $375,000 should be for endowment chiefly to increase salaries, and $125,000 for a new library building. The students and faculty subscribed $7,000 early in the campaign, and we entered upon the effort with confidence and enthusiasm. We hoped that aid might be forthcoming from the General Education Board. Some time previously Mr. John D. Rockefeller, impressed with the real crisis which advancing prices had created for institutions of higher learning, and showing that insight and generosity which have always characterized his giving, had placed $50,000,000 at the disposal of the General Education Board, both principal and interest to be used for the increase of professors' salaries. We looked forward with earnest hope to the possibility of help from this fund, and we were not disappointed, for in May 1920 the cheering news came that the General Education Board had made a conditional subscription of $125,000 towards the $375,000 of new endowment which we were endeavoring to raise. Furthermore, in order that salaries might at once be increased, the board promised us, as it did other institutions, an immediate annual grant—in our case, $6,250 for two years, subsequently extended for another year. In other words an income, figured at 5 percent, was to become immediately available from the

Rockefeller subscription. Success in the effort now seemed assured, although much work remained to be done. Alumni and friends rallied to the support of the College as never before. At the commencement of June 1922, we were able to announce the completion of the new endowment fund of $375,000. Enough more had been subscribed to pay most of the cost of the improvements in Sturtevant Hall beyond the amount of the insurance. The fund for the proposed new library building, however, had to wait.

It was also during these years that the Hiram K. Jones estate finally became available for the College. This amounted to about thirty-two thousand dollars which, according to the terms of the will, was added to the general endowment fund. Furthermore, it was about this time that the death of Hobart W. Williams added forty thousand dollars to our share of the Williams Scholarship Fund. Although our hopes for a new library had not been realized, these substantial additions to the endowment funds and the constantly increasing number of students, created a spirit of confidence and optimism such as the College had not known for years.

When Illinois College became co-educational in the fall of 1903, little was done for the women beyond admitting them to the classrooms and housing them in an old dormitory. It is true that a dean of women was appointed, but for financial reasons the office soon had to be abolished. Almost nothing could be done to promote the general social life and happiness of the women. Many of the older alumni still cherished the hope that co-education might prove only a temporary experiment at Illinois College. It is not surprising, therefore, that, in the absence of any substantial gifts for the purpose, our women students have been obliged to wait rather long for facilities which should have been theirs from the beginning.

It took several years for the women's literary societies to establish themselves as important factors in student life and a still longer time to secure attractive and comfortable quarters. When the girls from the Female Academy came to the Hill they brought with them one of their literary societies—Philomathian. However, this transplanted society for some reason lived a precarious existence and in time winked out. It was not long before another organization was started, Gamma Delta, the oldest of the existing women's societies. This society was organized in March 1911, the first regular meeting being held on the last day of the month in the old Y.M.C.A. room on the north side of the second floor of Beecher Hall. Sigma Phi Epsilon, the second oldest society among the women, was organized in January 1916. The number of women in college had been gradually increasing during the five years since Gamma Delta had been founded, and it was obvious that one women's society could no longer afford opportunity for membership to all the women students. Gamma Delta gave the movement its sympathy and support, even promising it would not pledge that year any freshman girls except those who were relatives of its own members. The first meeting was held on Saturday afternoon, January 22, 1916, in the old library room on the first floor of Academy Hall. Four years later Agora, a third women's society, was organized. The special object of this society was to emphasize the importance of scholastic attainments, to follow more closely the literary programs of the men's societies, and to be frankly democratic in its membership. The organization of the society was, in fact, somewhat of a protest against the pretensions of the other two. The first officially recorded meeting was held on a Sunday afternoon in February 1920.

The competition among these three girls' societies for members soon became very keen, and the results were not always conducive to the happiness of the girls or the best interests of the College. Some of the women on the faculty felt strongly that the situation would be greatly improved if girls were not taken into the societies until the end of their freshman year and if, instead, the girls of the freshman class had a society of their own to which every member of the class was eligible. The old societies, when the matter was presented to them, consented to the plan, which resulted in the organization of Alpha Eta Pi in the fall of 1921.

It proved impossible for the College to provide adequate quarters for these societies, and they were too young and weak financially to accomplish much themselves in the effort to secure halls. As early as 1913 when only one of the societies had been organized, Professor Stella Cole made some stirring remarks at an annual commencement banquet of Gamma Delta, urging that the time had come when the women of the College ought to launch a movement for a woman's

David A. Smith House. Drawing by Louise Boring Wood

building on the campus. The suggestion was received with enthusiasm by all present at the reunion and led, within a few months,
to the organization of the Woman's Building Association. No large
gifts were forthcoming, but the women never lost courage or patience. By selling sandwiches and candy after chapel and securing
subscriptions here and there among students, alumnae, and friends,
they began to accumulate a small fund. Some may have smiled at
the effort of the girls to raise a hundred thousand dollars by selling
sandwiches and candy, but none could fail to admire their pluck.
The exigencies of the World War halted their efforts temporarily, but
they never allowed trustees and friends to forget the cause.

When in 1922 the beautiful piece of property near the southeast corner of the campus known as the David A. Smith House seemed likely to come upon the market, the directors of the Woman's Building Association decided that, instead of proceeding with the efforts to raise funds for a new building on the campus, they would try to purchase this property and use it for the social and religious life of the girls of the College. Their plan succeeded even better than they dared to hope. They took possession of this property in the fall of 1924, and funds were soon forthcoming which not only paid off a mortgage but provided a substantial endowment for its maintenance.

In looking back over a quarter of a century that has elapsed since my joining the faculty of the College, I am impressed anew with the steady progress of those years. It took a few years to repair the leaky boat, which seemed at times on the point of sinking. Occasionally caught in a calm, now and again buffeted by storms, she has not gone forward with great speed, but she has sailed sturdily on. Attendance in the College has more than quadrupled, and the permanent endowment fund has grown from less than two hundred thousand dollars to well over a million dollars. Still more gratifying to me has been the steady maintenance of high ideals of scholarship during these years.

We are not only near the end of an old century but we stand on the threshold of a new era. The future beckons us to still greater achievement. Illinois College must remain a college in the best sense —small enough to conserve the advantages of such an institution but thoroughly well equipped for its task. Still greater plans are in prospect. God grant that in these plans for the future we may measure up to the example set by the noble men and women of the past, to their idealism and their willingness to sacrifice for a great cause.

PART 2

1925–1979

"Looking upon Evangelist very carefully, Christian said, 'Whither must I fly?' Then said Evangelist, pointing with his finger over a very wide field, 'Do you see yonder wicket-gate?' Christian said, 'No.' Then said Evangelist, 'Do you see yonder shining light?' And Christian said, 'I think I do.' Then said Evangelist, 'Keep that light in your eye, and go up directly thereto; so shalt thou see the gate, at which when thou knockest, it shall be told thee what thou shalt do.'"—John Bunyan, *Pilgrim's Progress*

16

Intermission: Of History, Written and Oral

When I go to the theater, I like the intermissions almost as much as the play, sometimes more. I have a chance to sort things out, think things through, put them into perspective, and best of all, talk them over with friends. I'd like to believe that readers of *Pioneer's Progress* are in that frame of mind about this point. They have journeyed through a hundred years of history and deserve a little break, a chance to put the book down and reflect, better still to talk over what they have read with some congenial soul, say a former classmate or colleague at old Illinois. If no such person is at hand, may I serve as the next best thing? In any event, I would enjoy talking about what I have done so far and what I intend to do hereafter.

I have concluded my abridgement of Rammelkamp's *Centennial History*, and before going on, I wish to pay tribute once again to the excellence of his work. He was thorough and accurate and fair in his judgments. Moreover, he placed the development of this one small college firmly in its proper setting and showed the interaction of institution and community in such important matters as the evolution of education on the American frontier, the concern for human rights in regard to the slavery issue, the role of the churches and especially the denominational rivalries that generated some progress and much divisive quarreling. Perhaps most important of all, Rammelkamp advanced the cause of Christian liberal education in the midwest by showing how a college devoted to that cause could survive and grow and prosper despite the pressures of secularism and the competition of the tax-supported public colleges and universities. I have found the *Centennial History* a fascinating chronicle.

I now embark on the continuation of that chronicle, using some of the same kinds of source materials that Rammelkamp used and some others that were not available to him. I should like to mention both classes of materials. The written materials available to me are similar to but even more abundant than those Rammelkamp had. Of primary importance are the minute books of the board of trustees and the faculty; in the one we can trace the making of the general policies of the College and in the other the making of its academic policies. There are also regular reports of presidents to trustees and alumni, there are collections of official College correspondence, and there are the catalogues which provide information about faculty and students, as well as curricular changes. All of these have been carefully composed and preserved. Naturally, they represent official views and ought to be examined along with the less carefully composed and more volatile records of student opinion as presented in the campus newspaper, the *Rambler*, and yearbook, the *Rig Veda*. Both of these spokesmen have been in continuous, though not always regular, publication throughout the whole of the period I am covering. Rammelkamp could draw on them only for the latter part of his century. These publications claim to represent student opinion, but of course they really represent the opinions of an articulate minority, usually responsible. Recently, there has been a student literary publication called *Forte* that represents an even smaller but not unimportant segment of the student body. In addition, there are the minute books of the men's and women's societies and in some cases the organized histories of individual societies, which throw light on campus social and intellectual life, but that light is sometimes partial and unsteady. Finally, there are the records of the Student Forum.

A most interesting sourcebook is the *Alumni Quarterly*, a periodical that Charles Henry Rammelkamp called into existence during the latter part of his administration and which was edited for a number of years by his widow when she was Alumni Secretary of the College. Since the Alumni Secretary is appointed by the President of the College, the publication is semiofficial, a kind of house organ. Nonetheless, anyone reviewing the fifty-some years of its publication would have to come to the conclusion that it has not been servile. It often has reported events quite candidly as well as thoroughly; at the very least it provides an official calendar of noteworthy events at the College. A leaflet called *IC Comments* is issued from time to time, and there are the regular recruiting mailings of the Admissions Office; these are revealing but not of prime importance. The Alumni Office has also kept a scrapbook of happenings on campus as they have been reported in the local newspapers, and that office has extensive files on individual alumni which can be of help to the historian.

President Rammelkamp must have loved photography and undoubtedly believed that the fruits of the camera enhanced the written record. There are 20 full-page cuts and no less than 275 lesser ones, all minutely and I suppose accurately identified: for example, members of the baseball team of 1886, the football team of 1903, the track squad of 1904, along with the class of 1891 as sophomores, the cast of *The Hobby Horse* produced in 1903, and many, many others. Hundreds of men and women, looking young and fresh but now long gone from this world, are not only identified with their pictures but are carefully indexed.

I have been admonished to include lots of pictures in the new history, with the dictum "one picture is worth a thousand words," but I respectfully decline. Like any other cliché, that one has its limitations. One might as well say that one hundred well chosen words are worth a thousand miscellaneous pictures. For the visually oriented, however, there are a few photographs and drawings in this volume. I wish to thank Louise Boring Wood, '34, and my wife, Dorothy Berry Frank, for permission to use their sketches of campus buildings. I should also like to thank Tom Smith who has made copies of the presidential portraits and photographs, and has done additional work for the dust jacket. The portrait of President Mundinger is by Bill Wade. The files of *Rigs* and *Ramblers* and *Alumni Quarterlies* must supply the further needs of nostalgia.

Ever since the development of meaningful symbols, writers have tended to place a very high value on the written word. And since Caxton, English-speaking readers have been much impressed by the product of movable type. We are only half-respectful of the historical methods of the author of *Beowulf*, to say nothing of Homer and Herodotus. "I saw it in print" has seemed to guarantee authenticity. A moment's thought should tell us that lies can be written as well as spoken, that half-truths are as commonplace in print as in conversation. Interestingly, in the last fifty years or so, there has been a change. The means of recording—and being able to refer back to— the human voice in all its marvelous varieties and nuances has become available to us, and we have used the device innocently and guilefully, frivolously and ponderously, sometimes furtively and dangerously.

Oral history has flourished, and popular acceptance of the medium has been demonstrated in the success of books like Studs Terkel's *Working* and *Hard Times*. On television, Walter Cronkite and Bill Moyers and David Frost have presented history as the makers of it choose to reveal it to us. Academic historians at first urged caution in the use of this art form, but many of them now are not only using it themselves but are offering seminars to show others how to use it. I have been dabbling with the use of the tape recorder for more than twenty years. Recently, I have applied the technique to record the recollections of former students, faculty, presidents, deans, and business managers of Illinois College.

It is fortunate that four of the six presidents I shall be discussing have been available and willing to be taped. More than that, some former faculty and staff who worked with the two deceased presidents were eager to be interviewed, along with many who knew more than one of the recent presidents. Numerous alumni of the past five or six decades have information and opinions; they have been willing to illuminate the written records and to supply the kind of information that doesn't get written down. It is not easy to categorize these recordings or to make reference to them, but I have been typing transcripts and filing them under four main headings: 1. Shapers; 2. Teachers; 3. Learners; 4. Tenders. Some participants fall into more than one of these classes, and I have placed them in the one that seemed most appropriate to me, with cross references to other possible classes. The names of these persons are given in Appendix D.

Much of the taping was done in the summer of 1975, when I took an IC Odyssey, my wife accompanying and abetting me. In one month, we covered 7,500 miles, with stopovers in Arkansas, Texas, New Mexico, Arizona, Nevada, California, Washington, Kansas, and Missouri; still later I made recordings in Washington, D.C., and in Massachusetts. In addition to getting much useful information and some fascinating opinions, I learned that no matter where I traveled, I was never far from someone eager to talk about Illinois College. Since I made the original odyssey, I have done further recordings with a variety of informed persons, as they became available on campus.

These taped interviews run from fifteen minutes to more than ten hours in length. They are not for publication, but they will be placed in the College archives—along with typescripts—for future historians to consult. They are necessarily a miscellaneous lot, but they form a fine background against which to examine the written record. I am aware that some of the people I have taped know more than others, some have better memories than others, and some may have purer motives than others. And I realize that however the record is made, the historian must validate his sources. Indeed, much depends on the sensitivity and patience and persistence and judgment of the interviewer.

I have six administrations to deal with, and four of them I have observed at close range; I believe this to be an advantage rather than a disadvantage. From a combination of firsthand and secondhand knowledge, I can state that each of the six administrations offers a special challenge to the historian. I must first deal with the almost legendary Rammelkamp administration. Dr. Rammelkamp wrote about the first twenty-some years of his administration, and I have given his first-person view of those years in abridged form. But he died in office and could not pass judgment on his total achievement. Even had he lived and written in retirement about the whole of his administration, he would have had difficulty evaluating his work, for obvious reasons. Next, I have to handle the rather brief and turbulent years of President Jaquith, a man of fine administrative background and large international experience; unfortunately, his background was not academic. That caused problems, as did the nationwide depression and the local bank failure.

Then I consider the sixteen-year administration of President Hudson, who had to preside over the College during the Hitler-Mussolini mania abroad and the social and political changes brought about by the Roosevelt New Deal at home. His were exciting but unpredictable times. During our involvement in World War II, the civilian enrollment at Illinois College shrank to eighty-seven students. When the war ended and the GIs, supported by a grateful nation, swarmed to this campus as to many others, Dr. Hudson had to see to the expansion of faculty, curriculum, classrooms, and laboratories, additional housing for veterans, many of whom had families—and all on short notice and in competition with every other college in the country.

After President Hudson retired, President Selden took over for two frantic years, trying to cope with the problems of declining enrollment, decreasing income, and rising expenses. His chief remedy seemed to be merger with MacMurray College across town, which was having somewhat similar problems. When President Selden's constituency rejected this solution, he had no recourse but to resign. President Caine came in after a brief hiatus; with bulldog determination he set about restoring the health of the College by looking within for solutions and for support. He succeeded in spectacular fashion. In his seventeen-year tenure, he built up enrollment, raised money and spent it cautiously, and added considerably to the physical plant. The administration of the incumbent is still creating its history, but Dr. Mundinger has shown a strong leaning toward the fiscal conservatism of his predecessor, along with a desire to widen the horizons of the College. I shall have to appraise his achievements somewhat tentatively, since they are in progress as I write.

I deal with these administrations in separate chapters, well knowing that important events in the history of a college cannot be compartmentalized chronologically. There are also many facets that I must take into consideration besides enrollments and budgets, endowments and buildings. Some of them are rather abstract, like matters of faculty recruitment and retention; student content and discontent; relations with the churches that helped to found us and have continued to give us support; relations with the seats of government in Jacksonville, Springfield, and Washington; relations with our sister college across town and with many other colleges and universities that have had influence upon us; and relations with alumni and trustees and our neighbors in Morgan County. It's a large order. But this I believe—or I could not write at all: that the history of this College is not only long but honorable, interesting because of its many problems, illuminating in the way it has met challenges to its fiscal and academic integrity. And the third half-century is as worthy of study as was the first century.

Various colleagues and friends have given me the benefit of their perceptions of these last fifty years by reading critically one or more of the ensuing chapters. I acknowledge their assistance gratefully; they cannot of course be held accountable for any errors that may remain, in spite of their efforts. My thanks for inquisitive scanning go to Walter R. Bellatti, Ernst Bone, Ruth Bump, Donald Eldred, Helen Foreman, Helen Hackett, Jean Hildner, Doris Hopper, Wallace Jamison, Eleanor Miller, Mary Jeanette Osborne, Richard Pratt, Ethel Seybold, Alma Smith, Malcolm Stewart, John S. Wright, and Iver Yeager. For other kinds of assistance with the manuscript I am indebted to Jack Bales, Virginia Green, Howard Jarratt, Richard Pratt, and Cindy Zattich. Finally, I should like to thank Vernon Sternberg, Director of the Southern Illinois University Press, for his thoughtful, sensitive editing of the whole manuscript of *Pioneer's Progress*.

Now back to the play.

17

President Rammelkamp: Partly Third Person,
1925–1932

President Rammelkamp's last seven years in office were largely spent consolidating the gains he had made in his first twenty years. He was not an innovator in curricular planning and in any case he had no desire to change the basic educational mission or practice of Illinois College. He seems not to have wished for personal fame, and he certainly was not an academic climber; he made no effort to use his fine early record as an administrator to move on to fresh fields. He wished to finish the job he had begun and to leave Illinois College financially secure and educationally sound.

After the student body had reached a certain number, about four hundred, he chose to stabilize it by limiting the number of freshmen admitted to one hundred and fifty. He wanted not more but better students. He sought to build an efficient and attractive physical plant, to gather a highly qualified faculty, and to increase the endowment so that the College could get and keep good students and teachers without significantly increasing costs and, above all, without making the institution elitist. To achieve these ends, he wished to call the attention of a wider audience to the merits of the College. The approaching centennial seemed to offer excellent opportunities for doing just that. He gave much time and energy to planning a dignified, wholly worthy celebration. Committees of trustees and faculty, alumni, students, and friends were appointed to carry out these intentions. Meanwhile, he continued to work on his *Centennial History*, which he regarded as the keystone to his program of gaining favorable notice for the College.

President Charles Henry Rammelkamp

He also knew that he had to raise more money, even though he had only recently, at Commencement, 1922, concluded a campaign for new endowment. In January 1925, with the approval of his board of trustees, he launched an active campaign to secure $1.5 million for a centennial building and endowment fund. To rally support for this drive he released one of the most popular members of the faculty, Professor John Griffith Ames, from his teaching duties for the 1925–26 academic year. "Johnny" was the only member of the faculty with a longer record of service to the College than Rammelkamp himself. He was widely known as a teacher of English and universally respected by alumni and friends of the College.

Plans for a new quadrangle were formulated; foremost needs were a library and a gymnasium. Also needed were better facilities for the women of the College, especially dormitories and equipment for athletics, and a new commons for the men. (As a sidelight, it may be noted that President Rammelkamp usually referred to the undergraduate sexes as "men" and "girls.") The campaign was geared to raise $750,000 for buildings and $750,000 for endowment; it was hoped the first half would be in hand by Commencement, 1927, and the second half by Commencement, 1929. Centennial fervor was counted on to give momentum to the drive.

At the very outset of this campaign for new buildings and increased endowment occurred a series of student-faculty confrontations that must have been deeply disturbing to the administration. In his *Centennial History*, Dr. Rammelkamp minimizes the difficulty saying: "The story of the recent years might be lengthened still further. The abolition of the 'Dorm Court' and of hazing deserves more than the mere mention, for these acts were really forward steps in the history of student life. I admire the common sense and wisdom shown by the students in joining with the faculty to meet these issues. If the pages of this book were unlimited, the picturesque 'Tie and Collar Rebellion' and the plan of student-faculty cooperative government, which grew out of it, would also deserve more than a word."

Granting that some good resulted from the struggle between students and faculty, it could not at the time have been a pleasant experience for the administration, which may be the reason Dr. Rammelkamp played it down. In my opinion, it does deserve more than a word, for it throws light on the way these things happened in the twenties, in comparison to the late sixties and early seventies. I shall present the story principally as it unfolded in the *Rambler*, the campus weekly that would soon celebrate its fiftieth anniversary.

During the 1924–25 academic year the *Rambler* editor was R. J. Schumann, who seems to have been a level-headed, unsensational editor; still, more than a hint of unrest appeared in his editorial "Freedom," published November 19. Mr. Schumann wrote: "One of the things that has distinguished Illinois College from other small colleges has been its freedom of thought and action. Perhaps we are mistaken, we sincerely hope we are, in believing that there has been a tendency in the last year or two to suppress that freedom. Any attempt to destroy the traditional atmosphere of freedom in Illinois College will result in widespread dissatisfaction." Later in the year, the faculty intervened in a matter of social discipline. Some faculty resolutions were passed and were presented to the students in chapel. An article published in the January 21 issue of the *Rambler* fully describes this intervention under the headline "Drastic Action Abolishes Dorm Court / Expulsion is Penalty in Faculty Rules." "Dorm Court" had a long tradition at Illinois College; it had been inaugurated in the Tanner administration as a form of group discipline. It gave undergraduates a sense of self-government, it gave them an opportunity to prosecute and defend specific cases, and it relieved the faculty of the necessity of regulating the social conduct of the students. It was a very good system when it worked, but like all other systems, it could be subverted and turned into a form of petty tyranny by upperclass bullies. Something of this kind had happened and the faculty decided to abolish the system. Hence the resolutions banning the "Dorm Court." An editorial in the same issue analyzes the new rules. What the faculty had done was to abolish hazing in all its forms; what the *Rambler* objected to was not the intention of the resolutions but the arbitrary manner in which the faculty had imposed them and the probable failure of the measures proposed to enforce the new rules. A letter in the same issue calls the faculty action "provocative of antagonism with the students in that they do not ask their co-operation in any way."

In later numbers of the *Rambler*, articles, editorials, and letters were published indicating a genuine desire on the part of responsible student leaders to develop new machinery for student government. Typical of this effort is the editor's statement: "The *Rambler* voices the hope that some form of student government will be adopted and that the attitude of all concerned will be such as to make it a success and a solution for some of the problems that have gone unsolved in the past." During the rest of that year, the *Rambler* ran a series of articles on how student government was managed on other campuses. Finally, on May 6, a draft constitution was published, but no action on it was reported that year. It would have required a two-thirds vote by the students and adoption by the faculty to put the constitution into effect; apparently all concerned were content to wait until the following year to try the new system.

The editor in 1925–26 was H. Clay Tate, who later became a prominent newspaperman in Bloomington, Illinois. He cut his journalistic teeth by putting out a lively *Rambler*. Once he had aroused interest in an issue, he saw to it that the interest did not die. His first target was the foreign language requirement, and in the September 30 issue, he ran an editorial entitled "'Heavy Heavy' hangs over your course of study." He began his crusade quietly and modestly: "One of the customs which has been handed down under the guise of a liberal education is the foreign language requirement in our American colleges. Latin, Greek, French and German might have been of use as disciplinary studies when the college course was limited, but at present there seem to be many more practical studies which could be used for the same purpose." After several paragraphs showing the uselessness of foreign languages to most American students, the writer concludes: "Illinois College has reduced the requirement from four to two years within recent times. May the remaining two be speedily erased from her curriculum."

On October 8 the target was more personal. A front-page article headlined "Faculty makes Cupid unwelcome at Illinois College!" begins: "Last Monday in Chapel, President Rammelkamp read a faculty resolution which aroused a great deal of interest among the students. The resolution advised against the marriage of students, but if such marriage take place, the consent of parents must be obtained." Some stern remarks by Dean George H. Scott were quoted, and the article concluded: "The faculty does not believe in secret marriages and inserted the clause which caused so much hilarity in chapel, 'Married students are expected to live together.'" Accompanying the article is a cartoon which shows Dean Scott planting his foot on the chest of a struggling student and pointing to a scroll on which is written:

Thou *Shalt Not*

I. Go without a collar and tie.

II. Get married.

III. Throw paper.

IV. Haze.

More was to be heard about these commandments, especially the first.

On October 15 there was another editorial on "College Requirements." This one enlarges the scope of the protest by urging the elimination of all requirements. It concludes: "Why not forget class records and parceled out doses for daily consumption; get big men to instill into the students the joy of following their own inclinations? Let us cease to waste four years in superficial and impractical study! Let us throw off this ancestral worship and delve into modern problems in a modern way!" Clearly the editor was enjoying himself, and he kept up an almost weekly barrage. He began to get letters agreeing and disagreeing with his stands, some of which he published. His October 22 editorial was labeled "Faculty Recognition" and it contained such inflammatory statements as: "Faculty rulings at Illinois College have brought the students to the explosive stage. It appears that the faculty is no longer for the benefit of the students. Students have no right which the faculty is bound to respect. Are we getting a liberal education administered by liberal minded men or are we being subjected to the whims of fanatics and the degradations of the ambitious?" The young man had learned something of the art of rhetoric, especially of the vituperative kind.

It may be appropriate to note that some months later Mr. Tate was invited to appear before the Alumni Association at their annual meeting in June 1926. At that time, he reported that there had been a rumor to the effect that the administrative forces of the College had endeavored to censor the material to be used in the *Rambler* but that this was a false impression, although one or two faculty members, as individuals, had endeavored to curb his authority as editor. No action was taken; the meeting was informative only.

Some other matters of moment occasionally distracted the editor; for example, he was interested in the centennial building and endowment campaign and the effort to create a new athletic conference with Augustana, Eureka, Illinois Wesleyan, Knox, and Monmouth. But not for long. He came back to his original targets and made lengthy reply to those who were benighted enough to support the foreign language requirement. One was a professor of modern languages; after knocking down each of the gentleman's arguments, he concluded: "The language professor is going to have to use new selling points before he can get the students of today to fall in line; in other words he is going to have to sing a new tune and get new words to go with that tune. The new words are going to have to be in harmony with the utilitarian idea of education, or the foreign language requirement is going to pass into the junk heap in the same way that obsolete machinery is disposed of." An editorial of December 10 restates the paper's position: "There are two theories of education; one is that it is a ritual, the other that it is an adventure. The present system at I. C. tends toward the former, while the change, as desired by a majority of those connected with the college, advocates the latter."

The *Rambler* of December 17 was put out by the freshman class, the centennial class. Perhaps that is why the editorial voice was so fresh and hopeful; a cheerful, confident note was sounded: "General opinion seems to be that our class has fallen into the spirit of the institution more easily than the average entering class. The new period, it is said, is one of transition. By the time the class of '29 becomes seniors, the new feeling will have reached its highest point.

All students are looking forward to the culmination of this spirit in the centennial celebration of '29."

That bright note must have cheered President Rammelkamp and Dean Scott and the faculty generally. But it was not to prevail. A new issue was introduced in the January 14, 1926, number. A proposal was made that tuition should be increased by ten dollars a year, with the increase being devoted to certain activities: five dollars for intramural athletics; two dollars for the *Rambler*; one dollar for the band; one dollar for the men's and women's glee clubs; and one dollar for the YMCA and YWCA programs. A student meeting was to be held for discussion of the proposal and a vote on it. The *Rambler* editorial commented: "Our tuition recently made a twenty-five dollar jump and now it is proposed to add another ten dollars. We are getting dangerously close to wiping out one of the big reasons for the existence of the small college. However, if the tuition is to be raised, it behooves the students to have a say as to how the increase is to be used. The budget as worked out seems adequate and comprehensive. It is for a good cause, but let us not readily increase our tuition. It is setting a bad precedent." No doubt the editor was interested in getting two dollars per student for his *Rambler*, but he was not quite ready to abandon principle.

The January 21 issue reported that "Student body holds stormy session." The session ran overtime, partly because a young woman moved that a part of the five-dollar allocation for intramural athletics be used to promote an intercollegiate program for women's athletics. Her motion to amend was vigorously debated and was passed, despite the objections of the Director of Athletics. Eventually, as reported in the January 28 *Rambler*, the original proposal, without the amendment, was adopted by "an overwhelming majority. One hundred and sixty stood up in favor of the proposal and fourteen stood opposed to it. A large number refused to vote on the proposition." A petition to implement the proposal was forwarded to the Board of Trustees.

A year later, December 14, 1926, when the trustees considered this petition, they modified the request. After considerable discussion, they voted to increase the tuition by two dollars, one dollar per student to go to the support of the College band, fifty cents per stu-

dent to the girls' glee club and fifty cents per student to the men's
glee club. "On account of the large number of students of slender
means who are working their way through college, the Trustees hesitated at this time to increase the tuition any further." No comment
was made on the appeal for funds for intramural athletics or the *Rambler*, but regarding the compulsory fees for the YM and YW organization, "members of the Board felt strongly that such religious
organizations should be kept on a strictly voluntary basis."

For a time this crusade and its probable success had a calming effect on the campus. The *Rambler* ran a euphoric editorial in its January 28 number entitled "New Illinois." Commenting on the plans
for the proposed new quadrangle issued by the Centennial Committee, the editor praised these efforts: "An institution of a hundred
years may have its slumps, but it can brave the greatest of trials
and survive. Illinois College is stronger today than it has ever been.
All hail to 'New Illinois.'"

If the administration was pleased with this olive branch extended
by the *Rambler*, once again the pleasure was not long-lived. On February 11, there was a cryptic report of a "joke on prexy"—the removal of the door on the College bell tower—and the week following an editorial "Why Chapel Jokes?" indicating further examples of
rowdiness. The editorial denounces these juvenile pranks and their
perpetrators, but closes with an admonishment: "Chapel jokes are
not desirable, but they are a crude way of registering disapproval.
And until the talent of the student is discovered and nourished by
the educational system, he is going to waste it away in misdirected
lines. How then abolish such pranks? First, provide a substitute;
second, let the student choose his own college; third, give him something interesting in the college of his choice. Until that is done, all
we can say is: play the jokes with discretion."

A March 18 editorial returns to the question of student government and says that nothing of worth has yet been achieved by the
students: "The initiative and recall would be retained by the faculty.
The boast of the faculty last year was their retention of all power
under the proposed student government plan. They have no intention of relinquishing that power." An April 8 news article says that
"by an overwhelming majority the student body voted to draw up

some form of student council," and the editor of the *Rambler* was made a member of the committee named to prepare a draft.

The April 22 issue indicates that the various controversies between students and faculty had at last reached a climax. A long editorial labeled "Broken Pledges" tries to put the matter into context by citing the general pledge that students had made when matriculating: "We agree to observe faithfully the College's rules and requirements." But the writer goes on to say: "In that pledge we understood that we were giving the faculty power to make certain rules for the proper administration of college affairs and to aid us in our efforts to get an education. We thought the faculty was concerned with what was in our heads and not what was around our necks. Few of us believed that enrollment in Illinois College constituted a repudiation of our rights as more or less intelligent and responsible human beings, and our privileges as American citizens. If these things are included in the pledge they should be specifically stated in it."

A side issue—the question of a dress code requiring the men to wear collars and neckties—had got mixed up with the larger question of student government and a first class brouhaha had resulted. Headlines in the April 22 edition screamed the story:

> "Sophomores protest Collar and Tie Rule
>   Send Resolutions to the Faculty"
>
> "Students uphold Sophomores in protest to Faculty"
>
> "Students and the Faculty end Collar
>   and Tie War in joint conference"

That conference reached a compromise solution, with the faculty backing down as gracefully as they could at so late a date: "Resolved, that when a Student Council acceptable to both students and faculty shall have been organized, the faculty will delegate regulations in matters of dress to said Council without faculty veto." The resolution was carried, signed by the Secretary of the Faculty, and delivered to the Student Association.

Further references to this row occur in subsequent issues, but they are not so hectic; they show a growing desire to "get along." The outside press had picked up the squabble and delighted in exploiting it. This was an irritation to President Rammelkamp and all those engaged in raising funds for the College.

On May 27, the *Rambler* reported: "Student body accepts Council Plan 118 to 6." The plan had been drawn up by a committee of six students and three faculty members. The constitution provided for methods of electing ten representative students; it also provided for a faculty council of ten to meet with the student group at regular intervals. "Unrestricted power in regulating dress is the only power consigned to the Council at the present time. A provision is made whereby the Council-elect may evolve further duties and powers, the same to be subject to the approval of both faculty and the student body." I wish I could state that the matter ended thus, but it did not. Incomprehensibly, the faculty rejected the proposal which had been negotiated by its own representatives, assuring further clashes when College reconvened. The faculty did repeal the collar and tie rule for the coming year, however, and left the way open for further consideration of "a plan of student government."

President Rammelkamp gave considerable attention to all of this in his June report to the Board of Trustees, saying among other things:

Certainly no episode in the whole century of Illinois College history ever attracted so much attention in the public press of the country; not even the vigorous fight which the early faculty made for the cause of human freedom spread so far on the editorial page. And yet how insignificant and unimportant the whole affair really was! Unfortunately, some good friends of the College seemed actually to have believed the exaggerated and distorted accounts which appeared in some sensational newspapers, but most friends, I hope, saw the humorous aspect of the episode and were able to read the truth between the lines.

The phase of the tempest which deserves more serious attention, however, is its bearing on the whole question of student-faculty relationships. It is, I believe, a reflection on all of us that such a violent controversy should occur over so small a matter. I am sure that the students of Illinois College are not burning with a desire to pose as last-ditch champions of slovenly habits, and I am equally positive that the faculty have no desire to dictate on such delicate matters as styles of dress. The machinery and spirit of college discipline must be improved so that such a tempest cannot reoccur.

That is all very well put, and probably both sides, in quiet moments, would have been ready to agree with Dr. Rammelkamp's analysis. In another part of the same report, the President refers to the controversy over curriculum:

I hope the day will not come when a student can graduate from Illinois College without enough training in the various large departments of knowledge to make him a broadly educated man.

To be specific, that means, in my opinion, a good training in English, including both literature and rhetoric so that he can appreciate good literature and express himself without disgrace to himself or his college; a training in some foreign language as an aid to his English if for no other reasons; some knowledge of history and the social sciences that will give him an appreciation of past civilization and of his own relation to contemporary society; nor of course, can a man be regarded as liberally educated who has not some knowledge of science and scientific methods of study. I believe that the future of the American Liberal Arts College depends on holding fast to these principles and ideals.

Again, beautifully put, whether you altogether agree or not. The philosophy is the culmination of nineteenth-century academic liberalism, with echoes of Matthew Arnold and John Henry Newman and just a pinch of Thomas Henry Huxley. Another witty Rammelkampian summary, from the same report, puts both students and faculty in their proper places: "It is perhaps an encouraging sign when students give attention to things educational. One certainly should not object to an expression of opinion from students on educational policies, even on the requirements for graduation. However, the responsibility for the curriculum of a college belongs to the faculty and if a faculty is not capable of assuming this responsibility, the remedy is not to surrender it to the students but to change the personnel of the faculty."

Now, more than fifty years later, one feels like crying out, "Bravo, Charles Henry!" At the same time, one is impressed by the gentility and articulateness of both sides in this controversy, and especially of the students who might have been expected to be less reasonable, more physical. No one threw a brick through the Dean's window or set fire to the President's shrubbery. There was not even a shutdown of classes or a boycott of chapel. Admittedly, not much was accomplished, but what was done, was done with a touch of class.

There is no direct evidence that the unrest on campus that year affected the fund-raising campaign then under way, but it must have had some effect. At the Board meeting that June, Dr. Rammelkamp had sadly to report that both the Carnegie Corporation and the General Education Board had declined to make grants to the Illinois College centennial building and endowment fund. At the very least, the business was a distraction at a crucial time. Professor Ames, as senior faculty member, was involved in numerous committee meetings dealing with these problems, even though he had been released from his teaching duties in order to arouse alumni enthusiasm for the proposed new buildings and endowment. And certainly the President had his attention diverted from his many time-consuming tasks.

The dramatic death of Dean Scott at the very opening of the 1926–27 academic year had a restraining effect, but also underlined the tension that remained on the campus. The account of that event given in the *Alumni Quarterly* does not make any allusion to the controversies of the preceding year, but the writer obviously had them in mind:

Dean Scott always had a message for the incoming class and he was very careful to explain to them in a clear comprehensive way the purpose of a college education and the great benefits to be derived therefrom. The great interest he took in the freshmen is forcefully demonstrated by the last talk he delivered, which was made Saturday morning while he was suffering the first attacks of his last illness.

According to the program of affairs he was to deliver the class of '30 an address at 9 o'clock in the chapel. He did not feel capable of doing it but as he considered it his duty he went to speak to them against the desires and wishes of a number of friends on the faculty. He was not able to stand but sat in his chair and talked to them of their college work. Soon after he was taken to his home, where within a short period of time he passed away.

At Dean Scott's funeral services, President Rammelkamp delivered a strong eulogy of the Dean and alluded obliquely to the problems we have been examining:

His devotion to scholarly ideals led him to be a champion of high standards in the College. He was not in favor of letting down the educational bars. He was a jealous guardian of the good name of the College in the educational world.

As Dean, Professor Scott was the chief disciplinary officer of the College. Responsibility for discipline is a delicate and heavy duty, involving intimate human contacts, that sometimes lead to misunderstanding. Furthermore, a dean or a college president often has to execute the decrees of a faculty or a board of trustees, even when he does not personally agree with them. I have a high regard for the manner in which Dean Scott discharged these delicate and difficult duties.

Whether or not the student-faculty controversy was responsible for the reluctance of donors to contribute—and it probably was not—there is no doubt that the campaign for the centennial building and endowment fund was lagging. In his annual report for 1926–27, President Rammelkamp put it bluntly:

Of the $300,000 subscribed, about $165,000 is available for the library, the rest being by special request of the donors designated for other purposes, chiefly for endowment, the David Smith House, and improvements to Sturtevant Hall. But of this $165,000 only about $70,000 has been paid in cash. Friends will therefore appreciate why we did not begin construction of the library this spring, as we had hoped to do. However, I do not despair.

Owing to economic conditions which do not need to be explained to people residing in this part of the country, we have not made as much progress during the past year in our centennial campaign for $750,000 as we had hoped. Furthermore, certain Eastern boards which have given generously in the past to the endowment of the College, have definitely withdrawn from their previous policy of making contributions to general college endowment and building funds. It seems that these boards, so far as their gifts indicate their policies, no longer intend to support the great constructive, educational work which the colleges of the country are doing, but plan rather to devote their funds to highly specialized and costly enterprises of the larger universities and of certain educational and scientific associations. We must face the fact that, here as elsewhere, we are thrown back on our own resources. If our centennial program is to be realized, we ourselves must accomplish the task. Let us resolve, with God's help, to do it.

Some good news was given out at that commencement. First, that the Chairman of the Board of Trustees, Mr. Andrew Russel, had offered to the College land adjacent to the campus and that it would be developed as playing fields; second, that Mrs. Eloise Pitner, widow of Dr. T. J. Pitner, class of 1862, was donating to the College her home, "Fairview." The money value of the gift was said to be about twenty thousand dollars, but "the beauty of its site and the stately grounds is beyond estimate." The site was just west of the main campus, a convenient location for future development; furthermore, the home had been built for Judge Samuel Lockwood, an early trustee of the College, so there were historic connections. These two gifts would not directly help the building and endowment campaign, but they were expected to greatly assist the development of the athletic program of the whole college and the improvement of the condition of women on campus.

Through it all, President Rammelkamp kept his courage up. Grave as the situation was, and decorous as his conduct usually was, he could clown a bit before the student body when the occasion seemed to demand levity. I have been told that he never entered the chapel without wearing his academic gown. But, reported the *Rambler* of February 9, 1928: "Bedlam reigned supreme here Monday morning when President C. H. Rammelkamp stepped into Jones Chapel with a spade, a shiny new one, upon his left shoulder. In a few words he explained that the implement was to be used for the very purpose for which it had been designed and that the new library would be started as soon as possible." He then announced a forty-thousand-dollar gift from an anonymous donor, one that would make it possible to go forward with the library.

In spite of that good fortune, the President could show little further progress, in his report for the year 1927–28:

Net subscriptions to the Centennial Building and Endowment Fund now total about $360,000. However, it is to be carefully noted that not all of the money subscribed has been collected. The important question is—what are we going to do about the completion of our Centennial Building and Endowment Campaign? The library, it is true, is assured and we are profoundly thankful for that much progress. But are we going to stop there? Or are we going to make a serious effort to complete the whole Centennial Fund? This whole fund, including provision for a new gymnasium and heating plant, was by formal resolution of the trustees, set at $750,000. [The reader may remember that the original fund had been set at $1,500,000, but somewhere along the line, when the response had not been encouraging, this sum had been halved.] To complete the Fund, we must therefore raise within the next year approximately $400,000. We may as well face facts. This goal cannot be reached unless some very substantial gifts are forthcoming. But why have we not a right to believe that the unique and important occasion of the Centennial of the College will inspire some alumnus or friend to make a gift that will insure the success of this larger campaign? Let us not despair. Let us have faith. Let us also be willing ourselves to make further sacrifices for the cause.

Professor Ames was once again given leave for the 1928–29 year and sent on the road to generate renewed interest and generosity among alumni and friends. He had some success, enough to insure a spirited centennial celebration. One of the highlights was the dedication of the new library building. It should be reported that the faculty sent a formal petition to the Board of Trustees, meeting in December 1928, requesting that they name the new building "The Rammelkamp Centennial Library." This suggestion was welcomed and given the unanimous approval of the Board, but when the President learned of it, he promptly asked the Board "in positive and strong language" to rescind their action. He then entered the meeting and moved that it be named "The Tanner Memorial Library," honoring the third president of the College, and it was so ordered.

One charming event of the centennial, under the direction of Professor Willis DeRyke, was the planting of one hundred elm trees. These were set out in various parts of the City of Jacksonville, an appropriate thank-you from gown to town. An event that did not take place was a special game: the Illinois College football team had challenged the Yale University reserves to meet them on the field of honor, centennial weekend. Yale politely declined the challenge, pointing out that the university trustees would not be likely to sanction so long a journey in the midst of their already arduous schedule.

Four days in October 1929 marked the culmination of Charles Henry Rammelkamp's presidency of Illinois College. Many are the printed descriptions that have come down to us of events that took place at that time, in the Jacksonville newspapers, the College *Rambler*, and the *Alumni Quarterly*. And those who witnessed the events still grow misty-eyes as they describe them to me in recorded conversations. I have chosen to compress some excerpts from a commemorative volume published in 1930 under the title *Centennial Celebration of the Founding of Illinois College*. Let us begin with an account of "The Parade of a Century."

After four days of leaden skies and ceaseless rain, Saturday, October 12, dawned bright and clear, a day of white, blue and gold—the right colors, those of Yale and Illinois—and a perfect setting to the Illinois College Centennial Celebration. In the City Square and on the streets the crowds were gathering to witness this pageant, soon to pass down the flag-trimmed streets, a chronicle in motion and color, a history of Illinois College.

Mounted heralds in their blue and white were seen advancing, and then the Reverend John Ellis and his wife, returning to Jacksonville after long years, followed by the Quaker pioneer, Thomas Lippincott, and that group of courageous young men, "The Yale Band." Before the interested spectators passed a log cabin, representing the homes of one hundred years ago, with citizens and children in the quaint costumes of 1829. Out of the shadows of the past came the first faculty of the College—Beecher, Sturtevant, Adams, Turner and Post.

Men and women of the present day saw the deep snow of a century ago mantling prairie and cabin. Also a prairie schooner, land vessel of adventure, bearing a pioneer family to a new world. On one float a sewing society of 1830 resumed their work, while on another float, an old-time church choir sang spiritedly. Members of the Ladies Education Society—oldest organization for women in the United States—were seen discussing the problems of the education of women; Governor and Mrs. Duncan bowed graciously from their carriage; in a straw-filled wagon, fearful travelers on the "Underground Railway" moved slowly past. Bands played when War Governor Yates presented his commission to General Grant and when William Jennings Bryan drove by, wearing his Junior Class hat. Young men in the rough clothes of pioneer days, Maypole dancers and Woodland Players in gay costumes, students on mules, horses, high-wheeled bicycles, in carriages and automobiles, riding to classrooms and proms, elaborate and colorful floats representing college, civic, patriotic and business organizations all graced the parade.

As a climax to all that had gone before, the last to appear was Mrs. Rammelkamp as the serene and stately figure of Alma Mater, in flowing robes of blue and white. Children, representing the Future with its responsibilities, its hopes and dreams, surrounded her. A century of life of the College had passed with its stirring events dramatically portrayed. The long procession winding through the elm-shaded streets presaged the traditions, the incidents and themes which would find repeated expression during the four golden days of the Centennial Celebration.

Other events of that first day included a football game, not with Yale, but with Monmouth College, which unfortunately we lost, an "I" Club banquet, a performance of *As You Like It*, under the direction of Professor Ames, and a Homecoming Dance.

On Sunday, October 13, there was a service of thanksgiving held in the convocation tent, with approximately two thousand persons attending. In addition to several local clergy participants, the Moderator of the National Council of Congregational Churches delivered the sermon. The anthem was Handel's "Hear Ye, Israel," sung by Helen Brown Read, of the Illinois Conservatory of Music, and a favorite Jacksonville artist. In the afternoon, the Tanner Memorial Library was dedicated, with Professor Edgar Johnson Goodspeed of the University of Chicago making the principal address, "Adventures with Books." That day ended with a reception at the David A. Smith House, presided over by members of the Woman's Building Association clothed in charming costumes of bygone days, crinolines and hoopskirts, with their hair worn in long curls or caught up with nets or with high combs which had once belonged to their mothers or grandmothers.

On Monday morning, October 14, an audience of two thousand gathered in the convocation tent to hear an address by Dr. Alexander Meiklejohn, chairman of the Experimental College of the University of Wisconsin, along with briefer statements by the Honorable Morton D. Hull, Member of Congress, and William Dawes, Chicago

Tanner Hall. Drawing by Louise Boring Wood

businessman. In the afternoon, there were addresses by Professor Edward Capps, classicist of Princeton, and President Livingston Farrand of Cornell. In the evening there was an alumni banquet with toasts and responses by Dr. George Baxter, trustee of the College, Mr. Frederick Tanner, son of the third president of the College, Chancellor Throop of Washington University, Dr. Ruth Fairbank of Johns Hopkins University Hospital, and others. Simultaneously, there was a reunion banquet of alumnae of the Jacksonville Female Academy, the Young Ladies Athenaeum, and the Illinois Conservatory of Music, with more toasts and responses, and, one hopes, equal though separate amenities. Probably there was no banqueting hall in Jacksonville big enough to accommodate all the celebrants.

The grand finale came on Tuesday, October 15, with an academic procession that included the representatives of 150 colleges, universities, and learned societies. The invocation was offered by Dr. C. P. McClelland, president of MacMurray College, who prayed long and fervently for the continued health and prosperity of Illinois College. President Rammelkamp delivered an address of welcome to the assembled delegates and friends; it was both cordial and scholarly as befitted the occasion. There were greetings from the private colleges by the president of Carleton College; from the public universities by the president of the University of Illinois; from the moderator of the Presbyterian Church in the U.S.A.; from the Governor of the

State of Illinois; and a letter from the President of the United States. The major address on that occasion was given by the president of Yale University. Finally, Illinois College awarded an extraordinary fourteen honorary degrees, complete with citations.

There was a centennial luncheon with more toasts, greetings and congratulations, followed by a reception at the President's home, and as a final observance, a round of love feasts by the literary societies. It was surely a noble celebration, but it is exhausting just to read about it. What must it have been like to take active part in it? to be responsible for all, including the weather and protocol, to go well?

Handsome tributes were paid this little college on the prairie during this burst of celebration. A student who entered college that fall was overwhelmed; she told me that she and her contemporaries thought that all those dignitaries had come to this campus from far places to pay homage to Dr. Rammelkamp, the father-figure of Illinois College. She was not altogether wrong. In recognition of his quarter century of unremitting work for the College, the Board of Trustees offered President Rammelkamp a year's leave and voted travel expenses for him and Mrs. Rammelkamp. Shortly after the centennial festivities had ended, they left the campus for a year of rest and recreation, the first sabbatical leave granted at Illinois College. The *Rambler* reported the itinerary of the presidential travels, the sailing from Hoboken on the U.S. Lines *George Washington* to Cherbourg, the prospective travels in France and Italy and the Near East. Alumni and former students, faculty and friends would be visited in Beirut and Constantinople, Athens and the Greek Islands. The return journey would be by way of the Balkans, Germany, and England. (During Dr. Rammelkamp's absence, Professor John Griffith Ames would serve as Acting President, a choice the *Rambler* endorsed.) The *Rambler* was also pleased to announce that the President "has kindly consented to write an article, occasionally, for publication."

Writing from Paris, Dr. Rammelkamp told of his travels during the first six weeks of his sabbatical; mentioning some of the delights of his visits to historical shrines, he makes a poignant revelation: "I am more sorry than ever that in an evil moment I deserted the muse of history to sit in a president's office." Despite the bantering tone, there is genuine regret in that remark. At the same time, there is genuine nostalgia in the letter: "Although we are wandering far afield, our heartstrings bind us to the old campus." Some weeks later, writing from Florence, he described an earlier visit to Chateau Thierry, where he had been welcomed by Dr. Julian Wadsworth, class of 1881, who was running a community house and social center for the residents of the town, an American memorial to our war dead. "This Illinois College man has not only performed a great practical service for the French people, but his institution stands as a symbol of brotherhood among the nations."

Somewhat later, writing from Athens, he describes the hospitality and special attention shown the Rammelkamps in part because of their connection with Edward Capps, Illinois College, class of 1887. (Professor Capps was also Mrs. Rammelkamp's brother, it should be noted.) Dr. Rammelkamp writes: "As we have traveled through various countries, we have been delighted to meet here and there old friends, especially Illinois College alumni who are contributing something of value to life, scholarship and humanity in the Old World."

Returning home in late summer, President Rammelkamp expressed the heartfelt thanks of himself and his wife to the Board of Trustees for the leave they had granted him, adding characteristically: "We can hardly overestimate what the trip meant to us, not only in rest and recreation, but especially in opportunities for new knowledge." The *Alumni Quarterly* of October 1930 carried a summary article describing the highlights of the ten months' pilgrimage; it is too concise to reveal much of interest to us now, but President Rammelkamp attached a word of greeting to alumni and former students which has an almost prophetic tone: "Our travels and studies in foreign lands have, I hope, given Mrs. Rammelkamp and me new energy and enthusiasm for the years that lie ahead, whether they be many or few."

For Charles Henry the years ahead were indeed to be few. There were, however, events of those years that deserve notice. A portrait of Edward Allen Tanner, third president of the College, was presented by his son, Mr. Frederick C. Tanner, class of 1898. Also presented to the College about this time was a portrait of Marian Brown

Tanner done by Marian Boyd Allen of Boston; it appears to be a warm likeness of a gracious lady. Portraits of Charles Henry Rammelkamp and Rhoda Jeanette Capps Rammelkamp were commissioned by friends of the College and executed by Edmund Giesbert of Chicago. These and other portraits in the possession of the College form an interesting collection of varied styles of portraiture and they keep alive the memory of those who have faithfully served Illinois College over the years.

Although unwilling to make any contribution toward the building of the new library, the Carnegie Corporation of New York did make a grant of ten thousand dollars for "development of the library through the purchase of books," which the Board "accepted with hearty thanks" at their December 1930 meeting. The Edward Capps Chair of Classics was funded as part of the centennial celebration. A member of the class of 1887, Edward Capps was a distinguished classicist who had served not only on the faculty of Illinois College but also of Yale, Chicago, and Princeton. Among many distinctions, he was one of the editors of the Loeb Classical Library, Minister to Greece in Woodrow Wilson's administration, head of the American School of Classical Studies in Athens, and director of the excavation of the ancient agora in Athens. Friends of Edward Capps in Greece as well as America joined to establish this chair in his honor.

The first incumbent of the chair, Raymond H. Lacey, was installed in formal ceremonies presided over by President Rammelkamp in early November 1930. Professor Louis Lord of Oberlin College was the prinicipal speaker on this occasion, delivering a graceful paper entitled, "Islands of the Blest." Professor Lacey made a suitable acknowledgement and read a letter from Professor Capps, who was unable to be present, expressing "the hope that the College may always foster with the exceptional care which in these days the liberal studies require, the ancient group of studies whose past has been so honorable and beneficent in education." For reasons that most readers are familiar with, that hope proved to be increasingly difficult of realization.

The gradual shrinkage of student interest in the classics would have distressed Dr. Rammelkamp had he lived to witness it, but that does not seem to have been the case with music. He personally en-

joyed the arts but did not find them essential to the educational
program of Illinois College. Reference was made earlier to the 1928
union of the conservatories of Illinois College and Illinois Woman's
College, soon to become MacMurray College. Dr. Rammelkamp
said that "this action caused some regret," but he justified it by saying that "Jacksonville is hardly large enough to provide patronage
for two music schools of high grade."

If one looks over the President's reports between the years 1923
and 1928, one finds regular deficits of a small but irritating kind in
the Conservatory accounts: $1143.97, $4319.80, $3738.00, $3749.00,
and $4841.06, respectively. Appended to one of those reports is
Rammelkamp's warning comment: "If the Conservatory of Music
cannot be made to pay its running expenses, some radical changes
will obviously have to be made." Generally a small surplus in the
over-all operations of the College covered the loss in the operation
of the Conservatory, but in 1927 the President had to report: "I regret that for the first time in sixteen years, I must report a deficit
in the financial operations of the College—$870.02. If the Conserva-
tory had simply paid its way there would, of course, have been no
deficit." The next year the Illinois College Conservatory was closed
out. I would hazard the guess that if the deficit had been occurring
in one of the academic disciplines another remedy would have been
found.

It is, I think, worth our while to examine briefly the terms on
which the merger was carried out. The contract is fairly complicated,
but the main points can be summarized thus: 1. It would take effect June 15, 1928, and would be in effect for a period of twenty-
five years. 2. The new conservatory, to be known as the Illinois
Conservatory of Music, would be under the direction of Illinois
Woman's College with an advisory committee consisting of members of the Boards of Trustees of both institutions, two from Illinois
College and three from Illinois Woman's College. 3. During the
period of the contract Illinois College would not conduct or sponsor
a school of music or employ any instructor of music, excepting for
directors of glee clubs and bands. The directors of the glee clubs
were to be members of the faculty of the Illinois Conservatory of
Music, unless the Conservatory had no one available for such duty,

in which case Illinois College might make its own choice. 4. All community choruses and orchestras were henceforth to be under the direction of the Illinois Conservatory of Music.

It is clear that Illinois College was so eager to "remedy" the deficits resulting from its instruction in music that it was willing to abandon the field altogether. True, there was to be a committee of trustees from the two colleges overseeing the whole operation, with the deciding vote however always in the control of the Illinois Woman's College. President Rammelkamp later reported that the arrangement "is proving on the whole satisfactory" but that "no meeting has ever been called of the joint Conservatory Committee of the two boards."

One might dismiss this arrangement as an unfortunate but necessary economic adjustment to the circumstance of time and place. It does, however, seem that a shorter period of time for a trial arrangement might have been negotiated. Failing that, there might have been greater care given to the need to give up so many options. For a period of twenty-five years, the College had almost no music on campus, except for a sporadic band and an occasional choir and an elementary music appreciation course taught by a faculty member of MacMurray College. I should like to add, however, that Illinois College was most fortunate to have teaching that one course a man of the calibre of Hugh Beggs, a fine pianist and an enthusiastic lover of music. Art fared no better during most of this period of decreed abstention from the arts. Thus a void developed that would have to be filled, with difficulty, at a later date.

An honor of more than personal importance came to Dr. Rammelkamp in May 1931, when he was granted the honorary degree of Doctor of Laws by the University of Illinois. The occasion was the inauguration of Harry Woodburn Chase as sixth president of the University of Illinois. Dr. Rammelkamp had been invited to extend greetings on behalf of the universities and colleges of the state. The unusual fact of this participation was that Charles Henry Rammelkamp had taken part in the inaugurations of President Chase's two predecessors, Edmund James in 1905 and David Kinley in 1920. Presenting Rammelkamp for his degree, Dean Babcock alluded to this distinction as well as others:

Charles Henry Rammelkamp, for twenty-six years president of
Illinois College and historian of the first century of its notable service
to higher education in Illinois and in the Mississippi Valley; staunch
supporter of historical scholarship as Trustee of the Illinois State Historical Society; and sagacious leader and councillor in educational
affairs in the North Central area. A son of New York, educated in
the broad traditions of Cornell University, and baptised into the
spirit of the West in California and in Illinois, he now welcomes for
the third time a new president of the University of Illinois who will
admit him to full membership in the Tribe of the Illini with all the
rights, privileges, and immunities thereunto belonging.

In his address, Dr. Rammelkamp noted the magnificent growth of
the University in both size and stature since he had first welcomed
President James, but he also noted the unique contributions of the
small colleges of the state and called on President Chase to continue
the fruitful relations that had been developed between public university and private college in the past.

Not all went smoothly during these final years of the Rammelkamp administration. The centennial fund had not been fully subscribed; so the development of Pitner Place for the women was not
undertaken; and the building of a new gymnasium had to be indefinitely postponed, although the Andrew Russel Field was gradually
improved and placed into use. The lack of a modern gymnasium
caused genuine inconvenience to the athletic program of the College.
There were makeshift arrangements for the use of the gymnasium
of the School for the Deaf, but this was a constant source of confusion and misunderstanding. The swimming team had no pool of
their own, either for practice or for meets, but were by the kindness
of the Superintendent of the School for the Deaf able to use that
school's pool.

There were also some internal frictions, within the Physical Education Department and between the Department and the administration and faculty. This matter was partly settled by the resignation
of William T. Harmon, the controversial Director of Athletics,
whose many and vehement supporters among students and alumni
brought pressure upon the administration and the board of trustees.
Even after a new Director of Athletics was appointed, there remained a legacy of suspicion that would surface in the next adminis-

tration. So far as I can determine, President Rammelkamp tried to remain neutral down to the end, even when appeals and counter-appeals were made to him while he was seriously ill. He seems to have valued sports as a means to *mens sana in corpore sano*, as an inculcator of wholesome college spirit, and as a part of the well-rounded life, but he would not permit athletics to assume such importance as to interfere with what he regarded as the main business of this or any college, the training of the mind.

Unquestionably the most significant and rewarding event of Rammelkamp's long administration, from an academic point of view, was the earning of a chapter of Phi Beta Kappa by Illinois College. How long this had been one of his goals is not certain, but knowing his methodical, careful planning in all matters, I assume that it had long been at the top of his list of desiderata. He wanted this mark of distinction very keenly and he worked for it consciously. In considering appointments for the faculty, he was pleased to uncover a wearer of the key among those eligible; it didn't assure appointment, but it helped. As an elected member of the Cornell University chapter, he attended triennial meetings of the United Chapters and he became acquainted with important members of the hierarchy. One of the reasons he worked so hard for the new library was his knowledge that this facility would be impressive to the Committee on Qualifications.

The report of Acting President Ames to the Board of Trustees in June 1932 summarizes the achievement very neatly: "The members of Phi Beta Kappa on the faculty resolutely waited until the completion of the new library before taking formal steps to bring the claims of Illinois College to the attention of the Senate of Phi Beta Kappa. From 1928 to 1931 several trips of inspection were made to the campus by the Secretary of Phi Beta Kappa and others. In 1930 a petition for a charter was sent to the officers by the members of the faculty who belonged to Phi Beta Kappa. This petition was approved by more than the requisite two-thirds of the chapters in the East Central District which comprises Ohio, Michigan, Indiana and Illinois. The petition was then approved by the Senate of Phi Beta Kappa, and finally by the Triennial Convention which met at Providence last September. [Charles Henry Rammelkamp was present at that meeting, of course.] The Epsilon of Illinois Chapter was installed on April 6, 1932." Thus Illinois College joined the select company which included at that time in the state of Illinois only the universities of Chicago, Illinois, and Northwestern and Knox College.

It is one of the dramatic ironies of the history of this college that Charles Henry Rammelkamp died the day before that event took place; he saw the promised land but he was not permitted to enter it. He was ill during the summer of 1931 and spent several weeks in hospital seeking relief and diagnosis. His painful seizures were attributed to gall stones, and he made frequent trips to St. Louis for consultation and treatment. It was eventually decided that surgery should be performed by the surgeon-in-chief at Barnes Hospital. An operation was performed in mid-October, but it was called "preliminary," and it was said that further surgery would be called for in the spring. Almost every issue of the *Rambler* carried news of the state of his convalescence, sometimes by letter from Mrs. Rammelkamp. After several setbacks, he did return home before Christmas, sent greetings to students and faculty, saying, "I feel confident I will join you in person after the holidays."

He was not able to do that, but kept sending hopeful messages and performing as much of the necessary work of his office as he could, with the help of his wife and his "agent," Professor Ames. The *Rambler* of March 5 reported that "Although still subject to relapses, President Rammelkamp has been growing stronger slowly, and was able to enjoy a part of the recent spring weather from the porch of his home. He celebrated his 58th birthday very quietly at home." In early April he sent the following message to the student body. It was read in chapel by Professor Ames:

During the past week my illness has so developed that the physicians have decreed an absolute "giving up" of all college business for the next two months. I am greatly disappointed in this, as I have been hoping each week that I might be able to announce a day for my return to my office. The complication which has arisen is serious, but not alarming, and I expect to be on hand in the fall.

In the meantime, I desire that all of your activities shall go on with their usual spirit and success. I may even look out of my window occasionally to enjoy a baseball game.

I wish, also, to express my deep appreciation of the spirit of loyalty and harmony which has characterized this year on the campus while I have been ill.

Devotedly yours,
C. H. Rammelkamp

A day later, April 5, he was dead of a cerebral thrombosis.

From all accounts, the College was nearly paralyzed, but it made every effort to carry on. At Mrs. Rammelkamp's request, the installation of the Epsilon Chapter of Phi Beta Kappa went on as scheduled, April 6, although the public banquet celebrating the event was cancelled. Many of the out-of-town delegates to the installation ceremonies, old friends of Charles Henry's, stayed for his funeral. Tributes and condolences poured in from all over the country, including those of the Governor of Illinois and other civic officials, from the academic world, including the president of the University of Illinois and other colleges and universities, the Secretary of the Association of American Colleges, from former colleagues, and of course from many alumni of the College. The funeral services were simple, with students and former students, faculty and trustees participating.

Charles Henry Rammelkamp was the second president of Illinois College to die in office, and this fact, along with the sense that his accomplishment, though splendid, was incomplete, gave special poignance to his death. I have tried throughout this chapter to evaluate the main contributions of his long and distinguished administration. I never knew him, but I have known and talked with many who did; I have also read much that was written about him. Perhaps the best way for me to summarize his career is to cite some of the tributes that were paid him, at the time of his death and later.

There were some formal, almost stilted, student tributes paid him in the *Rambler* at the time of his death:

Cautious even in his most progressive projects, President Rammelkamp would never sacrifice for ephemeral gains.

. . . .

Campus harmony and normality, athletics that place sportsmanship above victory, scholarship for the sake of learning and the betterment of human welfare—these are the goals Prexy has left us. We are staunch in the knowledge of an eminent past, we must be as staunch in the hope of a fair future that will fulfill the fondest wishes of the man who has given us no small portion of our college history.

Years later, although students of those times recalled his natural dignity, they have tended to recall also absurd things, lovable things, about the man. I have been told many stories of the pleasure he took in the annual November leaf-raking day, when students and faculty took an afternoon's holiday, formed teams, and competed to rake up previously marked sectors of the campus. There was much tomfoolery and occasional tossing of students and professors into piles of dried leaves; often there were bonfires, and then a picnic supper of hot dogs and cider, topped off by an informal dance in the old gymnasium. Mr. Rammelkamp was as playful as the youngsters on such occasions, and leaf-raking drew the College family together informally and intimately, as the Osage Orange Picnic had once done, before it became a carefully planned affair.

Another occasion recalled with much pleasure by old grads was the competition for "Prexy's Gumdrops," which took place during the late winter doldrums of February, along about the time of President Rammelkamp's birthday. In the earlier days when the campus population was quite small, the Rammelkamps invited the entire student body to their home for the evening. Each class would put on a skit, and the class that had the cleverest writers and performers would win a box of chocolates, known as "Prexy's Gumdrops." When the student body grew larger, the event was moved to the auditorium of Academy Hall, residence of the women. Somehow, away from the atmosphere of the president's home the skits grew more raucous and even rowdy, and were eventually discontinued. But not forgotten.

The alumni had their say concerning the man at Commencement, 1932. He was made one of them at that year's ceremonies, being awarded an honorary degree, Litt. D. *post obitum*. At the annual alumni luncheon, tributes to the late leader formed the major part of the program. Many of these were printed in the *Alumni Quarterly*, Summer 1932. Like the undergraduate tributes, some were solemn— and some were charmingly naive:

President Rammelkamp left nothing to chance. For twenty-seven years he moved steadily toward a sure goal. He possessed unlimited tenacity, gentle and considerate though his methods were. Such a man was not to be denied.

. . . .

I have lost a friend—the sort of friend one finds only once in a lifetime, too big to be snobbish, too true and sincere to slight even a poor, awkward country girl like me.

The Journal of the Illinois State Historical Society gave forty-five pages of its October 1932 issue to memorial tributes by a variety of hands: "Boyhood and Youth," by Merrill M. Barlow; "The Educator: An Appreciation," by Joe Patterson Smith; "Rammelkamp and his Board of Trustees," by Carl E. Black; "The Citizen," by Frank J. Heinl; and "Historical Contributions and Interests," by Clarence E. Carter. Dr. Black, who served as a trustee for many years, wrote:

In his Board of Trustees he carefully set up his several committees which he made real working units. Then he brought his plans to the appropriate committee. He always cemented to his proposals five or seven members of his Board of Trustees. Or if the committee could not support his proposal it was dropped for the time. He never tried to force any plan on his Board of Trustees until he was sure of it himself, and had the proper committee behind it. His methods were always simple, direct and complete.

He made membership on the board a pleasure and a privilege. All knew that he appreciated our suggestions and that he placed his own ideas before us completely for our honest criticism. The relations he established and maintained were delightful. He was so generous and so patient that support naturally flowed from his board to him.

Mr. Heinl and Mr. Carter wrote about his contributions to the Morgan County Historical Society, to the celebrations of the Illinois Centennial in 1918 and the Jacksonville Centennial in 1925, his service as trustee of the Illinois State Historical Library and director of the Illinois State Historical Society. Mr. Heinl, who was a member of the General Assembly of Illinois when Rammelkamp became president of Illinois College, notes that he "was attentive to educational legislation and particularly to the outlawing of diploma mills."

But no tributes paid him were more meaningful than those of the faculty he had presided over. They would have meant much to him, for no part of his administrative duties received more of his attention than did appointments to his faculty. He was proud of their success in the classroom and in their professional organizations. He brought to the faculty such long-time stalwarts as Robert Busey, Stella Cole, Raymond Lacey, Mary Louise Strong, and Leonora Tomlinson in the languages; Willis DeRyke, William Leavenworth, Earle Miller, and Isabel Smith in the sciences; Eleanor Miller, Frederick Oxtoby, Joe Patterson Smith, and John Stratton in the social studies; and Bill Harmon in physical education. Professor Joe Patterson Smith wrote of him:

He encouraged the faculty to attend the meetings of learned societies of which they were members both by attending the meetings of organizations he belonged to and by inducing the trustees to appropriate funds partially to defray the expense of such journeys.

He felt that all problems were capable of some satisfactory solution if a trained and disciplined mind considered all their ramifications. His deep human interest in the individual and his problems led many students and alumni to remark that Charles Henry Rammelkamp and Illinois College were synonymous.

I have left uncited numerous other judgments of this many-faceted man, but I should like to close this chapter by quoting from the eulogy of his closest friend and ally on the faculty. These words are drawn from the report of John Griffith Ames to the Board of Trustees in June 1932, two months after he had succeeded as Acting President:

Few can speak with more intimate knowledge than I of his character and his accomplishments inside the College which he loved so dearly, and for which he labored so unceasingly. I had the privilege and the honor of working with him throughout his entire years of devoted and self-sacrificing service, and what I say comes from the heart.

It was not given to him to found great institutions or to gather what in these days are considered vast endowments, but year by year we saw him steadily add to the slender endowment which the College had when he became president. Year by year we saw him balance his budgets and keep within them. The College business was always up so the trustees and faculty knew what to depend on. He never faltered, never lost heart, never complained. His reports were models of clearness, exactness and adequacy.

President Rammelkamp was noble with his faculty. Although always he was our guide, he was never dictatorial. To all our deliberations and debates he listened patiently and guided them skilfully, but in the end his constant word was, 'What does the faculty wish to do?' Of the students he was an equally excellent administrator, always ready to listen to their complaints, to answer their questions, and to help them solve their problems, and they admired and respected him deeply. Not the least of President Rammelkamp's achievements was his uniting in devoted service and loyalty to the College the large body of alumni and former students who, before he became President, were loyal indeed, but without a leader and not united.

With what zeal and devotion did President Rammelkamp guard the good name of Illinois College. How *proud* he was of her! In his history of Illinois College, a model of sound learning, he is prone to pass lightly over his own accomplishments and give unstinted praise to his predecessors. A smaller man would have written differently.

May God grant that his noble spirit may long guide the destinies of his loved College.

Depression: Failure of the Ayers National Bank

Anyone who lived through the Great Depression has vivid memories of that time and has no need of reminders from me. However, those who are too young to have such memories and want a sense of what it was like can hardly do better than to riffle through the pages of a magazine like *The Literary Digest*; failing that they can read the more accessible *Hard Times* by Studs Terkel, published in 1970. Persons with whom I have talked about the decade of 1929–39 at Illinois College have usually told me that Jacksonville was almost insulated from the national disaster. There was no single manufacturing plant employing a large portion of the working population that shut down or went into bankruptcy. The largest single employer was the family-owned Capps Clothing Company, Ltd., and it survived the thirties nicely—so nicely that when I arrived in Jacksonville in September 1939 Capps was having a gala centennial celebration, complete with parades and pageants and banquets.

Moreover, the town is in the midst of a rich agricultural area, and although prices of commodities had fallen and cash income was down and farm mortgages were being foreclosed, most people survived tolerably well. One student who lived at Academy Hall at the time told me that she remembered a year when the only fruit served in the commons there for months on end was watermelon. A student whose father raised melons had told the business manager of the College that he could pay his daughter's tuition in melons but not in cash. The business manager being both prudent and understanding made a deal, and the basement of Academy Hall was filled with watermelons that graced the tables of the commons for breakfast, lunch, and dinner. Forty years later, the woman who told me this story said that she still could not look at, let alone eat, a watermelon with any relish.

But even the low cost of living in the dormitories and eating in a budget commons was too much for some students. Some lived in private homes, caring for furnaces, doing laundry, acting as cooks and bottlewashers and babysitters. A number of young men lived in barn lofts scattered throughout the west end of town. These places were cold and unfurnished, without bathing or toilet facilities, but the boys got by, with a little scrounging of food and occasional baths here and there in friendly bathrooms. The director of athletics at the time had recruited some of his football team in the coal-mining towns downstate. The College had a policy, then and now, of no athletic scholarships, and couldn't have afforded them even if it had not had the policy. But Coach Van Meter was not willing to let these husky boys get away; so he started what was known as The Student Coal Company. He bought some old trucks, ordered coal from selected mines where the boys' fathers worked, and had the coal delivered by members of his football team. He even got the College contract for the Student Coal Company. There were some protests from local merchants over infringing practices of this kind, but on the whole town and gown were in this mess together, and they worked things out. In fact, a good many town businessmen employed students at depressed wages, to the mutual benefit of both parties.

Another buffer between Jacksonville and the economic troubles that were engulfing the country was the presence in town of three large state institutions, which had been here for nearly a century: the School for the Deaf, the School for the Blind, and the State Hospital for the Insane. They are here still, under different, more palatable names. Given their special missions, all of these institutions required rather large staffs, with a small cadre of highly trained professional people and large numbers of semiskilled custodial help. The payrolls of these institutions were not as large as they would be today, but the money came from outside the community, and it was very steady, and that steadiness helped to stabilize the economy of the whole community. Finally, the two local colleges also brought in money from outside and added to the modest prosperity of Jacksonville. There were salary cuts, to be sure, and some retrenchment all along the line, but there was no general depressed condition or despair.

Immediately after the death of President Rammelkamp, the Board of Trustees appointed Professor Ames acting president; they also created a committee on selection, hoping to be able to have a new president on campus the following fall. That was unlikely unless there was a candidate ready and waiting in the wings. Apparently there was none, although Professor Ames was well qualified through long acquaintance with the College and past experience with its administrative functions. He had spent two years on the campaign trail for the centennial building and endowment fund in 1925–26 and 1928–29, a year as acting president while the Rammelkamps were abroad in 1929–30, and he had been the president's "agent" during Rammelkamp's illness in 1931–32. He was, however, not of the executive temperament, having too much of Mr. Chips in him.

I remember that when I first came to Illinois College in the fall of 1939, the English department gave, as it had for many years, the Purdue Placement Test in English, to incoming freshmen. That test was one of those multiple-choice affairs, with lots of little squares to be filled in; largely on the basis of results in this test, we singled out a dozen or so students for an advanced placement section of freshman composition, with the rest going into regular sections. We had, I am happy to say, no remedial or "dumbbell" sections. There was on the test sheet a place marked "class" where apparently the student was to write some such thing as "freshman" or "class of '43." Mr. Ames asked me and my colleagues, Miss Hastings and Mr. Donahoe, to be very careful to have each candidate write in that spot his exact date of birth, as "3/12/21" or whatever. When we had all finished grading the exams and determined the relative level of preparation of our new students, Mr. Ames made out a separate 3 × 5 card for each student, with pertinent information recorded, and especially that birthdate. These he filed chronologically, not alphabetically; he carried the cards of the current month in his coat pocket.

Mr. Ames and I shared an office in Jones Chapel. He would occasionally ask me whether I knew a Clara Belle Miller, let us say. If I did, he would ask me to point her out as she came into Jones. He would then station himself at the chapel exit and he would hail her in a very courtly way and say, "Happy birthday, Miss Miller, and many happy returns of the day!" I saw this happen often, with both men and women, though I think he enjoyed it more with the women. There was usually a look of puzzlement, or at least surprise, on the face of the person addressed, followed by a warm smile and "Thanks!" It struck me then and it still does as one of those little important gestures of personal recognition that can be made on a small campus. It was the Johnny Ames, the Mr. Chips, touch.

This was the man at the helm when the greatest calamity ever to befall Illinois College struck. I would gladly omit this chapter if I could, but I cannot. I ask the reader to bear with me if I use an approach different from those I have used before or shall use hereafter. I mean to report the facts as accurately as I can, but I shall not spell out the names of some of the principals in this sad drama. I shall use titles instead. They are all, these unfortunate people, long dead, but they do have descendants who still have connections with the College and the community, and those people remain sensitive to the events I am about to relate. Readers who know the actual names will fill them in as they read, no doubt. But those who do not will be none the poorer.

The Ayers National Bank was the largest, most prestigious bank in the whole area. Ayers was thought to be as solid as a bank could be. It was the depository of most of the operating funds of Illinois College and of various ancillary organizations like the Athletic Association, the literary societies, the *Rambler*, and others. In its safe deposit vaults were the stocks and bonds and other securities of the College endowment. It was thought that the financial affairs of the College were in good hands. That is, until November 1932, when it was discovered that the College had placed great trust in three men who were in fact not worthy of that trust. All three were prominent citizens of Jacksonville, officers of the Ayers National Bank, and long identified with Illinois College in a variety of ways. All three were engaged in activities which would bring ruin to themselves and their families, bankruptcy to the bank, and near disaster to the College. To distinguish them without revealing their identity, let me call them by appropriate titles. First, the president of the Ayers National Bank; he had formerly been a trustee of the College, but had resigned when his friend William Jennings Bryan left the Board over the question of approaching Carnegie and Rockefeller for grants to the College. I shall refer to him as President. Second, the former chairman of the Illinois College Board of Trustees, who had only recently retired as chairman but remained on the board. He was a director of the Ayers Bank. I shall refer to him as Former Chairman. Third, a man who was cashier of the Ayers Bank, and was also treasurer of the College. I shall refer to him as Cashier/Treasurer. There were others involved, but these were the principal culprits, so far as this story is concerned.

The President and the Former Chairman ran, in addition to their capacities with the Ayers National Bank, a private investment company under their own names. I understand that their operations in this private venture were highly speculative; one of my informants told me they "ran a bucket shop." It seems that when their speculative ventures did not pan out, they had to borrow various sums of money to tide them over. To borrow money, they needed collateral. Here is where the Cashier/Treasurer came into the picture. He was younger and less affluent than the other two; he was also in the process of establishing himself in the financial circles of the community. Under the circumstances, he was vulnerable to any influence his seniors cared to bring upon him.

When the President and the Former Chairman needed to float a large loan, they would require the Cashier/Treasurer to remove from the College safety box in the Ayers Bank securities sufficient to use as collateral. How often this may have happened, I have been unable to discover, but it had apparently happened more than once over a period of years, without discovery. When the finance committee of the College Board of Trustees had reason to look into the deposit box—whether to clip some coupons or make a change in the College's holdings—the Cashier/Treasurer would be asked to meet the committee at an appointed hour for the purpose. If he knew that any of the College holdings were being used by the President and

Former Chairman in their private enterprise, he could stall for a time until the "borrowed" securities had been returned. In June of 1932, however, the President and Former Chairman had more than the usual need for collateral. They floated loans for $295,000 with three separate banks: $85,000 from one, $110,000 from another, and $100,000 from still another. As collateral they hypothecated $504,000 in negotiable bonds of the Illinois College endowment funds. It was not likely that the finance committee would want access to the College safety deposit box during the summer months, and it was expected that before they did, the loans could be paid off, and the half-million dollar parcel of securities repossessed.

Something went wrong, however, and the loans were not repaid, and the bonds were not repossessed. The whole tangled skein of deception began to unravel when one of the notes held by a Chicago bank came due and the President of the Ayers National Bank attempted to renew it. Inquiries were made that revealed irregularities; the officers of the Chicago bank called Dr. George Baxter, Chairman of Illinois College's Board of Trustees, into conference. After hearing the main outlines of this series of events, Dr. Baxter informed three of his colleagues on the board, and they met in Chicago to consider what to do.

Shortly thereafter, a special and urgent meeting of the Illinois College Board of Trustees was called in Jacksonville—the required three-day notice was waived—and Dr. Baxter reported the following facts to all his colleagues: that in the presence of the vice-president of the First National Bank of Chicago and the attorney for that bank, he had been informed by the president of the Ayers National Bank of Jacksonville that the Cashier/Treasurer had turned over to him certain bonds belonging to Illinois College in the amount of $504,000 par value and that the President in collusion with the Former Chairman had signed notes with three banks, respectively: the First National Bank of Chicago, the First National Bank of St. Louis, and the Stockyards National Bank, for the total sum of $295,000. Subsequently, this information was confirmed in the presence of Dr. Baxter and trustees Walter Bellatti, Harry Dunbaugh, and Frank Elliott, and Attorney Jacob L. Fox, by both the President and the Cashier/Treasurer. I have been told that the Former Chairman was in California at the time these events transpired but that his later testimony did not materially alter the confessions made by the other two.

The Board of Trustees of Illinois College thereupon took the following action: (1) Notification was sent to the three lending banks of the interest of Illinois College in the bonds used as collateral. (2) All other securities held by the Cashier/Treasurer on behalf of Illinois College were removed from his control and dispatched to the Harris Trust and Savings Bank of Chicago, where they were to be held in safekeeping. (3) The liquid funds of the College in a checking account at the Ayers National Bank were to be transferred to a new account at the Elliott State Bank of Jacksonville. (4) Conferences were held with the President, the Former Chairman, and the Cashier/Treasurer, as a result of which each man executed and delivered to the College a deed to his own residence property in Jacksonville and certain other properties, as partial restitution for the losses suffered by the College. (5) The College retained the services of an independent attorney [there were several highly competent lawyers on the Board] who would "protect the interests of the College" by pursuing every avenue that might lead to the restitution of the misappropriated securities. (6) Resignations from the Illinois College Board of Trustees were received from the Former Chairman and the Cashier/Treasurer. They were accepted.

These were the main actions taken by the Illinois College Board of Trustees at the special meeting, Sunday, November 20, 1932. The following Monday morning the Ayers National Bank did not open its doors. It was placed in receivership, and after several years of litigation, approximately 25 percent of the claims against it were paid off. The technicalities of the receivership and the litigation over it are not relevant to our inquiry, nor are the civil and criminal trials which resulted. The three men in question, pillars of Jacksonville and of Illinois College, were found guilty in varying degrees and received appropriate penalties under the law. These matters were to cause great anxiety and grief in the community and on the campus at the time and for many years thereafter. There were those who thought that if the College authorities had not acted so promptly and vigorously when the defalcation was first discovered, it was possible that the private investment company might have been able to pay off its loans, restore the College securities, and avoid bankruptcy and receivership. I am told that a prominent local attorney dismissed this kind of speculation indignantly: "When you see someone running down the street with the family silver, you don't just hope that he will return it when it has served his purpose. You yell 'Stop Thief!'" It should also be noted that any dallying of the trustees would have made them collaborators in the felony. It was not something to be trifled with.

It should be said here that the College eventually recovered all but about $140,000 of its lost funds. This happened over a period of years, and at considerable expense in money, time, and energy. The College contended, and the courts eventually upheld the contention, that securities removed from a bank's safety deposit vaults were in a different category from money lost to depositors in savings and checking accounts, through the bank's default. The College and many of its officers and employees suffered the latter kind of loss and were treated in the same way as everyone else, but the theft of the securities from deposit boxes placed that matter in a special category. Unfortunately, there were some in the community who, in spite of the decision of the courts, erroneously thought that the College had used its influence to win special treatment.

The immediate loss in income suffered by the College was about $30,000 a year, though that was later reduced by more than half. Acting President Ames had not only to suffer the trauma of these events, but he had also to report to the Board at their semiannual meeting, December 17, 1932:

The business manager of the College and I spent the entire evening of Tuesday, November 15, in going over the financial situation of the College, comparing all items of income and expense with those of a similar date of the year preceding. We retired full of joy in the confident expectation that continuing to operate as the College had been operating since last May, we could report to the Trustees in June a surplus larger than that of June, 1932. The spirit and atmosphere of the whole College, students as well as faculty, was unusually fine, enthusiastic and cooperative; student activities were flourishing, the football team had far surpassed its record of the previous year, the attendance was surprisingly larger, and the faculty were enthusiastic and wholeheartedly devoted to the work of instruction. Then, on November 21st, out of a clear sky fell the blow with which you are familiar, changing our prospects of a small surplus to a large deficit.

The Acting President and the Board went to work to repair as much of the damage as they could. Letters were dispatched to the General Education Board and to the Carnegie Corporation, pointing out the size and nature of the calamity that had befallen the College, and asking for special help, at least for a few years, while the College attempted through legal means to restore its lost endowment funds. Both foundations responded negatively, calling attention to the fact that other colleges and universities were suffering the effects of the general depression, and though sympathetic to the Illinois College cause, they could not make exceptions—they had no funds to help make up deficits.

Almost immediately, the authorities took steps to reduce expenditures, since income was inevitably going down. Acting President Ames, with the support of a faculty committee made up of Professors Stratton, Smith, and DeRyke, appealed to the Board not to further cut faculty salaries—a 5 percent reduction was already in effect. As the economics professor put it, in terms that the whole country was learning to consider respectable: "Better a temporarily unbalanced budget than a lowering of standards!" Nonetheless, an additional 5 percent cut was levied on the faculty and staff for the months of March, April, and May of 1933.

Nothing could be done about reducing the staff for the academic year then in progress, but "faculty adjustments" were decreed for the year 1933–34: the College would operate without a Dean, it would have to get along without an assistant professor in physics and mathematics, and three instructors in history, French, and Latin, respectively. In addition, leave of absence was granted to the Acting President (one suspects that Johnny Ames needed a leave by then) on terms that were something less than generous, although the minutes record that those terms were suggested by Mr. Ames himself. Very simply, the terms were these: the College would pay Mr. Ames's salary and he would pay that of his replacement.

As a result of these and other small retrenchments, the Chairman of the Board was able to announce to the College constituency at Commencement, 1933:

Loyal trustees, alumni and friends have generously come to the assistance of the College and helped make up the depleted income so that the Trustees point with pride to the fact that the College is ending the year without a deficit.

All of the friends of the College should know that whatever the ultimate shrinkage in the invested assets of the College may be as a result of the unauthorized hypothecation of the bonds, it will not operate to diminish in any way the amounts standing to the credit of the endowment funds of the College; that the endowment is and must be as abiding as the institution itself; and that the hundred and four years of its great history of service to education, its physical equipment, its buildings and campus, and its invested funds will continue to be behind every dollar contributed by friends and alumni.

Those were brave words but of course it wouldn't be as simple as all that. There are pathetic tales and wretched tales and some heroic tales told of this bleak event and its consequences to College and community. It can be summed up this way, I think: that the considerable monetary losses were wholly outweighed by the moral loss, the loss of confidence that the citizens of the community and the constituents of the College suffered, in themselves and each other. The malefactors were not off in New York or Chicago or even Springfield; they were right here in our midst and there was no gainsaying their guilt, nor explaining it away. The College was a principal loser, not only in the financial sense but in the larger sense of standing for real values, intellectually and socially. It was the shock of recognition that such things could happen here, in Jacksonville, done by Jacksonvillians. It took time to be reconciled to this tragic fact. But it was done, slowly and painfully, and genuine recovery did come. That was the eventual victory, and final triumph, for community and College.

19

President Jaquith, 1933–1937

While these unhappy events were unfolding, the Presidential Selection Committee of the Board of Trustees was trying to find a suitable person to become the seventh president of Illinois College. It must have been a very difficult task. The College certainly needed strong moral and fiscal leadership if it was to survive the disaster, but the reason for that need only complicated the task of attracting the right man. (I don't find any evidence that a woman was seriously considered, though I believe Mrs. Rammelkamp's name was mentioned.) What was needed was someone of stature and integrity from outside the community; someone young, vigorous, and ready to do battle for the cause of Christian liberal education; someone of vision who could see beyond the present morass and who could make new friends for the College while restoring the confidence of old friends. Search committees always set very high standards and then come as close as possible to realizing them.

There were said to be many candidates; the problem was to locate one with the above qualifications who was available, willing to dream the impossible dream, and then go to work to achieve it. A very interesting candidate was suggested by Professor Edward Capps of Princeton University. Dr. Capps's connections with Illinois College have been mentioned before, but deserve repeating at this juncture. A graduate of the College, he had served on its faculty, been for many years the chairman of the very successful Alumni Fund Association, and would later be elected a trustee of the College by the Alumni Association. In his honor the Capps Chair of Classics had been established in 1930. He also kept in intimate touch with the College throughout the years because he was President Rammelkamp's brother-in-law. In fact, Capps was to Rammelkamp what Theron Baldwin had been to Julian Sturtevant, an attentive listener, a thoughtful counselor. Who could more knowledgeably suggest the right man for the presidency at this critical time than Edward Capps?

It was planned by the Presidential Selection Committee to bring leading candidates to the campus on some appropriate assignment so that they could see and be seen by the academic community—the students, faculty, and trustees—without being known generally as candidates. In mid-December of 1932, less than a month after the collapse of the Ayers Bank, Harold Clarence Jaquith was thus brought to the campus for two days. As the *Rambler* stated later: "He stepped from a train at 4 A.M., December 16, after a night of hard travel, and yet appeared on the chapel platform at 9:45 A.M., looking fresh and cheery, to deliver one of the simplest and most interesting chapel talks of the year. With a few deft touches, by limiting his outline to three concrete, isolated pictures of the Near East, he yet managed to convey a complete and vivid panorama of the entire Near East and the relief work with which he has had so much to do. In the short time he spent on the campus—known to the student body as a distinguished visitor, not as a candidate for the presidency—he made so favorable an impression that the unanimity with which the Trustees made their offer to him could not fail to be duplicated among the students."

Born in Nashua, New Hampshire, and educated in the schools of that city, Mr. Jaquith was a graduate of Trinity College, Hartford, Connecticut. He held a Bachelor of Divinity degree from Union Theological Seminary and an M.A. in sociology from Columbia University. He began his career as Assistant Pastor in charge of Religious Education and Administration at the First Presbyterian Church of New York City. He had been involved with Near East relief during and after World War I and been director of overseas administration in Constantinople and Athens. (It was on this assignment that Edward Capps had met him, when Capps was working with the In-

President Harold C. Jaquith

ternational Red Cross.) At the time of his being considered for the presidency of Illinois College, he was Executive Officer and National Secretary of the Near East Foundation, with offices in New York.

He had published in *Current History, Review of Reviews, The Social Service Review*, and was a member of several learned societies. Save for his lack of a Ph.D. degree, he seemed admirably equipped in the academic sense. He was forty-four years old, married to a charming and cultivated woman of Russian origin, father of two young children, a member of the Presbyterian Church; socially, he was totally acceptable. He had been largely responsible for raising and spending thirty million dollars for work in the Near East. What more could one ask? He was offered the post as a result of action taken at the mid-winter meeting of the Illinois College Board of Trustees.

Accepting the challenge of a mid-career change of responsibilities, he wrote to the Chairman of the Board:

It has not been easy to make the decision to accept the Presidency of Illinois College. For sixteen years I have been happily affiliated with one task and associated with a group of friendly co-workers. My life has become entwined in a thousand silken threads, both in America and the Near East. I shall not try to untie them all, for the Near East with memories of the past and interesting changes of the present, will always remain a major interest in my outlook on world affairs.

Now, in turning westward, I know Mrs. Jaquith and I will make a host of new friends. We will find full satisfaction in new responsibilities and new objectives. We can only dedicate our best efforts to the common purpose to which you yourselves are committed.

Mr. Jaquith arrived in Jacksonville as president-elect on May 15, 1933, and was given a most cordial welcome. He had stopped off in Chicago to address the annual dinner meeting of the Chicago Alumni Society. He had been escorted down to Springfield by Acting President Ames and Business Manager Merrill Barlow. At Springfield he was welcomed by Faculty Secretary Earle Miller. Then he was brought to Jacksonville where the whole College family was assembled in the central square. A parade was formed and he was escorted to the president's house on campus. One of the placards in that parade bore the legend: "Everything's Jake now!"

He spent the rest of that first week getting acquainted and indoc-
trinated. A special chapel was arranged, where he was greeted by the
presidents of the four undergraduate classes, by a representative of
the women on the campus, and by the dean of the faculty, Raymond
Lacey. As reported in the *Rambler*, Dean Lacey's remarks were both
unsettling and reassuring: "This is a faculty on which there is no
agreement on almost every question. We speak our minds without
hesitation. As a body we pledge you our whole-hearted support."
(The phrasing of that first sentence does not sound like a dean's
phrasing, but the sentiment rings true enough; so we may let it pass.)
It is no wonder that Mr. Jaquith is reported to have said that "he felt
like a flyer landing in a strange country." He asked the students to
regard him for the time being as a person getting used to things,
rather than as a full-fledged president.

Other things he did that first week: he went to Springfield to hear
testimony given before a committee of the Illinois State Legislature
on a bill that would require the normal schools of Carbondale,
Charleston, DeKalb, Macomb, and Normal to charge tuition; he
threw out the first baseball at a home game; he accompanied the track
team to an out-of-town meet; he attended a reception and dance
given in his honor by the students; he tried to get acquainted with
campus, faculty, trustees, and townspeople. He must have felt thoroughly inducted by the time commencement came along, and he was
given the opportunity to make the principal address.

On that occasion, Dr. Jaquith paid tribute to the pioneers who had
founded the College and also to his immediate predecessors, President Rammelkamp and Acting President Ames. (I call him "Dr."
now because nearby Blackburn College was so thoughtful as to grant
him an honorary degree shortly before he addressed his first commencement at Illinois College.) Then Dr. Jaquith reviewed the state
of the world since 1914 when he had received his degree from Columbia University; he noted the false optimism of that prewar commencement and tried to find some useful lessons in the terrible war
and the great depression that followed the war: "We are penitent,
as never before, realizing that we all lived on false hopes, builded our
castles on sinking sands, leaned on breaking reeds, and have fallen
on a common disaster. We recognize that this depression, through

which we have passed or are passing, is something other than an inevitable business cycle. . . . We will fight to control the forces of our economic existence. We are in revolt against any theory of any group of persons that bids us supinely await an unhappy fate." He concluded this address by linking himself with the Illinois College faculty and in their behalf giving the graduating class a ringing send-off: "Let me assure you members of the senior class that each one of us who has transmitted to you our knowledge, our experience from life, will follow each of you with pride as you march onward, rejoicing that we have had some small part in inspiring and guiding you into a more abundant life, devoted to the good of all mankind." It was not exactly an original thesis, but it must have been thought a good beginning by those who were assembled in the College grove that afternoon. In view of these salutatory words, it will be interesting to trace the course of the next four years in the history of Illinois College.

The new president recognized that he was dwelling midst alien corn, and he decided to get well acquainted with his region and his constituency before making any radical moves. During the opening days of the fall term, he gave half his office time to interviewing individually each member of the freshman class; what he learned from these interviews has not come down to us, but certainly the freshmen must have sensed his earnestness and have been flattered by it. Upperclassmen were invited in small groups to the president's house and were entertained there by the Jaquiths and made to feel at home. Faculty members of the period have told me there was more social activity in the president's house than there had been for some time. (Of course, Dr. Rammelkamp's illness and his year abroad and before that his preoccupation with the College centennial had reduced the opportunities for entertaining during the later Rammelkamp years.) Both of the Jaquiths made special efforts to get acquainted in the community by addressing civic and church groups, he on topics relating to the Near East, and she describing various phases of life in Russia. They were doing public relations for the College as well as for themselves.

One of Dr. Jaquith's interesting experiments was the writing of a weekly column in the *Rambler*; it went under different titles, but was

usually just labeled "Prexy's Column." I have read all of them and
found them an interesting potpourri, containing some of his reflec-
tions on international affairs, on matters educational, on campus
athletic successes, and sometimes engaging in the kind of general
uplift that a Norman Vincent Peale or an Earl Nightengale might
effect. I have no way of measuring their impact on either students
or faculty, but I would guess it to have been rather small. Interest
in the column must have risen, especially when he took issue with
something that the *Rambler* had said editorially. There is no reason
why a president should not write occasionally for the campus newspaper, but I think it takes a very great deal of sensitivity and tact to
do it successfully on a regular basis. President Jaquith gave up the
practice after a time, and no one commented either favorably or unfavorably on this decision. I suspect both sides were relieved.

   Dr. Jaquith used the occasion of his inauguration November 10,
1933, to let the world know that Illinois College was ready to re-
establish its place in the world of higher education. It was one of the
more carefully planned inaugurations in the College's history. In
view of recent events, both locally and nationally—Franklin D.
Roosevelt had just been elected president of the United States—the
Board of Trustees thought that this should be something more than
the carriage ride through town that had placed Charles Henry Rammelkamp in the driver's seat more than a quarter century ago. Delegates representing more than seventy institutions of higher learning,
including Harvard, Yale, and Princeton, and church and learned societies attended the affair; there were messages of good will from
many others. The editor of the *New York Times*, a good friend of the
Jaquith family, sent a rather cute telegram: "The Presidents and the
Deans depart, Still stand the Jaquiths in our heart. We Finleys of
the Middle West Send you our New York, Near East, best." Other,
more conventional tributes were received and read at a banquet preceding the formal ceremonies.

   There was no place on campus large enough to hold the inaugural
assembly; so it was held in the auditorium of Jacksonville High
School. Following the academic procession, the President of Blackburn College offered the invocation, and then Dr. Baxter, Chairman

of the Illinois College Board of Trustees, made a graceful presentation of the new president to College and community, saying among other things:

> In the short space of time since he assumed the office of President, he has demonstrated to the board of trustees and faculty that our judgment of him was sound and that our confidence is well placed.
>
> It is my duty, as chairman of the Board of Trustees, and it is my personal privilege and pleasure, to formally and officially proclaim your appointment, Dr. Harold C. Jaquith, as President of Illinois College and to declare that you now assume the duties, responsibilities and honor which that high office confers upon you.

President Jaquith responded by saying that he hoped to continue the orderly progress of the College "to the end that it may be worthy of its history of one hundred and four years." He was grateful to have "the most sacred heirlooms" entrusted to his care. He went on to say:

> I am not unmindful that in the days that lie ahead of us, when more cooperation will be demanded to keep education abreast·of the changes that must inevitably come in industry, in business, in government, for a widening of the benefits of our mechanized, agricultural age, that colleges, universities and normal schools will face delicate problems of readjustment, supplementation and growth. . . .
>
> Neither am I unmindful of the problems that have arisen because of the increasing demand and rapid growth of various kinds of higher educational institutions. These problems concern the place and function of the university, the liberal arts college, the normal school, and an efficacious division of the duties of institutions of higher learning.

He made passing references to ruthless competition among these institutions for money and students and athletic prestige, and then he said:

> The technical knowledge required today is infinitely more exacting than ever before. The economic forces to be harnessed and controlled are larger and more titanic than even those of the last generation. New and closer association of people of the world place a new tension on human intercourse.
>
> We must live together in an old world and a new world. It is our

business to make life worth living today and tomorrow. Our task is to combine the old and the new with faith in the ultimate destiny of mankind in a common brotherhood for all, with the enthusiasm of youth "to set fire itself ablaze," to sustain the fires of courageous living in a doubtful, bewildered world, with satisfaction at the close of life that we have made the best contribution to the common good within the capacity of our individual personalities.

It would be hard to quarrel with those sentiments, but they are not specific enough to form a program for the development of Illinois College. The principal address of the evening was made by Robert Maynard Hutchins, the colorful and sometimes controversial president of the University of Chicago. He said some provocative things, as may be imagined: "Colleges have a tendency to ornament their catalogues with lists of Ph.D.'s instead of with good teachers. Here they are trying to look like universities. But at the same time they exhibit a contrary tendency, which frequently makes them look like high schools. Their attitude toward their students, and it is the attitude of most universities, too, suggests that they regard them as children, as receptacles for information, as persons who cannot learn, but must be taught." He concluded with a formula and a charge:

The depressing urge to conformity which James Bryce noted afflicting our American cities afflicts our institutions of higher learning too. There is a place, and a great place, for the college of liberal arts. But it will not be found by imitating the size, the staff, the student body, the curriculum or the atmosphere of the university, the high school, the junior college, the normal school, or any other educational unit. The college must discover the bases of a liberal education. Disdaining all others it must, as Illinois has done, adopt the policy of giving that education on the highest level to those who are qualified to achieve it. Never did the country need that service as much as it does today. The colleges, and this college, Mr. President, may perform it if they will. The Kingdom of Heaven is within you.

Just how President Jaquith understood President Hutchins' advice, I do not know, but he certainly did not follow it. And he may have been right not to, for it was an elitist college that Hutchins espoused.

It does appear that there was a desire on the part of the president to give new emphasis to the athletic program of the College. This may have been President Jaquith's way of attracting attention to the College, or it may have been an outcome of recent appointments in that department. In any case, the director of athletics, LaRue Van Meter, and his assistant, Ray Nusspickle, were both aggressive sponsors of sports, Teddy Roosevelt types, who thought that manly competitiveness was next to godliness. The president's interest in sports was expressed by his endorsement of a more ambitious program for the teams and high praise for the coaches. His support was rewarded by an unusual string of victories in almost all intercollegiate competition. In the year 1934–35, for example, the football team won six out of seven games played, losing only to Macomb Teachers by a narrow margin. The basketball team won all but one game and claimed its first Little Nineteen championship in history, with outstanding performances by men like "Too-Tall" Louis Lasiter and Vergil Fletcher. The President wrote: "The basketball team has shown real courage, ability, unity, and loyalty. It has reflected great credit to the College, and every student and faculty member is proud to share in its achievement. It has been superbly directed."

The baseball team performed well also, losing only to Normal and Eastern Teachers. The swimming team took the Little Nineteen championship several years running, though they had no pool of their own for practice or for competition. They became famous throughout the region as the "Poolless Wonders." Tennis also had a winning season, losing only to Normal and Macomb Teachers. In 1935–36 Illinois College teams won conference championships in swimming, golf, and baseball. If the President praised the teams and the coaches, the coaches reciprocated. When Ray Nusspickle moved on to the University of Illinois, where he became nationally famous as Ray Eliot, he paid high tribute to the administration of Illinois College: "It has been a pleasure to work in an institution that has been so capably directed by a person of the calibre of President H. C. Jaquith. His clear vision, his sincere cooperation, and his able guidance have been of the same inestimable aid in my department as they have been in all other divisions of the school."

President Jaquith not only encouraged Van Meter and Nusspickle on campus, but he was one of the leaders in the movement to create a new and more workable intercollegiate athletic conference. The so-called "Little Nineteen" was too big, too heterogeneous, too widely scattered geographically to be a workable small college conference. Moreover, the old conference included the normal schools, about which President Jaquith had almost an obsession. So, with the support of his faculty committee on athletics, he worked to produce a new and more effective conference. This meant the breakup of the Little Nineteen and the formation of the Illinois College Conference consisting of Augustana, Bradley, Illinois Wesleyan, Knox, Lake Forest, Millikin, Monmouth, North Central, Wheaton, and Illinois College. The new conference also required adoption of the freshman rule, which bars first-year men from varsity competition. In the long run, this tended to handicap the smaller colleges in the conference, including especially Illinois College, but the conference realignment must be regarded as one of President Jaquith's undeniable achievements while in office. Some of the faculty urged him to work for a conference that would develop more than athletic interchange, but in this he was not successful.

On academic matters, the new president's leadership was less firm. In his opening address of the 1933–34 academic year to the faculty, he made a plea for close cooperation between faculty and administration, and he even said that he wanted close contact between faculty and board members; to bring this about, he proposed a regular dinner meeting in connection with the midwinter meeting of the Board, so that faculty and trustees could discuss common problems. This was a novel idea, but it does not seem to have produced any clear-cut results.

Very early, the president asked chairmen of standing committees of the faculty to state in writing the purposes and procedures of their individual committees. This sounds like the "job-description" gimmick that business and government find so attractive. The most obvious outcome of this exercise seems to have been a complete overhaul of the faculty committee structure the following year, 1934–35. The thirteen standing committees of the faculty were cut back to seven, one of which was a new committee called the Administrative Council, chaired by the president, and including the deans of the College, of men, and of women. This makes sense from a purely administrative point of view, but it was a decided change from the Rammelkamp policy of asking: "What does the faculty wish to do?"

The other and even more threatening change was the establishment of a committee replacing the curriculum committee. The new committee would be known as the Educational Policies Committee, and it would consist of a representative cross section of the academic disciplines, under a chairman representing the administration. This committee still exists, and is generally regarded as the premier committee of the faculty, for almost all matters of academic policy are thrashed out there before being presented to the whole faculty for action. Today it is composed of two members from each of the three divisions of the curriculum—(1) language, literature, and the arts; (2) physical sciences; (3) social studies—elected by their own divisions for two-year terms on an alternating yearly basis. That is, there is always a senior member from each division and a junior member who will become senior member in his second year on the committee. This permits continuity of policy making along with orderly change. The committee is chaired by the academic dean of the College. This is how "ed-pol" has evolved, and it is, I believe, accepted as a fair and democratic way of establishing and developing curriculum.

President Jaquith's Educational Policies Committee was appointed by him, and he made himself chairman of the committee. I find no specific objections to this procedure in the minute books of the time, but I can imagine that it and other changes caused immediate and lasting misgivings. Of the thirteen former committees, seven of them were gone, along with their coveted chairmanships. The duties of the defunct committees were either assigned to existing committees or to faculty advisors, as was done with debate and music, for instance. Of the six committees that remained, one had been decidedly altered, with the president himself in the chair. I have come to the conclusion that this arbitrary reform—and I am sure that the president regarded it as a reform—marked the beginning of Dr. Jaquith's problems with his faculty that would eventually produce a serious split between administration and faculty and within the faculty itself.

Other changes were produced by other studies. Perhaps the most important study made on any campus is the one that is mandated by the decennial visit of the accrediting body of the region in which the college is located. Illinois College was one of the institutions that founded the North Central Association, and although for a time it became inactive, it has for most of its history been a strong supporter of the plan to have a supervisory body come onto the campus every ten years to examine the faculty, the curriculum, the library, laboratories, and various other facilities, and then judge them on a basis of comparison with ideal conditions, as well as those existing in other comparable institutions.

President Jaquith was facing this judgment by his peers in his second full year in office; he wanted to be ready for it, and no doubt many of the decisions he made were made with this in mind. The administrator always marches to the beat of a different drummer from that of his faculty. I can see him, trying to set a course for the future, with always the North Central visitation looming ahead.

Appended to the faculty minutes of 1934–35 is a document entitled "Aims and Purposes of Illinois College—A Symposium Prepared by the Faculty." It is a perfectly acceptable statement, but neither original nor exciting. It contains such bromides as: "In general Illinois College should provide the student with a cultural equipment essential to a broad and deep understanding of himself, his fellows, and the universe in which he lives. It should be the training ground of a self-disciplined citizenship, capable and willing to share fully in its opportunities and responsibilities." "It is not the purpose of a college to prepare a student to earn a living alone, but to teach individuals the fine art of living." It would be difficult even now to quarrel with such statements of purpose, but of course they need specific implementation if they are to be more than mere words. That's where the trouble comes.

Some curricular changes were discussed; a few of these were adopted by the faculty, but they did not long survive. An attempt was made to do something with art. The wife of an English instructor had offered a little work in the field in the 1933–34 year, and then in the fall of 1935 a young man with the extraordinary name of Homer Haggard Dasey was named instructor in art. He appears to have been an energetic fellow, to say the least. He took over a large room in Tanner basement and equipped it as a studio classroom for work in drawing, painting, and ceramics. He got enough work out of his students to mount a show at the Strawn Art Gallery of the Jacksonville Art Association in the spring, including figure drawing, oils, water colors, some clay sculptures, and a scale theatre model complete with a stage "equipped with border, spot and flood lights, all controlled from master switches and rheostats in the rear." The instructor himself showed water color portraits, including one of President Jaquith. Mr. Dasey offered to do student portraits, either from a photograph or a personal sitting. "A flat rate of $5.00 is charged except for graduating seniors, to whom the artist is extending a special rate of $4.00."

At the beginning of the 1935–36 year, announcement was made that the Chicago Academy of Fine Arts was accrediting the Illinois College Department of Art and would accept work done here at full value. According to a letter received from the managing director of the academy, "We are particularly pleased that we can make this commitment to you, and are able to do so largely because of the very timely and effective tendencies of the courses of study you have inaugurated and have been so successful with this past year." Mr. Dasey was selected to do murals for the Chicago Auto Show. He was something of a commercial artist as well as a professor. He did the portrait photography for the *Rig Veda* of 1936. That spring he visited New York and wrote a column for the *Rambler* about the Great White Way, complete with vivid impressions of panhandlers and burlesque queens. It was amusing, though not very dignified. He mounted another exhibit of student work at the Strawn Gallery just before commencement. Then this flamboyant and exotic character folded his tents and the brief flurry of art on the Illinois College campus came to an untimely end, at least for that time. Announcement was made that Mr. Dasey had decided to "go with Time and Fortune Publishing Co."

There was some change in the musical opportunities on campus, with the separate men's and women's glee clubs being merged into an all-college chorus. This arrangement does not appear to have advanced the cause of music on campus—or to have set it back much

either. There was activity in the area of drama, sparked by an editorial in the *Rambler* entitled "Ten Nights in a Barn Loft." The
reference here was to the very intimate theatre created in the barn
behind Russel House, a dormitory for women. After listing the de-
ficiencies in the heating facilities of the Little Theatre, the writer
says: "There are windows, there's that much to be said for the theatre. The windows are where the pigeons come in and leave. And
there is a raised platform with curtains which passes as a stage, but
there's probably no smaller or more cramped one to be found in any
other school, anywhere. It couldn't be any smaller and still hold
plays with more than two characters. There's one nice thing about
the stage, however. The shingle roof is so low that the actors can
stop leaks in it by reaching up between speeches and planting their
gum in the holes." Necessary improvements did come later, but it
has been one of the glories of the Illinois College Hilltoppers, a name
adopted about this time, that they have mounted excellent produc-
tions under less than ideal conditions.

There was some activity in the teacher-preparation department,
for certification as a teacher was a very appealing thing in those depression days. Students who had no real calling for the profession,
here as elsewhere, were preparing for such a career, just in case.
Illinois College even added a new course called Extracurricular Activities intended to prepare the prospective teacher to sponsor newspapers, debates, theatre activities, and the like, along with teaching
in the classroom. This proposal did not meet the favor of some of
the more conservative faculty, but it got enough votes to be given a
try.

Consideration was given to inaugurating a comprehensive examination program for all seniors. An *ad hoc* committee studied the
programs existing elsewhere, but an Illinois College program did not
materialize at that time. Study was also made of the possibility of
inaugurating a new course in general science intended for those who
were not "scientifically minded." This proposal had the strong endorsement of the president and was passed by the faculty without
enthusiasm. There is a penciled note on the margin of the faculty
minutes recording the adoption of the plan. The anonymous com-
mentator says that the meeting was "perfunctory" and was held

"merely to ratify the decision which the President had induced the science faculty to agree to."

Interest in debate fluctuated erratically during this period, partly because of the general retrenchment following the bank failure. The College withdrew from the forensic organization it had been affiliated with, and there were gloomy forecasts that debate was about to expire, yet an interesting revival took place, stimulated in part by the visits of two teams of English debaters. In November 1934, two men, one from the London School of Commerce, the other from University College, London, came to Jacksonville to debate Illinois College's champions, Willard Ice and Ralph Smith, on the subject: "Resolved, that science has not increased human happiness." The Englishmen upheld the affirmative, the Americans the negative. The English team was sponsored by the National Student Union of England, and was making appearances on the campuses of twenty-five American colleges and universities. Their witty, nonchalant style contrasted sharply with the more earnest, often plodding style of their American opponents. No decisions were rendered in these encounters, but the idea of debate as good clean fun was a tonic here and elsewhere, especially in view of the generally bleak climate of the depression era.

The next year a team from Oxford University came over and supported the proposition: "Resolved, that a written constitution is a hindrance rather than a safeguard to social progress." Against them, Illinois College sent Johnson Kanaday and Walter R. Bellatti. Moderator for the evening was Professor John G. Ames, himself an Oxonian. Again there was no decision, but the *Rambler* stated that it would have been difficult to reach a verdict, for it was "logic and clear presentation on the one hand against humor and brilliance of delivery on the other. For sheer entertainment the English were far superior to their younger and less experienced American adversaries."

In May of 1937 Illinois College joined Jacksonville High School and MacMurray College in hosting the seventh annual National Speech Tournament sponsored by the High School National Forensic League. The meet drew more than a thousand contestants and guests and lasted for a full week. Mr. Harold Gibson, class of 1930, a teacher at Jacksonville High School, was largely responsible for bringing this important convention to Jacksonville. It also helped to maintain interest in debate on the Illinois College campus.

The Jaquith administration was responsible for some important changes in housing arrangements on campus. By purchase, the College had acquired the home built by Julian Sturtevant back in 1852. It was placed into service in the fall of 1933 as Fayerweather House, having been given the name of the wife of Sturtevant, the pioneer who came out here from New England as a young bride. Fayerweather House is still in service as an honor dormitory for women.

The following year, two other gracious old homes, Lippincott House and Russel House, became dormitories for women; these had both been acquired in partial restitution of losses suffered in the Ayers Bank failure. Neither one is presently serving as a dormitory, Russell having been razed to make way for Pixley Hall, women's residence, and Lippincott having been sold to Dean and Mrs. Hildner, who for many years continued to make students welcome there. Another home acquired about the same time and under similar circumstances was used for a time as a dormitory for men. Because Admissions Director Ernst Bone and his wife lived there, it became popularly known as "The Bone Yard." It is no longer owned by the College.

In 1936, Elliott House was given to the College by Frank and William Elliott, in memory of their parents. It was a charming residence for women for a number of years, but is no longer possessed by the College. All of these homes are fondly remembered by the men and women who have lived in them at one time or another. It is true that they were not economical to operate, but they added greatly to the style of "Athens of the West" living that has long been a part of the Jacksonville setting of Illinois College.

It should also be recorded that the old Academy Hall went out of service as a woman's residence hall in 1932 and was finally razed in 1936. Some years later, the lot on which it stood was sold to the local school board and became the site of the Jacksonville High School gymnasium. All these housing changes came about as a consequence of chance or fate rather than as a matter of policy, but it took planning to launch them, and it took the gallant efforts of what were then called "house mothers," later known as "residence hall directors," to make them work so pleasantly.

During the Jaquith period there was a noteworthy growth on campus of concern for the world outside; the College became less provincial. The international interests of the Jaquiths themselves had much to do with this, no doubt, but so also did the presence on the faculty of men like Joe Patterson Smith and H. John Stratton, both of whom were constantly challenging their students to look beyond their books. Perhaps the greatest influence of all was the impact of the worldwide depression and the threat of totalitarian governments and their ideologies, along with the ever-growing probability of war.

Under these influences an International Relations Club was started, and lecturers like Clifton Utley of the Chicago Council on Foreign Relations were brought to campus to inform and stimulate student opinion and activity. There was a controversy over an international movement toward pacifism. As part of the observance of Armistice Day, 1935, one John Nevins Sayre, Chairman of the Fellowship of Reconciliation, came to the campus and urged students here to back the peace mobilization being organized by the National Student Federation of America. In a chapel talk, Mr. Sayre asked students: (1) to refuse to support the government in any future war; (2) to support neutrality legislation in Congress; (3) to work for the demilitarization of all colleges and universities by having compulsory ROTC outlawed; (4) to insist that colleges and universities become concerned about national policy making, especially as regards war. This presentation stirred up much campus discussion, as it was intended to do. The *Rambler* urged students to say a resounding No! to proposition number one, on the ground that we must always retain the right to defend our homeland.

At the same time, the *Rambler* expressed interest in an organization called Veterans of Future Wars which had its origin at Princeton and quickly founded chapters at sixty other colleges and universities. So far as I can determine, no chapter was organized on the Illinois College campus. A course called Contemporary Affairs and Personalities was offered not only to undergraduates but to citizens of the community. It was given jointly by President Jaquith and Professor Smith, with the former concentrating on the affairs and the latter on the personalities. It was so well attended that a larger classroom had to be found for it.

A local issue aroused much interest and controversy, too. This was the question of whether or not the City of Jacksonville should create its own light and power utility to compete with the private company that had a monopoly in the area. Two professors and two local attorneys debated the issue before an overflow crowd in Jones Chapel. In favor of the proposal were Edward Cleary, class of 1929, and Economics Professor John Stratton; opposed were Walter Bellatti, class of 1905, and Professor of History Joe Patterson Smith. Entirely aside from the interest of the proposition was the opportunity to see how profs would conduct themselves against each other and how they would fare against members of the legal profession. No decision was reached on this question; that would come later in a referendum. But not only contemporary events got attention. In the midst of all this discussion occurred the bimillenium of the Roman poet Horace. The Epsilon Chapter of Phi Beta Kappa arranged for the appearance on campus of Dean Shipley of Washington University to speak on "The Universality of Horace"; so a sense of perspective was not altogether lost.

The College also got involved with the National Youth Administration and the Civilian Conservation Corps. The former provided employment on campus and made it possible for needy students to stay in college and to do some worthwhile work. For example, the NYA underwrote part of the expense of creating a needed union library catalogue in Jacksonville. The development of athletic fields at the Morgan County Fair Grounds for use by the Illinois School for the Deaf, Illinois College, and the community was also a project of the NYA. The CCC established Camp Jacksonville and did various conservation jobs in Morgan County. While the unit was in existence it used the college gymnasium for basketball practice; some of the Illinois College professors lectured to the boys about a variety of subjects of cultural interest; students did some tutoring and helped the boys to publish *Camp Jacksonville News*. It is likely that both collegiate and noncollegiate youth profited by these kinds of cooperative ventures.

Other accomplishments of the Jaquith era included the restoration of part of the staff salary cuts; a 5 percent cut had been made in 1931 and a second 5 percent cut in 1933. A restoration of 5 percent was made by Board action in December 1935. To further boost faculty morale, there was consideration of a pension plan, group life insurance, and a sabbatical program. None of these had existed in any organized way, nor would they until a later date. Still, they were under consideration.

President Jaquith tried to keep up the work that had been done by President Rammelkamp to attach the alumni more firmly to the College; he faithfully attended regional meetings in New York, Chicago, St. Louis, and elsewhere. Perhaps the most important step taken in this direction was the appointment of Mrs. Rammelkamp as alumni secretary and editor of the *Alumni Quarterly*. Many people had thought of her as vice-president and secretary of state for the College during her husband's incumbency. Her unmatched acquaintance with the alumni and the high esteem in which she was held by the whole College community made her a superb choice for the difficult task of dealing with delicate problems.

In spite of the tightness of money in the country and especially in agricultural west-central Illinois, enrollment held up well. Indeed, at the opening of the 1936–37 year, the recorder's office indicated the highest enrollment in the College's history, 429 overall, including 176 freshmen. This was fortunate, in that the percentage of income from endowment had been steadily declining, from a high of 64 percent in the twenties to a low of 31 percent in the thirties. In one of his reports, President Jaquith said that the extremes were 70 percent and 30 percent. Tuition had become the main bulwark of the College finance, and a full college was almost a necessity, if further retrenchments were not to be made. True, some of those admitted during these depression days did not pay in cash, and some were tardy in their payments. And there may have been some admitted whose academic qualifications were questionable. Still, enrollment held up.

The early presidency of Harold Jaquith had not been a distinguished one, perhaps, but given the total set of circumstances, this was not surprising. On balance, during the first two Jaquith years, the College had held its ground. Now the time for a real advance had come, but it did not take place. On campus, Jaquith's lack of experience in the management of a faculty produced confusion. The Board of Trustees had to step in to settle a jurisdictional dispute in the dean's office, regarding the respective provinces of the dean of students and the dean of the College (or the dean of the faculty, as he preferred to be called). A very precise, legalistic document was produced on this occasion by one of the best legal minds on the Board, but it should not have been necessary. A president with experience in the academic world would have prevented the misunderstanding or, failing that, would have settled the dispute himself.

On another occasion, the Board found it necessary to lay down guidelines for the president himself, a humiliating experience, I should think. This document covered a number of points, the most pertinent of which were: (1) the president of the College shall not be a member of any faculty committee except the Administrative Council; (2) faculty committees shall be appointed by the president, subject to the confirmation of the faculty; (3) there shall be no expansion of any College department nor any additions to the present departments or extracurricular activity which involves any financial outlay, without approval of the Board of Trustees; (4) the Board believes that as a general rule it is unwise to employ members of the immediate family of members of the faculty or officers or trustees, and no such relatives shall hereafter be employed without special prior approval by the Board of Trustees; (5) on account of the condition of the College finances, the Board of Trustees requests that the president devote the major portion of his time and effort to the raising of additional funds for endowment and College expenses and to this end such assistance in administration of College affairs shall be provided as shall meet the approval of the finance committee and the faculty committee of the Board.

If ever there was a mailed fist cloaked in a velvet glove, that policy statement is surely it. It was adopted by a committee of the whole meeting held by the Board of Trustees on June 13, 1936. Mr. Jaquith was not present when it was drafted, but it was made known to him very promptly. In September 1936, at a faculty meeting over which the president presided, the statement was presented to the whole faculty by none other than the chairman of the board himself, Dr. Baxter. It was not incorporated into the faculty minutes, however, "because Dr. Baxter thought such incorporation would be unwise and unnecessary." The episode indicated a serious cleavage between president and board, and president and faculty.

Yet, President Jaquith seems to have been almost oblivious of the anxiety felt by his trustees and his faculty over his efforts to re-direct the course of the College. He charged up sacred academic hills with abandon. At the very commencement at which the Board drew up this statement, the President's Report to the Board of Trustees, June 13, 1936, must have incurred gasps and mutters, to say the least. Yet he went ahead and had it printed in the July 1936 *Alumni Quarterly*, for the whole world to see. Wrote Dr. Jaquith: "I trust that each member of the Board will read this rather long report carefully. It is important that each Trustee understand fully the problems confronting small privately supported, tuition-charging colleges in Illinois giving only Liberal Arts courses. It is important that each Trustee understand the problems confronting Illinois College. This report attempts to indicate the trends in education and their effect upon the curriculum, the student enrollment and the finances of the College." He goes on to say that he had refrained from speaking out on these matters until he had familiarized himself with the College and its surroundings, but now after more than three years on the job he feels that he can speak with confidence:

The liberal arts college, while retaining its definite objectives, cannot stand aside from the more general trends in the whole educational field and either serve its present student body or maintain its place as an essential unit in the larger whole. No individual college can isolate itself, without the risk of financial collapse and starvation from lack of student enrollment. Each college is a part of the larger whole. Any institution may be outstanding in certain departments, have unusual general excellence, have distinctive buildings and equipment, offer exceptional scholarship grants, but still, even with unlimited funds, it must conform sooner or later to the general trends in the educational field as a whole.

He goes on to interpret statistics gathered from the Illinois Department of Education, studies made at the University of Chicago, Princeton University, and elsewhere, including Illinois College, regarding registration in the different disciplines. His interpretation of these and his fear of the rapid growth of the teachers' colleges in Illinois and elsewhere led him to the conclusion that Illinois College would have to modify its curriculum and abandon its emphasis on the liberal arts. At least, that is how many of the faculty and trustees regarded such a passage as: "Probably the most common fallacy among those directly or indirectly interested in education is to impose as the essential curriculum and processes, their own training and personal experiences. While this is natural, it often fails to recognize the inevitable changes of time and differing conditions in the whole field of education or to recognize the individual interests and objectives of the student of today."

If there had been any doubts about President Jaquith's unfitness to lead Illinois College into its second century, statements such as were contained in this report dispelled them. It now became necessary, in the minds of the majority of the Board members, to seek out new leadership. In a private memorandum, a committee of the Board drew up a carefully worded evaluation of President Jaquith's administration, generous in places, temperate and firm elsewhere, and gave him a year's time to change his whole approach to the administration of Illinois College or to bow out gracefully. The former would have been improbable; the latter, though difficult, was finally accepted.

If, as many at the time thought, Harold Jaquith had been brought to Illinois College primarily to raise money, to restore the endowment funds lost by improper hypothecation of College securities, he had failed. His success with the Near East Relief Fund had no doubt given rise to false hopes. On his behalf, one may say that the times were different and the constituencies were different. But when, in addition to not raising enough money to satisfy the pressing needs of the College, he attempted to alter basic educational policies of Illinois College, the Board of Trustees terminated his services.

The Jaquiths departed Jacksonville in August, 1937, with much less fanfare than they had come four years earlier. There were those who felt relief, including probably the Jaquiths, but it was not a happy conclusion, it was a very sad one, and it would produce further unhappiness. The Jaquiths kept in touch with many friends in Jacksonville, while reestablishing themselves in the east. At the time of Dr. Jaquith's death, his successor wrote of him: "The sudden death on April 20, 1944 of Dr. Harold C. Jaquith, President of Illinois College from 1933 to 1937, brought sorrow to our college community. Dr. Jaquith assumed the presidency of the College shortly after the foundations of its financial structure had received a serious blow and he courageously undertook the tasks of recovery and reconstruction. From here he went to Trinity College, Hartford, Connecticut, as Provost, a post from which at the time of his death he had leave of absence for the period of the war in order to serve as educational director of the Office of Price Administration in Connecticut." It should be noted too that Mrs. Jaquith carved a distinguished career for herself as an interpreter at the United Nations.

20

President Hudson, 1937–1953

After the disappointments of the Jaquith presidency, the Board of Trustees decided to seek the kind of president who had served Illinois College—and other colleges—well in the past, the scholar-president. The scholar-president has not always been a success, but he has a better chance of success, especially in the small liberal arts college. If it is possible, he should find time to teach as well as administer and thus be in regular daily contact with students and faculty alike.

Both should feel free to approach him and examine educational problems with him. In time, then, the alumni will come to respect him, perhaps even love him. At the very least, a scholar-president should understand his faculty and be able to get along with them. Trustees will support him if he does not propose expensive new programs at every board meeting, and they will be more than supportive if he shows some ability at fund raising. As for relations with the community, he should conduct himself with dignity, speak with precision, and dress conservatively.

A man who seemed to have many of these qualifications and whom the trustees were able to persuade to accept the presidency at this continuing crisis in the College's career was Harris Gary Hudson. Born in Osaka, Japan, in June of 1888, of Presbyterian missionary parents, Gary Hudson had come to the United States as a boy for his education. He was thus no outlander. On his mother's side he was related to the Herndon family of Springfield, Illinois. It will be recalled that William Herndon had been withdrawn from Illinois College because his father did not approve of the abolitionist

President H. Gary Hudson

spirit that flourished on the college campus in the 1830s. Despite this, young Herndon continued to oppose the institution of slavery; he later became Lincoln's law partner and, still later, one of his biographers. Dr. Hudson was very conscious and proud of the Herndon-Lincoln connection. He was especially happy to have in his office at Illinois College a pair of swivel chairs from the Lincoln-Herndon office—the gift of Mrs. Logan Hay and her late husband, who had been a trustee of Illinois College. The President would occasionally let a favored guest sit in one of them.

Gary Hudson earned his B.A. at Millikin University in Decatur, Illinois, majoring in Latin and Greek and studying piano. His graduate study was begun at Northwestern University, and included three years as a Rhodes Scholar at Queen's College, Oxford, where he took a B.A. and an M.A. in history and philosophy. He rowed for Queen's and brought back his oar, which he displayed on the wall of his study in Barnes House, the president's home. The oar in his study somehow demonstrated that the scholar was not unmindful of the importance of the body, that Gary Hudson believed physical and intellectual strength go hand in hand. His Ph.D. in history was granted by the University of Chicago, where he produced a dissertation dealing with some problems in British history of the seventeenth century. A summary of this thesis was published in 1931 under the title, *A Study of Social Regulations in England under James I and Charles I: Drink and Tobacco*.

Hudson's graduate studies were by no means consecutive, for along the way to his final degree he taught in high schools in Illinois, at Watseka and Decatur, and in preparatory schools in New England, Phillips Andover Academy, and the Country Day School in Newton, Massachusetts. During World War I, he served abroad with the YMCA and later enlisted in the artillery. For four years he had been Professor of History and Dean of Blackburn College, Carlinville, Illinois. It was the president of that college—William Hudson, but no relation—who had first drawn the attention of the Illinois College Board of Trustees to Gary Hudson's potential as a successor to President Rammelkamp. It is an interesting fact that he had been considered by the same committee that eventually chose Harold Jaquith in 1932. At that time, however, Dr. Hudson did not wish to be a candidate. He had only recently taken his Ph.D. and been appointed to the faculty of a well-regarded woman's college, Sweet Briar at Lynchburg, Virginia. He had enjoyed one year of teaching there and did not wish to exchange the classroom for an administrator's office. I cannot help wondering how the history of the College might have been changed if he had accepted the post in 1932 rather than in 1937. But it is not profitable to speculate on such "iffy" questions, as Franklin Roosevelt used to remind us in those days.

Gary Hudson declined to be a candidate in 1932, but some of the trustees had kept him in mind and approached him again in June 1937. This time he decided to leave the safe confines of Sweet Briar and accept the challenge. In addition to his appreciation of scholarship and academic excellence, Hudson brought to Illinois College other attributes which he would be called on to exhibit frequently throughout the years of his presidency, namely, frugality, common sense, toughness, and an organized mind. He knew the long and honorable history of the College; in fact, he knew Rammelkamp himself in a curious way. He had made three tries for his Rhodes Scholarship before he got it; each time Rammelkamp was a member of the examining committee. Dr. Hudson told me that he remembered Rammelkamp very well from those experiences because, although the presidents of the University of Chicago, the University of Illinois, and Northwestern University were also on the committees, it was Rammelkamp who asked the penetrating, unexpected questions. On one occasion, Rammelkamp had asked him whether, in the light of his background and plans, he might not do better to go to Princeton and study classics under Edward Capps rather than try for Oxford. Hudson could not recall his answer, but it must have been a convincing one, for he got his Rhodes.

In addition to his other qualifications, Gary Hudson knew the geographical and cultural setting of Illinois College and also its constituency. He knew the problems it had been facing since Rammelkamp's death, and he was aware they were far from being solved. As one of his brothers said of him, "Gary was always a sucker for a challenge." So, he accepted the call in much the same spirit as his missionary parents had accepted the call to Japan.

His first words to the students, in a letter printed in the *Rambler*, were modest ones: "I have come here with no definite program that I wish to see carried out, nor with any predetermined purpose except to work with you to promote the welfare of Illinois College and its progress." He is quoted as telling the students at the opening chapel of the new year, "We believe that you will be happy if you are primarily interested in intellectual activity." That must have called forth interesting internal responses from the students who were getting their initial impression of the new head man.

The first issue of the *Rambler* of the 1937–38 school year carried a good deal of information about the new president, his wife, his family, and his career up to that point. The tone of the various articles is correct, cordial in a restrained way. There is nothing comparable to the enthusiasm that marked the arrival of President Jaquith. Indeed, there seems to have been a studied reserve in the acceptance of the new president. Over Mrs. Hudson's picture appeared the caption: "Moves In," and over Dr. Hudson's picture is: "Takes Over." Instead of an editorial welcoming the new president, there is an editorial paying tribute to the departed president. In it, Jaquith's praises were sung on several counts: that he made Illinois College coeducational in fact as well as in name, by improving the women's housing facilities, and by encouraging women to participate more fully in athletics and debate. And Mrs. Jaquith was said to have been "one of the most truly popular women ever associated with Illinois College." It was polite of the editor to say farewell to the Jaquiths so warmly; but it must have seemed a bit pointed, coming at that juncture. Perhaps there was no calculation behind those remarks, perhaps there was; it is not wise to underestimate the ingenuity of the undergraduate mind. In any case, there appears to have been a strong pro-Jaquith faction on the campus, consisting of both students and faculty. It apparently was not a majority, or even a strong minority, but it was very vocal.

Some of the ways in which this minority asserted itself were rather subtle; others were gross. Early that year, the director of athletics wrote a piece for the Chicago *Daily News* in which he gave high praise to the remarkable success Illinois College teams had had in Little Nineteen Conference competition—the conference was then in the process of breaking up—and he went on to say that "the successes of the teams were achieved under the handicaps of extremely poor facilities." As if this would not embarrass the administration sufficiently, he added: "Illinois College is not proud of the distinction of having the poorest athletic facilities in the state." Interestingly enough, he had not made such statements, in print at least, during the Jaquith administration, which might have been regarded as being rather more responsible for the inadequacies he was noting.

There were other evidences of disloyalty, culminating in a series of scurrilous mimeographed papers and pamphlets that appeared on and off campus; these were of course anonymous and difficult to trace. At length the *Rambler* took notice of this campaign and editorialized on the situation, condemning the "malicious propaganda" and the "virulent spirit" in which these attacks—against the new president and some of the faculty who supported him—were made. "We advocate an attempt to discover the author or authors of these writings and the immediate breaking off of any connection they may have with the school. Whether the authorities know it or not it is general campus opinion that more than students were involved. If this is the case, it is an intolerable situation. If it is not the case, the suspicion should be proven unfounded."

I do not wish to dwell overlong on these petty and unworthy activities, but they were certainly a major problem for President Hudson during his early days on campus. He and his wife said, more than once, "We were often discouraged, but we both were never discouraged at the same time." His toughness of character enabled him to endure a serious challenge that was mounted by those who had favored his predecessor. His sense of humor kept him from taking too solemn a view of his predicament. There was an exodus of both faculty and students during and following the first year of Gary Hudson's administration. Painful as it must have been at the time, this exodus did give the new president a chance to make major appointments of his own and also to establish new and more stringent admissions policies. Fortunately, he was able to rally to his cause most of the able faculty carried over from the Rammelkamp administration: persons like John Griffith Ames in English, Willis

DeRyke in biology, Raymond Lacey in classics, Earle Miller in mathematics, Eleanor Miller in psychology, Joe Patterson Smith in history, John Stratton in economics, Mary Louise Strong in German, Leonora Tomlinson in French. That gave him a strong nucleus. Then he reached out and brought in new blood from a variety of sources.

President Hudson had great faith in his ability to judge character and professional competence. Very early, he brought to the faculty people he had known elsewhere and whose qualities he admired, people like Ernest Hildner, who was at Western Illinois University, formerly Macomb Teachers. He had met Ernest years before when both were working in the British Public Records Office in London. In 1938, he invited him to join the Illinois College faculty as Dean of the College and Professor of History. It was a happy choice. Also in history, and education, he brought in John S. Wright, who had been a student at Blackburn College when Hudson was Dean there.

President Hudson also had strong convictions about the relative strengths of graduate schools. He told me once that the best places to look for people in English were the old line private universities of the East coast. And so, in 1939, he appointed Elizabeth Hastings of Yale and Charles Frank of Princeton; somewhat later, he brought in Ethel Seybold of Yale, Walter Gaylor of Harvard, and Edward Ives of Columbia—all these in English. In general, he thought it unwise to appoint to the faculty graduates of Illinois College. It could, he said, lead to inbreeding. Yet when he knew that an Illinois College graduate was especially well qualified for a post, he had no hesitation about breaking this rule. Examples of this practice were Chet Bone '36 and John Martin '32 in admissions, Arthur Hallerberg '40 in mathematics, and Ethel Seybold '29 in English. He devoted a great deal of time and energy to building a strong and loyal faculty. Even when he had to act quickly, he was careful in his choosing, so that there would be no need to repent at leisure. For instance, when Professor Oxtoby died suddenly in October 1941, the President brought to the campus as Professor of Religion and Chaplain Malcolm F. Stewart, who later became the Scarborough Professor of Religion and Philosophy and one of Hudson's most distinguished appointments. Although he thought the final responsibility of choosing lay with him, he was careful to consult with colleagues on the faculty, those who were in the same or similar disciplines and whose judgment he trusted.

I think it may be argued that the most important single act that a small college president performs is his selection of faculty. Much may be forgiven him if he performs that task well. Gary Hudson was proud of the faculty he assembled during his presidency. He made some mistakes (he admitted as much in his annual reports to the Board of Trustees, naming names), but on the whole he gathered around him a group of men and women who were competent in their disciplines and eager, enthusiastic teachers. There was a modest amount of scholarly activity as evidenced by the writing and presentation of papers, the attending of professional meetings, the keeping up with developments in their respective fields. But there was never pressure placed on faculty to prove their worth by publication or any other form of "productivity." There was healthy disagreement among the faculty on all manner of subjects, including politics and religion, but there were no running feuds between or within departments, or any clearcut division between teachers and administrators. How could there have been, when administrators, including the president, deans, and business manager, were almost always teaching too? (Hudson taught in the history department chiefly; he also collaborated with the English department in teaching the classics in translation.) Wherever possible, faculty were brought into the president's confidence on the operations of the College, either at regular faculty meetings or special ones, or through the committee structure of the faculty.

Moreover, there was no attempt to keep the faculty from fraternizing with members of the Board of Trustees. If abused, this practice can be mischievous, but in a town the size of Jacksonville, about twenty thousand during the Hudson administration, it is inevitable that trustees and faculty will mix, at church, at clubs, in the shops, in recreation and in politics. At any given time, about half the twenty-five-member Board of Trustees is made up of Jacksonville residents. They have more than one source of information about the

College, if they wish to take advantage of the opportunities, and most of them do. A president who tries to limit these opportunities is asking for trouble.

There were many problems facing Dr. Hudson in his early days. Perhaps the most immediate one was the matter of gaining the full support of the Board of Trustees. There was no opposition to Hudson on the Board, as there was among faculty and students, but he still had to gain the trustees' full confidence before he could hope to accomplish anything of consequence. The chief problem was this: when President Jaquith resigned in June of 1937, the chairman of the Board submitted his resignation as chairman, although he stayed on the Board. In his letter of resignation, Dr. Baxter was very careful to point out that he had retired and moved from Chicago to California and would thus find it difficult to give close and constant attention to College affairs. He thought that the office should not be merely an honorary one, but an active one. It was no secret that Jaquith's strongest support among the trustees came from George Baxter; he was the last one to be convinced of the need for a change. Nonetheless, Dr. Baxter asked that his resignation be acted on before a new president was chosen, so that no one could link his resignation with the choice. He was as "correct" in his position as a man could be.

Dr. Baxter had been chairman of the Board for five difficult years and could hardly be blamed for wanting relief. He had also been a generous patron of the College for an even longer period of time. The possibility of losing his good will was a serious matter for the Board and the new president. Let it be said to the honor of both Dr. Baxter and Dr. Hudson that they became warm personal friends and that Baxter's interest in the College remained at a very high level throughout the rest of his life.

Nonetheless, when Hudson assumed the presidency, there was no chairman to whom he could turn. It was not until a special meeting held in April of 1938 that the Board was able to persuade one of its members, Harry J. Dunbaugh, to accept the chairmanship, and then with some interesting reservations. Among them were: (1) his tenure was not to exceed three years, (2) his forte was not fund raising, and (3) the President was to have full authority to deal with

Baxter Hall. Drawing by Louise Boring Wood

faculty and there was to be no division on the Board or "gossip" about such matters. Mr. Dunbaugh was an able Chicago lawyer, who in spite of his insistence that his term should be for three years only, presided over the Board for the next seventeen years, with great dignity and absolute impartiality. President Hudson could not have found a more congenial chairman to work with; so that problem was happily solved.

Two problems related to the 1903 merger of the Jacksonville Female Academy with Illinois College gave difficulty. One was the matter of finance. At the time of the merger, there were those on both sides who doubted that the marriage would last and some who hoped that it would not. Some provision had to be made for the proper division of funds if dissolution became necessary. As a result, a special system of bookkeeping had been set up, so that resources of the old female academy could be identified and, if need be, separated. Moreover, there was a clear intention that income from the Jacksonville Female Academy funds should be spent specifically on the education of women at Illinois College. It was of course nearly impossible to determine what portion of the total endowment income of Illinois College came from Academy sources, and even had it been possible to make that determination fairly, it was quite impossible to say how it should be spent to the exclusive benefit of women on a coeducational campus. Chairman Dunbaugh wanted these affairs straightened out while there were still trustees of the former Jacksonville Female Academy alive who could consent to a new and workable arrangement.

The merger had been successful for thirty-four years, and there was little likelihood of its being terminated and a separate female academy reactivated. Therefore the assets of the Jacksonville Female Academy and Illinois College should be integrated, as the students had been; that point was successfully negotiated. However, in the remote possibility that Illinois College should abandon the educating of women, the Trustees of Illinois College agreed to assign a sum of $58,000 to the Board of Christian Education of the Presbyterian Church in the U.S.A.

The other matter resulting from the merger was more difficult of solution. It had to do with the religious commitment of the College. The local founders, the Rev. Mr. Ellis and others, were Presbyterians, while Sturtevant and the Yale Band were Congregationalists, but they had agreed to work together nonetheless. It will be remembered that at the time of the merger of Illinois College and the Jacksonville Female Academy, however, the College had become not only coeducational but "Presbyterian," that is, a majority of the trustees of the College were henceforth to be Presbyterians. This provision had been unpopular and apparently not strictly adhered to —it was as difficult to carry out as the division of income strictly for the use of women was—but it was still on the books. Chairman Dunbaugh wanted a clear understanding on this as well as on the division of income. (I think I should warn readers who are not interested in the church relations of the College that the next few pages may become tedious.)

Negotiations were made difficult by the fact that the Board of Christian Education of the Presbyterian Church in the U.S.A. was at that time becoming more inquisitive about the colleges that claimed affiliation with the Church and got support from it. It is understandable that a church, like a foundation or an individual donor, to say nothing of the federal government, should take an interest in the way its benefactions are being used. It is, however, a fine line to draw between interest and interference, and perhaps none could be established that would satisfy all parties. For the time being, no solution was realized.

At a later date, in May 1943, the Board of Christian Education adopted a set of standards which it desired its member colleges also to adopt. The Board defined what it meant by a "Presbyterian College" and then set forth the following provisions stating that each such college: (1) shall adopt a statement of purpose as a Christian College and indicate in its catalogue that it is affiliated with the Presbyterian Church in the U.S.A.; (2) shall employ on its faculty only men and women who are active members in good standing of some evangelical Christian church (This provision, it was noted, would not affect those already employed. Nonetheless, Hudson, calling on his familiarity with seventeenth-century English history, referred to this provision as a "Test Act."); (3) shall provide courses in biblical studies and require at least one for graduation; (4) shall submit annually to the Board of Christian Education complete financial information on forms supplied by the Board, and shall have an audit made by a certified public accountant; (5) shall be fully accredited by its regional accrediting agency.

President Hudson was present at the meetings when these policies were discussed; he vigorously objected to the phrasing of some of them and the intent of others. He had no quarrel with provisions number one and five, but he thought that number two was wrong in principle, number three was unwise because of its rigidity, and number four was offensive in that it required what any prudent college would do anyhow. His chief argument was that the Presbyterian Church should be reaching out for new college affiliations; such requirements as these would certainly not attract new colleges into the fold and might well drive out the stronger and more independent ones it already had. (There was some reason to believe that this might indeed be the intention. The fewer colleges that had to be assisted, the more money would be left for the others.) Hudson was able to achieve some modifications in the wording of items number two and three, and on that basis he agreed to recommend to his Board of Trustees that Illinois College should "go along with the majority." This was done rather reluctantly by the Illinois College Board, and thereafter President Hudson and Illinois College were regarded as not altogether safe and sound, but "on the outer fringes by Presbyterianism"—a phrase that rankled in Hudson's consciousness.

During the war and postwar years, the Board of Christian Education of the Presbyterian Church, U.S.A., not only made annual appropriations to the College, usually in the amount of five thousand dollars, but it also established a "restoration fund" intended to help its member colleges to regain ground lost as a result of the dislocations caused by the war. The allocation from this fund to Illinois College was fifty thousand dollars, paid over a period of several years. It was a Godsend, helping to meet the inevitable operating deficits during that difficult time. However, it was apparently felt by the trustees of Illinois College that the Board of Christian Education, or certain officers of that Board, were attempting to influence unduly the policies of the College, including the matter of appointing administration and faculty.

It took years for this matter to come to a head, but at the June 13, 1953, meeting of the Illinois College Board of Trustees, the last one of President Hudson's incumbency, there was an effort made to reconcile past differences, at least to come to an accommodation. Dr. E. Fay Campbell, Secretary of the Division of Higher Education of the Board of Christian Education of the Presbyterian Church, U.S.A., met with the Board of Trustees, at the invitation of Chairman Dunbaugh. Dr. Campbell told the trustees that an advisory committee of his body, the one that made investigations of member colleges, "feels not as close to Illinois College as it would like to be. . . . We are not wanting only pure Presbyterian colleges. We want a variety of types of colleges. But Illinois College is far to the left as regards liberalism theologically. . . . Illinois College is not in the main stream of our church."

Apparently this comment provoked a wide-ranging discussion, with the trustees restating their position of independence, though with all due respect to the Presbyterian Church, U.S.A., and with gratitude for the past financial assistance of the Board of Christian Education. Dr. Campbell said many times over that his Board did not want to control the college or shape its policies. What they would like was consultation, particularly in the selection of a new president.

The minutes indicate that the discussion became somewhat heated, so that adjournment for lunch at the president's house was welcomed. After that intermission, the minutes note that "everybody felt better when the Board reconvened." There was a motion made by President Hudson, to "thank the Presbyterian Board of Christian Education and Dr. Fay Campbell for his presence and presentation of the relationship of the Presbyterian Church, U.S.A. and Illinois College." A committee was appointed "to meet with representatives of the Synod of Illinois and members of the Advisory Committee of the Board of Christian Education of the Presbyterian Church, U.S.A." Immediately, another committee was appointed "to meet with the head of the Congregational Committee on Higher Education and the representatives of the Conference of the Congregational Churches of Illinois to study the relationship of Illinois College with the Congregational Church." Whatever else this meeting may have accomplished, there was clearly no intention on the part of the Illinois College Board to give up its traditional dual church relationship.

That was the inconclusive outcome of the controversy between College and Church during the Hudson presidency. It is interesting to note that about this time Dr. Hudson served as the elected president of the Presbyterian College Union. I asked him how that had happened, and he said he guessed it was because his "turn had come." Others have told me that some of the members admired Hudson's stand, even those who had not supported him, and wanted his leadership. In any case, his presidential address to the Union at Atlantic City was a stimulating one; it was tactfully worded, but it maintained the doctrine that Sturtevant had fought for almost a century earlier, namely that a college should have a strong religious commitment but that it should keep free of any direct denominational control.

I suppose that if I were being strictly chronological in presenting

these materials, I should conclude this discussion in the next chapter,
since it was in President Selden's first year in office that an "agreement" was reached by the Trustees of Illinois College and the Board
of Christian Education of the Presbyterian Church in the U.S.A. I
prefer to deal with it here, however, since the document was largely
phrased by President Hudson, or to meet his wishes. The text of the
"agreement" is given in full in the minutes of the Board of Trustees
meeting of December 12, 1953, when it was discussed at length.
It is given again, with minor revisions, in the minutes of the June 12,
1954, meeting, at which time it was ratified as if it were a treaty. If
it were not so long, I would give it verbatim, but the first half is
given over to a series of legalistic "whereases" which the reader can
imagine for himself. Then follows the meat of the whole matter:

Now, therefore it is mutually agreed:
　　1. That it is and will continue to be the declared policy of Illinois
College to adhere to the Christian purposes of Presbyterian Colleges
as set forth in the set of Standards established by vote of the General
Assembly of the Presbyterian Church in the U.S.A. in May 1943,
giving due consideration to any changes which may be made in these
standards.
　　2. That Illinois College through the Board of Trustees pledges
itself at all times to have as the President of the College a person of
strong avowed evangelical Christian faith.
　　3. That it is and will continue to be the declared policy of Illinois
College to use every reasonable effort at all times to have at least
three-fourths of the members of the Board of Trustees persons who
are members in good standing of evangelical Christian churches.
　　4. That the President of Illinois College shall periodically, at least
once in each calendar year, discuss with appropriate officials of the
Board of Christian Education of the Presbyterian Church in the
U.S.A., and also with appropriate officials of the Synod of Illinois,
matters of mutual interest and advantage, including matters relating
to the purposes and policies herein set forth, and that he will submit
annual reports to the Board and to the Synod.
　　5. That it is and will continue to be the declared policy of the
Board of Christian Education of the Presbyterian Church in the
U.S.A., so long as the purposes and policies set forth in this Agreement are adhered to by Illinois College, (a) to recognize Illinois College as a Presbyterian College, (b) to include Illinois College in its
published list of colleges approved by General Assembly, (c) to give

to Illinois College a share of the financial support given to these colleges in accord with the policy of the Board, (d) to assist Illinois College in procuring qualified students, and (e) to urge the Presbytery of Springfield and the Synod of Illinois, through the ministers of the respective churches, to encourage Presbyterians to contribute to the moral and financial support of Illinois College.

No doubt all parties concerned breathed sighs of relief after the document was duly executed. I leave it to those who like to see all i's dotted and all t's crossed to judge whether the Trustees of Illinois College or the Board of Christian Education of the Presbyterian Church in the U.S.A. made the greater concessions. It appears to me that both sides gave a bit, yet both got what they chiefly wanted—which is the way a lasting compromise should be reached.

I have been further enlightened by the "agreement" between Illinois College and the Congregational and Christian Conference of Illinois, the other group to be approached as a result of action taken at the June 1953 meeting of the Illinois College Board. There was a brief and amiable exchange of letters between the president of the College and the superintendent of the Congregational and Christian Conference of Illinois, ending: "Our Board of Trustees looks with favor upon the proposal of Illinois College that it be included in the list of institutions affiliated with the Congregational Christian Churches. . . . If there is anything further we can do to be helpful in this matter, please let us know."

There were other than church policy matters with which Hudson had to involve himself. He wanted very much to keep up enrollment, but he was unwilling to lower standards in order to do so. It was not just a matter of academic standards but of inequities in awarding scholarships and work assignments on campus. There had grown up a practice of "remitting" tuition to some students on a rather uncertain basis and a similar practice about assigning jobs to students who did not need the help as much as others did and then did not perform well in those jobs. Said Hudson of the first: "By means of partial remission of tuition fees, sometimes called 'unfunded scholarship grants,' we have been assisting students more than we can afford without detriment to our educational program." Of the other, he spoke even more bluntly: "Illinois College is no place for the lazy or incompetent student, nor is the College doing its full duty if it permits young people who have received from the College the gift of opportunity in the form of jobs, to acquire or become confirmed in habits of irresponsibility and shiftlessness." And finally, of both practices: "No college may jeopardize the quality of its educational program by impoverishing itself to help its students." The tightening-up process on these matters took some time and caused some muttering, but it was accomplished.

In his first report to the Board of Trustees given on December 11, 1937, the new president had commented on the growing competition among colleges and universities for students, and he stated his basic creed, on which he continued to operate throughout his presidency: "The strongest appeal, I believe, will be through a strong faculty presenting a broad program of education for the whole individual on his spiritual, aesthetic and physical sides as well as on the intellectual. In the long run, I believe that this appeal will build up a better student body in numbers and quality than the excellence of athletic teams or the variety of extra-curricular activities, valuable as they are in contributing to a college education. In other words, I believe that there is a considerable number of young people who would be attracted to a college which stands for intellectual and moral attainments. Such a college might be different enough to be conspicuous, I might almost say, unique."

The whole problem of recruiting students was becoming more competitive and more professional. In earlier days, the president and the dean were personally responsible for the promotion of enrollment. Sometimes other faculty members were asked to go on student safaris also. They called on schools and churches in the area, gave commencement addresses and sermons, and interviewed prospective students. This continued well into the Rammelkamp administration. The College was generally known downstate, and its academic standing was high. The methods of recruitment were somewhat hit or miss, but a new class always materialized in September.

But now, with the steady growth of the University of Illinois and the rapid growth of the teachers' colleges around the state, the private colleges had to become concerned about the competition and give some thought to the techniques of recruiting. The first professional of this kind at Illinois College was Charles Barlow '29, whose title was Dean of Men. The first person to be called Director of Admissions was Ernst Bone '36. The reports of these men to the president become ever more detailed, and they are regularly quoted in the president's report to the Board. In 1941 we learn not only that our average cost of recruiting a student for the entering class that fall was $51.06, a figure that "compares favorably" with figures from Carleton, Lake Forest, Monmouth, and others, all of which are given in charts. It is fascinating to discover that recruiting new students cost Illinois College $40 per boy and $142 per girl that year. The stated reason for the difference was that "many colleges are trying to make up losses in men students by taking more women than usual." An obvious hedge against the possibility of the United States getting involved in a general war.

"Admissions counsellors" were appointed to cover the Chicago area, more promotional mail was sent out, and more phone calls were made. Said President Hudson: "I confess to have once had a feeling that it is undignified for a college to seek students. But I have been wrong. High school students must be shown the value of a liberal education and the opportunities for intellectual and personal development that a college like this has to offer." Of course, the operation was an added expense, one that would grow with the years.

Some of the property owned by the College was unproductive and needed attention. The holdings of scattered farmlands had greatly increased during the thirties; they called either for disposal— at depressed prices—or professional management. Business Manager Merrill Barlow (he was the first to hold that title) had been handling details of fencing and fertilizing of croplands, selling corn and apples, securing satisfactory tenants, etc. He had some professional help, but the College holdings were too small and too scattered to justify a full-time manager. These various properties had been acquired not as a matter of calculated policy but, over the years, by bequest and gift, and more recently by foreclosure of mortgage loans which the College had made, wisely or unwisely. It was agreed by the finance committee that it would be better to take a loss on the book value of some of these properties in order to realize cash that could be invested and would produce income that could be counted on. In this way, more than forty thousand dollars worth of endowment funds had to be written off, but endowment income went up.

A piece of town property that caused concern was the so-called "Pitner Place," a fine old home on a lot of approximately five and one-half acres, located in the west end of Jacksonville, and given to the College in the late twenties, subject to an annuity. It had once been thought of as the site of a quadrangle for women, even though it was not adjacent to the main campus. The money for such a development was not then available, nor likely to become available in the foreseeable future. Moreover, since the acquisition of "Pitner Place," the College had acquired other more accessible properties for the housing of women. The house had sometimes been rented, sometimes vacant, but it never paid its way, because of the expense of upkeep and the necessity of paying an annuity to the donor. Thus when a developer suggested razing the old home (which had been the residence of Judge Lockwood, first chairman of the Illinois College Board of Trustees) and dividing the acreage into building lots, the finance committee had a difficult decision to make. The house was lovely, but the College simply couldn't afford to maintain it. They consulted Mrs. Eloise Pitner, the donor; she saw their dilemma and gave consent to the plan for development, under certain conditions which were met. Eighteen building lots were created, to be sold at fifteen hundred dollars each; when all were sold, the College would realize twenty-seven thousand dollars. With expenses of the transaction being estimated at seven thousand dollars, the net sum realized would be twenty thousand dollars, which happened to be the exact sum at which the property had been appraised when the College acquired it. Now, however, it would be producing income instead of being a liability. A neat lesson in economics for the president. Property matters of this kind are not matters of high educational policy, but they are important and they take much of a president's time and energy. He must become a jack-of-all trades, as Gary Hudson was discovering. He came to enjoy unsentimental appraisals.

Overshadowing all other problems were those that arose from the situation in Europe, which most Americans were watching with fascination and fear. President Hudson had to help the College prepare for the uncertainties of a war in which the United States would be greatly concerned and possibly closely involved. There are regular references to this possibility in his semiannual reports to the Board of Trustees, and they grow ever more pessimistic. In June 1940, he wrote: "While we do not expect that the United States will become involved in the war, such a possibility cannot be excluded. The faculty has already begun to consider the possible effects of this contingency." In December 1940, he reported on the desirability of entering into negotiations with the Civil Aviation Authority regarding the training of civilian pilots, in cooperation with Jacksonville Airport personnel.

In June 1941, he wrote: "As the emergency increases, our problems will certainly become more difficult. Undoubtedly our enrollment will be affected and members of the faculty will leave from time to time for military service." He thought that there would be some necessary changes in the curriculum, the introduction of summer school programs, and the probable acceleration of the usual four-year program for the baccalaureate to a three-year program. He said that there would be strong pressures to emphasize the physical sciences and to dilute or dissolve out of the picture the liberal arts program. But, said Hudson: "Illinois College with all her sister institutions must stand in determined defense of the principles of free inquiry and honest thought. . . . This conflict is not a conflict of arms alone. It is a conflict of ideals for human society, and the future of American democracy is more likely to be settled on the college and university campus than on the field of battle. . . . We are making every effort to quiet the students' restlessness and to induce them to remain in college. This policy is strongly urged upon us by Army men, government officials and industrial leaders."

To help him in forming policies to meet the emergency, he announced the creation of a new committee to be known as the Committee on the State of the College; it would consist of the president, the business manager, and three faculty members to be elected by their peers. Six months later, Pearl Harbor ended the uncertainty, but created other and more fearful problems. At the semiannual meeting, December 13, 1941, Chairman Dunbaugh read the following statement to the Illinois College Board of Trustees:

During the past few days this country has been plunged into a titanic World War. No man can predict the future. Nor can we foresee the effect upon Illinois College. Certain things are clear and worthy of emphasis.

First. As Administrators of the College, together with the Faculty, we must be true to the duty that is placed upon us, as guardians of the young men and women entrusted to our care. The life, the hope, of the nation rests in these young people. In all probability the time will come in this present emergency when the Board must consider cooperation with the Government, in some form or other, in the prosecution of the War. We must be sure, as never before, that, in our guidance of these students, we inspire them with love for, and unwavering belief in, true principles of democracy; that we do what lies within us to develop in them the sort of fibre and character that will make them thoughtful, strong citizens, and, so far as possible, leaders to a better way of life; that, in our advice to them, we exercise the understanding, moderation and sympathy which are due to youth just beginning to feel the full strength of manhood and womanhood; that, especially in the case of young men who are burning with desire to enlist in the service of their country, our counsels be considered, temperate and just. God grant that we do not fail.

Second. As trustees of the college property, we must conserve our resources. During the next few years, governmental burdens will undoubtedly make it impossible to appeal to the public for large funds. We must broaden among alumni and friends the base of our Sustaining Fund, and, by means of many small gifts, carry the institution through what almost certainly will be difficult financial years.

Third. Finally, we have cause to be thankful for the man who is the President of Illinois College. Four and a half years ago he came to us, to find a student body restless and disturbed, a faculty divided, a Board of Trustees shaken by a disrupting experience, and a community that had not recovered its traditional loyalty to the College since the time of the bank failure, thoughtlessly attributed by many to avoidable College action.

Today, he has solidly behind him the students, the faculty, the trustees and the community. He has expanded his acquaintance with the alumni from the Atlantic to the Pacific. He has steadfastly maintained high educational standards. He has brought the physical plant up to splendid condition. While other colleges have been losing students, he, without undue inducements, has sustained the enrollment. Year by year, through careful operation within the budget, he has steadily advanced the College to a strong financial condition.

Chairman Dunbaugh here inserted some specific details of Hudson's prudent management of the College finances, which may be summarized thus: in his first year, expenses exceeded income by ten thousand dollars; in his second year by five thousand dollars, in his third year by three thousand dollars; and in his fourth year there was the probability of a five hundred dollar surplus. And in each of the deficit years, special contributions had wiped out the budgeted deficits. Having cited these details, Chairman Dunbaugh concluded his statement: "This is the record of four years—a single college generation. With this record as a beacon light, and with President Hudson at the helm, Illinois College can look forward to the future, stormy though it may be, with hope and confidence." Mr. Dunbaugh's statement, inspirational yet low-key, was heartily endorsed by the Board of Trustees, and it may be regarded as having set the course for the College through the war years. It was certainly a vote of confidence in President Hudson.

The second semester of 1941–42 was accelerated so that students could complete as much work as possible before being called into service. Classes met on Saturdays as well as the usual Monday-to-Friday schedule; in order to carry out the schedule as originally planned, the first Saturday of the new semester was labelled "Monday," the second "Tuesday," and so on. Thus about three weeks were "saved," though it was difficult for some students—and some faculty—to adjust their internal calendars. But commencement occurred in May rather than in mid-June and there were a few more people around to celebrate it than there otherwise might have been.

There were some departures from the faculty; all who wished it were granted "leave for the duration." Included in that list, according to the president's report to the Board, May 1943, were John Stratton, who went to the Office of Price Administration; Eleanor Miller, research analyst with the Army Signal Corps; Charles Frank

with the U.S. Navy; John Wright with the U.S. Army; Alfred Lamb
with the U.S. Army Air Force; and Genevieve McCracken with the
American Red Cross. Malcolm Stewart stayed on, but assumed an
additional role as the "stated supply" pastor of the State Street Presbyterian Church in Jacksonville. Earlier, Eleanor McFall had signed
up with the United Services Organization, and Chet Bone had entered medical school under a U.S. Navy program. In his May 1943
report, the President stated that 510 alumni and former students were
in service, 95 outside the continental limits of the United States.
Four had already given their lives. (These lists would continue to
grow until the war was over.) One-third of the male student body
had left college for military service during the 1942–43 year. President Hudson said that he and the remaining faculty had "the startling
sensation of the College melting away about us."

The student body continued to melt away; the numbers of full-
time students during the war years are shown in the following table.
In Hudson's first year at the College (1937–38), there were 306 men,
93 women, or a total of 399 students. In the face of these fluctuations,
the President and faculty and student body worked together to maintain a respectable academic program and at the same time to "keep
the home fires burning" with extracurricular activities. But, in that
very low year, 1944–45, the men's societies ceased functioning, and
there were no intercollegiate athletics, though various forms of intramural and individual sports were carried on. The press, both *Rambler*
and *Rig*, shrank in size and coverage, but they continued to publish.
Everyone made the most of whatever sociability could be sustained,
and felt an extra measure of virtue in making do.

	Men	Women	Total
1942–43	249	69	318
1943–44	42	57	99
1944–45	37	50	87
1945–46	195	101	296

There were pressures to attempt to make the offerings of the College conform to the immediate needs of the day, which were chiefly
military and technical. Said President Hudson to his Board of Trust-

ees in response to those pressures: "We shall not be swept away by popular demands for courses of a highly technical or pseudo-military nature. Clearly recognizing where our strength lies, we shall do well what we can do, leaving to the training camp and to other institutions what can be done better and more quickly elsewhere."

The President attended conferences in Washington trying to find ways in which the College could serve the national interest and continue to survive as a liberal arts college. The Civilian Air Pilot Training Program was activated, and the College participated in the training of 45 Naval Aviation Cadets under the Civil Aeronautics Administration War Training Service. It also cooperated with the Army, Navy, and Marine Corps by encouraging students to enlist in various special programs. Many did this as the following list for 1942–43 shows.

Army Enlisted Reserve	24
Army Air Force Enlisted Reserve	9
Marine Corps Officers Reserve	9
Navy Enlisted Seamen's Training Program, V-1	27
Navy Aviation Cadets, V-5	3
Navy Deck Officers, V-7	19

In general, these programs allowed students to continue in college until such time as their respective services had need of them; then they were subject to immediate call to duty. It was a stopgap measure, both for students and for the College.

The most ambitious military program that Illinois College participated in was the so-called ASTP. According to President Hudson's report to the Trustees, June 26, 1943:

On June 17, representatives of colleges and universities in the area of the Sixth Service Command which had been cleared for participation in the Army Specialized Training Program met with representatives of the Army in conference in Chicago. There we were notified that Illinois College is to be one of the institutions in which a unit of the Basic Course will be established. The number of men was given as 200 to 250, although it was said that the number will probably be increased later. Unofficially we were told that instruction will begin on August 9, 1943, and that men in groups of 40 or 50 will be arriving here after July 19. The College will be responsible for instruction, housing, messing and medical care.

The length of the course will be three terms of 12 weeks each, with an interval of one week at the end of every term. The subjects to be taught will be mathematics, physics, geography, history, English and chemistry, with mechanical drawing substituted for chemistry in the third term. The men, none of whom are over 22 years of age, will be high school graduates, although some may have had a year, or possibly two years, in college. All will have had 13 weeks of basic military training. The Army's plan at present is to house the men in Crampton Hall and the gymnasium. The contract will be negotiated after instruction begins, since experience has shown that this is the best procedure for both parties.

The primary purpose of the program, as Army officers at the conference made very clear, will be to train soldiers, not to help colleges. Nevertheless, the Army desires that colleges receive full reimbursement of costs. For us the Army contract means keeping our faculty together and employed, assistance in the cost of operation and maintenance, and service to the national cause.

It was fortunate that ASTP 3670 was activated at Illinois College that year, for the civilian population of the campus dropped below 100 for the first time in many years. Housing 160 men in Crampton and 90 in the old gym was a large undertaking, but it was better for the soldiers than bivouacking in New Guinea or North Africa. The needs of instruction could not be met entirely with Illinois College faculty; so additional instructors were taken on. Somehow, all requirements, physical and mental, were met. The GIs marched to their classes in Jones and Sturtevant and to the messhall, which was Baxter. Classes and messing were separate from the civilians, but of course there was fraternizing.

The College had to get used to service ways of doing things— eternal lines, mystifying forms to be filled out, indefinite waiting for payment of accounts—the College had to borrow nearly $100,000 to care for staffing, messing, medical care, etc. The situation was, often enough, SNAFU. Eventually, though, accounts were settled to the satisfaction of both the Army and the College, although the interest the College paid on the bank loans it floated was not allowed as a legitimate charge.

The experiment was a lively, memorable one, even though it lasted only about nine months. The needs of the Army for replacements made it necessary to close out the ASTP venture abruptly and unceremoniously. In a special report to the Board of Trustees, April 1, 1944, President Hudson wrote:

The 3670th Service Unit, ASTP, comprising 250 men, was activated at Illinois College in mid-July, 1943. The men, ordered to duty with combat units, left here in the third week of March, 1944. The work of the College in teaching, feeding and housing these men was recognized by the Army authorities of the Sixth Service Command as "outstanding," and the results reflect great credit upon the members of the instructional, administrative and service staffs who loyally and unsparingly gave themselves to the task.

The Army has notified us that the termination of the contract will be effective on June 20 and has asked for proposed terms for a negotiated settlement of the amount payable for the incompleted portion. . . . Illinois College is in the position of a man who has been honorably discharged from the Army. Our services, given while there was need, are now no longer required.

I have been told that when the men in the unit got word of their imminent departure from Illinois College to places unknown and unspecified there was great sorrow among them. Some of them went on frustrated beer busts; others decided to make the most of whatever time was left them in the groves of academe. With only that incentive, they used the reading room of Tanner Library more assiduously than ever, during their final days on campus.

It is worth noting that when the war was over and the GIs could return to civilian life, a number of men of ASTP 3670 decided to use their educational privileges at Illinois College; most of these eventually received their degrees here. It was certainly an unusual way of recruiting students. Interestingly, as these words are being written, the first reunion of ASTP 3670 is taking place. The College welcomed back, thirty-five years later, as many of the men as could be traced and wanted to revisit old haunts and renew old acquaintance. A muster roll of the unit—and of the staff—as it existed in 1943–44 is printed in the College catalogue for 1944. I had sent a copy of that roll to the Adjutant-General of the Army, asking if it would be possible for the Army to indicate the survivors and to give their present addresses. I stated that my interest was historical, not commercial, or based on mere curiosity. The Adjutant-General forwarded my request to the National Personnel Records Center in St. Louis, Missouri. At length my request was denied on the grounds that "Department of Defense Directive 5400.11, Encl. 5, prohibits furnishing the public with rosters (lists) or compilations of names and home addresses, or single addresses of current or former servicemen and servicewomen." That appeared to end my inquiry. However, quite a few men of the old unit turned up at the ASTP reunion, with wives and fantastic stories of their experiences at Illinois College and elsewhere.

As the war drew to a close, President Hudson wrote, May 23, 1945, that even though enrollment was then one-fourth of normal, "Student activities are commencing to revive. The lights are beginning to come on again at Illinois College." An important factor was the quality of the student body. Using the results of the American Council on Education's Psychological Examination given to entering freshmen at 282 colleges and universities, he reported to the trustees: "This year our poorer students are as good as the average of other institutions, our average students are as good as the better students elsewhere, and our better students have notably high scores." He admitted that conditions were abnormal but he expected that "the general trend toward improvement of quality should continue."

He was pleased also to report that the faculty, after a two-year intensive study, had adopted some significant changes in curriculum. The college year, beginning in the fall of 1945, would be divided into three terms instead of two semesters, allowing for more offerings per instructor—four each per term for a total of twelve in place of five each per semester for a total of ten. This would require more work of both faculty and students—the statement was made soberly, not gleefully. The term system would also be more flexible for the scheduling of classes and, even more important, it would allow veterans to enter college at three different times of the year, rather than only two.

Under the new scheme a student in the first two years will pursue a curriculum of required subjects which is designed to afford a comprehensive basis for a truly liberal education, but which will permit sufficient latitude and flexibility in particular courses to accommodate individual differences of taste or capacity. In his last two years the student will devote most of his time to his field or fields of interest without restriction except such as is imposed by the subject matter itself. The field of concentration will be developed to suit his needs and purposes. . . . Several new course offerings have been provided in order to round out instruction in various fields. The new program is frankly experimental and will be modified as need arises.

While the program was new at Illinois College, it was based on studies of different approaches to the liberal arts being made in other institutions.

The President's presentation of the new program led him naturally to a matter that had long been on his mind. First came some comments on the raiding of faculties that was beginning to take place, in anticipation of the coming hordes of GIs. "Half the members of our present faculty, for the most part the ablest among them, have been approached by other institutions within the year. Some institutions which have made offers to members of our faculty seem to regard this College as if it were a jeep in an army salvage yard waiting to be stripped of every serviceable part." That comment led naturally to a crucial question that he wanted the Board to consider: "Our salary scale, relatively high when adopted, has not been changed in twenty years except to be reduced after the Ayers Bank failure. Part of the reduction was restored in 1936 but salaries are still 5% below the base rate. . . . Illinois College is surpassed by most of the other colleges in the state in buildings and equipment. It is superior in the strength and ability of its faculty alone. If that is lost, years will be required to regain the place which we have held. The life of Illinois College depends on retaining its excellent faculty."

Although he could not see the means for making any significant change in the salary scale, he proposed to restore the 5 percent salary cut still in force by way of adopting a retirement plan, namely that of the Teachers Insurance and Annuity Association of America, an outgrowth of Andrew Carnegie's teachers' pension fund. He wanted the Board also to approve a collective life insurance plan for members of the staff. These things had been talked about for years; now he urged the Board to do something about them. Hudson remained rather wary of the federal Social Security program, which was at that time voluntary for private educational institutions. When at a later date, the faculty voted in favor of participation in Social Security, he cheerfully acquiesced. He won approval of the Board for all of these fringe benefits, as they are sometimes called, and was able to hold on to faculty members who might otherwise have moved on to institutions that did offer these inducements. The President's Report for 1945–46 was almost buoyant in tone:

During the year Illinois College has come far toward recovery from conditions of the war years. With the return of men from military service the campus has assumed once more a natural appearance. Classes are full, the men's societies have been revived and nearly all student activities have gotten under way again. Intercollegiate athletics have taken the first difficult steps toward full resumption.

For next year, however, our problems have taken new forms. Instead of seeking students, we now must choose wisely from a flood of applicants. Instead of vacancies in dormitories, a shortage of housing for students, and for faculty as well, presents perplexing difficulties. Instead of members of the faculty leaving for other duties, scarcity of qualified teachers in almost every subject makes essential additional instructors unusually difficult to find. But these problems we welcome. They are problems of growth and vigorous life, not problems of war, deterioration and stagnation.

He could report that housing for veterans was being supplied by the Federal Public Housing Administration, and that it would house fifty-six single veterans in barracks-like quarters, and twenty-five married veterans in modified barracks, each containing a living room, kitchen, two bedrooms, and bath. Thus grew up the Illinois College Veterans Village, called by some "Fertile Valley," in the old orchard behind Russel House, on Park Street. These quarters—almost every college town in the United States had their counterparts —were not luxurious, but they were inexpensive and more than adequate for the veterans' purposes. Any profits made from their operation were to be refunded to the federal government; any losses were to be assumed by the colleges. It was a very fair arrangement. Many of the GIs who lived in them, especially the married ones, became sentimentally attached to them. One of the I.C. veterans told me years later, "They were as close to a man's castle as I had ever known."

To help provide classroom space for the GIs on campus, the government allocated another barracks-like structure, larger than the residences, which would contain eight classrooms, eleven faculty offices, and suitable toilet facilities. Thus "Federal Hall" was ready in September of 1947, and it served a useful purpose long after the veterans were gone. As the President reported: "The terms of the gift are very similar to those of the housing units: the College furnishes the site, plans and utilities up to the building; the government does the rest." The site chosen was northeast of Baxter, just west of where Ellis Hall now is, and the business manager, Mr. Arthur Samoore, laid it out in such a way that when the building was demolished, the concrete slab base would provide the foundation of an all-weather tennis court. It is so used today; thanks to the business manager's foresight, the College got a small future dividend from Uncle Sam.

Finding additional faculty, as the President noted, was not easy in a highly competitive market. Dr. Hudson found some very interesting ones, however. A notable example was Joachim Stenzel, German-born refugee from Hitler and the Nazis, who had served with the American Army in North Africa, become an American citizen, married an American girl, widow of an American soldier. Even with his accent, he was as American as apple pie. Stenzel's training was chiefly in the classics, but he was one of those people who could teach almost anything and do it well. He was for Illinois College an intellectual utility infielder. His attractiveness to the veterans was increased by the fact that he had been through many of the same experiences they had been through. In addition, he had served with the American legal staff at the Nuremberg trials of leading Nazis, as an interpreter. He could—and did—teach Latin and Greek, ancient history, German, all with great enthusiasm.

Perhaps the most vivid memories that veteran-students of that era still have are those of Professor Jesse L. Clements, the "Old Sarge." He came to the campus as Associate Professor of Education, Teacher Training Director, Placement Director, and as Veterans' Counsellor. He was adequate in the first three capacities, but he was superb in the last one. Let President Hudson describe him: "Himself a veteran of World War I and a father who lost his only child, a Marine killed in action on Iwo Jima, he has deep sympathy with the veterans, whose confidence he has won by patience and tact. He has helped them make out their applications for education and for subsistence, he has kept them informed of changes in policy in the Veterans Administration, and, in general, he has been tireless in securing for them all the benefits to which they are entitled. All of this has involved an immense amount of paper work. To his tact and good judgment with these men is due, in a large measure, the successful assimilation of veterans into the student body."

Anyone connected with the College during those postwar years is likely to look back on them as a very special era. Administrators were of course delighted to have students return in sufficient numbers to stimulate "growth and vigorous life," as President Hudson put it. Enrollment at Illinois College during the five postwar years was the greatest the College had ever known, and the veteran population was largely responsible. The following table tells the story of the veterans' impact on Illinois College.

	Men	Women	Total	Veterans
1946–47	419	133	552	64%
1947–48	455	131	586	53%
1948–49	439	124	563	41%
1949–50	381	130	511	33%
1950–51	291	110	401	21%

In addition, there were significant summer school enrollments in the summers of 1946 (134), 1947 (158), and 1948 (118). Illinois College held summer sessions largely for the benefit of the veterans who wanted to get on with their education as fast as they possibly could and into their careers and family lives. Moreover, the paper work required by the Veterans Administration took so long to process that a student at Illinois College who wanted to continue his education without interruption could scarcely have arranged to go elsewhere for the summer and then have returned to Illinois College for the fall term. It was a matter of necessity for the College as well as for the individual veterans.

Far more important than the numbers of students was the sense of purpose and maturity that pervaded the campus. No doubt there were some faculty members who were a little uneasy about being confronted by students in their twenties instead of their teens, students who came not directly from the farmlands and towns of Illinois, but from the battlefields of Europe and the South Pacific, students who were not pliable and amorphous, waiting the shaping hand of the professor but who had been disciplined by the rigors of camp and combat and were not about to accept pronouncements of fact and opinion simply because *magister dixit.*

Fortunately, the faculty was leavened with veterans, too, and those who had not been in service, had, many of them, the experience of dealing with the members of the ASTP unit, and all had had the opportunity of learning from their radios and their newspapers what the war experience was like—"the best reported war in human history," the journalists called it. Most important of all, the faculty was eager to understand what this generation of students had been through and to help them assimilate that experience into the main-stream of western culture and civilization. This may sound high-flown—it certainly was not a conscious, formulated program; it probably would not have worked if it had been—but I believe that it explains what happened at Illinois College and on the campuses of most of the colleges and universities of America following World War II. It accounts for one of the miracles of higher education in this country, when millions of young men and women, who in ordinary circumstances would not have thought of getting a college degree, suddenly found that it was possible and desirable, and might even be fun.

I believe that we can now look back on that period as one of the most truly revolutionary periods in our national life, a time when extraordinary—almost impossible—things could be accomplished by the individual human being within our democratic society. It was a time of rising hopes and a time of achieving those hopes. It took place in the afterglow of the most smashing victories—and not

merely military victories, though they were astounding—that the
United States had ever known. Each occupant of the classrooms of
America—teacher and taught—felt himself a part of the international
altruism of the Truman Doctrine and the Marshall Plan, NATO and
the United Nations, and all the rest of the idealistic schemes that
were being dreamed up and actually put into practice. Never mind
the fact that tarnish and corrosion dimmed those dreams. They
were glorious while they lasted, and education was part and parcel
of them. The excitement that existed on the campuses of America
was partly the result of those dreams, and partly the cause of them.

On the Illinois College campus, the administration, after organizing its housekeeping and taking care of the immediate needs of its
students, physical and intellectual, began to think of a more permanent kind of growth. From the time of his first accepting the
presidency, Dr. Hudson knew that Illinois College needed money—
money for buildings, for better equipping the library and laboratories, and for providing instruction in the aesthetic subjects. On
this latter point, he told the Trustees: "We should give instruction
in appreciation of the fine arts in order to develop intelligent listeners
and discriminating observers. Instruction in these subjects is definitely a part of education in the liberal arts, and if we offered it, we
would undoubtedly attract a desirable class of students, particularly
women."

More money was needed for raising faculty salaries, for promotion
and recruitment, and for endowment. Hudson knew the needs of the
College very well, and he made periodic efforts to meet them, but
he was never over-confident of his abilities as a money raiser. In
one of his semiannual reports to the Trustees, December 14, 1940, he
went into the matter at some length. He could envision three ways
of going about fund raising. One way was to leave it to the president,
but that would give him "divided and diffuse responsibilities. Moreover, the results of my efforts so far give no promise of my ability
to lead a financial campaign successfully." A second way would be
to employ a professional fund raiser. He thought that this was an
impersonal way for a small college to treat its alumni and friends,
and that "it involves a considerable financial commitment, with no
guarantee of success." A third way would be to add a competent

man to the College staff who would organize and direct such an appeal. That would involve a smaller initial commitment, it would lengthen the process, and it might not after all be satisfactory. Before any decision was made, we were in the war and it was decided that the time was not right. Almost plaintively, the President once asked, "Is there any right time for such an undertaking?"

For the duration, the only drive of any importance was to raise a sustaining fund, to take care of budgeted deficits and the renovation of Crampton Hall. He told the trustees that "mothers take one look at Crampton and depart. Few parents can evaluate faculty competence, but they can judge the adequacy of dorms in five minutes." Crampton was redecorated and refurbished at a cost of about fifteen thousand dollars. One other almost pathetic gesture was made toward the future building plans of the College. A building at the Illinois School for the Deaf was demolished about this time, and Illinois College purchased the salvageable brick for $782.75; with hauling charges, the cost was $970.25. Wrote the President to his Board: "When the brick has been cleaned and stacked, we shall be able either to sell it at a profit or to have it for our own use at a low cost." He pointed out that common brick was then going for $18 per thousand, and the price was rising. We were acquiring this brick for $5.50 per thousand—plus hauling and cleaning, of course. Students were amused and posted photographs of the I.C. brick pile, labeled "our new gymnasium." I have been told that the brick pile became a kind of penal colony for the ASTP unit. Soldiers might be sent there for so many hours of "cleaning brick" for minor infractions of Army regulations. Later they were sentenced to laying campus walks with these same bricks. At no cost to the College! Also during the war years, a student union was opened at what was known as "Kamm House." It was another fine old house on Mound Avenue, just across from Baxter Hall; it had been acquired very cheaply following a public auction. It soon became the campus hangout.

At a special Board meeting held October 10, 1944, a decision was made to experiment with the third alternative President Hudson had suggested earlier, namely to add "a competent man to the College staff" for the purpose of raising funds. Systematic solicitation was needed to meet the anticipated operating deficits "until things are

normal"; to bear the costs of "social security" for the staff; to renovate Beecher, Sturtevant, Jones, and Whipple; to provide increased
housing for students and faculty. Down the road were the long
anticipated new gymnasium, chapel, and heating plant; all of these
had been in Rammelkamp's centennial building fund plans but had
not been realized.

The person employed to implement these ambitious plans was
Irving E. W. Olson, a hard-working but somewhat ineffective fund
raiser, as it turned out. His major acquisition was a residence in
Pennsylvania, the gift of a good Christian woman who believed in
the kind of education she was told was going on out in Jacksonville,
Illinois. She deeded her house over to the College with an annuity
and possession until her death should occur. When that did occur,
certain of her relatives went to court to recover the property, and
litigation ensued. The property was eventually awarded to the College and sold, but the experience was not a pleasant or profitable
one.

One other acquisition was made about this time. The esteemed
hostelry of the west end of town, The Colonial Inn, was offered
for sale and purchased by the College for about twenty-five thousand
dollars. For a number of years it served as a dormitory for women,
and later for student nurses at Passavant Hospital who were taking
some of their class work at Illinois College. This latter arrangement
was mutually satisfactory to College and Hospital for a number of
years.

President Hudson was not happy about the efforts that were being
made to strengthen the material standing of the College, but he had
no alternatives to suggest. He respected Mr. Olson and was sure that
he was a hard worker, though not a very successful one. He said
to his Board in May of 1945: "I propose to keep on this course, but
I shall not hold this position indefinitely. If I do not see results in a
reasonable length of time, I shall give way to someone who can raise
the money we need."

At length, in January of 1946, the Trustees decided to try the professional approach and hired the New York firm of Marts and
Lundy, Inc. to conduct a concentrated drive to raise funds for a new
gymnasium. A representative of that firm came to Jacksonville and

organized a campaign that used all the techniques of the big city—brochures and letters and telephone calls, regional territories, teams with captains, and the like. The local campaign was kicked off with a dinner for workers, at the State Street Presbyterian Church, with Ray Eliot (University of Illinois football coach and former coach at Illinois College) making an inspirational "Go! Go!" speech. Other meetings were held around the country to whip up enthusiasm.

But when the results finally came in, eighteen months later, they were not what was hoped for. Approximately $110,000 was raised, but at a cost of $46,500; belated contributions to the fund altered these figures slightly. Said President Hudson: "I am frankly disappointed in the results obtained by the campaign. Much hard work went into its prosecution and I am at a loss to understand why it did not have a greater measure of success, unless the inertia resulting from the lapse of more than twenty years since the last previous solicitation for the College was too great to overcome in eighteen months. We could not know without making the attempt. . . . The campaign, if it has done nothing else, has restored contact between us and many alumni with whom we had lost touch. It has undoubtedly proved to be good public relations."

Mr. Olson was retained for a while to "mop up," as the vulgar professional jargon has it. A decision was made to build as much as could be built with what had been raised, but when the second firm of architects prepared the specifications and bids were let, they came in very much above the architects' estimates. Further economies were negotiated with the low bidder, and the Memorial Gymnasium was at long last begun. Said the President: "In my opinion this was a wise step. Although all the funds needed for the first unit are not in hand, the further postponement of construction would have resulted in such discouragement among our friends and in the community that it probably would have been impossible to secure a substantial amount in additional gifts within the next ten or fifteen years." The first phase of the gymnasium was placed in use in the fall of 1951.

It is somewhat ironic that Dr. Hudson's major money raising effort was devoted to the physical education side of the College, for that was not his chief interest, as the reader must have sensed. There

The Memorial Gymnasium. Drawing by Dorothy B. Frank

were some students and some alumni who thought that he did not give sports sufficient emphasis. While he certainly did not over-emphasize the role of intercollegiate athletics, I think it only fair to note that in his administration the teams representing the College were adequately equipped and physically cared for and that they were well regarded by the College community, students, faculty, and alumni. He appointed coaches who liked to win, but not at any cost, men of the calibre of Alf Lamb, Al Miller, and Joe Brooks. If these men and their teams did not often bring fame to the College, they always upheld its good name, on and off the field. The President in his annual reports to the Trustees spoke with cordiality of teams that enjoyed moderate success and with compassion of those that had losing seasons. The report of 1946-47 is typical: "Our teams have been a credit to Illinois College. Exhibiting clean sportsmanship, they have played hard and courageously against formidable odds, never losing their morale in defeat after defeat and always respected by their opponents who have never dared to take them lightly."

A second campaign known as the Forward Movement was conducted in the last years of the Hudson administration. Its purpose was to finance the restoration of Beecher Hall—a simultaneous campaign was conducted by the Sigs and the Phis to assist in the interior redecoration of their halls—and to supply funds toward the building of a new dormitory. Dr. Harold Gibson '30 and Mr. Russell Kohr, director of public relations, organized this effort. The campaign was successful, in part because the College qualified for a $200,000 federal loan, at a very low interest rate, to be amortized over a forty-year period.

President Hudson did not have the heart for large-scale fund raising, and he knew it; that kind of job seemed to require a Madison Avenue bustle that was repugnant to him. It is therefore pleasant to record that in his last years Gary Hudson was rewarded for his perseverance and integrity by receiving the largest bequest for the College in its history until that time. This was the William and Charlotte Gardner estate. An inventory of that estate dated January 1, 1950, shows gross assets of $389,785, with taxes and other expenses of $81,627, leaving a net of $308,161. Few outside his family and close friends knew how humanely Gary and his wife, Ruth, had cared for the social and intellectual needs of Judge and Mrs. Gardner, and for how long a period of time. There was friendship and affection between the Hudsons and the Gardners, but certainly the pilgrimages of the Hudsons to Red Oak, Iowa, went far beyond the requirements of friendship. The Judge had told Gary that his considerable estate would one day come to the College, and Gary showed his gratitude in the name of the College as well as in the name of personal friendship. That was the kind of fund raising Gary Hudson did well. The William and Charlotte Gardner Chair in History was established in memory of these generous friends, and the new men's dormitory mentioned above was named for them.

President Hudson had returned to the plan of appointing to the staff someone to assist him with the tasks of fund raising. In the fall of 1949, Mr. Russell V. Kohr became the president's right hand, with the title Director of Public Relations. He not only assisted the President by making contacts with possible donors and following up on them but did a variety of other things. At one point when the College had engaged a young and inexperienced director of admissions, Mr. Kohr, who had been an admissions man at Northwestern University before coming to Illinois College, oversaw that department. He was both an idea man and a leg man. There have been regular successors in this role at the College: men like Leonard Wilson, John Pearson, Larry Bienert, Charles Bellatti, and Howard Jarratt, whose functions have not always been perfectly understood or appreciated by the students, faculty, and alumni, but to whom a succession of presidents has been indebted. At the same time, all presidents of the College have discovered that, finally, the decisions must be made by the president himself, that the letters and calls that produce results are the president's. Donors of great magnitude and of little magnitude want the personal attention of *numero uno*, to use the expressive slang phrase.

A development of the early fifties reinforces this opinion. The Federation of Illinois Colleges, taking a cue from successes in the state of Indiana, began systematic solicitation of the corporations within Illinois in 1951. The president had to be personally involved in this solicitation, as he told his Trustees: "The college presidents make their calls in pairs, pointing out that free American business and higher education have a fundamental community of interest and that higher taxes for the unnecessary duplication of educational facilities by the tax-supported colleges and universities are inevitable unless the private institutions are kept strong." This approach has provided steady and growing support for meeting the operating expenses of private institutions in the state of Illinois. An equitable division of the contributions has been worked out, and all the beneficiaries seem to be happy with the plan.

The early fifties were made especially difficult for educational institutions by the Cold War and by McCarthyism, and most of all by the Korean conflict. These phenomena had different specific points of origin, but they arose from the common miasma of national and international suspicions. The vision glorious of the immediate postwar era had faded, and Americans had lost faith in their ability to create a brave new world here at home as well as abroad. In place of confidence among faculty and students, there was restlessness and insecurity. On top of all that came a wave of inflation that wiped out the financial gains that had been made by the families of students and faculty alike. In addition to all other problems the lower birth rate of the Thirties began to show up in the enrollment figures. Thus, after the veterans were largely taken care of, there began a new decline in the student population of Illinois College, as shown in the following table.

	Men	*Women*	*Total*
1951–52	219	64	283
1952–53	188	62	250
1953–54	161	61	222

At the beginning of the decline, Illinois College made application for an Army ROTC unit and later for an Air Force ROTC unit; in both cases the application was turned down on the ground that the College was "too small to warrant the assignment of the requisite staff for a unit." That may have been fortunate, for an ROTC unit on a small campus is bound to wield considerable impact on the host institution, as experience on some American campuses during the Sixties will attest.

Alternative programs were experimented with. Adult Education was attempted. It had a modest success, but not enough to offset the declines in the regular registration. The program for nurses, in association with the Passavant Area Memorial Hospital was continued and expanded. A "three-two" program was set up with the Illinois Institute of Technology. Under this program, a student took three years of work at Illinois College and two years at the Illinois Institute of Technology; at the end of five years, if all went well, and it usually did, the student received two degrees, a B.S. degree from Illinois College and the appropriate engineering degree from Illinois Tech. According to the official statement of the College, "The advantages of the plan from the student's point of view are (1) that with a solid foundation in the liberal arts he may become a better engineer than with only narrow technical training, (2) that he has three years in which without loss of time he may change his goal if he finds that his capabilities suggest another profession than engineering, and (3) that the actual pecuniary cost is less than for four years at an engineering school." The College did have to make some curricular changes, but they were not many nor extensive, and it was hoped that the program would attract students who might not have considered enrolling in a liberal arts college. Other programs of a similar kind have since been undertaken with the Missouri School of Mines (now the University of Missouri at Rolla) and with the University of Illinois. These are sound programs, but they have not notably increased enrollment at Illinois College.

The Illinois College Community Development Program was begun in September of 1950, by the College sociology department in cooperation with the Division for Youth and Community Service of the Illinois Department of Public Welfare. The College and the Department of Public Welfare were concerned about "the democratic processes of self-government, particularly as related to small communities." Each agency had certain advantages to offer in launching such an effort, and these would be increased if they worked in concert. The fact that one was a private agency and the other a public agency only made their cooperation more promising.

The College is located in the heart of a number of typical small communities that might profit from studies made and actions suggested; many of its students come from small communities and, after graduation, return to them. The state has many public welfare interests in the communities of west central Illinois, and these are often operated independently, without much awareness of the needs of others. Moreover, the state operates three important welfare institutions in Jacksonville—the then School for the Deaf, the School for the Blind, and the State Hospital—and all these institutions have highly skilled personnel who could contribute to such a program and would be pleased to have the opportunity. The concept of the Community Development Program was a worthy one.

In addition to training a considerable number of students in the field of rural sociology, the program performed numerous services to the communities where it operated, such as helping Chapin (pop. 550) find a doctor, assisting in the development of Youth Centers in Pittsfield (pop. 3,600), Waverly (1,400) and White Hall (3,100). In some cases, it acted as a catalyst to get citizens together to discuss their local problems, and perhaps to take action on them.

Over a period of several years, Illinois College bulletins were issued describing the projects being undertaken, the persons involved in them, and the success—or lack of success—those projects met with. In addition to the sponsorship of the College and the Illinois Department of Public Welfare, the program won small grants of money from the Chicago Community Trust and the Moorman Foundation of Quincy. Dr. Malcolm Stewart was adviser to the program, and at different stages, Illinois College sociologists Lloyd Gohn, Severyn Bruyn, and Phillips Ruopp were associated with the operation. So also were many community leaders from the YMCA, the three state institutions in Jacksonville, and the churches and social agencies of Morgan County. While it operated, the program had the support of President Hudson and later President Selden; it served many useful purposes, educational and social. But it never became a bureaucracy or attained a vested interest in the College or the community. When it had served its purposes and interest in it declined, it was allowed to expire, without unwarranted mourning.

About to arrive at the three-score and five mark, the time set by Board action for faculty retirement, President Hudson, at the semi-annual meeting of the trustees on December 13, 1952, stated his intention to retire on July 1, 1953. He wrote: "While the president does not have tenure in the same sense as other members of the faculty, he was included among those covered by the retirement plan. If the principle of the plan is beneficial to the College, as I believe it is, it applies with greater force to the president than to any other officer. The duties of his office impose an unremitting tax upon the energy and resources of the incumbent, far greater than even a generation ago. More than the members of other professions a college president requires for the proper discharge of his duties a combination of vigor, patience, boldness and resourceful imagination for which even long experience is no substitute."

He believed that he had earned his retirement, and the trustees reluctantly agreed. The last months of the Hudsons on campus were among the happiest they had known there. They were feted, as they should have been. They received many gifts large and small. Among those of interest to posterity was a portrait of President Hudson by the Chicago artist, Christian Abrahamson. At its unveiling, Dr. Hudson noted that in the portrait he is wearing appropriate academic regalia—his doctoral robe and his Oxford hood—and that the book he is cradling in his left hand is a "beloved copy of Thomas Moore's translation of *The Odes of Anacreon.*" That portrait hangs in the Faculty-Trustee Room of Tanner Hall. The Board also presented Dr. Hudson a generous purse and the "equity in the College car" that he had been driving for the last two years!

There were other memorable moments, as when Ruth Hudson was invited by the president of the Chicago alumni society to address their annual banquet meeting. She made a graceful little speech entitled "The President's Wife." After referring to Maggie, wife of John Shand, politician, in Barrie's play *What Every Woman Knows*, Mrs. Hudson said:

Like Maggie, the wife of the president would do well to work quietly in the background. There is a constant danger of being thought a Mrs. President. And yet, on a campus such as ours, it is inevitable that the wife of the president is aware of all the crises, the frustrations, and the disappointments, as well as the successes of her husband.

Happy is that president's wife who is born with a sense of humor and is able to maintain it under all circumstances. She must show no surprise if her Lennox dinner plates, missing all summer, turn up in Sigma Pi Hall in September with bits of food from the Love Feast of June. She must show no surprise if the carved mahogany ball atop the newell post in the hall of the president's house has been gone all winter only to reappear in a skit at Phi Alpha Open Meeting in May.

The *Alumni Quarterly*, July 1953, presented a "Presidential Portrait" of its own, complete with delightful photographs out of the Hudson family album, including one of Gary, age *circa* eight, seated at the family organ in Osaka, with mother, father, and siblings gathered around singing hymns; another of Gary as a soldier; another with Ruth and daughters Elizabeth and Ann before a glowing fire in the grate at the president's house; and one of Ruth and Gary at the grand piano in the living room. The article reviews the Hudson years compactly and affectionately, concluding: "They will be much missed at the College, and we have tried to tell them so. Truly the good wishes of a unified College go with them."

Perhaps that note of unification is the right one to strike in closing this chapter. As one reviews the Hudson years from 1937 to 1953, a "long lap," as he called it, that achievement outweighs all others. He himself liked metaphors of Marathon, the long pull that depended on stability and endurance. Going through some of his papers in preparation for writing this chapter, I came across a letter to him from his brother Donald, dated June 29, 1937. That of course was the very time when Dr. Hudson was considering whether or not to accept the presidency of Illinois College. Brother Donald was strongly in favor of his doing this; he concluded his letter in this way: "You asked what becomes of ex-presidents. I thought you knew. They grow old gracefully, and they mellow with age. They also grow Van Dykes and speak in soft tones. They live to be seventy and eighty years old and write books about their experiences. They have summer cottages upon Lake Michigan and finally they take the form of bronze plaques in the Library."

Not all of these things have happened, but the comment seems almost prophetic, even to the bronze plaque in the library. There is such a plaque in the Schewe Library, on the wall of the H. Gary Hudson Faculty Research Room. It was dedicated on January 16, 1978, with due ceremony and the incantation of one of Gary Hudson's favorite phrases from the *Aeneid: "Procul, O, procul este, profani!"* That is to say, "Far away, keep far away, O ye uninitiated!"

That is a lively epitaph for the man and his enduring influence on liberal education at Illinois College.

21

President Selden, 1953–1955

In a letter addressed to the alumni of Illinois College, January 1, 1953, President Hudson had announced his retirement, saying: "As in a relay race, there is a certain space in which the baton must be passed from the hand of one runner to the hand of the next. I have run a long lap and it is time for a fresh runner to enter the race. If I hold the baton too long, I may stumble or fall, causing my successor to lose stride. It is time for Illinois College to secure a new president with fresh vigor, fresh ideas and fresh skills."

The man to whom Gary Hudson passed the baton nine months later was William Kirkpatrick Selden. Forty years old, the youngest of five children, born and raised in Oil City, Pennsylvania, Selden was a graduate of Princeton University, class of 1934. There, among other things, he had been business manager of the *Daily Princetonian* and had had the great good fortune to attract the notice of Dean Christian Gauss, one of the ablest and most beloved of Princeton's collegiate hierarchy. For three years after graduation, young Selden learned the ways of academic administration under the direction of this master craftsman. Following his years at Princeton, Selden worked for nearly a year at Eastman Kodak before returning to campus life, accepting a post at Brown University. He spent seven years at Brown in administrative work, as Assistant Director of Admissions, Assistant Dean, and finally as Assistant to the President. Next he went to Northwestern University, where he spent eight years more in administration work, specializing in admissions. He also worked with Naval ROTC projects and was an adviser to the

Fund for the Advancement of Education, a division of the Ford Foundation.

No doubt all this experience in the "business" side of the academic world had impressed the Illinois College Committee on the Selection of a President, chaired by Dr. F. G. Norbury. Dr. Norbury reported to his fellow trustees that his committee had considered more than two hundred names submitted to it. Nine candidates had been interviewed and seven brought to the campus before a decision was reached to recommend William K. Selden. There was no doubt that Selden had been intimately connected with good institutions, all in the independent sector of higher education, though they were not small colleges.

Perhaps the thing that most impressed the trustees and faculty who met Bill Selden—he preferred the informal "Bill"—was his buoyancy, his almost boyish enthusiasm. His family, consisting of his wife Ginny, a Smith College graduate, and two boys, Van and Jebs, were also tremendous assets. It was a handsome, outgoing family that settled into the president's house in September of 1953. The transition from one administration to another had never been more smoothly, more gracefully made. There was none of the trauma that had followed the death of President Rammelkamp in 1932 or the abrupt departure of President Jaquith in 1937.

But, by the time of his inauguration, which took place on December 11, 1953, President Selden had begun to realize fully the magnitude of the task he had undertaken. The ceremony that evening was marked by "distinctive simplicity and dignity," according to the *Alumni Quarterly*. Chairman Dunbaugh welcomed William K. Selden as "a man qualified by his wide educational experience, his belief in the liberal arts college, his lovable personality, his Christian faith, and by his consecration to the future of Illinois College," and proclaimed him with all due ceremony "ninth President of Illinois College." Mr. Selden responded by paying homage to the founders, their courage and vision, but, he said, it would take more than courage and vision today. "Every college, and Illinois College is no exception, in these days of inflation, needs—desperately needs—financial support in sums that only a few years past would have been considered fanciful and illusionary. . . . As we look to the future we

President William K. Selden

can gain courage from the past. We have today in Jacksonville the factors and the forces ready to make in this community a great center of education. . . . We must not fail to bequeath to future generations what the Yale Band visualized. . . . In this, with your help, we shall not fail."

In the Winter 1954 *Alumni Quarterly* that reported the inauguration of President Selden, there is a reprint of an editorial that had appeared in the St. Louis *Post-Dispatch*, written by Irving Dilliard, under the title "Elm Trees and Ideals." After noting the approaching installation of President Selden, Mr. Dilliard wrote: "Undoubtedly Dr. Selden will have his eye on the approaching 125th anniversary and the role of his institution in the future. Yet he will be better able to see ahead if he looks back now and then at the work of his early forerunners—men with names like Beecher, Lockwood and Turner, Baldwin, Blackburn and Brooks. For the pioneers at Jacksonville planted not only elm trees from New England but ideals as well. President Selden, who takes over now, has a charge to keep and a tradition to cherish."

That was an interesting note to strike, in view of the approaches the new president was even then contemplating. A little later, in his first annual report to the trustees he had some startling suggestions. Parts of that report were published in the Summer 1954 *Alumni Quarterly* under the title "To Think Anew and Act Anew":

You are seeing some changes on this campus. . . . Frequently change is hard to accept. "If only things could remain as they are, life would be so much simpler!" But life is neither simple nor static; rather it is dynamic and full of changes; changes, for which we must continually be preparing. . . .

"Dogmas of the quiet past are inadequate for the stormy present. The occasion is piled high with difficulties and we must rise with the occasion. As our case is new, so we must think anew and act anew." President Lincoln included that statement in a message to Congress in December, 1862 in a proposal for compensated emancipation, yet its appropriateness is applicable again in this, the heart of the land of Lincoln where an entire community is affected by two colleges as they think anew and as they act anew.

"To dream of a golden age not in the past but in the future"— that may be the privilege of college presidents but it is also an opportunity for the entire college community.

It was shrewd of Mr. Selden to cite Abraham Lincoln as a text for a grand scheme which would be revealed in the coming year of 1954–55. Before looking into that scheme in detail, I should like to note some of the solutions Mr. Selden applied to the immediate problems the College was facing.

One of the first things President Selden did after he arrived on campus was to have surveys made by the Building and Grounds Committee of the Board of Trustees, in order to assess the state of the College plant. That committee called on two professionals, Hugh Gibson, Jacksonville contractor and graduate of Illinois College, and Richard Wyeth, a plant engineer of Springfield. Mr. Gibson submitted a detailed report, building by building, need by need. His conclusion was that to restore campus buildings to "practical standards of a modern college" would cost approximately one-half million dollars. Mr. Wyeth used the Gibson report as a basis for his own less detailed report, but after concurring with the Gibson report, he wrote: "All your buildings have been suffering from an acute case of 'falling-down maintenance.' It seems quite evident to me that, for a considerable number of years, only those things which have literally collapsed have been repaired."

An early decision was made to get rid of those buildings that would be expensive to repair and maintain and to restore the rest to respectable condition. The old gymnasium, the Old Club House, and Kamm House (the student union) were designated as obsolete and no longer needed, since a new gymnasium was already in operation and a new dormitory containing a student union would be ready for use by September 1954. Also doomed were some "huts" along Lincoln Avenue, formerly part of the "Veterans Village" of the postwar years. These buildings would not be missed, none of them being of either aesthetic or historic value. It is true that the Old Club House was second only to Beecher in age and that it was the home of Gamma Nu, but even Nuers were not attached to it, and would be willing to settle for other, and almost certainly better quarters. The old gymnasium had a certain quaintness that reminded some people of the Governor's Palace at Williamsburg, but there was little sentiment about it either.

The decision to redecorate Crampton and house women there after the new men's dormitory was completed was generally hailed as a sound one. Until enrollment went up markedly, there was no need for two large dormitories for men, yet Crampton rehabilitated would be a real asset, looking toward future growth. By using Crampton for women, the women's residences—Elliott, Fayerweather, and Russel, charming but expensive to operate—could be closed or turned to other uses, faculty housing perhaps. The whole program seemed eminently sensible.

I remember returning to the campus in September 1954, after a year's leave of absence, and feeling that a rebirth had taken place; the slightly seedy look of the recent past was gone, and there was fresh paint everywhere. "Fresh vigor, fresh ideas and fresh skills" was what President Hudson had called for. President Selden had also supplied fresh paint, and there was new hope in people's faces. But of course, these were cosmetic changes and much more was needed, if the bright future were to become more than an illusion. In the last years of the Hudson administration, an effort had been made to open conversations with MacMurray College about cooperative efforts to enrich the offerings at both colleges and yet reduce expenses. It was, for instance, foolish for the two college libraries to duplicate holdings, except for basic reference works, standard classics, widely read periodicals, and the like. Yet, because there was no clearing house, much duplication occurred, unwittingly. Both colleges had need of basic courses in English and history and mathematics, in foreign languages and the natural sciences. In each of those fields, however, advanced courses might be given, some at the one and some at the other, to the great advantage of both colleges and their students. Neither college could afford a good program in classics— since the war Illinois College had barely kept a makeshift program going—or in the earth sciences or anthropology. And there were numerous other instances where cooperative effort would have paid off. The question was especially pertinent at that time because the "conservatory agreement" of 1928 expired in 1953, and there were those who thought that Illinois College should once again develop a program in music.

Moreover, MacMurray College had had a change of administration in 1952 and the new president, Dr. Louis W. Norris, was eager to talk cooperation with Illinois College. So, during Hudson's last year and Norris's first year, there was much exploration of the possibilities. The two presidents sought to develop separate but shared "pools of excellence." To this end, they appointed faculty committees to work both separately and jointly, on the potentials of exchange. As a first step, they organized an exchange program on the basis of what already existed at the two colleges. Then they developed "Principles for Exchange of Students and Faculty between MacMurray College and Illinois College agreed upon by President Norris and President Hudson, June 30, 1953."

Exchange of Students

1. Where students enrolled in MacMurray College register also at Illinois College, or vice versa, the college of their primary registration shall collect the tuition and pay the college of secondary registration at the rate of $15. per semester hour, or $10. per term hour respectively.
2. Each college shall calculate and pay tuition due the other semi-annually.
3. Students are subject to the academic and social regulations of the college, or colleges, in which they are enrolled. Should disciplinary action beyond academic penalties be necessary, responsibility for its execution rests with the college of their primary registration. The college of secondary registration should, however, make a report of violations at issue, and may make recommendations for action needed.
4. Where transportation between campuses is furnished, the responsibility for it belongs to the college of the student's primary registration. Its cost will be shared in proportion to the number of students from each college.
5. Fees incidental to a particular course shall be paid at the college where the instruction is given.

Professors Teaching in the Exchange Programs

1. Professors are subject to the regulations and traditions of the college in which their instruction is given. They shall be regarded as voting members of the faculty in the college of their primary employment.
2. Fifteen credit hours of teaching shall be regarded as a normal load at MacMurray and sixteen credit hours at Illinois College.

    (a) Laboratory work shall be counted at the rate of three clock hours for two credit hours.

    (b) Other responsibilities considered a part of a professor's normal load shall be given such rating as may be determined by consultation between the President and Dean of the college of his primary employment and the professor involved.

3. In determining the salary paid for such exchange of services, the credit hours taught shall be counted as part of the regular load of the professor.

    (a) The college borrowing the professor shall pay that part of the salary at the salary rate of the college of his or her primary employment which is represented by the credit hours of instruction offered and at the rate of salary paid by the college of primary employment.

    (b) In cases where instruction at either college would mean, by virtue of exchanged services, additional hours above his normal load, salary for the overload shall be paid at the rate per hour which the professor receives for a normal load.

    (c) One term credit hour at Illinois College shall be counted $\frac{2}{3}$ of a semester credit hour at MacMurray College.

    (d) The number of credit hours taught in either institution, i.e., overload or underload, shall be calculated on the basis of the full year, and the salary adjusted accordingly.

4. Total salary payments shall be made at the college of primary employment. Tax and annuity calculations shall be made as if the total work of the professor were done at the college of primary employment.

    (a) Each college shall calculate and pay the salary payments due the other semi-annually, viz., December 31 and June 30.

This document sounds as if it had been drawn by the business managers of the two colleges, with legal counsel. Nonetheless, it was well to work out these details at the very start so that no misunderstandings would later occur and mar the working arrangements between the colleges. It should be pointed out that at the time these agreements were entered into, the tuition rates and the salary scales at the two colleges were very similar, so that there was no haggling necessary on those scores.

    This agreement, be it noted, was entered into on June 30, 1953, and signed by both presidents; it was thus one of the last official acts of Gary Hudson's presidency. It was, of course, a nuts and bolts arrangement, but it was a beginning, and more imaginative things could be attempted if this sort of approach worked well. In its first year, 1953–54, it had some success, but not as much as had been hoped for. Many reasons were given for its less than satisfactory success, but the most convincing one had to do with the calendars of the two institutions. Illinois College was on the quarter or term system, adopted to better serve the veteran population of the late forties and early fifties; MacMurray was on the semester system and always had been. What this meant was that examinations and vacations occurred at different times on the two campuses, so that a student trying to take work at both colleges was bound to have some conflicts. Perhaps if the separate but joint committees of the two faculties had worked at this problem more diligently, they might have found solutions, but they didn't. Instead, they reported that unless comparable calendars could be arranged, it was hopeless to attempt to increase student exchanges between the two campuses.

A compromise was reached; Illinois College returned to the semester system which it had abandoned a decade ago. The changeover was voted by the Illinois College faculty—not unanimously—and it was to take effect in September 1955. There was some grumbling about this on the Illinois College campus by students and faculty alike, those who much preferred the quarter system. Some of the grumbling came over the fact that Illinois College had given up something important but had got nothing in return.

Illinois College had had a "self-study" program going during Hudson's last several years. It was thought by members of the Committee on Self Study that they would make more and faster progress if their study could be funded. A large sum was not needed but enough to give committee members some released time, some secretarial help, perhaps some travel money to observe innovative programs at work on other campuses. What academic doesn't dream of such rewards for committee work? In any case, an application had been made to the Fund for the Advancement of Education for a grant to assist in this study. It was denied. Mr. Selden thought that such an application would have a much better chance of being funded if it came from both colleges. A joint Illinois-MacMurray application was prepared for submission to the Fund for the Advancement of Education, but it also failed to win approval. Then the two colleges asked the North Central Association to authorize a study by some of their experts, the cost to be shared equally by the two colleges. (The study was partly underwritten by a local manufacturing company, Nesco, which had an interest in the welfare of both colleges.) This request was granted. The study was made by Professor M. G. Neale, College of Education, the University of Minnesota; Charles J. Turck, President, Macalester College; and Harry Wells, Vice-President, Northwestern University, and the results published on May 25, 1954.

The title of the twenty-five page analysis and set of recommendations was: "A Co-ordinated Educational Program for Illinois College and MacMurray College, Jacksonville, Illinois." The study committee examined pertinent documents at both colleges, was given access to their financial records, consulted with the faculty self-study committees of both colleges, and conferred at length with the two presidents about their respective problems. The report sets forth significant statistics about enrollments of the past five years, curricula, educational goals, future prospects, etc. After making this analysis in a very objective way, the committee made these specific suggestions regarding possible future cooperation between the institutions:

1. Let art be taught by MacMurray College only.

2. Let biology, for the present, be given on both campuses.

3. Let chemistry be confined to Illinois College. (The laboratories there must be cleaned up. MacMurray would continue chemistry courses for home economics.)

4. Let economics and business administration be confined to Illinois College, and secretarial studies and office management to MacMurray, but with the introductory course in economics given on both campuses.

5. Let education be divided into elementary and seondary, with elementary at MacMurray and secondary at Illinois, and full exchange of students permitted in both fields.

6. Let English be maintained on both campuses, with different advanced courses given on each campus, and full exchange of students permitted.

7. Let the classics be given only at Illinois.

8. Let modern foreign languages be centered at Illinois, with first and/or second year courses in French (perhaps other languages) to be given at MacMurray also. Perhaps add Russian at Illinois.

9. Let geography be given only at Illinois.

10. Let government or political science be maintained at both colleges.

11. Let history be maintained at both colleges.

12. Let mathematics center at Illinois, with introductory courses at MacMurray.

13. Let music center at MacMurray, but each college needs its own choir. Illinois must have a band, but it should not duplicate other music offerings.

14. Philosophy and religion should be coordinated at both campuses, and the coordinated department can offer work on each campus. Additional personnel for this department would seem to be indicated.

15. Physical education would necessarily be maintained on both campuses.

16. Let physics be confined to Illinois College.

17. Let psychology be given in both colleges.

18. Let sociology be given in both colleges.

19. Let speech and drama be given in both colleges in and through a co-ordinated department.

The report says further: "The above plan does not merge the colleges or the faculties, and maintains more departments than strict economy would require. However, it is important that each college should have a representative number of basic departments organized and functioning on its own campus." Many other questions were considered, and the report specifically ruled out a student referendum on the matter "because of the difficulty of giving the students complete background information and because of the stake in the two institutions held by elements of the clientele other than students."

Pointing to the success of cooperative ventures at Hobart and William Smith Colleges, Tulane and Newcomb, Centre College and the Kentucky College for Women, and on a larger scale, Harvard and Radcliffe, the report recommended that the two colleges continue to operate as separate entities, but ultimately that they form "the Affiliated or Associated Colleges of Jacksonville, Illinois" and be ready "to join in financial campaigns, statewide publicity, and even in the joint solicitation of students."

The committee report says further that "each of these colleges faces a serious financial challenge if it is to weather the next eight or ten years." After commenting favorably on some aspects of the Illinois College campus, the report says: "Many of the buildings are obsolete, several are obsolescent, and no adequate program of repairs has been recently in effect." Elsewhere, the report says: "The physical facilities of MacMurray College appear to be above average for North Central institutions in its group," but "financially, MacMurray could become even more hazardous than Illinois College. MacMurray has encumbered its future growth by borrowing against assets which may not be available for many years. As a result of this, income which might have been available to the budget is foreclosed."

I imagine that some of these blunt statements made painful reading for trustees on both campuses, but they appear to be impartially given, and they come from men of stature in the field of higher education. The report makes eight further recommendations, of which, in the light of the controversy that was to develop in the coming months on both campuses and in the community, these three are especially pertinent:

Since setting up a long-range program of institutional cooperation would require a long period of time, the committee recommends that the two colleges extend at once cooperative activities in their educational programs and student social life.
Establish in Jacksonville and among the clientele the concept of the *Jacksonville Affiliated Colleges*.
In conclusion, the committee desires to point out that to establish the concept of the *Jacksonville Affiliated Colleges* there will need to be complete confidence on the part of the citizens of Jacksonville, the college trustees, and the administration and faculty of each institu-

tion. To assure this, the committee recommends the appointment of a liaison committee, with representatives of all groups concerned, clothed with considerable responsibility to resolve interrelated problems as they arise.

In none of the eight recommendations, of which I have given the last three, is there mention of merger or fusion; and hasty action is specifically ruled out.

I think it is imperative for the reader to be acquainted with the main provisions of this report if he is to understand the furore that arose over attempts to implement the North Central Association Program for Illinois College and MacMurray College during the academic year of 1954–55. Some of the people who contributed to the furore tended to overlook this background material; misunderstandings arose, and things were said and done that now, almost a quarter century later, do not seem reasonable. Positions were taken, and sides were chosen up, and longtime friendships were bruised, if not broken. To establish an exact chronology of the events is not easy, but there is a helpful document that I shall draw on. I doubt that many people know of its existence, but it was composed shortly after the events by one of the principal participants in them. It is "A Case Study used at the Harvard Institute for College and University Administrators," prepared in 1955–56. The Harvard Institute was established to give guidance to new college presidents, letting them participate in an intensive study of an actual collegiate incident and discuss it among themselves with the intention of seeing how and why certain problems occurred and perhaps of suggesting better ways of dealing with such problems. To protect the privacy of the institutions and individuals involved, the names of persons and places were usually fictionalized, though the events themselves were portrayed with as much fidelity as possible.

As one who lived through the experience and played an active role in it, I have examined this case study very carefully and I think I can say that it is a generally accurate account of what happened in Jacksonville, Illinois, during the year 1954–55, insofar as relations between Illinois College and MacMurray College are concerned. I would have written the story differently and so, no doubt, would every other person who took part in it, but I think we could all agree on the main outlines, even though details would differ and the conclusions would differ.

The case study in question is forty pages long; its inclusion *in toto* would magnify the incident out of all proportion to its importance in this history. It presents an abbreviated history of the two colleges, here called Shields College (Illinois College) and Reynolds College (MacMurray College). The town, instead of being Jacksonville, Illinois, is Rotan, Iowa. The respective presidents are named Dale (Selden) and Briscoe (Norris). There are tables and statistics regarding enrollments, balance sheets of assets and plants, make-up of faculties and boards of trustees. All these details check out with the actual situations of Illinois College and MacMurray College at the time. So does the account of the North Central Association Program, which is presented very much as I have given it above, including the nineteen recommendations, word for word.

As I recall, it was the understanding of the Illinois College faculty committee that the proposed "Coordinated Educational Program" was to be the basis for further intensive study by the faculty committees on cooperation. The Illinois College committee met both separately and jointly with their MacMurray counterparts. During the fall semester of 1954–55, committee members reported back to their Illinois College colleagues, formally and informally; I believe the same procedure was used at MacMurray. In any case, there was a cordial, business-like exchange of information and views between the two faculties. The "complete confidence" the North Central report called for appeared to be developing, at the faculty level.

A few trustees from both institutions kept in touch, but it is much more difficult for widely scattered trustees, with very divergent interests, to meet together or even to exchange views by letter or telephone. Apparently, they delegated their interest and authority to the elected presidents, who had greater opportunities for meetings and discussions. The respective presidents conferred with each other and from time to time with members of their boards who had shown special concern for improving the financial and academic situations of their colleges. It does not appear, however, that there was any significant exchange of information between the administrative authorities and the faculty committees. They appear to have been pursuing rather different courses, though ostensibly attempting to solve the same series of problems. The faculty committees were in search of ways to improve educational exchange that would enrich the programs at both colleges and at the same time result in economies. The administrative authorities had apparently already decided that such solutions would not work and that there was only one way to deal with the economic problems of the two colleges, and that was to merge them and deal with the academic questions once the merger was complete.

To return to the Harvard case study, there is, I think, little point in fictionalizing my summary of it. More than twenty years have gone by since these events occurred, and personal sensitivities should have become less acute. So I shall speak of the institutions by their real names. I shall summarize statements, but if they seem to be of special importance, I shall give them at length in Appendix A, "Resource Materials."

At a joint meeting of faculty and trustees on December 5, 1953, shortly before the inauguration of President Selden, the new president said some unsettling things and raised some awkward questions:

Faculty salaries are low. The faculty is loyal and will stay with us, but salaries and conditions of employment must be improved or we will not be able to attract adequate replacements and additions to the faculty.

The reputation of the College is good but reputation lags. Our reputation is based largely on what Illinois College has done and not so much on what we are doing now.

Can this College survive? Should this College survive? It has survived for 125 years because people believed in what it stood for and what it attempted to do. We must set our sights on what we hope to accomplish, and not concentrate on the form in which we will do it.

If we do not have the determination to succeed, we should bury the College. The 125th anniversary can provide an appropriate setting. But I for one am not ready to pound that last nail into the coffin.

That was strong medicine, meant to arouse both faculty and trustees to a sense of urgency regarding the future of the College. The President made four specific proposals: (1) to approve a campaign to raise four million dollars as part of the 125th anniversary celebration;

(2) to approve the 125th anniversary program for the academic development of the College; (3) to approve the proposal that Illinois College and MacMurray College cooperate as closely as possible for the benefit of education offered by each institution; and (4) to approve the appointment of an Illinois Board Committee to consult with a MacMurray Board Committee regarding further cooperation between the two institutions. The reader will note that there is still no mention of merger or fusion of the two colleges.

Two statements that appear in the Harvard case study should be quoted here because they reveal important views of President Selden. "The Board of Trustees of Illinois College was made up of twenty-one members, most of whom were quite old, and all members of the Board except two were alumni of Illinois College. The Board of Trustees of Illinois College had customarily left operations of the College to the President and had, themselves, exerted very little original thinking and leadership to the College." The other statement is also revealing. "Historically, the faculty was the dominating force of Illinois College, as had been demonstrated in earlier years when the faculty participated in the removal of several presidents of the College." Both of these are overstatements, in fact and in tone, but they represent the point of view held by President Selden.

During the late summer and early fall of 1954, according to the Harvard case study, the joint Trustee Committee on Coordination of the two colleges met twice, to consider the development of "The Associated Colleges" and the suggestion made by the President of Illinois College and the Chairman of its Board that there be a merger of the two schools. At the close of the regular faculty meeting of Illinois College early in October 1954, in response to a question regarding rumors that Illinois College was considering an agreement with MacMurray College by which Illinois College would give up its women students, President Selden said that he was not at liberty to discuss the matter at that time, but that he would give a full report at a special faculty meeting later. As had been agreed between the presidents of the two colleges and the chairmen of their respective Boards, the proposed agreement between MacMurray College and Illinois College creating "The Associated Colleges" was to be acted upon by both Boards on October 15, 1954. The agreement is a lengthy one, full of "whereases" and "now therefores" but the meat of the matter occurs in the following clauses:

Illinois College and MacMurray College do hereby create and become members of an association to be named THE ASSOCIATED COLLEGES.

Illinois College shall assume the primary responsibility for the education of men and MacMurray College shall assume the primary responsibility for the education of women.

After September 1, 1955, all entering men shall be admitted to Illinois College and all entering women shall be admitted to MacMurray College.

New appointments to either faculty shall be made only after mutual consultation between the administrative heads of the Colleges and after consideration of the joint needs of the two faculties.

The work of the Associated Colleges shall be facilitated hereafter by a Coordinating Committee of eight members, to be selected as follows: Three by the Board of Trustees of Illinois College, three by the Board of Trustees of MacMurray College, and two to include the respective Presidents of the two Colleges.

In order that any other educational institution may become a member of the Associated Colleges, approval thereof must be granted by the Board of Trustees of Illinois College and the Board of Trustees of MacMurray College, upon recommendation of the Coordinating Committee.

This agreement between Illinois College and MacMurray College shall be in force until and including June 30, 1960, and shall expire on that date unless renewed, extended or revised.

Special Illinois College faculty meetings were held on October 7 and October 13. At the first, President Selden, as he had promised, gave the provisions of the proposed agreement. After lengthy discussion, particularly of Article 3, that would have required Illinois College to give up its women, the faculty created a special committee to draft a statement that would represent "the sense of the meeting" regarding those provisions. At the second, a five-page draft was presented, in two parts, with part 1 regarding the matter of coeducation being presented as of primary importance, and part 2 having five subsections, relevant to the question, but not wholly in faculty provenance. For full text, see Appendix A, "Resource Materials." Both parts passed without dissent, and the president was asked to submit them to the Board.

At the board meeting of October 15, 1954, the MacMurray College Board of Trustees approved the proposal altogether, but the Illinois College Board refused to approve the portion of the agreement which stated that after September 1, 1955, all women would enter MacMurray College and all men would be enrolled at Illinois College. In rejecting this part of the agreement, the primary purpose of the proposal, so far as MacMurray College was concerned, was defeated by the Illinois College trustees, although the latter suggested that committees study further the possibility of coordination and cooperation between the two schools. And there the matter appeared to have ended. However, on January 8, 1955, the chairman of the Illinois College Board invited seven senior faculty members to meet with him, two other members of the Board, and President Selden. At that time, the faculty members were informed that the Board had passed a resolution the day before authorizing a reconstituted committee of the Board of Trustees to explore further the possibility of an absolute merger with MacMurray College. The faculty members present expressed strong opposition to this proposal, and there was continued unrest among all the faculty members.

On January 28, 1955, Professor Frank of the English Department at Illinois College, after consulting with President Selden and showing him a draft statement of his personal anxieties regarding the negotiations with MacMurray, asked for permission to share his views with his colleagues. President Selden read over the statement and agreed to recognize Professor Frank at the end of the faculty meeting scheduled for that afternoon. The full text will be found in Appendix A, "Resource Materials," but perhaps the concluding paragraph should be included here.

If this Faculty had a solemn duty last fall to inform the Board of Trustees of our position regarding that proposal, we have just as solemn a duty now, and since secrecy is no longer an issue, there is no reason why we should not discuss the matter fully with all who have a concern for the College. We are a peaceful faculty, even docile; we are ready to be led, but we do not like to be dragged or driven. Once the Board makes its *final* decision, we must either abide by that decision or resign, but until that time we have a duty to help them *explore* every phase of this proposal. If each individual will perform that duty, according to his own conscience, with honor and with candor, I have no doubt of the outcome.

That statement was discussed on and off campus, and a week later, Professor Stewart of the religion and philosophy department and Professor Wright of the history department asked for a meeting with Chairman Dunbaugh and President Selden. At that meeting, the professors presented to the chairman and the president a bill of particulars entitled "An Assessment of the Present Situation at Illinois College." (The full text of that statement is also given in Appendix A, "Resource Materials.")

The meeting of these four persons lasted two and one-half hours. Mr. Dunbaugh was shocked by the memorandum and the conversation that followed it. He understood that the representatives of the faculty were "demanding" two things: a prompt decision on the question of merger with MacMurray so that members of the Illinois College faculty could decide whether to stay or to look elsewhere for employment for the following academic year, and concurrently, the resignation of President Selden. Later that evening, Mr. Dunbaugh and Mr. Selden met with four other trustees to consider how to respond to the memorandum. Unfortunately, the memorandum had not been presented to the faculty, so that, while it represented the views of many, it carried only the avowed endorsement of the two professors who presented it. In addition, it had not been signed, even by the two professors who presented it. This was a mere oversight, but the document was sometimes referred to thereafter as an "anonymous assessment." The professors believed that their personal delivery of the document removed any possibility of such a misunderstanding. The professors had offered what they thought to be a candid "assessment"; the trustees had received what they took to be an "ultimatum." They referred to the incident as a "faculty uprising." Their decision was to back the president.

At a hastily called special meeting of the faculty held the next morning, Chairman Dunbaugh reviewed the situation as he saw it. He told the faculty—every member was present—that all that President Selden had done, he had done "in accordance with the wishes or instructions of the Trustees," and that therefore the Board was standing behind the president. However, so far as further negotiations regarding merger with MacMurray were concerned, the Board would probably, by formal action at a later date, abandon them "for the present and the foreseeable future."

In an attempt to restore a measure of amity between faculty and administration and trustees, a further statement was drawn up by Professor Wright, who had taken part in the meeting with President Selden and Chairman Dunbaugh. (The text is given in Appendix A, "Resource Materials.") It was presented to the whole faculty at another special meeting and signed by eighteen of them. Nonsigners were not necessarily opposed to this attempt to restore amity, but they were offended by the fact that members of the faculty, without first consulting them, had held a meeting with the chairman and the president. In fact, three members of the faculty specifically disassociated themselves from the whole controversy, transmitting a minority report to the Board. Thus, the faculty, which had once been acting in accord, wound up in disarray.

In any case, the rift had gone too far to be repaired. President Selden resigned, saying to the Board: "I wish to express officially to the Board my sincere apologies for leading all of us into these difficulties unprepared for the sudden and unexpected turn of events. I admit readily my impatience and too energetic desire for a rapid improvement in the affairs of this College. In addition, I confess to a lack of appreciation for the intangible values at Illinois College held in such high regard by some of the faculty and for the loyalties of some of the alumni to many of these values. And also, I must point out my complete inability to comprehend the rivalry, even deep bitterness, between the two colleges." After examining the underlying causes of the confrontation, as he saw them, the President continued:

It was in the field of overall educational objectives and policy in which there was confusion of thinking and acting. In this realm the Board of Trustees must be supreme. The Board is legally and morally responsible for the College and must not be circumscribed in exercising its responsibilites.
This winter the Board was so circumscribed for a number of dif-

ferent reasons, some of which I will enumerate: (1) the impatient
actions of the President; (2) lack of thorough study, discussions and
planning for the important propositions under consideration; (3) a
Board of Trustees unaccustomed to assuming leadership and giving
direction for the future of the College; (4) a faculty which has been
accustomed and permitted to criticize any policies of the Board and
in some cases with abandon and lack of propriety.

In this statement to the Board, President Selden suggested some
ways of restoring what he considered a proper balance between
board, administration and faculty. Some of the same things were
stated more vehemently in his final message to the faculty on May
2, 1955. The president recapitulated the situation at some length,
quoting in support of his position Professor George W. Horton's
declaration, "I feel as strongly as any member of the Board of Trustees feels that the Faculty of Illinois College has been out of line in
its actions of the last few months." President Selden concluded his
twenty-minute valedictory thus:

My resignation was accepted this last Saturday. Now, the concern
is to hold together a Board of Trustees, a group of people who have
been devoted to and interested in this College in a period when a
large number are disgusted with the attitude and action of a few
people on this faculty.
This is a Christian College. We all have duties, responsibilities
and moral obligations. The faculty of a Christian college, I am sure,
know how to pray, and to each of you I urge that you go home
or to your church and pray before your altar, pray for a knowledge
of what your individual responsibilities, obligations and duties may
be in the same manner as some of us have been doing for the past
several months.
May the Lord make his face to shine upon you and bring you in-
ward peace. Amen.
The meeting is adjourned.

Thus ended the two-year tenure of President William K. Selden. It
was not a successful tenure, but it clarified some issues and it made
possible the setting of a new course for the College under the administration to follow. If the reader has read the preceding pages
with care, including the appendices, he will have identified those

issues in his own mind and will perhaps have reached conclusions on them.

Crosstown rivalries are common and they are not necessarily bad. In this case, the outcome had unfortunate aspects such as the breaking off of the promising academic cooperation between the two colleges, but there were also benign results. Illinois College kept her women and maintained genuine coeducation rather than reverting to all-maleness. And as a direct result of this incident, MacMurray College founded a co-ordinate college for men, and eventually became genuinely coeducational. Jacksonville now has two healthy coeducational colleges, and it is not impossible that the friendly rivalry that exists today, socially and athletically, may eventually lead to a renewed and wholesome academic cooperation.

The matter of governance that was referred to in President Selden's statements to the Board and to the faculty is perhaps the most important issue that was contested during the Selden administration. I have tried to represent the differing views on the issue fairly and fully in the quotations from trustees, administration, and faculty. That each group has its special province is undeniable, but the boundaries of those provinces could not and can not be firmly and arbitrarily established. There is a large commons where the boundaries overlap, where all three have legitimate interests. Anyone who now reads between the lines of the quoted statements can see that this was the case, but at the time all the participants had somewhat blurred vision. I have talked with a number of them while working on this chapter, and I am convinced that they were all honorable men, seeking what they thought was best for the College and genuinely surprised that not everyone agreed on what was best.

President Selden saw an opportunity to fashion a new and more prosperous institution out of the materials of what he thought to be two faltering institutions; as he himself said, though, he was impatient, he wanted to work an overnight miracle. The faculty and students and alumni of Illinois College were not willing to give up so many things they cherished just to provide a quick solution for the kind of problem the College had faced many times before. The Board of Trustees was caught between irreconcilable views of what

Illinois College should be. They vacillated and tried to find middle ground; in the end they backed the man they had elected to lead the College, though they seem not to have been certain that he was leading in the right direction.

The most immediate good thing that came out of this muddle was an extraordinary renewal of alumni support for the old College. There were many men and many women who rallied round and wrote letters to the chairman of the Board and other trustees, to administrators and faculty, stating their views and offering help. Many of them were bewildered by the claims and counterclaims and rumors they heard, but if the College was threatened, they wanted to come to its support. The principal organizer of the alumni fund raising effort was Mr. E. Dwight Smith, '31, President of the Alumni Association, who could by commencement, 1955, report almost eighty thousand dollars in pledges, of which more than forty thousand dollars had been paid in cash. With that demonstration of loyalty as a stimulus, the Board of Trustees took heart and began the search for a new president.

22

President Caine, 1956–1973

President Selden's resignation was accepted by the Board of Trustees in late April of 1955 and was made known to the world at that year's commencement. It was the inevitable consequence of the yearlong struggle over the College's future. Mr. Selden's proposals for that future having been rejected, he resigned. This he did promptly and without agonizing, for he was a man of quick judgment and speedy execution. He regretted the necessity for this act, he told me twenty years later, but "my coming to Illinois College was a mistake; it was a mismarriage." Without much of a backwards glance, he moved to the world of Washington, D.C. as Executive Secretary of the newly created National Commission on Accrediting, an administrative post that called for his kind of energy.

But the College was left rudderless. Not only did Mr. Selden resign from the presidency, but Mr. Dunbaugh resigned as chairman of the Board of Trustees. He noted that his term had begun in April 1938—the reader may remember that he had said he would serve only for three years—and that seventeen years at the helm was long enough. Moreover, he pointed out that he would soon become seventy-eight years of age, and "a younger man should take over." These two reasons were cogent enough, but he added: "The unfortunate circumstances leading to the retirement of Dr. Selden from the Presidency of the College present, to my mind, a compelling reason for my retirement. These circumstances add up, in substance, to a repudiation (on the part of the Faculty and of many alumni) of my long-range policies for the College." Mr. Dunbaugh did agree, however, to remain on the Board, a decision that was most welcome to his fellow trustees and also to the faculty and the alumni. Dr. Fred Hoskins, class of 1926, who had come on the Board as an alumni trustee in 1952 and been elected a permanent member in 1955, was named chairman to succeed Mr. Dunbaugh.

A Committee on Selection of a new president, Dr. Ellsworth Black, chairman, was appointed to undertake the search, and an interim committee composed of two trustees and Dean Hildner was named "to carry on the functions of the College." They were informally known as The Triumvirate, but by mid-August the Board thought better of having the College administered by a committee, and Dean Hildner was appointed acting president. He had done more than anyone else to hold the College together during the last days of the Selden administration and was a good choice to run the College until a new president could be found. Partly as a result of the uncertainties regarding the future of the College and the tensions created by the disagreements that had occurred, eight members of the faculty, in various disciplines—chemistry, economics, English, French, history, physical education, and speech—resigned within the next year. In addition, two members of the staff—the alumni secretary and the director of development—also resigned. In a small college, such a turnover of key people is deeply disturbing.

Acting President Hildner, conscious of the importance of alumni support in a period of crisis and transition, addressed a message to that body: "The interest shown by the Alumni in every phase of the activities of the College is a source of encouragement to those of us who are dealing daily with its problems. Never have we felt more keenly the loyalty and devotion of those of you we have been privileged to know on the campus. I extend my personal thanks to those who have participated or who will participate in these enterprises so necessary for the health and wellbeing of the College." The College as a whole rallied to the cause, while the search for new leadership went on. Enrollment went up almost 20 percent in the fall of 1955. The intensified fund-raising campaign by E. Dwight Smith, '31, was carried on by Walter R. Bellatti, '36. Replacements were found for departed staff, and morale was boosted by the assurance that the College was not going to lose its identity and by the sense of urgency

President L. Vernon Caine

that existed. Finally, on January 10, 1956, Chairman Hoskins announced the appointment of L. Vernon Caine as the tenth president of Illinois College.

Vernon Caine came to Illinois College from Macalester College, St. Paul, Minnesota, a well-regarded liberal arts college. His background included a B.S. degree, with a major in chemistry and physics, from Jamestown College, and an M.A. in educational administration from the University of Minnesota. He had studied also at the University of Wisconsin, Columbia University, and New York University; he had in 1950 received an honorary degree of Doctor of Laws from his alma mater, Jamestown College. He was a willing worker in the Presbyterian Church in the U.S.A. and very active in civic and social affairs wherever he had lived. His family consisted of his wife Elizabeth, a graduate of Huron College, with graduate work at the Universities of Iowa and Minnesota, and three sons, the eldest a first-year law student, the second a sophomore at Macalester, and the youngest still in high school. All who met the Caines regarded them as a very solid, attractive family.

One of Vernon Caine's characteristics that impressed the trustees and faculty who got acquainted with him before his appointment was announced was his directness. He answered questions with conviction and without equivocation; there was no nonsense about the man. He had heard, he said, good things and bad things about the College; among the latter was that it "was a graveyard for presidents." But the heritage of the College, and the people who had been associated with it made it "worth a gamble." He told me recently that on his first visit to the campus at Thanksgiving time, 1955, he spent several days in Jacksonville and took a good look around. He found the college buildings "not well maintained," but he was much impressed with the faculty. "I think that was the thing that impressed me the most." He sized up the Board and the faculty and he looked over the town, and he found them all "full of potential." He told me that he had heard from various sources that "nobody knew who was in charge of what." He said, "I wanted it clearly understood that the president was the administrative officer and not the faculty, not the Board of Trustees. If the trustees decided they were going to do something, it was up to me to carry out their orders. I think the most important fact in whatever success we had was that the Board stuck to that."

He wrote to the Alumni Association shortly before taking office: (1) "To be a successor to Edward Beecher and all the other great men who have occupied this position is an invitation not to be taken lightly." (2) "A Phi Beta Kappa chapter is a scholastic recommendation of priceless value. Since a college is first and foremost an academic institution, its standing in that regard is a primary consideration with me. I was greatly impressed with the academic competency of the faculty. I can be proud to head a college of this quality." (3) "I am sure that my administration will put increased emphasis on the Christian aspects of the College." Before Dr. Caine had been in office a year, the Alumni Secretary responded enthusiastically: "Our new President shows an understanding of the College. He appreciates the heritage handed down to us by our founders and their successors. He has dedicated himself not to change for change's sake, not to complacency in the name of tradition, but rather to build on the solid foundation of the past. The future looks bright. We have faith, but much work remains."

By October 1956, when he was officially installed as the tenth president of Illinois College, Vernon Caine was in control. At the formal ceremonies of inauguration, attended by "nearly two hundred representatives of colleges and universities, learned societies and religious and educational organizations," as well as trustees, faculty, students, and townspeople, the principal address was given by Dr. Charles J. Turck, president of Macalester College, under whom Dr. Caine had served for six years. It was the same Dr. Turck who had been a member of the three-man committee of the North Central Association that had made the study of Illinois College and Mac-Murray College, with a view toward improving the cooperative program between them. Dr. Turck was an excellent choice for that occasion, since he knew the man who was being installed and the institution which was accepting his leadership. "This College," Dr. Turck declared, "has something to say—and its motivation toward progress is essentially Christian. It insists upon freedom of thought, of study, of teaching. It is designed not to indoctrinate, but to lead in a pilgrimage of ideas."

Dr. Hoskins, who, since taking office as chairman of the Illinois College Board, had become Minister and Secretary of the General Council of the Congregational Churches of the United States, officially proclaimed Vernon Caine's installation, saying, "As symbols of your office I place in your hands a scholar's hat, a copy of the Holy Bible, and a gavel indicating orderliness with seemliness." And then he pronounced a benediction on the new president and presented him to the large audience that filled the arena of the Memorial Gymnasium.

President Caine's inaugural address was carefully orchestrated. Without making specific reference to the recent troubles on campus, he showed that he was thoroughly aware of them, and that he thought he knew how to deal with them:

Those who have come to know me in the brief time I have lived in Jacksonville must be aware that I will not make the too common mistake of new administrators in thinking that progress begins where I came in. I am not here to outline any grandiose plans to bring to pass greater advance in the next few years than came about in the combined lifetime of my predecessors. We are going ahead. We have enormous resources of good will among those who know us. We have a good endowment, a beautiful campus, a loyal and unusually distinguished body of alumni, an academic reputation well above the average.

Wisdom consists of foreseeing and planning for new developments and not being forced by circumstance to make changes simply to survive. "Where there is no vision, people perish." I advocate the forward look, the cautious venture, the willingness to be among the first in the procession. This is good Illinois College doctrine. This College came into being because of venturesome souls.

I favor as best for us and our people a rather strict liberal arts program, but we do not degrade liberal arts when we serve the needs of the kind of students we want most. The most thoughtful and the most able student wants to see in his education some tangible progress toward his vocational goal.

At Illinois College we shall continue the time-honored policy of admitting persons without regard for race or color, and we shall judge their admission scrupulously on the basis of intellectual ability and character. We shall promote worthy extracurricular activities including intercollegiate athletics, but we shall not permit the tail to wag the dog.

America needs both the independent and the tax-supported institutions; it would be a catastrophe to lose either. We need not decide which is the more necessary; both are necessary.

As far as I am concerned, I doubt whether the sacrifice, the worry, and the sweat necessary to maintain this College are justified if we do not hold central the Christian concern of our founding fathers. Let the taxpayers take care of higher education if we do no more than duplicate the public program.

Illinois College stands at the threshold of a new day rich in opportunity for growth in service to God and man. Let us, as we look back on what has been and move forward into an unknown future, resolve that with God's help this College shall continue to be a significant, constructive force. May we so labor here that in some future day when we are but history, our record will be such as to inspire those who come after us to achievements of service far greater than even our present dreams.

It is always interesting to compare public pronouncements made to large general audiences to those made privately to small specific audiences at about the same time. To his Board of Trustees at a meeting held just before his inauguration, Dr. Caine said some things that are not less confident, but are couched in different terms. After thanking members of the Board for their "generosity, consideration, friendliness, and wisdom," he said: "I came to Illinois College only after very careful consideration persuaded me that this College had, in spite of many problems and potential difficulties, a significant role to play in the educational world of the immediate future. Like Winston Churchill, who once said he had no intention of presiding at the liquidation of the British Empire, I had no idea of coming to Illinois College if it seemed at all likely that the decline and fall of this institution was a possibility. In fact, I decided to come only because the prospects of success for the College seemed to be excellent. I have had no valid reason to regret this decision."

I have no doubt that the trustees were glad to hear these sentiments and that they responded eagerly to such hard-headedness as President Caine showed in his analysis of specific problems:

For 1955–56 Illinois College had a substantial increase in enrollment. We anticipate a further increase next year. In order to operate efficiently as a business institution, the gross enrollment should be not less than 450 students. As our enrollment increases, we ought to be at the same time more selective in order to maintain the traditional quality of work here at Illinois College. We must do something about both the quality and quantity of our students. This constitutes one of our major problems which must have considerable attention.

The financial condition of Illinois College is much improved. The audit for 1955–56 will show some surplus in the operating fund. Not since 1949–50 has income including gifts been sufficient to meet all costs. In the intervening years it has been necessary either to carry a deficit or to sell assets of the College in order to balance the budget. It is a comfort to all of us to know that we are in solvent operation and that the prospects for next year are also favorable.

The previous administration had been reporting the College in desperate financial condition. In less than a year's time, the new administration was exuding confidence. The trustees must have felt that they had brought in a magician. But it was not done with mirrors. Dr. Caine simply made a practice of looking at things with an auditor's eye. For example:

Regarding the dining hall, it seems that there is little or no excuse for subsidizing the feeding of students. When facilities are provided as a gift, it is reasonable to expect that costs of operation should be borne by the revenue. The cost of operating the dining hall does not now and has not in the past reflected administration overhead. Even without considering this overhead, Baxter Hall has lost thousands of dollars in recent years, but the dining hall is no longer a financial liability to the College.

It was that kind of seepage of funds that Vernon Caine spotted and quickly corrected; lots of little seepages corrected make for solvency.

President Caine was aware of larger policy matters also. He knew of the strained relations that had existed between Illinois College and church governing boards, especially the Board of Christian Education of the Presbyterian Church. He proposed to improve relations by restating the College's religious commitment. He recommended to the Board that in addition to the one required course in religion or philosophy, each student should be required to take six hours of religion, beginning with the class entering in the fall of 1956. Fur-

Rammelkamp Chapel. Drawing by Louise Boring Wood

thermore, he wanted a renewed adherence to required chapel for graduation from Illinois College. Excuses from chapel on any grounds were to be minimized, and fines for nonattendance were to be abolished. This practice, he contended, simply permitted those who could afford it to buy their way out of a requirement. The commitment to religious emphasis at Illinois College was to be a firm one and not easily evaded. "If a student is fundamentally opposed to regulations clearly announced, his option is to register somewhere else," he stated in *Illinois College Comments*.

Once the College had convinced Presbyterians and Congregationalists of its genuine commitment to a Christian emphasis, it would be possible and proper to ask the churches to increase their financial aid to the College. President Caine was vigorous in his appeals for such aid and he was generally successful. The funds for a new chapel, to be named after President Rammelkamp, had been accumulating slowly for a period of ten years. He stepped up the campaign and secured considerable grants from both churches, from the Christian Higher Education Fund of the Congregational Christian Churches, and from the Board of Christian Education of the United Presbyterian Church, U.S.A. Construction of the Rammelkamp Chapel was begun in the spring of 1961, and the building was dedicated April 23, 1962, less than a month before the death of Mrs. Rammelkamp, who had long dreamed of this memorial to her husband, and who was present for the dedication.

The chapel was made part of a building campaign called "A Forward Step for Illinois College." In announcing this drive, which was very largely under his control, with help from trustees and alumni, President Caine pointed out that in the years between 1953 and 1959, the enrollment at the College had doubled and that with the steadily growing college-age population of the sixties, it would continue to grow. The College could attract more students if it was prepared to receive them. He did not want unlimited expansion, but he thought an enrollment of about eight hundred was possible and desirable. To care for such an enrollment the College would need, in addition to Rammelkamp Chapel, a new science building, a swimming pool addition to Memorial Gymnasium, and new dormitories.

Vernon Caine was the buildingest president the College had yet known. The ten-year "Forward Step" initiated by him in 1958 produced the following buildings:

  1962—Rammelkamp Chapel; an addition to Ellis Hall, women's residence
  1963—Crispin Science Hall
  1964—swimming pool addition to the Memorial Gymnasium

1965—Turner Hall, a residence for men

1966—Pixley Hall, a residence for women; addition to Baxter Hall, nearly doubling the dining capacity

1967—Student Center, later appropriately named for Dr. Caine.

In addition, Sturtevant Hall was renovated, a little theater was created in the former Jones Chapel, Whipple Hall was rejuvenated and made more useful, tennis courts and parking areas were created. More than three million dollars was spent on these projects; this is surely a remarkable accomplishment for a college that was thought to be in perilous condition when Dr. Caine arrived.

Where did the money come from? No single rich benefactor came to the rescue, no large foundation offered support. Many sources in addition to the churches mentioned in connection with the chapel were tapped, over a period of ten years. The dormitories were made possible by low-interest, long-term loans from the federal government, which was eager to provide facilities for the rising college generations. The major investment in such buildings is amortized by the fees charged for rental, of course, but the loans did not cover the full cost of the buildings, nor the expense of equipping and furnishing them.

The state-wide canvasses of business corporations conducted by the Associated Colleges of Illinois were continued, with encouraging results. These funds are used for operating expenses, rather than capital expansion, but they free other funds for building. An annual Jacksonville campaign known as CACHE (Campaign for the Advancement of Community Higher Education) was initiated in 1961. Teams of local citizens make a one-day appeal to the business community of the city, pointing out the economic advantages of having two independent colleges in Jacksonville. There is almost no administrative expense, and the proceeds are equally divided between Illinois College and MacMurray College. The amount thus raised has grown steadily over the years, and it provides substantial aid for both colleges' operating expenses. (See Appendix A)

Traditionally, the Board of Trustees of Illinois College has not been willing to go ahead with any building project unless the money for it was in hand, or very nearly so. This policy may be over-conservative, but it is certainly prudent. Gifts vary from year to year, but the year 1963 is perhaps a typical one. The sources of gift income for Illinois College that year are shown in the following table. These have been the four main categories of Illinois College's income other than income from student tuition and fees, government grants, and invested endowment funds. A president must appeal to a very diverse constituency if he is to keep the College solvent. Vernon Caine was diligent and persistent in his pursuit of all these sources, and his methods paid off so well that he kept his annual reports consistently in the black.

Nonalumni	$180,624	38%
Alumni	164,765	35%
Business and Foundations	66,346	14%
Churches	59,161	13%

	1967–68	1971–72
Professor	$10,000–15,000	$12,500–18,500
Associate Professor	8,500–12,000	11,000–15,000
Assistant Professor	7,500–10,000	9,000–13,000
Instructor	6,000–8,000	8,000–10,000

He also managed to keep pay scales attractive enough to retain faculty and staff, for the most part. President Hudson had been able to restore faculty salaries to their pre-Depression levels and then to increase them modestly, but not spectacularly. He had also initiated certain fringe benefits like Social Security, hospitalization insurance, and a guaranteed pension plan, through the Teachers Insurance and Annuity Association. During the Caine administration all of these, in keeping with inflation and competition with other colleges and universities, rose steadily. At the end of President Caine's first year in office, 1956, the Board of Trustees established the following salary scale for faculty: professor, $4,500–5,500; associate professor, $4,000–5,000; assistant professor, $3,800–4,500; instructor, $3,500–4,000. Representative scales during other years of the Caine administration are shown in the table above. Actual salaries tended to be the average of these low-high figures, and the variations gave the President some leeway in his negotiations with individual instructors. No reader needs to be told, I expect, that these salary scales were greatly affected by the inflation of the times and that they were, compared to those of urban universities, modest. Even so, they reflect President Caine's concern for the economic welfare of his faculty.

Other inducements were made to attract and keep a strong faculty. A regular item in the annual budget, approved by the Board, was a sum set aside for faculty travel to professional meetings. These sums were controlled by an elected faculty travel committee, which established guidelines, allocated, and administered the funds. "Class enrichment" funds were also made available, so that an instructor could take a class on a field trip, or to see a performance of a classic play, or to hear a distinguished lecturer at a nearby college or university. These funds were likewise administered by the faculty travel committee. Ventures of this kind are inexpensive, but they are sound investments if an administration is at all concerned about student and faculty morale.

In 1969, a faculty award was established in memory of Harry J. Dunbaugh, former chairman of the Board. This is the Dunbaugh Distinguished Professorship to be awarded each year to a faculty member who is adjudged by a committee of students to be an outstanding teacher. Certain qualifications were established by the donor, Mrs. Dunbaugh, but the nominations are made by a rather large group of representative students, and then a smaller committee of upperclass students makes the choice. The award consists of a generous check, an individual plaque, and the inscription of the recipient's name on a permanent roster that lists the names of all the Dunbaugh professors. The student committee, if it chooses, can ask the advice of the president and the dean of the College, since they are not eligible to receive the award. So long as the students take their responsibilities seriously—and they always have—there is no likelihood that the competition will become a mere popularity contest. On the contrary, the Dunbaugh Distinguished Professorship is regarded by both students and faculty as a very great honor; it has been especially prized by those who knew Harry J. Dunbaugh.

Perhaps the greatest stimulus to faculty morale given during the Caine administration was the establishment of a regular, funded sabbatical program for faculty members of long service and some scholarly ambitions, allowing them time off for study, reflection, writing, and travel. In general, the candidate for a sabbatical must have served on the faculty for six years or more, have formulated a program that will increase his competence and teaching effectiveness, and submit this plan to an elected committee of his peers. If the committee finds the proposal a worthy one, and there are funds available, the College then grants the candidate full salary and benefits for six months, or half salary and benefits for a year. Anyone chosen for such a grant is expected to return to the campus for two years of service after the sabbatical is completed. The program was originally funded by the Board of Trustees, but in 1970, Mr. Kenneth Danskin, '26, made a gift of one hundred thousand dollars to the College, for the purpose of partially funding the sabbatical program. A difficulty has arisen because of the rising costs of unemployment compensation and the terms on which such compensation is granted. A temporary appointee to fill the place of a professor on sabbatical may claim such compensation and the College may be required to pay it. This greatly increases the cost of the sabbatical program. It is unlikely that legislators anticipated this possibility; perhaps they will find a way to alleviate it.

Partly to avoid the misunderstandings that had arisen between faculty and Board of Trustees during the Selden administration, two new organizations of the faculty were created during President Caine's tenure. The Illinois College Senate is composed of all full professors, and it is intended to represent the collective wisdom of the senior members of the faculty. It elects its own officers and calls its own meetings, often at the request of the president when he wants advice. It is an advisory body. Matters of appointment, advancement in rank, tenure, and termination of service are discussed and recommendations are made to the administration. The Senate also recommends persons for honorary degrees to the Board of Trustees. It organizes and sponsors an annual series of faculty lectures, elects the Bellatti Scholar—a member of the senior class who exhibits a high degree of scholarship, active participation in student affairs, and a concern for the welfare of the College—and other things of this kind. It has on a few occasions acted as a last court of appeal for faculty grievances and on student disciplinary matters where the usual procedures did not produce a satisfactory result. One might say that it is a stabilizing unit of governance, important more because of what it stands for rather than for what it does.

The second organization has a more elaborate structure, greater pretensions, but it has had less success. This is known as the Teaching Faculty Organization. It was established to permit all faculty members, not just senior members, to communicate with the Board of Trustees, via the president of the College. It may hold meetings without the presence of administrative officers of the College, and it provides for its leadership by a rather complicated system. The intention of the Teaching Faculty Organization was a worthy one, but it has not functioned effectively, largely because the teaching faculty is already busy with other duties. When they have found time to deliberate and debate they have found themselves not always in sufficient agreement to pursue any particular goal. Although the Teaching Faculty Organization is so egalitarian that it has not been able to speak with unity, it still exists and is still recognized by the Board of Trustees as a valid voice of the faculty, should it choose to speak.

Another voluntary organization has been in existence since the mid-1960s and has had modest success. This is a chapter of the American Association of University Professors. When its officers are vigorous, it functions; when they are not, it exists. AAUP has the enormous potential of bringing to bear on local academic problems the prestige and power of a highly respected national organization. At Illinois College, no appeal for assistance from outside has ever been made, but merely as a potential organ of a concerned faculty, AAUP serves a useful purpose. As a local debating society, it is influential, and its occasional joint meetings with the MacMurray chapter have been fruitful.

During President Caine's administration, the number of cultural opportunities offered Illinois College students and faculty were increased, not necessarily by him, but certainly with his support. For example, on the retirement of Professor Joe Patterson Smith, a committee of alumni, colleagues, and friends raised funds to endow a lectureship that would keep alive this great teacher's influence on the campus. His interests being especially in the field of history and government, the lectureship was established to bring to the College distinguished scholars and government officials who give public lectures, hold seminars, and conduct interviews with advanced students in the field. Similarly, the Epsilon Chapter of Phi Beta Kappa, with financial support from the College, has been able to bring to the campus each year a visiting scholar of national repute, from one of many disciplines. Individual departments have also from time to time arranged for appearances by noteworthy persons in their disciplines, to stimulate student interest in the world of scholarship. It is not easy to assess the effect of these events, but at least on some students the results have been satisfying.

For a number of years, the College provided a center for the annual exhibit and competition of the Southwestern District Science Exposition. This one-day competition brought hundreds of high school students and their teachers to the campus each spring. The College provided exhibition space in the Memorial Gymnasium and seminar rooms for the reading of papers in Crispin Science Hall. The College science faculty and selected students performed many necessary chores for these conventions, from helping to set up exhibits to judging them and moderating panel discussions. These annual conventions gave valuable experience to young scientists, both from the high schools and from the College.

In 1965, a Visiting Asian Professors Program was initiated at Illinois College, funded by the Fulbright Program, the Asia Foundation, and the U.S. State Department. Scholars of distinction were brought to the United States and sent to several American colleges for two-month residency programs. The presentations of these scholars varied widely in relevance and comprehensibility, but they were always stimulating to the community, and Illinois College was most fortunate to have been one of the American institutions chosen to host these visits. For a period of several years, Illinois College had on its campus men and women from Burma, Ceylon, India, Japan, Kashmir, Korea, Nepal, the Philippines, and Taiwan. In the corn, hog, and soybean center of the United States, merely to hear their accents and observe their costumes was stimulating; they provided our students with an opportunity to widen their cultural horizons authentically.

Concerts were provided, both off campus and on, for those with musical interests. Some of these have been funded by the Student Forum, some by administrative allocation, and some by friends of the College. An interesting example of this kind of activity has been the Illinois College subscription to the Jacksonville-MacMurray concert series, an annual program of four or five professional recitals by artists as diverse as Leontyne Price, Burl Ives, Myra Hess, and Andrès Segovia; and by groups as different as the Columbus Boys' Choir, Boris Goldovsky's opera theatre, and the Preservation Hall jazz combine. For many years, Illinois College has purchased a block of fifty tickets to these concerts, making them available to students on a first-come, first-served basis. The College has also made Rammelkamp Chapel available to the Jacksonville Symphony Society for rehearsal and concert. Both students and staff have played in the orchestra, and a good many Illinois College people attend their concerts.

An event of significance was held on campus in the spring of 1969. Anticipating the effort of the state of Illinois to convene a special constitutional convention to rewrite the 1870 constitution, the Illinois College department of history and government convened a Model Constitutional Convention in Jacksonville, April 24–26. The student delegates formed eighteen working committees to deal with eight major areas that would be of prime concern to the Constitutional Convention authorized by act of the voters of Illinois in a November 1968 referendum. It was no mere mock convention held in the Illinois College gymnasium. Lieutenant Governor Paul Simon gave the keynote address, Senator Charles Percy praised the students' accomplishment at the concluding banquet, and Governor Richard Ogilvie a few weeks later received a delegation of students who presented their draft of a proposed new constitution. The whole exercise was an example of purposeful student inquiry and action.

Professors Hildner and Zeigler, assisted by members of the Illinois College faculty and members of other participating faculties, gave the students professional guidance, but the student delegates worked hard and effectively and ran their own show. The fact that this con-

structive activity occurred during the height of nationwide student
protest made it the more significant. As a journalist, Al Seiler, who
covered the convention for his paper, *The Pike Press*, of Pittsfield,
Illinois, remarked:

> It was a warm, sunny Spring afternoon—ideal weather to set off
> a fire bomb in a college library, invade and destroy a college presi-
> dent's office, march, protest, wave signs, or demonstrate. On certain
> college campuses of the nation that's exactly what was happening.
> But on the campus of Illinois College in Jacksonville last Friday after-
> noon 116 students from 24 colleges and universities throughout
> Illinois were engaged in their own kind of "protest." What they were
> protesting, and that's not really an accurate term, is the present Illi-
> nois State Constitution.
>
> We'd venture the I.C. convention delegates have a far greater
> knowledge of our state constitution, its weaknesses, and the need for
> its improvement than the average adult citizen of the state. And
> probably it's appropriate that these young people are better informed
> about our state constitution and more interested in its reform than
> their elders, because they'll be living longer with its features—good
> or bad.

Just how much effect this draft constitution had on the convention
members who were later to draft a new document for Illinois would
be impossible to measure, but its effect on the students who convened in Jacksonville for those three days was no doubt salubrious.

Worthwhile films have been shown on campus, sponsored by
various College organizations. The Student Forum has sponsored
weekend showings of classic films, and the administration secured
the Kenneth Clark "Civilisation" series of BBC films, made possible
by grants from the National Endowment for the Humanities, the
National Gallery of Art, and the Xerox Corporation. When that
series was first shown, it was thought that one screening would suffice, but so many students, faculty and townspeople showed up that
each of the thirteen films had to be shown four times. That series
and others like Bronowski's "Ascent of Man" have been shown frequently. Also, departments arrange for showings of films of special
interest to their students.

Students brought their own performers on campus for Forum-
sponsored programs. Tastes in these matters seem to be volatile

Crispin Science Hall. Drawing by Dorothy B. Frank

and unpredictable, so that it is difficult to assess the impact of these events. From time to time, "big names" made appearances on the Illinois College campus, as they do regularly at the large universities. More than student support was needed to pay for these billings, and it was not always sufficient to cover costs. Sometimes the Student Forum activities fund was depleted by a single concert that did not attract paying customers. President Caine was notoriously unsympathetic to student promoters who overspent their budgets.

As the reader will have observed, Vernon Caine was energetic in his efforts to pull the College together; he made it stable without sacrificing its academic excellence. Nonetheless, he received criticism for some of his acts, and especially for his methods, which were regarded as authoritarian. Authority came under attack in the sixties, but Dr. Caine stubbornly resisted all such attacks; he insisted on his right to exercise his authority.

We appear to have passed the zenith of student discontent and protest, and there may even be a tendency to forget that it existed. But readers who were on campuses anywhere in America between 1963 and 1973 will remember the demonstrations of that decade; anyone who watched television or who read *Time* or *Newsweek* still feels a tremor of fear, a shudder of despair at the sound of names like Berkeley and Kent State, Columbia and Cornell, My Lai and Cambodia. Details may have become blurred, but the general feelings of outrage and bafflement and discouragement come flooding back.

Every college president had to face the anger of students for policies and acts over which he had no control and by which he was thwarted as much as his protesting students. Many presidents gave up in despair, and some—like President Nason of Swarthmore—

were very real casualties of a crisis in our national life. Students had
many reasons for their unhappiness, and they had few ways of vent-
ing their frustrations. The college president, sometimes dean, the
military recruiter, or the representative of Dow Chemical or DuPont
all became targets of convenience. The army recruiter or the industrial representative could leave the campus, but the president and the
dean had to stick it out.

President Caine thought that the students who criticized him when
he had done so much for them and the College were being grossly
unfair, and he was justified to think so, but the students needed a
target of convenience, and he was very visible and always available.
Some of the criticism was absurd, but some of it was legitimate,
and it did occasionally produce positive effects.

Vernon Caine had a thread of boastfulness in his character—like
Beowulf before going into battle, he would sometimes exult publicly. He often told the students—and the faculty—how much he had
done for them, and then he expected them to be grateful. If he had
been more subtle about it, he might have been forgiven, but he was
not subtle. He just laid it on the line, and usually to a captive audience in convocation or faculty meeting. He had been informed by the
A. N. Marquis Company, publishers of *Who's Who in America*, that
Illinois College had an extraordinarily high percentage of its alumni
listed in that prestigious volume. When the students were restless
over some decree of the administration, Dr. Caine would wave
Who's Who before them like a battle standard.

It was said by some of the faculty that he was autocratic and inflexible in his dealings with them, particularly the younger, nontenured faculty. There is some evidence that points this way, but if
one examines all the evidence, the charge is not very substantial.
There were cases of so-called harassment of teachers who took an
inordinate length of time to get the Ph.D.'s they were "on the verge
of" when they were first appointed. Yet, the stimulus given by Dr.
Caine sometimes had happy results, both for the individual and the
College. There were some instances of faculty who, to supplement
their income, took outside employment, without first consulting the
president. Again, Dr. Caine's irritation with this practice was shared
by many others, particularly among the trustees. I cannot find any

evidence that the president ever interfered with the academic freedom of any teacher.

Students sometimes complained that Dr. Caine regarded them as children, unable to manage their own affairs. Remembering the improvident guarantees they made to certain entertainers who drew audiences too small to cover the costs of their concerts, he may have felt justified. A *cause célèbre* of this sort arose after the Surgeon-General's report on the hazards of cigarette smoking was published. President Caine did not smoke, but he took this report very seriously. Without consulting student wishes, he had all the cigarette-vending machines removed from the campus. The act was arbitrary but not capricious. Dr. Caine did not ban smoking by students, but he "removed temptation," as he put it. He said that the College had no obligation to sell, or permit the sale of, dangerous substances on the campus. If students wished to buy them, they would have to go off campus to get them. There was, of course, no convenient source of supply nearby—at the time. But a student married couple who owned a house across from the campus enclosed their front hall, installed cigarette-vending machines in it, and left the entrance to their home open and lighted twenty-four hours a day. They helped put themselves through college by pandering to the bad habits of other students. This mild act of defiance was made notorious by the *Rambler's* featuring a large photograph of the house on its front page, with the caption "Where To Go" and an arrow pointing to the front door of 212 Park Street.

There was another celebrated case regarding the removal of a rather large stump from the center of the campus. The stump was occasioned by the Dutch Elm disease that devastated Jacksonville's lovely trees in the sixties. The dead trees had to be taken down, but there was a delay before the stump remover came to finish off the job. By that time, the stump had become the campus center for protests of all kinds—especially against required chapel. The stump was equidistant from the library, the chapel, and the dining hall. One day, March 16, 1966, just about lunch time, one of those horrendous machines that chew up stumps arrived in the middle of the campus and the operator began to obliterate the stump. He became hungry and stopped work when he was about half-way through and went off somewhere for lunch. When the students came out of Baxter Dining Hall and saw the ruins of their favorite protest spot, they started a protest. They made signs reading "Save Our Stump!" and about two hundred of them held hands and formed circles and swayed and sang "We Shall Overcome." When the stump obliterator came back from lunch and wanted to finish his job, several of the men flung themselves on the half-stump and shouted, "Over my dead body!" Messages were sent to the homes of the business manager, the dean, and the president, alerting them to the impasse. The president arrived first and, appreciating the humor of the protest, he sent the stump obliterator to other stumps. The sacred stump has been rotting away there for more than a decade, a symbol of one small student success over authority.

A recurring cause of student discontent during the Caine administration was required attendance at chapel. Objections to this requirement had been voiced by many generations of students before Dr. Caine arrived on campus, but they were either ignored or answered with the reminder that students knew before coming to Illinois College that chapel attendance was expected, and so there was no reason to complain about it. During the late sixties, however, the protests were more frequent and took more purposeful forms. There were meetings at the stump just prior to the chapel hour, and some sign of protest would be agreed upon—to stand up for the opening hymn and not sit down again for the rest of the service, to kneel for prayer —not a Presbyterian or Congregational practice—and look up fervently at the clergyman offering the prayer, to take a sign-in card at the beginning of chapel and not return it at the end, and other variations of peaceful dissent. On one occasion, there was a planned exodus just after the beginning of the service; almost two hundred students walked out quietly. The main point of the student opposition was that attendance might be required but worship could not be required and that attending chapel without worship was a mockery of the religious commitment of the College. If attendance was to be in partial fulfillment of some educational goal, then the meeting should be clearly secular and informative.

The constant agitation of the students caused the faculty to study the situation, after which they made a series of recommendations to

Caine Student Center. Drawing by Dorothy B. Frank

the Board of Trustees. The end result was a clear-cut distinction between an educational gathering called convocation, with a certain number of required attendances, and a purely voluntary service of worship to be called chapel. The Board adopted this proposal, and thus took much of the sting out of student protest at Illinois College.

There was no violent, destructive demonstration on the Illinois College campus during the whole of this period. There was, however, one shattering performance in convocation that produced general revulsion. It occurred at the first convocation of the second semester of the 1970–71 year. At this convocation the whole faculty processed in full academic regalia to seats in the front rows of Rammelkamp Chapel; the chaplain, dean, and president were seated on the platform. There had apparently been a plan to disrupt this ceremony even before the processional; it continued sporadically during the various parts of the ritual, gaining strength and ribaldry during the presidential address. According to the *Rambler* account: "For the first time in 142 years, Illinois College's second semester opening convocation was marred by protest and disruptions. . . . The crowd responded loudly, using noise-makers, musical instruments, and balloons. . . . The disruption continued until Dr. Iver F. Yeager, Professor of Religion, rose from his seat with the faculty and spoke to the students. He deplored the demonstrations. . . . The faculty and many students applauded his statement."

There were hearings on the disturbance held by the Faculty Committee on Discipline, and eventually action was taken against nine students who were known to be involved in provoking the outburst. Disciplinary action was meted out to eight of the students, ranging from a two-week suspension to letters of reprimand. The students involved were known, of course, as "The Convo Nine," and there was some expression of sympathy for them, but not much. The action included "social probation for the remainder of the semester" for six students, including the elected head of the Student Forum. As a consequence, he was removed from office. Although the faculty vote on this action was not unanimous, the verdict of the disciplinary committee and the penalties invoked were supported by a substantial majority. What was more important, the student body accepted the decision as a just one. There was no more of that vulgar, mindless kind of dissent during the Caine administration. Disagreement thereafter was channeled through accepted democratic procedures.

Partly through these same channels, there were some curricular changes made during the latter part of the Caine administration. Perhaps the most important ones came about through the forming of a Student Educational Policies Committee, parallel to that of the faculty. This committee considers student requests for new courses, new procedures, and the like. When it has suggestions to make, it holds a joint meeting with the faculty committee and the suggestions are discussed jointly. If and when agreement is reached, the faculty committee brings the suggested changes to the faculty floor, where they are acted upon and usually adopted. Thus the limited use of pass-fail courses has been inaugurated. This procedure permits upperclass students to take advanced courses outside their fields of concentration without risking their grade-point averages in competition with those specializing in the field. There are limits placed on this practice, but it has the desirable quality of encouraging students to broaden their educational opportunities.

The most important product of this joint student-faculty exploration of the curriculum has been the development of a core course required of all freshmen. The course is entitled Interdisciplinary Studies 191–192. It was inaugurated in the fall of 1970, after two years of study by a faculty committee, with student advice; it is intended to make students, especially freshmen, more aware of the complexity of their world by taking a look at several problems, from several different points of view. The theme of the first course was "Man in Change," and the readings included Skinner's *Walden Two*,

Bronowski's *The Identity of Man*, Barry Commoner's *Science and Survival*, Raymond Mack's *Transforming America: Changing Social Patterns*, and the *Saturday Review*. Lectures and films and discussions interpreted the themes of the course. Two hundred and fifty freshmen took the course under the guidance of seven professors drawn from the three divisions of the curriculum, who moderated the discussion meetings of small sections. The lectures were given by a number of Illinois College faculty and by visitors from the University of California, Northwestern University, and Washington University, and by officials of state and local government.

As a required course, Interdisciplinary Studies 191–192 has been under close scrutiny by students and faculty alike; it has changed its format and content from year to year. After a few years' trial, a faculty committee, with the help of students who had taken the course, made a thorough study of the course's content and methods; it suggested some changes but recommended strongly that the course be continued. Perhaps the significance of the course lies chiefly in the fact that it is a genuine group-learning experience for both students and faculty and that in a time when American higher education was getting more and more fragmented and specialized Illinois College had the courage to initiate and foster a course of broad, liberal inquiry.

In the spring of 1972, President Caine announced his intention of retiring from office at the end of the 1972–73 year. Like President Hudson before him, he stated that he wished to retire at the same age as was required of the faculty. His early announcement gave the Board of Trustees ample time to search for his successor, and it also gave students, faculty, and alumni time to reconsider the Caine years at the helm. I think this exercise led to greater understanding on all sides of the role of the presidency at Illinois College. I have already cited the material gains of Dr. Caine's stewardship, his careful use of the resources of the College, his extraordinary expansion of enrollment, plant, and prosperity. The College grew under him, in size and strength. There was also, especially in his last year on campus, a growing affection for the president and his charming wife, Elizabeth. They had been, during all of their residence at Barnes House, gracious in their entertainment of students, faculty, parents, alumni, trustees, and townspeople. As the time for saying goodbye approached, their fine qualities were reassessed and newly appreciated. There were recognitions by the Student Forum, the *Rambler*, the faculty, the Jacksonville Alumni Association and other alumni groups, and the Board of Trustees. The Jacksonville Chamber of Commerce sponsored a public recognition dinner, attended by four hundred people. MacMurray College held a special convocation at which it granted Vernon Caine the honorary degree of Doctor of Laws.

Best of all, Vernon and Elizabeth Caine could relax and enjoy the tributes that were paid them, secure in the knowledge that they had indeed earned them. For more than seventeen years they had served Illinois College faithfully and well.

23

President Mundinger, 1973—

In his last two annual reports to the trustees of the College, President Caine made some interesting observations and gave some advice useful both to the Board Members and to his successor. In August of 1972 he wrote:

It is likely that the present administration will be viewed in the perspective of history as much as a launching pad for future greatness as for any accomplishments of its own.
. . . .
The problem for the Trustees now is to see that plans are carried out under new leadership without retreat in the areas of good will, prestige, purpose, and solvency. The time for consolidation of position is over. The College can now move ahead, but not necessarily in the same manner or precisely in the same areas as in the recent past.

In May of 1973, by which time his successor had been chosen, President Caine waxed eloquent in his farewell address to the Board. The following excerpts are taken from that message:

We ought always to try to see that character and idealism and motivation to service are part of the method and the message of the College. We need men and women more than we need technicians.
. . . .
A trend in recent times in the academic world has been the decentralization of administrative power. The plight of colleges and uni-

versities today is in part the result of the idea that almost everybody ought to have a part in making decisions.

. . . .

By the very nature of his position, the president is the most vulnerable of all college employees. He has neither tenure nor protective colleagues. That a president can operate effectively long in opposition to faculty, students or the community is a myth. There is a built-in safeguard against presidential tyranny.

Very soon after Dr. Caine had announced his planned retirement, the Board named a presidential search committee, which was chaired by Lyndle Hess, class of 1930, and member of the Board since 1961. Mr. Hess wanted the broadest possible consensus before reaching a decision; so he called for advisory committees of the faculty, the student body, and the alumni to join the Board in its search for a new president. Never had the College been in better shape to attract an outstanding man, and never had it had so much time to spend on the process; moreover, the Board gave the committee a free hand and sufficient funding to carry out its assignment.

There were several organizational meetings of the four-constituency group, to establish goals and guidelines. At these meetings, all persons were listened to by the Board committee, which would have the final responsibility. Without doubt, this was a wise procedure. Another very sound decision made by Mr. Hess was to employ a consulting firm to do some of the leg work for the committee; to sound out prospective candidates and to make inquiries about them; to inform the Committee of probable strengths and weaknesses. This procedure for locating top executives has long been employed in the business world, but it is not so common in the academic world. There were, I believe, some of the Illinois College people who were dubious about it at the start, but I think that by the time the screening process was completed, everyone was convinced of the validity of the method.

After several months of looking over *vitae* of possible candidates, discussing them, and hearing reports from the consultant, the committee members were in agreement on the three top candidates available; these candidates were invited to Jacksonville to see and be seen. Each one was entertained and interviewed by students, faculty, alumni, and trustees—the interviews were not limited to persons formally on the committee—and then each group made its separate evaluation. I believe that every member of the general committee was slightly apprehensive that other groups might have different perspectives and reach different conclusions. It was therefore exhilarating to get together and discover that each group had come to the same decision, that the best possible man to lead Illinois College into its sesquicentennial celebration and subsequent development was Donald Charles Mundinger.

Dr. Mundinger had taken his B.S. in Education from Concordia Teachers College in River Forest, Illinois, an M.A. from Northwestern University, and a Ph.D. in political science from Washington University. He had taught at various levels from elementary school up through graduate school. He had held various fellowships, including a post-doctoral fellowship at the University of Michigan, and he had taught at several colleges and universities. Before coming to Illinois College he had been Dean of the College of Arts and Sciences and later Vice-President for Academic Affairs at Valparaiso University in Indiana. He had been Director of Valparaiso's Community Research Center, and he had spent a year abroad, establishing the university's overseas study centers at Cambridge, England, and Reutlingen, Germany. He had touched just about all the academic bases; he had climbed the ladder steadily and well. Beyond that, he was a strong churchman, Lutheran Church, Missouri Synod, a strong family man with an energetic wife and three lively children. He held memberships in the American Political Science Association, the Indiana Academy of Social Sciences, the American Association of University Professors, and Rotary International.

Personal meetings with Donald Mundinger by students, faculty, alumni, and trustees confirmed the written reports about him. He was a big man in every sense of the word—physically, intellectually, spiritually. Perhaps the one question mark in the minds of some was his church affiliation. A generation earlier, the Lutheran affiliation might have disqualified him at Illinois College, but given the trends of the sixties among almost all the Christian sects toward tolerance and understanding, it offered almost no problem. As an Illinois College graduate said to me recently, after being awarded an Alumni

President Donald C. Mundinger

Citation, "When a Presbyterian college honors a Roman Catholic like me and the presentation is made by a Missouri Synod Lutheran —believe me, that's ecumenism!"

Personally, Dr. Mundinger came across as a man of confidence, of enduring inner resources, stamina, and courage. He listened well, really listened, and held his peace; if a response was called for, he gave it quietly. He seemed to be a contemplative man, a reader and a ponderer. And yet he was not withdrawn, but easy in crowds, one who was sensitive to the mood of the moment, and ready to enjoy that mood. Everyone who got acquainted with him in those early meetings seemed to feel that he had established a personal relationship with Dr. Mundinger, one that would grow. I suppose the most striking quality of all was the sense of identification between the man and the institution. Although he had never been on the campus before, he seemed immediately to belong.

When, after his formal election by the Board, he was presented to a gathering of trustees, faculty, and students, he said very simply, "My decision to come to Illinois College was easy. It's the type of college I'd like to be affiliated with." The *Rambler* editorialized: "The Search Committee and its three advisory groups were unanimous in their choice of Dr. Mundinger. It's an astonishing, optimistic sign that such a large group of opinionated, diverse intellects would be so united in their vision of what Illinois College needed, and who the proper person was to fulfill those needs. We look forward with anticipation to the Mundinger presidency, and look forward to years of better communication between students and administration."

I think I should note here the thoughtful and courteous conduct of Vernon Caine at this time. He was as helpful to his successor as he could be, answering his questions candidly, but not trying to indoctrinate him. The temptation to do this must have been strong in a man of Dr. Caine's temperament, but he put it behind him. He communicated with Dr. Mundinger in a supportive way. Although he and Elizabeth had decided to make Jacksonville their home in retirement—the ties of seventeen years were strong ones—he accepted a succession of appointments as administrative consultant to colleges that were having problems about which he knew a great deal. He spent most of his first year of retirement in North Dakota, of his

second in Texas, and of his third in Tennessee; so he was out of town
for Donald Mundinger's first three years in office. It was an effective
way for Dr. Caine to use the talents he had developed at Illinois
College, and it also gave Dr. Mundinger a chance to find his way
into his job without being second-guessed by a veteran.

When he took over the reins of the College in September 1973,
President Mundinger made a brief but effective speech, addressing
himself to the questions of the moment, but also placing those questions in a larger perspective: "I am suggesting that more than ever
before, liberal arts colleges contain the germ of hope for the world."
As a political scientist he showed a penchant for weaving phrases
from speeches given by men he admired into a local context, as for
example, "While we should not change because of fear, we should
not fear to change." And in his special charge to the faculty, at the
opening Convocation, he said, "We are not here to be served, but to
serve."

If one looks through the issues of the *Rambler*, 1973–74, one is impressed by a sense that the College was moving purposefully toward
a less regimented kind of social life. It was not a panicky movement,
brought on by confrontation, but a planned response to reasonable
requests made by students and faculty alike, as the following examples show.

"*Women Get Key Rights.*"—What this meant was that the women
were at last being treated as if they were as responsible as the men;
that they could come and go from the dorms without formal signing
in and out.

"*Women May Move Off Campus.*"—Under certain conditions,
similar to those observed by the men. There was also a relaxation
of Baxter Hall dining rules, to make the eating process less formal
and more enjoyable.

"*Chaperones Abolished.*"—A move that was at least as welcome to
the faculty as it was to the students, and was long overdue. The idea
that every scheduled dance or party had to be monitored by two or
more faculty members was Victorian, and equally abhorrent to the
students who had to find chaperones and the faculty who felt obliged
to put in an appearance at functions where they were not wanted—
and did not want to be.

Perhaps the ultimate in Illinois College's entry into the collegiate world of the Seventies came in March of 1974. The *Rambler* announced it with banner headlines: "STREAKING HITS I.C." A premature spring had come to Jacksonville, and the students responded with primitive exuberance. Festivities began rather uncertainly after dinner on the evening of March 6 when a few males, wearing face masks and towel-turbans, ran a few nervous steps in the nude between a couple of men's dormitories on Mound Avenue. Interest picked up, small crowds gathered, and rhythmic chanting encouraged greater abandonment and wider involvement. Soon the exhibition included bicycles and convertibles, solos and group demonstrations, with growing enthusiasm among the spectators, who now numbered several hundred. The dean of the College was alerted, and he is said to have cautioned: "Everyone have a good time, but don't catch cold!" And the president is reported to have said, "As long as the streakers keep moving, it's all right." (To his trustees a few days later, President Mundinger made light of the affair, but he pointed out that any attempt to put a stop to the streaking would have "elicited a strong reaction from the crowd.")

The next night, the celebration was renewed, with much larger crowds, radio and television coverage—though this was said to be disappointing. Word was received that participants from MacMurray College wanted to join in, and they were heartily welcomed. The event became the country's "first intercollegiate streak." The Jacksonville police came to the campus to control traffic, vehicular as well as human. Some feared that they really wanted to put a stop to the whole business, but a spokesman for the department said: "We want the kids to have a good time. We only ask you keep the streets clear for the safety factor." Given the conservatism of the College and the community, this was a remarkable demonstration of the new social freedoms of the age. There was some muttering and complaining, but anyone who wandered across the campus on the nights of March 6 and 7, 1974, must have been struck by the general feeling of good will, good humor, and good sense. In the midst of the festering of Vietnam and Watergate, these rites of spring on the bucolic campus of Illinois College were wholesome, cathartic experiences. They symbolized an earthy return to sanity.

Winter returned to Jacksonville on March 8, and the ardor of the students was cooled. Clothes were resumed along with studies, and Illinois College prepared to inaugurate Donald Mundinger officially. On that occasion, March 21, 1974, there was the usual academic procession, and a keynote address by Yale University's Stirling Professor of Religious Studies, Yaroslav Pelikan, a personal friend of Donald Mundinger's. After that, the new president was invested and admonished, praised and warned, by representatives of the trustees, the alumni, the faculty, and the student body. He responded to all of these optimistically:

The main challenge for Illinois College is the challenge of mission. We must with daring read the current revolution of rising expectation and prepare for its full impact. The coming decade will be especially treacherous. We will be ahead of the times because we lavish our resources on the development of minds and hearts sensitive to the humane, as we also teach vocational and professional skills.
. . . .
Illinois College will succeed and she will receive her share, and more, of honor and recognition.
. . . .
It is in this spirit of a future dedicated to man, the improvement of his mind and spirit, that I with confidence and joy accept the tokens of office of the President of Illinois Collge.

Several presidents have told me that at the beginning of their administrations they were uncertain where to start. It was not possible to single out a problem and attack it and then move on to others in an orderly way. Everything needed doing at once. Still, a start had to be made somewhere, even though other things kept demanding attention. President Mundinger appears to have decided that admissions was his first priority. President Caine had also faced that problem very early; he came in at the postwar nadir and had built up enrollment steadily. Still, in his last years President Caine witnessed some decline in enrollment.

Dr. Mundinger decided to have a close look at the personnel and policies of the admissions office. He saw that more money would have to be spent there and that a more dynamic image had to be

Schewe Library. Drawing by Dorothy B. Frank

created for the College. The long-time director of admissions was due for retirement; so there was a good chance of achieving these goals painlessly. President Mundinger enlarged the staff and appointed personable young people to it. All of them were recent graduates of the College; they knew its faults and its virtues. They were trained to tell the truth, even to turn prospects away, if it did not seem likely that Illinois College was the right place for them. The new director and his staff were given more travel money, more telephone money—and they were encouraged to use it imaginatively.

The rather prim stationery of the College was made to look more contemporary, with a new logo, and the logo was used on all the promotional material that was sent out, including a blue T-shirt with white logo, sent to all applicants who are admitted to the College A new slogan was created: "The thing that sets us apart is the people we bring together." That might not qualify for a Pulitzer prize in poetry, but it slips off the tongue pleasantly and creates a positive image. For many years the people who have had to meet the public and sell the College have said that once you get thirty miles from

Jacksonville, Illinois College is confused with the University of Illinois, Eastern, Western, Southern, and Northern Illinois universities, and others. The fact that the College is located in Jacksonville only adds to the confusion.

Over the years, there have been several well-meaning attempts to change the name of the College to avoid this kind of confusion. President Mundinger has not adopted this form of escapism but has encouraged students and faculty and alumni to think of the College as unique—"premier" both in time and quality. It is too early to say that this ploy has worked, but it has a better chance of success than changing the name of the College would have.

There has been some attempt made to broaden the College's constituency. Spreading out from Morgan County and the usual areas of Chicago and St. Louis, Springfield and Quincy, etc., there has been a special effort made to attract students from Kansas City and Indianapolis. There have always been a few students from foreign countries, but never many at any one time. Congressman Paul Findley, a member of the Board, has urged a program to attract students from overseas; perhaps something will come of this. It takes time to build regional and foreign constituencies, but once they are established, they tend to nurture themselves.

Next to admissions, and related to it, is the problem of retention. Studies have been made at every college in the country to find out why students leave before they have earned a degree. Since the end of the national draft, male students especially have been under less compulsion to go to college at all, let alone remain at any particular one. What used to be known as "drifting" is now known by other, more respectable names, and it is even encouraged in some quarters. "Laying out" has also become an acceptable practice. If a young man or woman can profit from working at some worthwhile job, or from travel, or from contemplation, few people now will be critical, not even parents. But these practices are not panaceas, and they do make the job of college administrators infinitely more difficult by the uncertainties they give rise to.

One way of holding good students is to give them some things that are intellectually challenging. Few developments of our times have intrigued students more than the many uses of computers. Illinois College has never attempted to run programs in competition with the technical and engineering schools of the country—even the 3–2 program described earlier is meant to supplement rather than compete with engineering schools—but there are still many opportunities for using the computer imaginatively in a liberal arts setting. For a time we had access on our campus to a computer at MacMurray College. When that arrangement was discontinued, a grant from the Illinois Board of Higher Education made it possible for us to hook in with a more sophisticated system known as PLATO (Program Logic for Automatic Teaching Operations) at the University of Illinois. Several of our faculty and a number of our students have taken advantage of the program. At its inauguration, Illinois College was the only private college in the state to offer this opportunity.

Another exciting experience called "The Women's Collegium" was made possible by a grant from the Helena Rubinstein Foundation. A local committee of students and faculty, under the chairmanship of Professor Carole Ryan, has organized a series of lectures, panel discussions, and workshops dealing with the special concerns of women—though men are urged to participate. Books have been bought and films have been shown that explore these concerns. Personalities that are nationally known, like Shana Alexander and Betty Friedan, have participated in these explorations, along with many others of lesser note but sometimes greater impact.

A grant from the Danforth Foundation made possible a "Black Awareness Week," which sought to educate a student body that is not hostile or even indifferent to the condition of blacks, but is generally not very well informed. Illinois College, by principle, from the time of its founding, has been conscious of racial discrimination and its evil effects, but it has never made a practice of recruiting blacks or offering programs that would attract them. It welcomed blacks cordially long before 1954 made this a matter of national consciousness, blacks who wish the experience of genuine integration, on a "come as you are" basis. There is no post from which blacks have ever been excluded, no society or team that would not gladly accept them as colleagues. Most blacks who have come here have come because they liked the atmosphere, not because they were filling some quota. The results have been unspectacular, but deeply satisfying. The black awareness week reinforced this sense of belonging.

All students, regardless of sex, race, or creed, have a keen sense of their identity and their individual rights. This had been taken for granted on the Illinois College campus, but had not been spelled out. In President Mundinger's first year, there was great interest shown in drafting a document that would achieve this goal. Student and faculty committees worked on the problem and produced a four-page, eleven-article Bill of Student Rights that any of the founding fathers might have been pleased to sign. (For text, see Appendix A, "Resource Materials.") After adoption by the student body, it was ratified by the faculty at a special meeting held April 22, 1974. The Board of Trustees received it at their annual meeting that year and discussed it with interest. They took no action on it, however, believing it to concern matters which were wholly in the provenance of the administration, faculty, and student body.

Another matter of campus concern was the College calendar. In the past this had been an administrative matter, with some faculty involvement. Students have a legitimate interest in the calendar, of course, but they were not usually consulted on it, except perhaps for setting the date of Homecoming. Although there was no clear-cut consensus, there was a good deal of interest shown in the possibility of beginning the academic year and ending it several weeks earlier. This would make it possible to have semester final exams before Christmas break, eliminating the short but grim period between the break and finals; the earlier commencement date would allow seniors to get into the job market sooner, and give them every possible advantage there. It would also improve the chances of other students to line up summer jobs in May rather than in June, by which time many of the temporary summer jobs have been filled. The opening of College in late August in the humid, hot weather of central Illinois was the main drawback. Nonetheless, the advantages outweighed that disadvantage, and a calendar change was proposed and adopted, by joint administrative-faculty-student consultation and action.

The convocation requirement for graduation continues to come under scrutiny. Like his predecessors, President Mundinger believes that there is a very real advantage to having stated formal meetings of the whole student body. It is one of the symbols of community that a large institution cannot possibly duplicate and for that reason —as well as many substantive reasons—the convocation requirement should be kept. One way of making it more palatable is to improve the quality of the programs offered; every administration has tried to do this. I think that a neutral observer would agree that in recent years the quality of convocations at Illinois College has been varied but relatively high. A second way of making convocation more meaningful to the student body is to involve students both in the planning and the execution of the programs. Students are not necessarily prejudiced in favor of student participants, but if there is a note of competition—such as in the debates between literary societies, or the competition for prizes in oratory, etc.—they are likely to be interested.

An occasional stressing of ritual is also a way of arousing some student curiosity. At the opening of each semester, there is a full-dress parade of the faculty into Rammelkamp Chapel, and the ritual of pronouncing the College "in session for the first semester of the 149th year," or whatever, is indulged in by the whole community, with some fanfare. The flag of the United States and the banner of Illinois College are borne at the head of the procession by the student marshals, and the faculty are led to their seats by the faculty marshal, and so forth. There is appropriate music, including processional and recessional marches, an anthem by the choir and the singing of the Alma Mater by all—or almost all—present. In the first semester opening, the president himself sounds the keynote of the year in an address. President Mundinger has produced an interesting variation for the second semester opening convocation. He takes that opportunity of officially installing the holder of one of the endowed chairs and having the recipient of the honor give an address, on a subject of his choosing. Thus, Iver Yeager was installed as the Scarborough Professor of Religion and Philosophy in January of 1976. In 1977, Don Filson was installed in the Strawn Chair of Chemistry, which had not been occupied since 1947. In 1978, Charles Frank was installed as the first A. Boyd Pixley Professor of Humanities. In each case, the person installed gave an address that dealt with his discipline or some special concern of his.

Another ritualistic form of convocation is the honors convocation, at the end of the year, shortly before the ritual of commencement. This practice dates back to the Caine administration, but it has been given new emphasis. There used to be just one honors convocation, but the crowded agenda has made it necessary to divide it into two parts, in successive weeks: academic honors and athletic honors. Both of these recognize the achievements of students, from election to Phi Beta Kappa to letters in various intercollegiate sports, from listing in *Who's Who in American Colleges and Universities* to a fellowship at the University of Illinois. The Dunbaugh Distinguished Professor award is the fitting climax of the academic convocation, since it is granted by decision of committee representing the students.

Other methods of enlivening the convocation experience have been used, as for example granting double attendance for certain evening concerts, lectures, and performances. Also, the variety of the programming has been improved by a joint student-faculty committee. The number of credits required for convocation credit has been given careful attention, as well as the ways of acquiring the credits. Admittedly, some of these experiments dilute the "community" aspect of the experience, but they do not sacrifice it altogether. There are probably always going to be a few students who will complain of having to meet any "cultural" requirement, but so far the successive administrations have held firm to the requirement as a reasonable demand on the academic community of the College.

In his first five years, President Mundinger succeeded in forging a strong admissions policy and had some success in improving the retention record of the College; he thus stabilized enrollment. He appears to be happy with the current figure of about eight hundred. Like his predecessors, he would like to broaden the base of the constituency without endangering the traditional homogeneity of the College population. This is a delicate balance. His program for improving the quality of the education offered at Illinois College is, at the time of writing, still taking shape, but it appears to be based on a strengthening of the fine arts within the liberal arts context.

McGaw Fine Arts Center. Drawing by Dorothy B. Frank

On the physical side, a number of important additions have been made to College facilities. Of primary importance is the Schewe Library, a truly beautiful building with excellent facilities, such as the audio-visual room, the seminar rooms, the overnight study room, and the Hudson Faculty Research Room. Perhaps the greatest improvement in the Schewe Library as compared to the Tanner Library is the scattering of the study areas among the stacks instead of having them concentrated in one large, central room. The Mason Grosvenor Reading Room of Tanner was a handsome room, but it was not conducive to genuine study. There were too many distractions.

By the way, that room has been essentially maintained in the renovation of Tanner Hall. The architect who devised the new uses for the reading room without greatly altering its appearance was ingenious, to say the least. Seminar rooms, faculty offices, and a large, lobby-like reception room provide additional meeting places for students and faculty and visitors. The acoustical problem has not, however, been wholly solved. Elsewhere, the restructuring of Tanner has been very successful. The administrative functions of the College are more than adequately housed, and the first impressions of visitors are more favorable than they once were.

The Memorial Gymnasium is now completed, more than twenty years after it was begun. The physical education plant is probably as good as that of any small college in the state; it is a far cry from what it was in the thirties. It took a long while to achieve this adequacy, but it has been done.

In connection with the sesquicentennial celebration, there are further planned additions to the College's physical equipment. Most eagerly awaited is the new Fine Arts Center, now well into the planning stage. This will provide a really adequate small theater, ample space and facilities for music and art. There is no intention of offering professional training in any of the arts but rather to offer a full experience of man's creative expression as part of the well-rounded life. Illinois College has always tried to recognize this aspect of a complete education, but it has not been able to afford it. The situation is about to change.

A word should be said about the fine arts at Illinois College, as they have been, and as they may become. I have indicated earlier that the merger of the two conservatories of music in 1928 had the effect of taking Illinois College out of competition with MacMurray College in the whole area for a full generation or more. It is true that the theatre has always been lively on the Hill, but those working in it have not had the advantage of a good setting or equipment. The new theatre in the McGaw Fine Arts Center should remedy this deficiency, without turning the theatre program into a pre-professional one. The emphasis will continue to be on the theatre as one branch of man's artistic striving, not on the commercial aspects of entertainment.

As for art itself, there has been a quarter-century of strictly limited commitment to the teaching of painting and sculpture, of the crafts of weaving, ceramics and jewelry making, and of the history of art. Studio space has been found in the old gymnasium, Tanner, Russel House, Gardner, etc. In other words, the art department got whatever space was left over when every other department was taken care of. The personnel commitment was also minimal. For many years, the College has had a working arrangement with the Jacksonville Art Association, which called for the joint appointment of one person who would act as the director of the Strawn Art Gallery and the instructor of art at Illinois College. Often this worked very well, for the person who took the post was usually young and enthusiastic and willing to work very hard at two rather different tasks, with sometimes conflicting demands. That person got an excellent apprenticeship in both teaching and organizing and mounting exhibitions; on the basis of those experiences he could decide whether to go into teaching or museum work. The students had certain advantages too; they learned from a generalist, and were often called on to help him with his too heavy schedule. But no one stayed on the job very long, and so continuity of program could not develop, at either College or gallery. The facilities in the new art center will be infinitely better than anything Illinois College has known before, and it should be possible to attract artists who will enjoy teaching in them and who will want to stay for a while. The advantages to our students are obvious. As in the case of the theatre, the program in the art department will not be directed toward training professional artists but rather at making our students more aware of their heritage and more willing to participate in the arts, actively or passively.

Likewise with the music program. The College has long supported choral singing and some forms of instrumental performance, in the form of a band, and participation in the Jacksonville Symphony Orchestra. It has provided the experience of listening to music, both live and recorded. It has given courses in the appreciation of music, its history, and, to some degree, its theory. There is now a stronger movement toward performance. The gift of a harpsichord by the A. C. Hart family, the class of 1977 gift of a new grand piano for Rammelkamp Chapel, and, most of all, the installation of a fine pipe organ in Rammelkamp are signs of this desirable movement. The various practice and performance rooms in the fine arts center will reinforce all of these signs. There should be a renaissance of joyful noises on the Illinois College campus. Again, as in the case of theatre and art, there is no intention of creating a professional music school here, only a demonstration that music is an essential part of the human experience, of the liberating arts.

The recent establishment of the Claridge Lectureship, through the efforts of the English department and generous patrons of the realm of letters, is related to the growing emphasis on the creative arts. The first two Claridge lectures brought to the campus figures of importance in the literary world, men like Jonathan Wordsworth of Oxford University, collateral descendant of the poet William and recognized critic of his work, for a series of lectures and seminars; and the Pulitzer Prize poet Howard Nemerov, for a public reading and private consultations with students. All of these opportunities have greatly increased the cultural awareness of large numbers of students, and they give evidence of this administration's desire to enrich the creative quality of the College.

It is not possible at this point to evaluate the contributions President Mundinger has made and will make to the history of Illinois College. One may, however, point to the success he and the College have had in their initial tests by outside examiners. In the spring of 1975, the decennial visit of the North Central Accrediting Association occurred. A large committee of faculty, with five subcommittees, under the general supervision of Dean Wallace Jamison, made a thorough study of all phases of the College's operations and prepared a report on them. The visiting committee of the North Central Association made its own evaluation, of course, but the members were favorably impressed, not only by what they found but by the general awareness of the faculty and staff of the mission of the College, its strengths and weaknesses. The committee's report cited some "concerns" along with their general approval of what was happening educationally at Illinois College. In summary, they said, "Illinois College has a strong sense of mission; faculty are unusually devoted to the institution and exhibit a genuine concern for and responsiveness to student needs; the faculty make innovative use of facilities, resources, and programs in the Greater Jacksonville area; faculty demonstrate an unusual initiative to participate in programs contributing to their professional growth; the College enjoys reasonable stability in its financial position and enrollment; there is growing involvement of faculty and students in the governance of the College." A short time later, a much larger group from the Illinois Office of Education made a searching examination of our teacher preparation program. On the basis of their initial findings, they granted "provisional" approval, and then a bit later, after some clarifications and changes had been made, they issued an "unqualified" approval of the teacher preparation program of Illinois College. Even when you are confident that you are doing a first-rate job, it is reassuring to have confirmation of this kind.

At the same time, it is also reassuring to know that President Mundinger, who has not yet faced a serious crisis in his administration, is not overconfident, not a victim of *hubris*. In his keynote address of the first convocation of the 1976–77 academic year, he raised the question "Is Small Really So Beautiful?" He wanted the College family to know that while we boast of our knowing each other and caring for each other, smallness is not "an assured blessing."

Small will be beautiful at Illinois College only if individuals—administration, students, faculty—are prepared to take advantage of the opportunities which are inherent in smallness.

As I start my fourth year at Illinois College, I sometimes sense a kind of complacency with who we are, what we are, with the quality we have achieved. This is an uncomfortable feeling.

That is probably as good a note to end this chapter on as I can find. Any college president who can look down the road ahead without some nervousness has probably outlasted his usefulness. One wishes a long presidency for Donald Mundinger, not just for his personal happiness, though that should be considered, but for the good of Illinois College. As one looks back over one hundred and fifty years, he sees quite clearly that the good days of the past have occurred in the long presidencies, those of men like Sturtevant, Rammelkamp, Hudson, and Caine. May Mundinger join those worthies in their longevity.

24

Epilogue: Illinois College, Where Are You Going?

It may be foolhardy to attempt to look into the future and predict what will happen in the next fifty years at Illinois College. It would be safer to repeat Rammelkamp's generalized conclusion: "The future beckons us to still greater achievement. Illinois College must remain a college in the best sense—small enough to conserve the advantages of such an institution but thoroughly well equipped for its task." I think many who love the old College would settle for this centennial pronouncement, and then let each reader imagine for himself just how the College will achieve that worthy goal. But can we not be a little more explicit? I think we can, and I am willing to take the risk. Those who care not for this kind of risk may consider *Pioneer's Progress* concluded with the preceding quotation. The rest of us will go on, cautiously.

After tracing the record of one hundred and fifty years, I am tremendously impressed by the stamina of the College. It has faced all kinds of crises during those years, survived them, and come out stronger than it went in. It should have expired back in the 1830s, in the 1860s, in the 1890s; in this century it tottered on the brink of extinction in 1905, 1932, 1944, and again in 1955. No one could blame Beecher, Sturtevant, or Tanner if they had given up in despair. Nor could Rammelkamp, or Hudson, or Caine be condemned, if any of them had decided that the time had come to cease collegiate operations here. But they did not give up, and the College did not die. To adapt the noble words of William Faulkner on a solemn occasion, the College has not merely "endured," it has "prevailed."

Good. But how will it acquit itself in the next fifty years? Let me look with you at some of the problems that appear to lie ahead and hazard some guesses about ways of dealing with them. Neither the statements of problems nor the ways of dealing with them have any official sanction; they are personal projections, based on my study of the past and my experience of a considerable part of it.

Let me begin with the basic elements of any educational institution —students and faculty. The student body of the College grew from a mere handful in 1830 to approximately 100 in 1900. By 1929, enrollment had been stabilized at about 400; this number seems to have been regarded as ideal until World War II, when the uncertainties of the times caused a drop in student population to 87. After recovery from that low point, and taking advantage of the postwar growth of college-bound youth, the Illinois College optimum was set at roughly 800, and there it remains today. Assuming that this figure will continue to be accepted as ideal, there are still questions regarding the way in which the complement should be filled. A study of enrollment statistics and percentages shows that Illinois College has always drawn very heavily on Jacksonville and Morgan County and thereafter on certain population centers in Illinois— Chicago, Springfield, Decatur, Quincy, and Rockford—for the major part of its student body. The College has been happy to have a few pockets in the East and in the St. Louis area from which it has drawn in the past, principally because it had an alumnus in the area who recruited actively, usually a clergyman or a teacher.

A somewhat similar situation has affected the enrollment of minority students and foreign students. They have been warmly welcomed and treated with special care when they have come, but they have not come in large numbers. I believe that a greater effort to diversify should be made in the future and that it will be made. Educationally, a more varied mix, culturally, ethnically, and geographically, will produce superior results. There are risks to such a policy, if it should be adopted, and they should be carefully calculated. Surely one of the reasons why Illinois College moved through the late sixties and early seventies with so little confrontation and disruption was the homogeneous character of its student body. That student body has been a conservative one in almost every respect.

The liberal student is welcomed, listened to and accepted, but not much followed; he or she is tolerated. Even the radical student turns up occasionally and is not scorned; he just feels rather lonely. If he achieves an influential office, he finds that in his hands its influence is muted. A change toward diversity in recruiting policies would probably alter this pattern, but a moderate shift might well provide intellectual ferment without spoiling the whole brew. Whatever the makeup of the student body, it will remain desirable to keep open the lines of communication between students, faculty, administration, and trustees. The present incumbent in the president's office appears to have established a good balance in that respect and to have achieved acceptance by the student body without losing control of his power to make decisions.

Much the same thing can be said about relations between the president and the faculty at the present time. There are always problems in this realm, as any reader must have sensed in following the story of the first century and a half. Professors are harder to deal with than students, for a number of reasons. For one thing, they last longer. They are often as mature and able as the president himself, frequently more learned and experienced. They are conscious of their collective power; they usually have strong ideas on how a college should be run and are very capable of expressing them. So long as the opportunities for expression are not repressed, the exchange of ideas between teachers and administrators is likely to be cordial, urbane, and fruitful; occasionally there will be disagreement and dissonance. Regular faculty meetings attended by all full-time members of the faculty and presided over by the president himself will keep the lines of communication open between administration and staff. The existence of the Illinois College Senate as an advisory body provides an excellent buffer, both for the president and the faculty. An active chapter of the AAUP gives constructive criticism, and even the dormant Teaching Faculty Organization is a valuable means of direct communication between faculty and the Board of Trustees, should that become necessary. In the recent past, however, the trustees have been eager to keep open the lines of communication with both the faculty and the student body, not merely through ceremonial receptions and luncheons but through working committees, where real problems can be explored thoroughly.

What are the faculty problems in need of solution? Two principal ones should be addressed. The first has to do with the teaching load. By long tradition at Illinois College, that has been fixed at fifteen credit hours, usually five three-hour courses. If that involves five different courses, as it sometimes does, it is a heavy load, especially for younger members of the faculty. The faculty argument is that a fifteen-hour load allows little time for anything that could be regarded as research, and, especially for the less experienced teacher, does not even allow adequate time for proper preparation of class work. The administration argument is that to reduce the teaching load to twelve credit hours will either mean a 20 percent reduction in course offerings or the addition of 20 percent more faculty. The former is likely to be unacceptable both to students and faculty; the latter will cost so much that it will preclude salary increases and other benefits, unless of course the income of the College is greatly increased, either by raising the tuition charged or by finding other large new sources of operating income. Neither of these can be easily accomplished; so an impasse is reached. A compromise solution must be seriously pursued.

Another problem that affects faculty morale is the matter of tenure. Essentially, this is the academic equivalent of seniority in the business and industrial worlds. A faculty member on tenure cannot be dismissed without demonstrable cause; this, in turn, gives the tenured professor a sense of security and allows him to speak his mind without fear of the displeasure of his president or dean or chairman. It is a vital support of academic freedom, the most precious of the professor's rights. The matter is even more acute in the seventies because of the tightness of the market, the limited job opportunities at the college and university level. Young Ph.D.'s nowadays have difficulty finding jobs, and once they do, they hang on to them until they achieve tenure, and having achieved it, they do not readily change jobs. The result is that there are more and more posts held by tenured professors, and institutions have less and less opportunity to bring in new blood, which is needed if a faculty is not to grow stagnant. Administrators have tended to respond to this situation by making new appointments in nontenured tracks, usually "three years and out." It is not easy for a young instructor to give excellent service day in and day out if he knows that however fine his teaching his services will inevitably be terminated at the end of three years. On the other hand, the institution cannot remain healthy if it permits itself to be indefinitely committed to an unchanging staff. There is no easy solution to this problem either; tact is required on both sides, and an understanding that exceptions will be made. The administration of Illinois College has shown that it is not inflexible in these cases, and it must continue to do so. The College must strive to improve those programs that clearly stimulate the faculty to excellence in their teaching and research, such as the sabbatical program and the appropriation of money for travel to professional meetings and in support of research. A program of exchange of faculty with institutions of a similar character in other parts of the country might be worth exploring. Faculty morale at Illinois College is on the whole good, but it cannot be neglected, even benignly.

The curriculum of the College is under constant study, both from within and from without, especially through the visitations of experts from the North Central Accrediting Association and the Illinois Office of Education. If these visits achieve nothing else, they require the resident faculty to examine itself and its program, critically and regularly. Changes ought not to be made whimsically or faddishly, but change should not be resisted merely to maintain a tradition. The basic liberal arts are still at the core of the Illinois College program and will almost certainly continue to keep their central position. At the same time, all of the administrations of this century, including the long-lived ones as well as the short-lived ones, have attempted to introduce some elements of vocationalism or professionalism. Thus Rammelkamp introduced a program for training teachers, Hudson sponsored cooperation with the military establishment both during and after World War II, and he launched the Community Development Program. Both Hudson and Caine encouraged cooperative programs with the School for the Deaf, the School for the Blind (now the Illinois State School for the Visually Impaired), the State Hospital (now the Jacksonville Area Mental Health and

Developmental Agency), and Passavant Hospital. Caine and Mundinger have looked with favor upon various kinds of internship programs in the community, programs of study abroad, and cooperation with MacMurray College, under mutually beneficial circumstances. Thoughtfully planned and carefully administered, all these programs can give liberal arts students additional valuable experiences in the educational, professional, and business worlds, without lessening the value of a liberal education for its own sake. They also keep the liberal arts program from becoming or appearing to become, as its detractors like to claim, dilettantist. Unquestionably, the most notable curricular innovation of the Mundinger administration has been the renewed emphasis on the fine arts. This has shown itself in recent appointments in music and art and, even more, in the provision of adequate facilities to pursue the arts. The McGaw Fine Arts Center is the most visible of these new facilities, but the accoustical renovation of Rammelkamp Chapel and the installation of a fine pipe organ in the Chapel are other visible signs of this new approach. The fruits will be tasted in the years to come.

In past years, the trustees of the College have been most active and visible on two occasions: when a new president was being sought, or when a money-raising campaign was being launched. These are certainly important occasions, but the Board should be visible at other times; in fact, it should be an ever-present part of the life of the College. Recent activities of the Illinois College Board of Trustees seem to show an awareness of that function. There has been much greater interaction between the Board and the resident College family than ever before, especially in the planning and the execution of the Schewe Library, the McGaw Fine Arts Center, and the sesquicentennial celebrations. This has been a healthy development for the whole College family. In electing new members, the Board might consider in addition to the traditional clergy, doctors, lawyers, and business men, a few topnotch artists and educators, in order to give a still broader outlook for the future of the College.

All recent presidents have cultivated the alumni of the College and have done much to cement the good relationships originally developed by President Rammelkamp. Here one can only urge the continuation of policies that are already in being. Some special ap-

proaches have been tried recently: the Century Club, the President's
Club, the Founders' Circle, and the Society of 1829. It is too early to
assess their effectiveness, but they appear to be succeeding. Another
special group that is being encouraged is the Parents' Association.
Still another venture that seems to be having some success is the
appeal to special interests of a desirable kind, instead of having only
large drives for major improvements. The recent limited campaigns
for the David A. Smith House, the Courtney Crouch Wright memorial garden, and the Friends of the Library all have produced excellent results, and have given alumni and friends a chance to participate
in providing the College with things they as individuals would like
to see on campus. Such special campaigns can complicate the whole
matter of fund-raising, but so far they seem to have been kept in
balance with the larger needs of the College.

The relations of College and community have been remarkably
close ever since the Rev. John Millot Ellis entered into correspondence with the Yale Band, back in 1829. The situation has never been
better described than it was by President Sturtevant in June 1858
when he reported to Theron Baldwin on the great success of his
fund-raising in the area of Jacksonville: "Illinois College dwells
among its own people. *It is at home.*" Still later, the Osage Orange
picnic was, and still is, an expression of the special relationship between College and community. The community supports the athletic events and dramatic and musical performances of the College;
citizens swell the attendance at lectures and films; they use the tennis
courts and occasionally other facilities of the College, such as the
gymnasium and chapel. Perhaps the only time during the past century when relations have been seriously strained was at the time of
the Ayers Bank failure. But the recriminations of that event are long
since ended, and Illinois College is very much at home in its community. Not only are Illinois College people active in the churches,
service organizations and clubs of the community but in local politics as well. In the city-wide elections of April 1973, nine new alder-
men were elected to the City Council, six of whom had Illinois College connections—two were members of the senior class, two were
members of faculty and staff, and two were alumni. The relationship

is further reinforced by the financial support given to the College by local business and industry.

It is no doubt this close relationship between the community and the College that has made the state-supported community college unnecessary in the Jacksonville-Morgan County area. As a result of legislative action, Illinois began some years ago to develop a state-wide system of junior or community colleges. The intention was to provide every region of the state with educational opportunities for all high school graduates who wished to continue their education. The concept was and is a sound one, and it has had considerable success. There are, however, certain areas in the state that are already well provided with facilities for higher education, Jacksonville and Morgan County being among them. These areas have chosen not to form their own community college districts, and they have resisted the attempts made to affiliate them with nearby community colleges. Bills have been introduced into the House and Senate that would force these reluctant areas into the community college system, even though referenda have shown an overwhelming negative response to these attempts. The last effort to affiliate the school districts of the Jacksonville area with Lincolnland Community College was rejected by votes of from 9–1 to as high as 14–1. Agitators for a "complete" statewide system of community colleges will no doubt continue to work for the plan in spite of the expressed will of the people. Illinois College and other independent colleges will have to continue to make their case that they are serving the needs of their districts and at the same time helping local taxpayers to avoid expensive and un-needed duplication. It is to be hoped that the executive and legislative branches in Springfield will continue to see the justice and wisdom of this stand.

Perhaps the most encouraging sign of all for the future of the College is the nature of the gifts and grants that have recently been made to it, indicating confidence in the mission of Illinois College. In addition to those generous bequests of Judge and Mrs. Gardner, Mr. and Mrs. A. Boyd Pixley, and the more recent major gift of the Lawrence Sibert family, have been the signal benefactions of Karl H. and Louise H. Schewe that made possible the new library, and of

Mary W. and Foster G. McGaw that provided the new arts center. These are welcomed not only for their splendid additions to the plant of Illinois College but also because they show clearly that what the College has been doing this century and a half is admired and appreciated not only by her own graduates but also by thoughtful and generous patrons outside her immediate circle. Much the same kind of cachet has been placed upon the College by the several foundations, the Kresge and Rubinstein foundations among others, that have made special grants in recent years.

Thus, for many reasons, the future of Illinois College looks bright. Even the most optimistic of observers, however, must practice caution in making predictions. The wheel of fortune is always on the move and it depresses as well as exalts. It loves to humble the proud and the complacent. Although Illinois College has much to be proud of, she has no reason for complacency; she must frankly acknowledge that much remains to be done. "The future beckons us to still greater achievement."

Appendices
Index

A Note on the Appendices

Although many readers are indifferent to them, appendices are very important to others. The information that follows will, I hope, be of use to the latter kind. In Appendix A, I have not repeated the material already available in Rammelkamp. His bibliography of manuscript and printed materials, pages 535–41, should be consulted by all serious students. So also should his reproduction of the Charter of Illinois College, pages 543–48. Some additions should be made to his listing of background materials. The *History of Morgan County*, originally published by Donnelly, Loyd & Co., Chicago, 1878, was republished by the Jacksonville Area Genealogical and Historical Society in 1975. Ernest G. Hildner, Jr., wrote a brief history of Jacksonville for the Elliott State Bank, published in 1966. *Morgan County, Illinois: the Twentieth Century* was edited by E. G. Hildner, Jr., and a committee of local historians, and published by the Morgan County Commissioners in 1968. A *Family History of Morgan County* was put together by a committee under the editorship of E. G. Hildner, Jr., and Helen Hinde, and published by the Taylor Publishing Co. of Dallas, Texas, in 1977. A fascinating study of Jacksonville's early development by Don Harrison Doyle was published in 1978 by the University of Illinois Press, under the title, *The Social Order of a Frontier Community: Jacksonville, Illinois, 1825–70*.

Works of special interest to friends of Illinois College are Harold E. Gibson's *Sigma Pi Society of Illinois College, 1843–1971*, Dan Runkle's *History of Football at Illinois College, 1879–1968*, and Dacey R. Smith's *Charley's World*, 1969, which contains an amusing account of life on the campus in the 1920s. Douglas Brockhouse '69 wrote a history of Phi Alpha, 1929–1969, and Ken Bradbury '71 performed a similar service for Pi Pi Rho, 1929–1967; both of these are available in the Schewe Library. Other societies have briefer accounts prepared for their members. Several unpublished theses that deal with Illinois College are available in the library. Margaret Blakely submitted a thesis to the University of Chicago in 1945 for the M.S. degree, entitled "Illinois College: Present Status and Recommendations for the Future." Doris Broehl Hopper submitted an M.A. thesis to Western Illinois University in 1971, entitled "The Speech Department at Illinois College, 1829–1971." Donald E. Polzin submitted an M.A. thesis to the University of Illinois in 1952, entitled "Curricular and Extra-curricular Speech Training at Illinois College, 1829–1900." George W. Horton, Jr., is currently at work on a thesis to be submitted to the University of Oklahoma for the Ph.D. degree, entitled "The Development of a College Mathematics Curriculum: Illinois College, 1830–1930."

A Faculty Handbook is made available to new members of the faculty when they are appointed; it is periodically revised in accordance with actions taken by the trustees and the faculty. Likewise there is a guidebook for students known as the IC Blue Book, which is regularly revised. The Office of Alumni Affairs publishes occasional directories, listing former students by class and by geographical area. It is interesting to note that although our students have usually been drawn from a rather limited area, once graduated, they spread out all over the world.

I had originally intended to have appendices listing those alumni of the College who served in the armed forces of the United States during World War II and the Korean and Vietnam conflicts. Their numbers are very large, and I soon realized that without the cooperation of the Department of Defense, Veterans Administration, and other holders of personnel records I could not hope to produce accurate and complete lists. As I have already related, in dealing with the ASTP unit in Chapter 20, I was denied access to those records. However, Appendix B, listing the trustees of the College from 1925 to 1979 and Appendix C, giving information about the faculty for the same period, should prove helpful.

Mr. John Power detected a slight error in Rammelkamp's reporting of the beginnings of the *College Rambler*; on page 289, Rammelkamp states: "The first number of the *College Rambler* appeared in January, 1878." Mr. Power has located a news item in the Jacksonville *Journal* of Sunday, December 16, 1877, giving the following account:

COLLEGE RAMBLER

The above is the title of a new publication, the first number of which was issued from the press, in this city, during the past week. It is edited by Messrs. E. B. Palmer, H. W. Johnston, C. L. Morse, J. F. Downing and C. R. Morrison—students of Illinois College. It is a 20-page pamphlet and is to be printed monthly. It is printed at the *Journal* office, and of course is neatly done. The first number was hastily gotten out, but its neat and newsy appearance is entirely creditable to the young gentlemen entrusted with its responsibility. In addition to editorials, it contains contributed articles by Dr. J. M. Sturtevant, H. W. Milligan and others, together with spicy locals, clippings and interesting miscellaneous matter. The business men have patronized it liberally with advertisements, and its success is as assured as its career promises to be useful.

No doubt I have committed more heinous errors in *Pioneer's Progress*. If they are reported to me, I shall make note of them in a copy to be kept in the Illinois College Collection of the library. If the first edition of this history is exhausted, I shall correct all such errors in later editions. In any case, there will be at least one corrected copy in existence.

Appendix A
Resource Materials

Part 1: Chapters 2 through 15 of *Pioneer's Progress* are abridgements of *Illinois College, A Centennial History*, as follows:

Part 2: I have cited major sources in Chapter 16, "Intermission: Of History, Written and Oral." To document statements specifically would be pretentious and not very useful, since the reader would not have access to a great deal of the material I have drawn on. I should like to say that Illinois College continues to keep a very large amount of relevant historical material, along with some that grows increasingly irrelevant. The original minute books of the trustees and faculty are locked in the Tanner Hall vault and can be consulted only with the permission of the president of the College. The correspondence of presidents, deans, etc. is stored in the basement of Tanner Hall and kept in roughly chronological order. Some of the miscellaneous stored material needs sorting, pruning, and cataloguing, a task for a skilled archivist.

I have reduced the bulk of the text by placing some documents in the appendices rather than quoting them at length in the text itself. The decisions were not always easy. No one can hope to please all readers in matters of this kind. I can only hope that I shall have the approbation of some of my readers much of the time. I should like to acknowledge valuable assistance given me in the preparation of these back-of-the-book materials by Vernon Caine, Wilmith Gillham, and Helen Hinde. As elsewhere, I am totally responsible for any errors that may remain.

Chapter 18: Depression: Failure of the Ayers National Bank

In addition to the sources cited in the text, I have had numerous conversations with people who lived through these difficult years in Jacksonville. Of course, many of the people who were most knowledgeable are long dead. However, a most valuable source turned up in the vault of Illinois College, a memorandum dictated by Mr. Frank Elliott shortly after the defalcation of the College securities became known. Mr. Elliott was a distinguished Chicago banker and a member of the Illinois College Board of Trustees. His careful, dispassionate account of the events described in this chapter is invaluable.

Chapter 20: President Selden

I have had correspondence with Mr. Selden that has helped me to verify and clarify certain events in this chapter, and I should call attention to an interview held with him in Wellesley, Massachusetts, August 4, 1975. At that time, we reviewed together the events of his presidency. He stated that "the College was not receptive to what I then thought would make it a more substantial educational institution." He told me that he had envisaged the possibility of creating a sort of Claremont cluster of colleges including, among others, Eureka and McKendree and possibly Shurtleff. All of these colleges

were having financial problems, largely the result of declining enrollments. The plan for the Associated Colleges does make allowance
for admitting other institutions, but since the primary ones did not
unite, no such opportunity developed. Another revelation was that
President Selden had assured President Norris of MacMurray College that if the merger went through, he, Selden, would resign so
that there could be no misapprehension about which of the presidents
was to preside over the Associated Colleges. I do not think that this
commitment, had it been known at the time, would have been reassuring to the faculty of Illinois College. I should say, further, that it
was Mr. Selden who first called my attention to the Harvard case
study mentioned several times in this chapter. When I was organizing the materials for this chapter, I asked President John J. Wittich,
current president of MacMurray College, whether there were materials at his disposal that might throw additional light on the attempt
to merge the two colleges. President Wittich was cordial and understanding but unable to release to me any materials dealing with the
subject. I do not think it likely that there is anything in the MacMurray archives that would materially alter my account of the effort, but
I do wish to thank President Wittich for his effort to assist me.

Re: p. 284, bottom: "A statement from the faculty of Illinois College
to the Board of Trustees, transmitted by the president." This represents the sense of the meeting of the faculty discussion of October
7, 1954, prepared by a committee composed of President Selden,
Mr. Wright (Chairman of the Committee on Cooperation with
MacMurray), Mrs. Miller (Chairman of the Illinois College Self-
Study Committee), and Members of the Administrative Council—
Mrs. Bruyn, Mr. Frank, Mr. Hildner, Mr. Horton, and Mr. Ricks,
business-manager. The statement was presented to the whole faculty
on October 13, adopted, and forwarded. It reads as follows:

The Faculty of Illinois College wishes to express to the Board of
Trustees of Illinois College its deep gratitude for the privilege of
examining and discussing the Proposed Agreement with MacMurray
College regarding the establishment of the Associated Midwest Col-
leges. It wishes further to express its thanks to the President of the
College for his full and candid presentation not only of the agree-

ment, but of the situation which led to its formulation. Having had this opportunity, the Faculty regards it as a solemn duty to convey to the Board its collective opinion of the proposal. It should be pointed out that no vote was taken regarding the proposal itself, since that is clearly a responsibility of the Board of Trustees.

The proposals in Article 3, however, are inconsistent with our idea of good educational policy for Illinois College. Coeducation, as it has been observed on the Illinois College campus for the past fifty-one years, is becoming increasingly common in colleges all over the country. This pattern of coeducation involves men and women living on the same campus as well as attending the same classes. In this part of the country, such bona fide coeducation seems a particularly desirable educational policy.

The Faculty of Illinois College believes in cooperation with Mac-Murray College, and has demonstrated its belief consistently and whole-heartedly. Exchanges of students and faculty are taking place to the financial advantage of both institutions and the educational benefit of their students. Your faculty voted unanimously to shift from the term system, although many of us prefer that system, to the semester system in order to facilitate cooperation. This step is easily the most extensive adjustment to cooperation made by either college, since it involves a complete reorganization of the curriculum. Since this change will not take place until September, 1955, its effects cannot yet be judged. Your faculty believes that cooperation built upon the foundations already laid will produce great advantages to Illinois College and MacMurray College, and that we should give them an adequate trial before proceeding to more drastic innovations.

We do not believe that the proposals of Article 3 are necessary for continued and expanded cooperation between the two colleges. We should like to call your attention to the report of the North Central Association Committee which significantly omits any suggestion that Illinois College give up her women students. In fact, in private conversation with several of us, two members of this committee specifically advised against such a policy at this time.

We are concerned with this proposal primarily as a matter of educational policy. We are, however, taking the liberty of commenting on certain related matters which, while not exactly in the realm of educational policy, are intimately connected with it. We are asking the President to transmit these additional comments to you, if in his opinion, they are pertinent to your discussion.

We realize that the ultimate decision must rest with the Board of Trustees, and that you have many factors to take into consideration. We sincerely hope and believe, however, that you will consider with great care these propositions which we of the Faculty believe to be of supreme importance to the present and future welfare of Illinois College, a concern which we share with you.

Respectfully submitted,
THE FACULTY OF ILLINOIS COLLEGE
E. B. Miller, Secretary

Postscript containing comments on related matters:

I. THE MATTER OF FINANCE. The Faculty realizes that the financial situation of the College is not comfortable. We further recognize that action of some kind must be taken to correct this condition, but believe that there are several possible corrective measures that have not been fully explored, measures that do not call for a change from our present coeducational system.

II. RECRUITMENT OF STUDENTS. At a time when the number of students at Illinois College is lower than we could wish, the proposal would appear to restrict still further our opportunity of attracting more and better students, and would almost certainly drive away many of those we already have. Many men and many women come to Illinois College precisely because it is a bona fide coeducational college. A shift in our policy of admission would surely be a serious blow to the size of the Illinois College undergraduate body, nor would it necessarily result in any appreciable gain to MacMurray College. It is extremely doubtful that the most active cooperation of the MacMurray admissions counsellors could bring to Illinois College enough men to compensate for the loss of our women. How then are we to make up the loss of men who would prefer to go where there is real rather than nominal coeducation?

III. THE SENTIMENT OF THE ALUMNI AND FRIENDS OF THE COLLEGE. The ideal of *Alma Mater* is deeply rooted in all who have ever gone to college. Colleges have always set before their students, alumni and friends the figure of a fostering, sheltering Mother. *Alma Mater* is to a college what patriotism is to a nation, and no one scoffs at patriotism, particularly in time of emergency. The wonderfully loyal alumnae of Illinois College will almost certainly regard this step as a renunciation of them; and they will not be easily reconciled. You don't find yourself a new *Alma Mater* fifty, thirty, ten or two years out of college. Should this proposal be accepted, most of them will regard *Alma Mater* as dead. No one can predict the reaction of our alumni, but it is hardly likely that many will be pleased by a divorce in the family.

IV. A QUESTION OF EQUITY. A contract or agreement should be based on certain principles of equity. As we examined the terms of this particular contract, it seemed to us that in almost every respect Illinois College sacrificed mountains of *quid* for molehills of *quo*. Moreover, the *quid* that we give is tangible; the *quo* that we get is largely intangible and could prove illusory. If this be the case, is such an agreement likely to prove lasting?

V. IN CASE OF FAILURE. As the formulating committee recognized, an agreement of this kind might not work, and it therefore called for a review of the terms of the contract at the end of five years. At this time, presumably, the contract might be continued along its present lines, it might be revised, or it might be abrogated. Let us assume that both parties to the contract labor faithfully and hard to make a success of the agreement, yet that it does not produce the results that were anticipated, and that the contract is terminated by mutual consent. What then will be the relative situation of the two colleges? Clearly, Illinois College will have given up what it cannot easily regain, and MacMurray College will have gained what it does not want. The Board and Faculty of MacMurray can await this possible outcome with equanimity, but can the Board and Faculty of Illinois College?

Re: p. 285, last paragraph: "Statement of Professor Charles E. Frank, January 28, 1955." The full text is:

Mr. President and Colleagues:

These past few weeks have been difficult for us all. I know I have been asking myself over and over again: "Shall I speak up firmly, or shall I bite my tongue and be still? Shall I stand up and be counted, or shall I run for the nearest cover?" These are hard questions for most of us because they must be answered not just on their merits, but with our wives and children in mind. We must think of our individual future careers at the same time as we think of the future of this College. The words of the Cavalier poet on going off to the wars keep coming to mind:

> I could not love thee, dear, so much
> Loved I not honor more.

With poetry in mind and the last remains of this month's salary jingling in my pocket, I have put down in chronological order some of the events of this past year. I have found it soothing to do this; at the same time, some of the confusion has been removed, and I have found it possible to come to a decision. Let me review these events with you in the hope that the process will have a similar soothing and strengthening effect on you.

The academic year of 1954–55 opened auspiciously at Illinois College. Much had been done during the summer to improve the appearance of the campus. Numerous eyesores were gone, two of the old buildings had been restored, and a new one was almost ready to be dedicated. The Freshman class was substantially larger than the previous year's, and morale among the students was high. There was mutual respect and good will between administration and faculty. It was a joy to return to this campus.

At the close of the regular October faculty meeting, a cloud appeared, no bigger than your hand. For various reasons that cloud has grown, perhaps been encouraged to grow, until it now threatens a storm that could destroy the College. In response to a question regarding rumors that Illinois College was considering an agreement with MacMurray College by which Illinois College would give up its women students, President Selden said that he was not at liberty to discuss the matter. When he could give a full report, he would call a special meeting of the faculty for that purpose.

Later that same week the President called a special meeting and read the Proposed Agreement regarding the establishment of the Associated Colleges, Article 3 of which contained the controversial clause requiring Illinois College to give up its women students. Although there were other clauses which caused concern, the one regarding women was generally believed to be the crux of the matter. The Faculty expressed itself as being strongly opposed to Article 3 of the Proposed Agreement and directed the Administrative Council, to which body was added the Chairman of the Faculty Committee on Cooperation with MacMurray College, and the Chairman of the Illinois College Self-Study Committee, to draw up a statement of its position.

This committee prepared such a statement (the President being in attendance when the final wording was agreed upon), submitted it to the Faculty, which approved it and forwarded it to the Board of Trustees, via the President of the College. The statement was in two parts, the first being a firm but temperate endorsement of coeducation as a matter of academic policy. The second part noted several serious objections to the Proposed Agreement, objections which were not specifically in the realm of academic policy, but which many members of the Faculty wished to call to the attention of the Board. Wishing to assure the President of its confidence in him, the Faculty placed these comments in a postscript, requesting the President, at his discretion, to present these comments to the Board. The

President attended several meetings at which these comments were made and he was quite aware that they were regarded as important. Nonetheless, he apparently exercised his right of suppressing them, so that the Board of Trustees heard only a part of the Faculty's objections to the Proposed Agreement. However, since the Board rejected the Proposed Agreement and reaffirmed its adherence to coeducation on the Illinois College campus, and since the President appeared to accept the Board's decision with good grace, the matter appeared to be closed. It was disappointing but not surprising to learn subsequently that the MacMurray College administration wanted all or nothing, that cooperation without capitulation was impossible. It was assumed by the Faculty that the President had turned his full attention to Illinois College and would now devote all his energy and talent to the many but not insuperable problems facing the College. The Faculty returned to its appointed tasks, believing that we were all—Trustees, Administration, and Faculty—once again pulling together, toward a common goal, a better Illinois College.

At the Convocation on the evening of January 7, 1955, honoring the 125 years of this College's proud and independent existence, we were reminded of the faith and courage of the founders who did so much with so little, and encouraged to believe that we with so much more might strive to do at least as much. Yet, in his address, though the President spoke of the College as a trim ship, there were hints that he thought she was on the point of foundering.

These hints were confirmed on the morning of January 8 when seven senior professors of the Faculty were called to a meeting with the President of the College, the Chairman of the Board of Trustees, and two other members of the Board. We were informed at that meeting that the Board had the day before passed a resolution authorizing a reconstructed committee of the Board of Trustees to explore the possibility of an absolute merger with MacMurray College. While the word "explore" was in the resolution, our questions were answered as if the principle was settled and only the details remained to be worked out. For the most part, we were stunned by this apparent reversal on the part of both the President of the College and of the Board of Trustees, and our feeble remonstrances seemed to fall into an echo chamber, out of which came a standard response: "That will be up to the new board of trustees." We were not encouraged to discuss the matter further, but we were not asked to keep it secret.

At first discussion was desultory, but then we learned that members of the Board meant no more than what they said when they authorized the committee to *explore*, that some of them felt that only by full exploration could anyone know exactly what was to be gained and what was to be lost by merger; that in any case, it was imperative to settle the matter once and for all. Our present situation, then, seems to be this: there are few who really *desire* a merger, either on the board or on the faculty or among the alumni and friends of the College. There are some who have been persuaded that merger is the only way out of a desperate situation and that it would be well to submit to it with whatever grace we can muster. And there are many who believe it to be unnecessary and undesirable from every point of view, and who are ready to support an independent Illinois College, but who will not support a submerged or hybrid college.

If this Faculty had a solemn duty last fall to inform the Board of Trustees of our position regarding that proposal, we have just as solemn a duty now, and since secrecy is no longer an issue, there is no reason why we should not discuss the matter fully with all who have a concern for the College. We are a peaceful faculty, even docile; we are ready to be led, but we do not like to be dragged or driven. Once the Board makes its *final* decision, we must either abide by that decision or resign, but until that time we have a duty to help them *explore* every phase of this proposal. If each individual will perform that duty, according to his own conscience, with honor and with candor, I have no doubt of the outcome.

Re: p. 286, l. 12: "An Assessment of the Present Situation at Illinois College presented to Chairman Dunbaugh and President Selden by Professor of Religion and Philosophy Malcolm F. Stewart and Professor of History John S. Wright, February 4, 1955." The full text is:

In assessing the present situation at Illinois College there are complicated and involved factors many of which are probably not known. The attempt here is only to look at the situation as objectively as possible from the point of view of some who are involved in it. In this there is no attempt to accuse, to blame or in any way to cast aspersions upon the honesty, integrity or sense of purpose of anyone. The seriousness of the situation, however, cannot be overestimated.

1. There is no question in the minds of anyone that the Board of Trustees is acting wholly within its right in this matter. There does, however, seem to be an apparent disregard of certain basic principles:
   a. a college is not just an organization but is essentially a highly complicated system of personal relations and loyalties formed and maintained through the years;
   b. Board action can consolidate organization and legal structure

but no such action can create a college; in fact, such action may well destroy a college;

c. efforts leading to cooperation between two colleges must work *through* the system of personal relations and loyalties and not above or around them. Such cooperation can proceed only as fast and as far as the loyalties and sentiments of the persons involved will permit;

d. it has been clearly evident since last October that any basis of cooperation must be predicated upon the principle that coeducation *must* be maintained on the campus of Illinois College in the full meaning of the term as it now exists;

e. any cooperation between two colleges *must* proceed from the ground up and *cannot* proceed faster than it can be accepted by the persons who comprise the college;

f. speed in a cooperative venture is warranted only as a desperation move and can be effective only when all persons involved are convinced that the college cannot exist otherwise. If all persons are not convinced of that, then to move too fast will arouse deep feelings, undermine confidence, create divisions and destroy the very fabric of the college itself.

2. The present situation has seriously shaken the confidence of the faculty, the students and many of the alumni and even the citizens of the community in the administration. This has been occasioned by a number of factors:

a. apparent discrepancies in statements made by the administration to various people and even to the same people at different times relative to such matters as:
   (1) the status of women on the campus;
   (2) the attitude toward coeducation;
   (3) the commitments made to MacMurray College;
   (4) the interpretation of the budget;
   (5) the import of the action of the Board of Trustees and the meaning of the resolution;

b. the apparent attempt always to paint the blackest picture possible concerning the position of Illinois College;

c. the apparent bending of all efforts in the direction of cooperation or consolidation with MacMurray College rather than toward strengthening Illinois College;

d. the apparent discrepancy between the attitude expressed following the Board action relative to the proposed agreement of last October and the fact that immediately negotiations were started leading to this present situation;

e. the apparent failure to understand or appreciate the deep loyalties, feelings, sentiments and personal relations that made Illinois College what it is;

f. attempting to move too rapidly without stopping to absorb and consolidate gains which have been made;

g. the failure to use and channel the enthusiasm and commitment of the faculty in the direction started last fall in the strengthening of the College and its program;

h. the failure to maintain the morale and enthusiasm of the student body, which was very high last fall;

i. the alienation of individuals at certain crucial points through either misunderstandings or other reasons;

j. the giving of part information and then the unwillingness to answer critical questions completely;

k. the apparent motivation by fear of the collapse of the College rather than by faith in its future;

l. the failure to realize the point at which feelings, loyalties and confidence become strained;

m. the apparent unwillingness to explore other means of strengthening the position of Illinois College than through cooperation with MacMurray College;

n. the failure adequately to assess the true nature of the attitudes and feelings existing between the two colleges.

3. At this immediate point and under present conditions Illinois College stands to lose many of its faculty and some, at least, of its students, recruitment will be increasingly difficult, promotion will be impaired and the morale of all concerned will continue to go down.

4. The lack of confidence is being reflected in many ways at the present time:

a. in the general atmosphere which reflects a restrained tenseness;

b. in the freedom of destructive criticism which has grown just in the past few days;

c. in bringing up all the petty irritations which were overlooked in the past;

d. in magnifying past mistakes and small errors in judgment;

e. in the willingness to believe or accept anything adverse whether there is any foundation for it or not.

5. It would seem that if Illinois College insists on the guarantee that it will remain, in fact, coeducational there is no possibility for any agreement to be reached between the two schools. If that guarantee is not included, Illinois College as it is will virtually cease to exist and it will take years to build and strengthen a new institution formed from consolidation.

6. If consolidation is not effected, Illinois College has already been immeasurably weakened and much valuable time, energy and resource has been lost which could have been spent on strengthening the College during this year and the years to come.

7. This second period of uncertainty pressing so closely upon the heels of the first one last October has proved too much. Only a certain amount of turmoil and uncertainty can be tolerated without serious loss to the College and without reflecting on the judgment of the administration.

8. It is imperative that steps be taken immediately to stabilize the situation, to eliminate the uncertainty and to provide a condition in which students, faculty and alumni can again be welded together within that delicate fabric of personal relations, loyalties, sentiments, faith, trust and confidence which is Illinois College.

Re: p. 287, l. 10: "A Statement read by Professor John S. Wright to the Faculty of Illinois College, February 7, 1955":

We, the undersigned, aware that recent efforts to assess the present state of the College may have been open to misinterpretation, and mindful of the present delicate situation, wish to state what should be obvious: that we have a deep concern for Illinois College.

We believe that there is now greater awareness of the intangible as well as the tangible factors in the light of which all decisions affecting the future of Illinois College must be made; we appreciate the opportunity to express our attitude to the Board of Trustees in whose collective judgment we have every confidence; and we have every expectation for the future of Illinois College.

We, therefore, resolve that, during the interim in which discussions are taking place, we will continue every effort to eliminate tensions and to maintain stability to the end that a correct and acceptable decision may be reached.

We further resolve that if a firm and dynamic program is formulated to build and strengthen Illinois College on the basis of the existing traditions, then such a program will have our enthusiastic and wholehearted support.

Chapter 22: President Caine

Re: p. 301, ACI and CACHE canvasses

Associated Colleges of Illinois

Twenty-nine independent colleges of the state benefit from the many services of this organization. Its goal is "to provide the member colleges with sufficient funds so that essential programs and services need not be curtailed, nor standards compromised, and so that these colleges will not become dependent upon State or Federal funds." The organization has been in operation since 1952–53. In recent years its cash disbursements to Illinois College have been as follows:

1965–66	$28,745	1973–74	35,768	1970–71	33,567
1967–68	34,064	1975–76	40,178	1972–73	40,165
1969–70	37,043	1977–78	40,487	1974–75	38,092
1971–72	35,044	1966–67	$34,560	1976–77	39,458
		1968–69	35,024		

Committee for the Advancement of Community Higher Education
"CACHE, Inc. was established in 1962 as a community campaign for dollar support of the annual budgets of both Illinois College and MacMurray College. The original plan was presented to local trustees of both colleges and to members of the Chamber of Commerce, and it was enthusiastically adopted as an opportunity for the business and professional community to express their confidence and support of higher education in Jacksonville." Sums received by Illinois College:

1962	$3,951	1963	$5,398	1964	$7,724	1965	$7,838
1966	8,282	1967	7,875	1968	7,850	1969	7,870
1970	7,208	1971	8,460	1972	8,900	1973	10,025
1974	10,000	1975	10,000	1976	13,500	1977	13,700

Chapter 23: President Mundinger
Re: p. 328, l. 10: "Bill of Student Rights" produced during President Mundinger's first year, which reads as follows:
Illinois College Student Bill of Rights
As citizens, students have the same duties and obligations as do other citizens, and enjoy the same freedom of speech, press, religion, peaceful assembly and petition that other citizens enjoy. In all of its

dealings with students, the College will respect the rights guaranteed to students by the Constitution and laws of the United States and the State of Illinois.

The academic community of students, faculty, and administration, in the spirit of mutual respect and cooperation, shall reflect the interdependency of rights and responsibilities on the part of every element of the community. The responsibility to secure and to respect general conditions conducive to the freedom to learn is shared by all members of the academic community.

ARTICLE I

Students have the following rights concerning participation in decision making:

A.	the right to formal participation in an advisory manner through student representation, in the making of policy decisions directly affecting them; and

B.	the right, through a duly representative student government, to make final decisions concerning Forum and Forum related student affairs.

ARTICLE II

A.	Students have the right to accurate and plainly stated information which enables them to understand clearly:
1.	the general qualifications for establishing and maintaining acceptable academic standing;
2.	the graduation requirements for their particular curriculum and major;
3.	the basic procedural course requirements and the course grading system set by the individual faculty member for his course, to be spelled out in writing within the first full week of classes.

B.	Students have the right to know:
1.	what authority has promulgated any regulations;
2.	the basis for the regulation directly affecting the student, or the reason for withholding such information;
3.	the possible avenues for changing such regulations; and
4.	the appellate process involved with such regulations.

C.	If official statements of duly constituted authorities of the College and duly constituted student authorities conflict in matters of student affairs, those conflicting statements shall be resolved by a student-faculty-administration committee consisting of four faculty and/or administration members appointed by the President of the College, four students elected by the Student Forum, and a ninth member to be chosen by the eight members so chosen. The ninth member, who shall serve as chairman, may be either a faculty member or student.

ARTICLE III

Students have the following rights regarding person and residence:

A.   the right to remain free from campus detention as a form of disciplinary action;
B.   the right to remain free from duress and coercion;
C.   the right to remain free from unwarranted entrance of his residence. The privacy of a resident's room shall always be respected (except in the conduct of routine housekeeping, maintenance functions and emergencies);
D.   the right to remain free from search and seizure of his person, place and property without reasonable cause. In the case of a warranted search, the student shall be informed of who conducted the search and why;
E.   the right to remain free from unauthorized use of his dormitory residence;
F.   the right to safe habitation on the college campus.

ARTICLE IV

Students shall be extended the following protection when appearing before a disciplinary body:

A.   the right to be informed in writing of the specific charges being brought against them and the right, on request, of at least ten days to prepare for these proceedings;
B.   the right to counsel before and during all proceedings;
C.   the right to a speedy and fair hearing;
D.   the right to refuse to answer self-incriminating questions;
E.   the right to present statements in their own defense if they choose;
F.   the right to be presumed innocent until proved guilty;
G.   the right to an appeal, upon request;
H.   the right to remain free from disciplinary action until the case has been closed except when further activities of the students would endanger members of the college community or the college itself;
I.   the right to confront and/or question witnesses against them.

ARTICLE V

Students have the following rights in the classroom:

A.   the right to take reasoned exception to the views offered in any course of study;
B.   the right to protection through orderly procedures against prejudiced or capricious academic evaluation;

C. the right to confidential retention by instructors of information about student views, beliefs, and political associations; and
D. the right to refuse to answer questions concerning their personal views, political associations, and other questions of a personal nature not germane to the course.

ARTICLE VI

Student rights regarding confidentiality of academic, disciplinary, medical, and financial records shall be determined within the professional guidelines of the American Association of Collegiate Registrars and Admissions Officers.

ARTICLE VII

Students have the right to associate or organize. Each group has the following privileges:
A. the privilege to choose an advisor;
B. the privilege to use the College facilities within conditions prescribed by the College;
C. the privilege to invite and hear any person of its choosing providing that it does not interfere with the essential college program;
D. the privilege to examine and discuss, pass resolutions, distribute leaflets, circulate petitions, and take other lawful action to express opinions, providing any of these do not disrupt any regular and essential College program; and
E. the privilege to support causes by orderly means outside of classroom situations.

ARTICLE VIII

Student communications have the following rights:
A. the right to publish all editorials or news commentaries that are not libelous, degrading, or slanderous to individuals, groups, or Illinois College; and
B. the right to written notification by the Board of Publications, the Student Forum, and the Board of Trustees of regulations governing student communications.

ARTICLE IX

Students shall be free from discrimination based on sex, age, race, religion, creed, and national origin.

ARTICLE X

The enumeration of certain student rights in this Bill shall not be construed to deny or disparage others held by each student. No right specified by this Bill is meant to be construed as enabling students to infringe upon the individual rights of another member of the academic community.

ARTICLE XI
A. This Bill of Rights shall become operative upon receiving a
    two-thirds vote of the members of the Student Forum and two-
    thirds of the votes cast in the student referendum, and with the
    concurrence of the faculty and administration, and the Board of
    Trustees.
B. Amendments to this document may be proposed by any one of
    the aforementioned parties and will be approved in the same
    manner as adoption.

Appendix B
Members of the Faculty, 1925–1979

Included in the following list are those who were accorded the privilege of voting at faculty meetings, 1925–1979. Part-time and special appointees such as the visiting Asian scholars are not included, nor are the nonteaching staff. The privilege of speaking and voting carries with it the possibility of influencing academic policies of the College; whether it is exercised or not, that privilege deserves recognition. Degrees shown are those held at the time of service at Illinois College; many took additional degrees later.

Ahlers, Rolf W. B.A., Drew University; B.D., Princeton Theological Seminary; Th.D., University of Hamburg. Religion. 1966–72. Dunbaugh Distinguished Professor, 1970

Allison, J. Clement. B.F.A., Ohio Wesleyan University; M.A., Wayne State University. Art. 1963–66

Ames, John Griffith. A.B., Johns Hopkins University; Litt. B., Oxford University; Litt. D., Illinois College. English. 1900–1944. Acting President, 1929–30; 1932–33. Emeritus, 1944–45

Anderson, Charters H. B.A., University of Minnesota; M.A., Mankato State College. Speech and Dramatics. 1970–71

Anderson, Henry A. B.A., Concordia College; M.S., University of Minnesota. Biology. 1961–62

Anderson, N. Arthur. B.S., B.S. Ed., Central Missouri State Teachers College; M.A., University of Missouri. Chemistry. 1949–56

Anderson, Stanley C. A.B., Carleton College. English and Public Speaking. 1926–28

Anderson, William A. B.A., North Park College; M.S.E., Northern
Illinois University. Physical Education. 1971–74

Armstrong, Frederick C. B.A., Southern Illinois University; M.A.,
Michigan State University. Economics. 1951–52

Arthur, John. B.A., University of Tulsa. Art. 1966–69

Augustine, Mary Ellen. A.B., Oberlin College. Physical Education,
English. 1924–26

Austerud, Stella M. Ph.B., Ph.M., University of Wisconsin. Geography. 1943–44

Baker, Roy T. B. A., Southwestern College; M.S., Kansas State
Teachers College. Speech, Dean of Students. 1956–61

Bales, James E. A.B., Illinois College; M.L.S., University of Illinois. Library. 1976–

Barlow, Charles C. A.B., Illinois College; M.Litt., University of
Pittsburgh. Education. 1962–71. Dean of Men, 1936–38. Emeritus, 1971–

Barrett, Robert M. A.B., Colgate University; M.A., Stanford University. English. 1970–71

Beasley, Claude N. B.P.E., M.Ed., Springfield College (Massachusetts). Physical Education, Director of Athletics. 1939–47

Berwanger, Eugene H. B.A., M.A., Illinois State University;
Ph.D., University of Illinois. History and Government. 1964–67

Bibbee, Paul C. B.S., M.S., West Virginia University; Ph.D., Cornell University. Biology. 1965–66

Black, Richard R. B.F.A., Drake University; M.S.A.E., University
of Wisconsin. Art. 1956–60

Blackwood, Glenn R. B.A., Sterling College; M.S., University of
Wisconsin. Economics and Business Administration. 1959–76

Blake, J. C. B.S., University of Colorado; Ph.D., Yale University.
Chemistry. 1926–27

Blakely, Margaret. B.A., Grinnell College; diploma, University of
Wisconsin Library School. Library. 1939–45

Bleckley, Erwin C. B.A., M.A., University of Oklahoma. Modern
Languages (French). 1967–

Blumenthal, Ilse H. B.A., Hunter College; M.A., Columbia University. Modern Languages (German). 1966–69

Boehme, Isabelle S. B.A., M.S.L.S., University of Illinois. Library. 1972–

Bolton, Rhoda R. A.B., Illinois College; M.F.A., Yale University. English and Speech. 1944–45

Boston, Alvin D. A.B., Illinois College; M.S., Tulane University; Ph.D., Ohio State University. Chemistry, Strawn Professor. 1938–43

Bowen, Ballard L. B.S., M.A., New York State College for Teachers. Psychology and Education. 1925–27

Boyd, H. Wayne. A.B., Indiana University. Art. 1950–51

Boyd, Philip S. B.Sc., St. Lawrence University; A.M., Cornell University. History and Political Science. 1934–36

Bragdon, Earl D. A.B., University of Maine; M.A., Ph.D., Indiana University. History and Government. 1964–65

Brauer, Marian C. A.B., Mount Holyoke; M.A., Cornell University. English. Dean of Women. 1942–44

Brewer, Nancy L. B.A., B.S., Ph.D., University of Chicago. Biology. 1963–65

Brewer, Robert H. A.B., Hanover College; Ph.D., University of Chicago. Biology. 1963–65

Brogan, Howard O. A.B., Grinnell College; A.M., University of Iowa. English. 1937–39

Brooks, E. Joseph. B.A., M.S., University of Illinois. Physical Education, Director of Athletics. 1947–53, 1955–. Dean of Students, 1955–56

Brothers, Chester R. A.B., A.M., Indiana University; A.M., Columbia University. Chemistry. 1956–60

Brown, Ruth M. A.B., A.M., Northwestern University; Ph.D., State University of Iowa. Greek and Latin, Collins Instructor. 1925–29, 1933–41

Bruyn, Severyn T. B.S., M.A., Ph.D., University of Illinois. Sociology. 1952–66

Bump, Ruth E. F. A.B., Olivet College; M.A., University of Wyoming. English. 1957–

Burney, Thomas G. B.A., State University of Iowa; B.D., McCormick Theological Seminary; M.S., University of Wisconsin. Philosophy. 1962–63

Burt, Patricia A. B.S., Murray State University; M.S., Eastern Illinois University. Physical Education. 1976–78

Busey, Robert O. A.B., University of Illinois; A.M., Ph.D., Harvard University. Modern Languages (Spanish). 1921–44. Emeritus, 1944–67

Caldwell, Henry H. A.B., Illinois College; A.M., Columbia University. English and Public Speaking. 1922–26

Calhoun, Arthur W. A.B., University of Pittsburgh; M.A., University of Wisconsin; Ph.D., Clark University. Sociology. 1957–58

Campbell, Cloyce, B.S., M.A., Ph.D., University of Iowa. Economics. 1950–56

Capps, H. Porter. A.B., University of Michigan. English. 1947–48

Chappalear, Claude S. B.S., Greenville College; Ph.D., Columbia University. Psychology and Education. Dean of the College. 1927–33

Chien, Wilbur S. B.S., University of Nanking; M.S., University of Wisconsin; Ph.D., Ohio State University. Economics and Business Administration. 1960–

Clavey, Paul E. A.B., Illinois College; M.A., Northwestern University. English. 1954–55

Cleary, Grace H. B.A., University of Utah; M.L.S., Texas Woman's University. Library. 1970–76

Clements, Jesse L. B.S., McKendree College; M.A. in Ed., University of Illinois; M.Ed., DePaul University. Education. Director of Placement, Veteran's Counsellor. 1946–57

Clugston, Philip R. A.B., Wabash College; M.A., University of Wisconsin. English. 1925–26

Cohan, Peter. B.A., Augustana College; M.F.A., Northern Illinois University. Art. 1977–

Collias, Elsie C. B.A., Heidelberg College; M.S., Ph.D., University of Wisconsin. Biology. 1953–57

Collias, Nicholas E. B.S., Ph.D., University of Chicago. Biology, Hitchcock Professor. 1953–58

Collins, Edward M. B.S., M.A., Ph.D., Princeton University. Chemistry, Strawn Professor. 1943–48

Conklin, Mary C. B.A., M.Ed., Boston University. Biology. 1962–63

Cooke, Francis W. A.B., College of William and Mary; M.S., Ph.D., University of Illinois. Physics. 1937–42

Coulter, William A. B.A., University of Virginia; M.A., Ph.D., Princeton University. English. 1976–77

Cozart, Karen E. B.A., Denison University; M.A., University of Denver. Library. 1971–72

Cross, William M. B.A., Valparaiso University; M.A., University of Chicago; B.D., Lutheran School of Theology; Ph.D., South Dakota State University. Sociology. 1972–

Crouthamel, James L. A.B., Franklin and Marshall College; Ph.D., University of Rochester. History and Government. 1956–58

Cummings, Mary Louise. A.B., Illinois College; M.A., University of Illinois; M.A., University of Iowa. Mathematics. 1926–33, 1943–44

Curtis, Nelson D. B.A., Western Michigan University; A.M., University of Michigan. Modern Languages (French). 1960–62

Dargan, Marion. A.B., Wofford College; A.M., Columbia University; Ph.D., University of Chicago. History. 1925–28

Dasey, Homer H. Chicago Academy of Fine Arts. Art. 1934–36

Davis, James E. A.B., M.A., Wayne State University; Ph.D., University of Michigan. History. 1971–

Davis, Marjorie A. A.B., Colorado College; A.M. Indiana University. Greek and Latin. 1929–33

DeGaris, Louise. A.B., Smith College. Physical Education and English. 1926–31

DeRyke, Willis. A.B., A.M., Indiana University; Ph.D., State University of Iowa. Biology, Hitchcock Professor. 1926–53. Emeritus, 1953–71

Desreumaux, James O. B.B.A., Wisconsin State University; M.B.A., University of Texas. Economics and Business. 1972–75

Diwoky, Fred F. B.S., Oregon Agricultural College; M.S., University of Wisconsin. Chemistry. 1927–28

Donahoe, Ned. A.B., Illinois College. Speech and Drama. 1938–43

Dreer, Herman. A.B., Bowdoin College; M.A., Ph.D., University of Chicago. English. 1963–64

Dudley, Lloyd P. B.A., Wabash College; M.A., University of Southern California. Speech and Forensics. 1947–56

Dummer, E. Heyse. A.B., Concordia Seminary; A.M., University of Wisconsin; Ph.D., Northwestern University. Modern Languages (German). 1958–63

Eldred, Donald R. B.A., University of Dubuque; M.A., Northwestern University. English and Speech. Dean of Students. 1961–

Elick, Gerald E. B.A., University of Missouri; M.S., University of Arkansas. Biology and Chemistry. 1964–67

Elwood, Kent D. B.A., Ph.D., Northwestern University. Psychology. 1975–

Emmons, Glenroy. B.A., Louisiana Polytechnic Institute; M.A., Tulane University; Ph.D., University of New Mexico. Modern Languages (Spanish). 1956–58

Erickson, Rick L. B.M.W., Milton College; M.Mus., Northwestern University; M.T.S., Garrett Theological Seminary. Music. 1977–

Erickson, Stanton J. B.S., M.S., Southern Methodist University. Biology. 1956–57

Evans, Robert J. B.S., University of Nebraska; Ph.D., University of Washington. Chemistry. 1966–

Everson, Ida G. A.B., Barnard College; M.A., Ph.D., Columbia University. English. 1968–69

Filson, Don P. B.A., Park College, M.S., Ph.D., University of Illinois. Chemistry, Strawn Professor. 1960–

Fisher, J. Elliott. A.B., Oberlin College; M.A., Columbia University. Sociology. 1969–70

Ford, Raymond A. B.A., George Pepperdine College; M.A., Redlands University. Speech and Forensics. 1963–

Fosnaugh, Ruth L. A.B., A.M., University of Illinois. Modern Languages (Spanish). 1966–77. Emerita. 1977–

Franchere, Hoyt C. A.B., A.M., University of Iowa. English and Speech. 1929–37

Frank, Charles E. A.B., Haverford College; A.M., Ph.D., Princeton

University. English, Pixley Professor of Humanities. 1939–55, 1957–. Dunbaugh Distinguished Professor, 1973

Frank, Dorothy B. B.F.A., Moore College of Art; diploma, Fontainbleau School of Fine Arts. Art. 1951–53, 1955–56

Franz, Edgar A. B.A., M.S., University of Iowa. Mathematics. 1965–. Dunbaugh Distinguished Professor, 1974

Fraser, Ralph S. A.B., Boston University; M.A., Syracuse University; Ph.D., University of Illinois. Modern Languages (German). 1954–58

Freeman, Lois I. A.B., MacMurray College; M.Ed., University of Illinois. Education. 1973–77

Frees, Octavia K. A.B., Adelphi College; M.A., Cornell University. Speech and Dramatics. 1946–55

Fry, Deborah Kolditz. B.A., M.A., University of Illinois. Modern Languages (Spanish). 1977–

Fry, Richard T. B.A., Grinnell College; M.A., Ph.D., University of Minnesota. History. 1967–

Fuller, Harold Q. A.B., Wabash College; A.M., Ph.D., University of Illinois. Mathematics and Physics. 1933–37

Gaddis, Shirley. A.B., M.S., University of Iowa. Chemistry. 1943–44

Garnett, W. Leslie. B.A., Iowa State College; M.A., Ph.D., State University of Iowa. English. 1964–66

Gaylor, Walter. B.S., Pennsylvania State College; M.A., Harvard University. English. 1947–50

Gilmour, Stephen D. A.B., M.A., Indiana University. Modern Languages (German). 1963–65

Gohn, Lloyd. B.S., Washington University. Sociology. 1947–52

Gooch, Margaret M. B.A., Texas Christian University; Ph.D., University of North Carolina. English. 1971–72

Gottschalk, Donald E. A.B., Illinois Wesleyan University; M.S., Illinois State University. Education and Psychology. 1965–67

Graber, Richard A. B.A., Tabor College; M.S., Kansas State Teachers College, Ed.D., Oklahoma State University. Education. 1971–

Graham, Joseph D. A.B., University of Michigan; M.A., Columbia University. Speech and Dramatics. 1953–54

Grant, Robert C. B.S., Bradley University; M.S., University of Illinois. Education. 1971–72

Gray, Eunice T. A.B., Stanford University. English. Dean of Women. 1929–30

Gustine, Don A. B.S., Western Illinois University; M.S., Southern Illinois University. Physical Education. 1967–70

Gutekunst, Helmut C. B.S., Illinois Wesleyan University; M.S., Washington University. Chemistry. 1957–71

Hallerberg, Arthur E. A.B., Illinois College; A.M., University of Illinois; Ed.D., University of Michigan. Mathematics. 1942–60

Halvorson, Anna M. B.A., Jamestown College; M.B.A., University of Denver. Economics and Business. 1956–59

Hammond, Norma M. A.B., Oberlin College; B.S. in L.S., Western Reserve University. Library. 1945–49

Hancock, Robert A. Jr. B.A., University of Massachusetts; M.S., Ph.D., Kansas State University. Psychology. 1977–78

Harmon, William T. A.B., A.M., Illinois College. Physical Education, Director of Athletics. 1910–32

Hart, Myrtle G. A.B., Lawrence College; diploma in Library Science, University of Wisconsin. Library. 1925–28

Hassenplug, J. Fred. B.S., U.S. Naval Academy; M.S., Purdue University. Mathematics. 1960–61

Hastings, Elizabeth T. A.B., A.M., Brown University; Ph.D., Yale University. English. 1939–51

Hatton, Lester E., Jr. B.S., M.S., Oregon State University. Biology. 1966–69

Hawkins, John. B.A., University of Minnesota. Art. 1957–59

Healy, David F. B.A., M.A., Ph.D., University of Wisconsin. History. 1960–64

Heckart, Harold A. B.S., Tri-State College; A.M., University of Missouri; Ph. D., Iowa State University. Mathematics. 1962–64

Hildner, Ernest G., Jr. A.B., A.M., Ph.D., University of Michigan. History and Geography, Gardner Professor. 1938–72. Dean of the College, 1938–58. Acting President, 1955–56. Dunbaugh Distinguished Professor, 1971. Emeritus, 1972–77

Hobbs, Barbara K. B.A., Lawrence College; M.A., State University of Iowa. Art. 1947–50

Holcomb, Martin J. A.B., Bethany College; M.A., Northwestern University. Speech. 1972–73

Hopper, Doris B. A.B., Illinois College; M.A., Western Illinois University. Speech. Dean of Women, Associate Dean of Students. 1958–

Horton, George W. B.S., Illinois Wesleyan University; M.S., University of Wisconsin. Physics. 1946–62. Emeritus, 1962–75

Horton, George W., Jr. B.A., Wabash College; M.S., Oklahoma A. & M. College. Mathematics. 1962–64, 1968–

Horvath, Attila S. LL.D., University of Budapest. Sociology. 1966–68

House, Floyd N. B.A., M.A., University of Colorado; Ph.D., University of Chicago. Sociology. 1964–65

Ives, Edward D. A.B., Hamilton College; M.A., Columbia University. English. 1950–53

Jamison, Wallace N. A.B., Westminster College (Pa.); Th.B., Princeton Theological Seminary; Ph.D., University of Edinburgh. History. Dean of the College. 1970–

Jenks, Jessie P. A.B., Coe College; B.L.S., University of Illinois. Library. 1928–39

Johnson, Keach D. A.B., Illinois College; M.A., University of Illinois. History and Education. 1941–44

Johnson, Shirley. B.A., Jamestown College; M.A. University of Denver. Library. 1967–70

Jones, Royce P. B.A., M.A., Texas Christian University; B.D., Duke University; Ph.D., University of Oklahoma. Philosophy. 1974–

Jones, William B. A.B., A.M., Georgetown College; A.M., University of Illinois; Litt.D., Columbia College. English. 1953–54

Judd, Lawrence C. B.A., Rice University; B.D., Yale Divinity School; M.S., Ph.D., Cornell University. Sociology. 1970–

Keating, Barry J. B.A., Swarthmore College; M.S., University of Connecticut; Ph.D., New York University. Psychology. 1976–77

Kerr, Daniel E. A.B., Coe College; B.D., Princeton Theological Seminary; A.M., Princeton University; D.D., Lincoln College. Religion, Chaplain. 1948–51

King, Ralph S. B.S., Eureka College; M.S., University of Michigan. Chemistry. 1956–57

King, Theodore I. B.S., M.B.A., Western Michigan University. Economics and Business Administration. 1975–

Kirk, Carey H. A.B., Princeton University; M.A., University of Virginia; Ph.D., Vanderbilt University. English. 1972–

Koch, John B. B.A., Blackburn College; M.A., Ph.D., University of Arkansas. Economics and Business Administration. 1960–67

Kohl, Elizabeth A. A.B., Macalester College; M.A., University of Kansas. Modern Languages (French). 1966–67

Kohlhoff, Dean W. A.B., Valparaiso University; M.A., Washington University. History and Government. 1962–64

Koss, David H. B.A., North Central College; B.D., Evangelical Theological Seminary; Th.M., Princeton Theological Seminary; Ph.D., Northwestern University. Religion. 1972–

Kreutzer, Valerie S. Staatsexamen, Paedagogische Hochschule, Karlsruhe; M.A., Duke University. Modern Languages (German). 1965–66

Krumboltz, Orus F. B.S., Iowa State College; A.M., George Washington University; Ph.D., University of Chicago. Chemistry. 1937–38

Lacey, Raymond H. A.B., A.M., Syracuse University; A.M., Johns Hopkins University; Ph.D., Princeton University. Greek and Latin, Capps Professor. 1917–47. Dean of the College, 1933–36. Dean of the Faculty, 1936–38. Emeritus, 1947–57

Lamb, Alfred. A.B., Illinois College. Physical Education. 1937–42

Landuyt, Bernard. B.Ed., Macomb Teachers College; M.A., University of Iowa. Economics. 1936–37

Lane, Larry Gay. B.A., Union University; M.A., Tulane University. Modern Languages (Spanish). 1961–63

Langfitt, John N. A.B., Stanford University; B.D., San Francisco Theological Seminary; Th.D., Graduate Theological Union. Religion, Chaplain. 1971–

Larson, Anna Marie. B.A., College of St. Catherine; M.S., Syracuse University; Ph.D., Oregon State University. Biology. 1970–73

Lauer, Dennis E. B.S., M.S., University of Kansas. Physics. 1963–65

Lauter, Felix H. B.S., Southwestern College; M.S., Ph.D., Louisiana State University. Biology. 1958–62

Leam, Harold S. A.B., Muhlenberg College; A.M., Lehigh University. English. 1967–76. Dunbaugh Distinguished Professor, 1975

Leavenworth, William S. B.S., M.S., Hamilton College. Chemistry, Strawn Professor. 1919–38. Emeritus, 1938–43

Leonard, Ruth. B.S., Kansas State Agricultural College; M.S., University of Chicago. Mathematics. 1926–27

Lindstrom, David E. B.Sc., University of Nebraska; M.Sc., University of Wisconsin; Ph.D., University of Illinois. Sociology. 1969–70

Linville, Ralph B., A.B., Ball State Teachers College; A.M., Indiana University. Chemistry. 1930–37

Livingstone, Courtenay R., A.B., DePauw University; A.M., Indiana University. Education. 1943–44

Long, James D., B.S., M.A., Sam Houston State Teachers College; Ph.D., University of Texas. Biology. 1956–59

Lukacs, Eugene. Ph.D., University of Vienna. Physics. 1942–44

Lynn, Alvin W., B.S., M.A., Rutgers University. History and Government. 1965–71

MacClintock, William D. A.B., A.M., Kentucky Wesleyan University. English. 1926–30. Acting Dean of the College, 1926–27

Magruder, Susan L. B.S., Eastern Illinois University; M.A., East Carolina University. Physical Education. 1978–

Mann, George. B.S., Arkansas State College; M.S., University of Mississippi. Physics. 1965–

Mann, Jewell A. A.B., Evansville College; A.M., University of Illinois. Education. 1967–71

Martin, Edgar W. A.B., Washburn University; A.M., Ph.D., University of Chicago. Economics and Business Administration. 1946–47

Martin, Robert J. B.S., M.S., University of Illinois. Psychology.
    1971–72
Martin, Ruth. *See* Brown, Ruth M.
McClelland, W. Robert. A.B., Macalester College; B.D., Mc-
    Cormick Seminary. Religion, Chaplain. 1962–70
McCracken, Genevieve. B.S., M.S., Louisiana State University.
    Physical Education. 1942–43, 1948–55. Dean of Women, 1948–
    55
McFall, Eleanor. A.B., Grinnell College; A.M., Northwestern Uni-
    versity. Physical Education. Dean of Women. 1938–42
McGeath, Marion S. B.S., M.S., Illinois State University. Psy-
    chology. 1972–75
McLachlan, Robert W. A.B., M.S., State University of Iowa.
    Chemistry. 1928–30
McNamara, Joseph L. A.B., A.M., Harvard University. English.
    1932–34
Meek, Louis F. B.S., Kansas State University; B.Th., Omaha Pres-
    byterian Theological Seminary; M.A., Adams State College;
    Ph.D., University of Wyoming. Psychology. 1964–75. Emeritus,
    1976–
Merris, William. B.S., Illinois College; M.S., Northern Illinois Uni-
    versity. Physical Education. 1958–
Miller, Albert J. B.S., Millikin University; M.S., University of Illi-
    nois. Physical Education, Director of Athletics. 1946–56
Miller, Earle B. A.B., University of Colorado; A.M., University
    of Chicago. Mathematics, Hitchcock Professor. 1927–62
Miller, Edeltrud S. A.B., Pacific College; A.M., University of
    Washington. Modern Languages (French). 1959–60
Miller, Eleanor O. B.S., A.M., Northwestern University; Ph.D.,
    University of Wisconsin. Psychology. 1927–64. Dean of Women,
    1944–48. Emerita, 1964–
Minnear, Festus L. B.S., Muskingum College; M.S., University
    of Pennsylvania; Ph.D., Ohio State University. Chemistry. 1966–
    67
Mintz, Grafton K. A.B., Bucknell University; M.A., Ohio State
    University. English. 1955–57
Moehn, Loren D. A.B., Carthage College; M.S., Southern Illinois

University; Ph.D., University of Illinois. Biology. 1969–. Dunbaugh Distinguished Professor, 1978

Moore, Geraldine. B.A., M.A., State University of Iowa. Modern Languages (Spanish). 1958–61

Morford, Dale D. A.B., Indiana University; A.M., University of Wisconsin. History. 1926–27

Morgan, Lee. B.S., Northwestern University; M.A., State University of Iowa. Speech and Dramatics. 1957–59

Mosher, Judy K. B.S., M.S., Western Illinois University. Physical Education. 1975–76

Moulder, Bennett C. B.S., Eastern Illinois University; M.S., University of Illinois; Ph.D., University of Tennessee. Biology. 1969–

Muller, Marcel N. B.A., Université de Liège; M.A., University of Wisconsin. Modern Languages (French). 1954–56

Nichols, Nathan L. A.B., Western State Teachers College of Michigan. Physics. 1943–44

Nusspickel, Raymond E. B.S., University of Illinois; M.A., Columbia University. Physical Education. 1932–37

Orland, Charlotte. B.A., Ohio Wesleyan University. History. 1926–27

Owen, Mabel. B.S., A.M., University of Missouri. English. 1945–47

Oxtoby, Frederic B. A.B., University of Michigan; B.D., McCormick Theological Seminary; A.M., University of Chicago; D.D., Alma College. Religion and Philosophy, Scarborough Professor. 1927–41

Pasel, Lawrence. B.A., Illinois Wesleyan University; M.A., Columbia University. Economics. 1947–50

Pautz, Roger C. B.A., Augsberg College; M.A., M.F.A., University of Iowa. Art. 1969–72

Pearson, Robert W. B.S., M.S., University of Illinois. Biology. 1962–63

Peterson, William M. A.B., A.M., Brown University. English. 1948–49

Pilcher, Frederick. B.S., Washburn University; M.S., University of Kansas. Physics. 1962–

Platt, R. Clinton. B.A., Albion College. Modern Languages and Classics. 1951–53

Poage, George R. Ph.B., A.M., Ph.D., University of Chicago. History. 1918–25

Polzin, Donald E. A.B., Illinois College; A.M., University of Illinois. Speech and Dramatics. 1955–57

Pratt, Richard L. A.B., Illinois College; M.A., University of Denver. Library. 1969–

Primus, John C. A.B., Macalester College; M.A., University of Minnesota. Economics and Business Administration. 1956–60

Rainbolt, Mary Louise. B.S., Oklahoma Baptist University; M.S., Oklahoma State University; Ph.D., University of Oklahoma. Biology. 1965–

Ramsay, David Craig. B.A., M.A., University of Maryland. History and Political Science. 1978–

Rasmussen, Gary G. B.S., M.S., University of Illinois. Physical Education, Economics. 1966–67

Raub, Nellie T. B.S., A.M., Purdue University. English. Dean of Women. 1926–29

Ravely, Melville F. B.S., Jamestown College; M.S., Ph.D., State University of Iowa. Chemistry. 1938–47

Reagan, M. Darrell. B.A., Baylor University. Speech and Dramatics. 1959–63

Rencurrell, Jose. B.A., Instituto Santa Clara; M.A., Kansas State Teachers College; LL.D., Havana University. Modern Languages (Spanish). 1965–67

Ritter, Deckard. A.B., A.M., Ed.D., New York University; B.S.L.S., Western Reserve University. Library. 1949–61

Robinson, Sue. B.A., Southwestern University; M.S., Wichita University; Ed.D., Oklahoma State University. Education. 1977–

Rogal, Richard F. B.A., University of Hawaii; M.A., Ph.D. University of South Dakota. Psychology. 1971–

de Roover, Raymond A. M.B.A., Institut Superieur de Commerce,

Antwerp; M.B.A., Harvard University. Economics and Business Administration. 1943–44

Rosenberg, Hans. Ph.D., University of Berlin. History and Political Science. 1936–38

Rowland, Thomas L. A.B., Illinois College; M.S., Southern Connecticut State College. Physical Education. 1973–

Rule, Andrew K. A.B., A.M., University of New Zealand; B.D., Princeton Theological Seminary; Ph.D., University of Edinburgh. Religion and Philosophy, Scarborough Professor. 1923–27

Ruopp, Phillips B. Diplomas in Economics, Political Science, and Anthropology, Oxford University. Sociology. 1953–55

Russell, Cyril B. B.A., North Dakota State Teachers College; B.D., Nashota House Seminary; M.A. in L.S., University of Michigan. Library. 1961–66

Ryan, Carole M. A.B., Illinois College; Certificate, University of Grenoble; A.M., University of Illinois. Modern Languages (French). 1962–

Samoore, Arthur S. B.S., M.S., University of Illinois. Economics, Business Manager. 1943–52

Sampson, Helen. A.B., Buena Vista College; M.A., University of Iowa. English and Speech. 1943–44

Sanchez, Rufino R. B.A., Instituto de Marianao; Ph.D., University of Havana. Modern Languages (Spanish). 1963–65

Saylor, Dennis E. Th.B., Midwest Bible School; B.A., Taylor University; M.A., Ball State University. Psychology. 1968–70

Schneider, George W. B.S., Case School of Applied Science; M.S., State University of Iowa. Mathematics and Physics. 1923–33

Schroder, Fridtjof C. B.A., Luther College; M.A., University of Iowa. Art. 1946–47

Scott, Charles E. B.F.A., Memphis Academy of Arts. Art. 1960–63

Scott, George H. A.B., University of Illinois, A.M., Harvard University. Mathematics and Physics, Hitchcock Professor. 1919–26. Dean of the College, 1920–26

Scranton, Robert L. A.B., Mount Union College; A.M., Ph.D., University of Chicago. Classics. 1939–40

Seator, Lynette H. B.S., Western Illinois University; M.A., Ph.D., University of Illinois. Modern Languages (Spanish). 1967–. Dunbaugh Distinguished Professor, 1976

Seybold, Ethel L. A.B., Illinois College; A.M., University of Missouri; M.A., Ph.D., Yale University. English. 1943–44, 1946–75. Emerita, 1975–

Seybold, Mary Anice. A.B., Illinois College; M.A., University of Illinois. Mathematics. 1943–44

Sherwin, Jane K. B.A., Rockford College; M.A., Middlebury College. Modern Languages (Spanish). 1953–56

Shope, John H. A.B., Catawba College; B.D., Eastern Theological Seminary; M.A., Columbia University; Ph.D., University of Pittsburgh. Sociology. 1968–69

Shwe, Maung Hla. B.A., Ohio Wesleyan University; M.A. University of Colorado. History and Government. 1958–60

Silvernail, Walter L. A.B., Park College; A.M., Ph.D., University of Missouri. Chemistry. 1949–51, 1953–56

Simmonds, E. S. B.S., M.S., University of Illinois. Education. 1957–61

Simmons, Jerold L. B.A., Kearney State College; M.A., University of Nebraska; Ph.D., University of Minnesota. History. 1971–72

Singh, Vidyapati. B.Com., M.A., University of Calcutta; Ph.D., Western Reserve University. Economics and Business Administration. 1959–60, 1967–

Smith, Isabel S. A.B., Oberlin College; M.S., Ph.D., University of Chicago. Biology. 1903–27. Emerita, 1927–48

Smith, J. Robert. B.A., M.A., Ph.D., University of Illinois. Modern Languages (German). 1969–

Smith, Joe Patterson. B.S., Ph.D., University of Chicago. History and Government, Gardner Professor. 1927–62. Emeritus, 1962–63

Smith, May Alice. A.B., William Penn College; M.S., State University of Iowa. Biology. 1959–62

Smith, Thomas D. B.S., M.B.A., Arkansas State University. Economics and Business Administration. 1976–

Smock, George E. A.B., DePauw University; A.M., University of Chicago. English and Speech. 1928–29

Solstad, Kenneth D. B.A., Yale University; M.A., Ph.D., University of California. English. 1971–72

Sorenson, John P. B.S., M.A., Northeast Missouri State Teachers College. Music. 1970–76

Specht, R. John, Jr. B.Mus.Ed., Westminster College (Pennsylvania); M.A., Western Reserve University. Music and English. 1964–70

Sperber, Brigitta. B.A., B.S. in Ed., M.A., Ohio State University. Modern Languages (French). 1947–50

Staley, Geraldine. A.B., Butler University; B.A. in Th., Pasadena College of Theatre Arts; M.S., Purdue University. Speech and Dramatics. 1961–

Steckel, Clyde J. A.B., Butler University; B.D., Chicago Theological Seminary. Religion, Chaplain. 1956–62

Stenzel, Joachim. Ph.D., University of Florence. Greek and Latin, Capps Professor. 1946–50, 1953–54

Stevens, Mark E. B.A., Baldwin-Wallace College; M.A., Bowling Green State University. Psychology. 1978–

Stewart, Malcolm F. A.B., College of Wooster; M.A., McCormick Seminary; Ph.D., State University of Iowa. Religion and Philosophy, Scarborough Professor, 1941–74. Dunbaugh Distinguished Professor, 1972. Emeritus, 1974–

Stowell, Ernest E. B.A., M.A., University of Washington; Ph.D., Centro de Estudios Universitarios de Mexico. Modern Languages (Spanish). 1947–53

Stratton, H. John. A.B., Evansville College; Ph.D., University of Chicago. Economics and Business. 1928–45

Stratton, Martha. A.B., Evansville College. Government and Physical Education. 1942–43, 1946–49

Strong, Mary Louise. B.L., University of Wisconsin; A.M., University of California. Modern Languages (German). 1922–51

Studer, Kenneth E. B.A., Bowling Green State University; B.D., Westminster Theological Seminary. Sociology. 1967–71

Sturges, Herbert A. A.B., A.M., Oberlin College. Mathematics and Physics. 1930–31

Sullivan, Virgil R. B.S., M.S., Ph.D., University of Illinois. Chemistry. 1948–49

Swanson, Kenneth E. B.A., Kansas Wesleyan University; M.A., Wichita State University. Sociology. 1971–72

Teach, Ruth. A.B., Manchester College; B.S.L.S., University of Illinois. Library. 1942–43
Thompson, Mary I. B.S., M.S., University of Illinois. Physical Education. 1931–38
Thompson, Wallace B. B.S., M.S., West Texas State University. Biology. 1967–68
Thoms, Robert D. B.D., Trinity Seminary; B.A., M.A., University of Northern Iowa. Library. 1966–69
Thrash, James R. A.B., Ohio State University; M.S. in L.S., Western Reserve University. Library. 1970–71
Tomlinson, Leonora, A.B., Bryn Mawr College; A.M. Northwestern University. Modern Languages (French). 1925–54. Emerita, 1954–
Tong, Ts'ing-Hi. B.A., Southern Illinois University; M.S., DePaul University. Mathematics. 1964–
Tracey, Donald R. B.A., M.A., Ph.D., University of Maryland. History. 1972–
Trainor, Charles R. B.A., Dartmouth College; B.A., M.A. Cambridge University; Ph.D. Yale University. English. 1977–
Tucker, Boyd W. A.B., Asbury College; A.M., Northwestern University. Religion. 1947–48
Ture, Norman B. A.B., Indiana University; A.M., University of Chicago. Economics. 1947–50
Turner, Frederick B. A.B., A.M., University of California. Biology and Chemistry. 1952–53

Van Meter, LaRue. A.B., Illinois Wesleyan University; A.M., University of Illinois. Physical Education and Sociology, Director of Athletics. 1932–38
Vriesen, Calvin W. B.S., M.S., University of Minnesota. Chemistry. 1947–49

Wagner, Raymond G. B.A., Lawrence College, M.A., University of Wisconsin. Economics. 1943–44

Warner, Lewis W. B.A., University of Mississippi, M.A., University of Florida. English. 1955–57

Wassermann, Felix M. Ph.D., University of Freiburg. Classics. 1950–51

Watt, John. B.A., Nebraska Wesleyan; M.S., Iowa State University; Ph.D., University of Nebraska. Biology. 1968–69

Williams, Clara B. A.B., Indiana University; A.M., Columbia University. English. Dean of Women. 1930–38

Williams, Ralph M. A.B., Ohio State University; M.B.A., Indiana University. Economics and Business Administration. 1968–69

Willis, Frank M. A.B., University of Denver. Library. 1941–42

Wilson, George E. B.S., Eastern Illinois University; M.A., University of Illinois. Modern Languages (Spanish). 1970–71

Wolf, Harry D. B.S., Kansas State Normal School; A.M., Ph.D., University of Chicago. Economics. 1923–24, 1926–28

Wooley, Wesley T. B.S., M.S., M.Ed., University of Illinois. Education. 1961–62

Workman, Clark M. B.B.A., M.A., University of Iowa. Economics. 1971–72

Wright, John S. A.B., A.M., University of Illinois; Ph.D., University of Chicago. History and Government. 1938–56

Yagol, Nathan. A.B., A.M., Emory University. Chemistry and Physics. 1943–44

Yeager, Iver F. A.B., Macalester College; A.M., Ph.D., University of Chicago. Religion and Philosophy, Scarborough Professor. 1958–. Dean of the College, 1958–70. Dunbaugh Distinguished Professor, 1977

York, Ruth B. B.A., M.A., University of Iowa. Modern Languages (French). 1956–59

Young, William H. B.A., B.B.A., M.B.A., University of Texas. Economics. 1924–26

Zaleski, Anthony M. B.S., Murray State University; M.F.A., Miami University. Art. 1972–77

Zeigler, Elizabeth R. A.B., Monmouth College; M.A., University of Michigan. Political Science. 1965–78. Emerita, 1978–

Zimmerman, Ruth M. B.A., Gustavus Adolphus College; M.A., University of Florida. English. 1966–67

Appendix C
The Trustees of Illinois College, 1925–1979

The role of the trustees of Illinois College has, over the years, been a very large one. The fact that the board has been self-perpetuating has given it a homogeneous, conservative character. The date immediately following a name represents the class to which that person belonged. If there is an H before the date, that indicates an honorary degree granted at that year's commencement. WA indicates attendance at Whipple Academy. Alumni of the College have always predominated on the Board, and, in general, preference has been given to residents of Jacksonville and the Midwest, so that there have been few non-participating trustees. At the same time, there has been a leavening of members from the East and the West. The length of tenure of members elected by the Board has often been quite long, as will be observed. Trustees elected by the Alumni Association have, in the last half century, had three-year and five-year tours of duty; some of them have been elected by the Board to continue service when their tours of duty as alumni trustees were completed.

Asterisks following dates indicate years of service as alumni trustees.

Adams, Albyn Worthington, 1921. St. Louis, Missouri. 1950–53*
Alley, William J. Springfield. 1975–
Ames, John Griffith. Acting President. 1929–30, 1932–33
Armstrong, Edward H., 1950. Springfield. 1969–72*
Ayers, John A., 1869. Jacksonville. 1901–28

Barber, Clayton, 1901. Springfield. 1941–44*
Barber, John A., 1894. Springfield. 1923–34*, 1934–39
Barge, James S. Springfield. 1977–
Barnes, James M., 1921. Jacksonville; Washington, D.C. 1929–33,*
    1948–51,* 1952–58
Baxter, Dr. George E., 1896. Chicago; Glendora, California. 1924–
    61. Chairman, 1932–37. Emeritus, 1961–66
Bellatti, Walter, 1905. Jacksonville. 1920–63
Bellatti, Walter R., 1936. Jacksonville. 1963–
Bergen, John J., 1863. Virginia. 1913–30
Black, Dr. Carl E., 1883. Jacksonville. 1906–46
Black, Dr. Ellsworth, 1916. Jacksonville. 1946–70. Emeritus, 1970–
    73
Bone, Dr. Ernst C., 1936. Jacksonville. 1953–56,* 1965–68*
Brady, Harry B. Jacksonville. 1907–29
Brown, William Barr, 1905. Jacksonville. 1920–31
Burr, W. Brown, 1900. Chicago. 1939–43
Burrus, Thomas M., 1971. Arenzville. 1976–81*

Caine, L. Vernon. President of the College. 1956–73
Capps, Edward, 1877. Princeton, New Jersey. 1935–38,* 1938–48
Capps, Harry M., 1890. Jacksonville. 1901–49
Capps, Robert M., 1917. Jacksonville. 1946–68
Clark, William N., 1940. Chicago. 1957–. Chairman, 1966–
Cornelson, Paul F. St. Louis, Missouri. 1975–
Coultas, James C., 1943. Jacksonville. 1957–60,* 1978–
Covert, William C. Philadelphia, Pa. 1916–26
Cully, Byron O., 1922. Freeport. 1937–40,* 1964–67*

Deatherage, Fred E., 1935. Columbus, Ohio. 1961–64*
DeVries, Calvin. Danville. 1965–68
Dewey, Dr. Grace, JFA. Jacksonville. 1928–46
Dillon, Doris S., 1920. Roodhouse. 1963–66*
Downing, John F., 1879. Kansas City, Missouri. 1909–28,* 1928–33
Dunbaugh, Harry J., 1899. Chicago. 1913–23,* 1932–59. Chair-
    man, 1938–55. Emeritus, 1959–69

Elliott, F. Osborne. Jacksonville. 1960–

Elliott, Frank R., 1899. Chicago. 1918–59. Emeritus, 1959–69

Engelbach, Dr. Friedrich, 1924. Jacksonville. 1947–50*

Eppenberger, Emily Hurd. St. Louis, Missouri. 1964–75. Emerita, 1975–

Ewert, Richard H., 1934. St. Paul, Minnesota. 1967–

Fairbank, Dr. Ruth E., 1911. Holyoke, Massachusetts. 1938–41*

Fansler, Thomas L. Philadelphia, Pa. 1916–36

Findley, Paul, 1943. Pittsfield and Washington, D.C. 1963–

Foreman, Helen Cleary, 1925. Jacksonville. 1954–57*

Foreman, Orville N., 1925. Jacksonville. 1940–43*

Frackleton, David W., 1894. Cleveland, Ohio. 1916–23,* 1935–59

French, Arthur J., 1927. Jacksonville. 1954–77

Funk, Donald S. Springfield. 1946–67

Goebel, William G., 1903. Jacksonville. 1915–32

Goltra, Edward F., 1884. St. Louis, Missouri. 1910–39

Gordon, Carl O., 1908. Jacksonville. 1925–41

Govert, George W., 1895. Quincy. 1920–32

Green, Hugh P., 1909. Jacksonville and Springfield. 1939–42*

Gussner, William P., 1963. Jacksonville and St. Louis. 1972–75*

Hamilton, E. Bentley, 1902. Peoria. 1923–35,* 1935–50

Hamm, Robert D., 1940. Jacksonville. 1973–78*

Hart, Arthur C., 1925. Arenzville. 1960–76. Emeritus, 1976–

Hartman, Dr. Robert R., 1935. Jacksonville. 1960–63,* 1963–

Hatch, Pascal E. Springfield. 1922–52

Hartong, Jack R., 1939. Jacksonville. 1966–69*

Hess, Lyndle W., 1930. Chicago and Hamburg. 1961–

Hoskins, Fred, 1926. Oak Park and New York, N.Y. 1952–55,* 1955–66. Chairman, 1955–66

Hudnut, William H., Jr. Springfield and Rochester, N.Y. 1942–46

Hudson, H. Gary. President of the College. 1937–53

Jaquith, Harold C. President of the College. 1933–37

Johnson, Charles A., 1897. Jacksonville. 1946–54. Emeritus, 1954–66

Jones, Ray Carlton, H1961. Chicago and Sioux Falls, S.D. 1968–

Kennedy, Melville T., 1904. Champaign. 1936–39*
Kirby, Harry N., 1897. Newtown, Connecticut. 1939–53
Kurth, Andrew E. Springfield. 1960–64

Lanphier, Charles H. Springfield. 1959–67
Lanphier, Robert C. Springfield. 1916–37
Leonhard, Emma Mae, 1912. Jacksonville. 1958–61*
Lindsay, Patricia Quinn, 1965. Springfield. 1974–79*
Lohman, Carol Coultas, 1945. Springfield. 1971–74,* 1974–

McNamara, Robert C. Chicago. 1950–56
Marbach, William H. Jacksonville and Chicago. 1922–34
Martin, Harold R. Bloomington. 1956–60. Emeritus, 1960–
Meeks, James A., 1889. Danville and Washington, D.C. 1930–46
Meenan, Harold G. Decatur. 1975–
Mellon, Eugene H., 1923. Champaign. 1943–46,* 1955–58*
Mills, Richard H., 1951. Virginia. 1978–83*
Milligan, D. O., 1930. Des Moines, Iowa. 1957–74. Emeritus, 1974–
Mitchell, Thomas F., 1949. New York, N.Y. 1962–65*
Morrison, Frank, WA. Pittsburgh, Pa. 1952–55
Mundinger, Donald C. President of the College. 1973–

Norbury, Dr. F. Garm, 1912. Jacksonville. 1928–62

Oxtoby, Robert B., 1943. Springfield. 1956–59,* 1959–78

Parker, Reed. Chicago. 1974–
Pixley, Ruth Badger, 1918. Chicago and LaJolla, California. 1934–37.* 1937–64. Emerita, 1964–66

Rainey, Henry T., H1931. Carrollton and Washington, D.C. 1932–34

Rammelkamp, Charles H. President of the College. 1905–32
Rantz, Frank R., 1917. Jacksonville. 1953–60
Reneker, Robert W. Chicago. 1968–73
Reynolds, Rosalie Sibert, 1947. Sycamore. 1977–82*
Robinson, Carl E., 1909. Jacksonville. 1924–64
Rowe, Harris, 1947. Jacksonville. 1967–70*
Rundquist, Anita Turner. Butler. 1976–
Russel, Andrew. Jacksonville. 1904–32. Chairman, 1911–32

Scott, Dr. Harvey D., 1942. Jacksonville. 1973–76*
Selden, William K. President of the College. 1953–55
Sibert, Robert F., 1936. Jacksonville. 1968–
Siefkin, Forest D., 1912. Glencoe. 1942–45,* 1947–59. Emeritus,
    1959–64
Smith, Arthur B. Belleville. 1969–76. Emeritus, 1976–
Smith, Frances McReynolds, 1933. Washington D.C. and Santa
    Cruz, California. 1968–75
Smith, J. Fairbank, 1916. San Francisco, California. 1949–52*
Smith, Rufus Z., 1944. Ottawa, Canada, and Washington, D.C.
    1970–73*
Smith, Thomas W., 1887. Hibbing, Minnesota. 1907–29
Smucker, James R. Chicago. 1966–68
Stearns, Raymond P., 1927. Urbana. 1944–47*
Stoddard, Bela M. Monticello. 1947–52
Stubbs, Robert L. Peoria. 1954–65
Sullivan, William J., 1941. Indianapolis, Indiana. 1972–

Tanner, Frederick, 1898. New York, N.Y. 1910–22,* 1933–36,*
    1936–37
Tate, H. Clay, 1927. Bloomington. 1946–49,* 1959–62*
Thomas, Benjamin P. H1947. Springfield. 1953–56
Thwaite, Walter E., Jr. Chicago. 1961–63

van Rosendal, Dorothy Graef, 1930. Jacksonville. 1968–71*

Wayne, Richard H. Chicago. 1960–68
Williamson, Dr. Arthur R., 1951. Lincoln. 1975–80*

Wilton, William E., 1939. St. Louis, Missouri. 1968–
Wood, Robert J. New York, N.Y. 1967–
Wright, Ben S., 1929. Toledo, Ohio. 1951–54*
Wright, Courtney Crouch, 1912. Jacksonville. 1945–48*

Appendix D
Persons Who Participated in the Illinois College Oral History

The persons listed below taped interviews with me prior to September 1978. They are placed in one of the four categories which should be self-explanatory, with the possible exception of "Tenders"; in that grouping I have placed administrators who have carried out rather than made policy. Several names appear more than once, with primary listing in the category that has seemed to me most appropriate. For the record, I have given the date and place of each interview.

It would be interesting to get additions, modifications and corrections to the text by informed persons. Hence, I invite anyone who can correct, add to or subtract from anything I have written or who wishes to comment pertinently upon it to get in touch with me. I shall add all such contributions to the Oral History of Illinois College in the Schewe Library archives.

Shapers

President L. Vernon Caine: July 15, 1975, Jacksonville, Illinois

President H. Gary Hudson: June 21–23, 1975, Santa Barbara, California

President Donald C. Mundinger: March 25, 1977, Jacksonville, Illinois

President William K. Selden: August 4, 1975, Wellesley, Massachusetts

Teachers

Professor Charles C. Barlow. *See* Tenders
Mr. Paul Clavey. *See* Learners
Professor Eleanor O. Miller: May 31, 1975, Jacksonville, Illinois
Professor Joachim Stenzel: June 27, 1975, San Jose, California
Professor Leonora Tomlinson: June 18, 1975, Paradise Valley, Arizona
Professor John S. Wright: June 20, 1975, Las Vegas, Nevada

Learners

Andrilenos, Joyce James: 1938, July 1, 1975, Seattle, Washington
Barlow, Charles C., 1929. *See* Tenders
Barlow, Merrill M., 1926. *See* Tenders
Becker, James A., 1948: July 1, 1975, Seattle, Washington
Becker, Martha Cloyd, 1950: July 1, 1975, Seattle, Washington
Bellatti, Charles, 1949. *See* Tenders
Black, Ione Linder, 1916: June 4, 1975, Jacksonville, Illinois
Bolton, Rhoda Rammelkamp, 1930: August 1977, Old Mission, Michigan
Booth, Caroline Hammond, 1948: June 28, 1975, Oakland, California
Browning, Rufus, 1940: April 7, 1976, Bethesda, Maryland
Busey, Harold M., 1939: June 27, 1976, Jacksonville, Illinois
Clavey, Paul, 1951: June 11, 1975, Harrison, Arkansas
Cleary, Edward W., 1929: June 18, 1975, Tempe, Arizona
Cully, John W., 1950: June 28, 1975, Oakland, California
Danskin, Kenneth A., 1929: June 13, 1975, Houston, Texas
Gamon, Mary Stein, 1928: July 1, 1975, Seattle, Washington
Gard, S. Wayne, 1921: June 13, 1975, Dallas, Texas
Hutchinson, Loren K., 1941: August 15, 1976, Standish, Maine
Hutchinson, Marjorie Von Tobel, 1942: August 15, 1976, Standish, Maine
Koehler, Ward, 1950: June 15, 1975, El Paso, Texas
Marx, Joe C., 1949: June 28, 1975, Oakland, California
Miller, Larry D., 1954. *See* Tenders

Nelson, Mary Pinkerton, 1938: April 7, 1976, Bethesda, Maryland
Niebur, L. Benjamin, 1941: April 7, 1976, Bethesda, Maryland
Pearson, Carol Leischner, 1963: July 6, 1975, Lindsborg, Kansas
Rammelkamp, Charles H., Jr., 1933: August 1977, Old Mission, Michigan
Rammelkamp, Julian S., 1939: August 1977, Old Mission, Michigan
Riva, James, 1951: June 16, 1975, Albuquerque, New Mexico
Riva, Marcella Taylor, 1950: June 16, 1975, Albuquerque, New Mexico
Scott, Franklin D., 1922: June 24, 1975, Claremont, California
Scott, C. Lavinia, 1927: June 24, 1975, Claremont, California
Smith, Frances McReynolds, 1933: June 26, 1975, Santa Cruz, California
Smith, J. Fairbank, 1916: June 27, 1975, San Francisco, California
Smith, Malcolm, 1932: April 7, 1976, Bethesda, Maryland
Spencer, Don S., 1967: July 7, 1975, Fulton, Missouri
Staniforth, Gwendolyn, 1954: June 28, 1975, Oakland, California
Stenzel, Jane, 1951: June 27, 1975, San Jose, California
Vuylsteke, Richard, 1966: January 4, 1977, Jacksonville, Illinois
Wood, William R., 1927: January 3, 1976, Jacksonville, Illinois

Tenders
Barlow, Charles C.: September 16, 1976, Jacksonville, Illinois
Barlow, Merrill M.: May 21, 1976, Jacksonville, Illinois
Bellatti, Charles M.: February 2, 1977, Jacksonville, Illinois
Gillham, Mrs. Wilmith: March 26, 1976, Jacksonville, Illinois
Hildner, Ernest G., Jr.: November 24, 1975, Jacksonville, Illinois
Kohr, Russell V.: September 27, 1975, Jacksonville, Illinois
Miller, Larry D.: July 7, 1975, Fulton, Missouri
Pearson, A. John: July 6, 1975, Lindsborg, Kansas
Samoore, Arthur S.: May 11, 1976, Jacksonville, Illinois
Van Horn, Jack: October 27, 1977, Jacksonville, Illinois
Van Meter, Larue: May 28, 1976, Jacksonville, Illinois

Index